The History Of England From The Norman Conquest To The Death Of John (1066-1216)

by

George Burton Adams

Double 9
BOOKS

The History Of England From The Norman Conquest To The Death Of John
(1066-1216)
by George Burton Adams

ISBN: 978-93-59393-07-0

Published by

DOUBLE 9 BOOKS
2/13-B, Ansari Road
Daryaganj, New Delhi – 110002
info@double9books.com
www.double9books.com
Tel. 011-40042856

ABOUT THE AUTHOR

American medievalist historian George Burton Adams was born in Vermont on June 3, 1851, and he passed away on May 26, 1925. From 1888 until 1925, he was a professor at Yale University. He was renowned for his written works as well as his 1908 lecture as president of the American Historical Association, in which he bemoaned the social sciences' intrusion into the study of history. James Harvey Robinson would subsequently contest this assertion. Additionally, he was crucial in the founding of the American Historical Review. Adams was elected a fellow of the American Academy of Arts and Sciences in 1918 as well as a member of the American Antiquarian Society in 1899.

CONTENTS

CHAPTER I.
THE CONQUEST

The battle of the 14th of October, 1066, was decisive of the struggle for the throne of England, but William of Normandy was in no haste to gather in the results of the victory which he had won The judgment of heaven had been pronounced in the case between him and Harold, and there was no mistaking the verdict. The Saxon army was routed and flying. It could hardly rally short of London, but there was no real pursuit. The Normans spent the night on the battlefield, and William's own tent was pitched on the hill which the enemy had held, and in the midst of the Saxon wounded, a position of some danger, against which his friend and adviser, Walter Giffard, remonstrated in vain. On the next day he fell back with his army to Hastings. Here he remained five days waiting, the Saxon Chronicle tells us, for the nation to make known its submission; waiting, it is more likely, for reinforcements which were coming from Normandy. So keen a mind as William's probably did not misjudge the situation. With the only real army against him broken to pieces, with the only leaders around whom a new army could rally dead, he could afford to wait. He may not have understood the rallying power of the Saxon soldiery, but he probably knew very well the character of the public men of England, who were left alive to head and direct a new resistance. The only candidate for the throne upon whom all parties could unite was a boy of no pronounced character and no experience. The leaders of the nobility who should have stood forth in such a crisis as the natural leaders of the nation were men who had shown in the clearest way their readiness to sacrifice England to their personal ambitions or grievances. At the head of the Church were men of but little higher character and no greater capacity for leadership, undisguised pluralists who could not avoid the charge of disregarding in their own selfish interests the laws they were bound to administer. London, where the greater part of the fugitives had gathered, could hardly have settled upon the next step to be taken when William began his advance, five days after the battle. His first objective point was the great fortress of Dover, which dominated that important landing-place upon the coast. On the way he stopped to give an example of what those might expect who made themselves his enemies, by punishing the town of Romney, which had ventured to beat off with some vigour a body of Normans, probably one that had tried to land there by mistake.

Dover had been a strong fortress for centuries, perched on its cliffs as high as an arrow can be shot, says one who may have been present at these events, and it had been recently strengthened with new work. William doubtless expected a difficult task, and he was correspondingly pleased to find the garrison ready to surrender without a blow, an omen even more promising than the victory he had gained over Harold. If William had given at Romney an example of what would follow stubborn resistance, he gave at Dover an example of how he proposed to deal with those who would submit, not merely in his treatment of the surrendered garrison of the castle, but in his payment of the losses of the citizens; for his army, disappointed of the plunder which would have followed the taking of the place by force, had burned the town or part of it. At Dover William remained a week, and here his army was attacked by a foe often more deadly to the armies of the Middle Ages than the enemies they had come out to fight. Too much fresh meat and unaccustomed water led to an outbreak of dysentery which carried off many and weakened others, who had to be left behind when William set out again. But these losses were balanced by reinforcements from Normandy, which joined him here or soon afterwards. His next advance was towards Canterbury, but it had hardly begun when delegations came up to meet him, bringing the submission of that city and of other places in Kent. Soon after leaving Dover the duke himself fell ill, very possibly with the prevailing disease, but if we may judge by what seems to be our best evidence, he did not allow this to interrupt his advance, but pushed on towards London with only a brief stop at any point.[1] Nor is there any certain evidence to be had of extensive harrying of the country on this march. His army was obliged to live on what it could take from the inhabitants, and this foraging was unquestionably accompanied with much unnecessary plundering; but there is no convincing evidence of any systematic laying waste of large districts to bring about a submission which everything would show to be coming of itself, and it was not like William to ravage without need. He certainly hesitated at no cruelty of the sort at times, but we can clearly enough see reasons of policy in most at least of the cases, which may have made the action seem to him necessary. Nearly all are instances either of defensive action or of vengeance, but that he should systematically ravage the country when events were carrying out his plan as rapidly as could be expected, we have no reason to consider in accordance with William's policy or temper. In the meantime, as the invading army was slowly drawing near to London, opinion there had settled, for the time at least, upon a line of policy. Surviving leaders who had been defeated in the great battle, men high in rank who had been absent, some purposely standing aloof while the issue was decided, had gathered in the city. Edwin and Morcar, the great earls of north and middle England, heads of the house that was the rival of Harold's, who seem to have been willing to see him and his power destroyed, had now come in, having learned the result of the battle. The two archbishops were there, and certain of the bishops, though which they were we cannot surely tell. Other names we do not know, unless it be that of Esegar, Harold's staller and portreeve of London, the hero of a doubtful story of negotiations with the approaching enemy. But other nobles and men of influence in the state were certainly there, though their names are not recorded. Nor was a military force lacking, even if the "army" of Edwin and Morcar was under independent and not trustworthy command. It is clear that the tone of public opinion was for further resistance, and the citizens were not afraid to go out to attack the Conqueror on his first approach to their neighbourhood. But from all our sources of information the fatal fact stands out plainly, of divided counsels and lack of leadership. William of Malmesbury believed, nearly two generations later, and we must agree with him, that if the English could have put aside "the discord of civil strife," and have "united in a common policy, they could have amended the ruin of the fatherland." But there was too much self-seeking and a lack of patriotism. Edwin and Morcar went about trying to persuade people that one or the other of them should be made king. Some of the bishops appear to have opposed the choice of any king. No dominating personality arose to compel agreement and to give direction and power to the popular impulse. England was conquered, not by the superior force and genius of the Norman, but by the failure of her own men in a great crisis of her history.

The need of haste seems an element in the situation, and under the combined pressure of the rapid approach of the enemy and of the public opinion of the city—citizens and shipmen are both mentioned—the leaders of Church and State finally came to an agreement that Edgar atheling should be made king. It was the only possible step except that of immediate submission. Grandson of Edmund Ironside, the king who had offered stubborn and most skilful resistance to an earlier foreign invader, heir of a house that had been royal since the race had had a history, all men could unite upon him, and upon him alone, if there must be a king. But there was no other argument in his favour. Neither the blood of his grandfather nor the school of adversity had made of him the man to deal with such a situation. In later life he impressed people as a well-mannered, agreeable, and frank man, but no one ever detected in him the stuff of which heroes are made. He was never consecrated king, though the act would have strengthened his position, and one wonders if the fact is evidence that the leaders had yielded only to a popular pressure in agreeing upon him against their own preference, or merely of the haste and confusion of events. One act of sovereignty only is attributed to him, the confirmation of Brand, who had been chosen by the monks Abbot of Peterborough, in succession to Leofric, of the house of Edwin and Morcar, who had been present at the battle of Hastings and had died soon after. William interpreted this reference of the election to Edgar for confirmation as an act of hostility to himself, and fined the new abbot heavily, but to us the incident is of value as evidence of the character of the movement, which tried to find a national king in this last male of Cerdic's line.

From Canterbury the invading army advanced directly upon London, and took up a position in its neighbourhood. From this station a body of five hundred horsemen was sent forward to reconnoitre the approaches to the city, and the second battle of the conquest followed, if we may call that a battle which seems to have been merely one-sided. At any rate, the citizens intended to offer battle, and crossed the river and advanced against the enemy in regular formation, but the Norman knights made short work of the burgher battalions, and drove them back into the city with great slaughter. The suburb on the south bank of the Thames fell into the hands of the enemy, who burned down at least a part of it. William gained, however, no further success at this point. London was not yet ready to submit, and the river seems to have been an impassable barrier. To find a crossing the Norman march was continued up the river, the country suffering as before from the foraging of the army. The desired crossing was found at Wallingford, not far below Oxford and nearly fifty miles above London. That he could have crossed the river nearer the city than this, if he had wished, seems probable, and considerations of strategy may very likely have governed William's movements. Particularly might this be the case if he had learned that Edwin and Morcar, with their army, had abandoned the new king and retired northward, as some of the best of modern scholars have believed, though upon what is certainly not the best of evidence. If this was so, a little more time would surely convince the Londoners that submission was the best policy, and the best position for William to occupy would be between the city and this army in the north, a position which he could easily reach, as he did, from his crossing at Wallingford. If the earls had not abandoned London, this was still the best position, cutting them off from their own country and the city from the region whence reinforcements must come if they came at all. A long sweep about a hostile city was favourite strategy of William's.

From some point along this line of march between Dover and Wallingford, William had detached a force to secure the submission of Winchester. This city was of considerable importance, both because it was the old royal residence and still the financial centre of the state, and because it was the abode of Edith, the queen of Edward the Confessor, to whom it had been assigned as part of her dower. The submission of the city seems to have been immediate and entirely satisfactory to William, who confirmed the widowed Lady of England in her rights and showed later some favour to the monks of the new minster. William of Poitiers, the duke's chaplain, who possibly accompanied the army on this march,[2] and wrote an account of these events not long afterwards, tells us that at Wallingford Stigand, Archbishop of Canterbury, came in and made submission to his master. There is no reason to doubt this statement, though it has been called in question. The best English chroniclers omit his name from the list of those who submitted when London surrendered. The tide of success had been flowing strongly one way since the Normans landed. The condition of things in London afforded no real hope that this tide could be checked. A man of Stigand's type could be depended upon to see that if William's success was inevitable, an early submission would be better than a late one. If Stigand went over to William at Wallingford, it is a clear commentary on the helplessness of the party of resistance in London.

From Wallingford William continued his leisurely march, leaving a trail of devastation behind him through Oxfordshire, Buckinghamshire, and Hertfordshire, where he turned south towards London. But the city was now convinced of the impossibility of resistance and was ready to yield to the inevitable. How near the enemy was allowed to approach before the step of actual surrender was taken is not quite certain. The generally accepted opinion, on the authority of English chroniclers, is that the embassy from London went to meet William at Berkhampsted, thirty miles away, but if we could accept the suggestion which has been made that Little Berkhampsted was the place intended, the distance would agree better with the express statement of the chaplain, William of Poitiers, that the city was in sight from the place of conference. It is hard to avoid accepting William's statement, for it is precisely the kind of thing which the men of the duke's army—which had been so long approaching the city and thinking of its capture—would be likely to notice and remember. It also agrees better with the probabilities of the case. Thirty miles was still a safe distance, especially in those days, and would allow much time for further debate and for the unexpected to happen. Wherever the act of submission occurred, it was in form complete and final for the city and for the chief men of England. Edgar came to offer his useless and imperfect crown; Aldred, Archbishop of York, was there to complete the submission of the Church; bishops of several sees were also present, and chief men of the state, among whom Edwin and Morcar are mentioned by one of the chroniclers who had earlier sent them home to the north. Possibly he is right in both statements, and the earls had returned to make their peace when they saw that resistance was hopeless. These men William received most kindly and with good promises, and Edgar in particular he embraced and treated like a son.

This deputation from London, headed by their nominal king, came to offer the crown to William. For him and for the Normans the decisive moment of the expedition was now come. A definite answer must be made. According to the account we are following, a kind of council of war of the Norman and other barons and the leaders of the army seems to have been held, and to this council William submitted the question whether it would be better to take the crown now, or to wait until the country was more completely subdued and until his wife Matilda could be present to share the honour with him. This is the question which we are told was proposed, but the considerations which seem to have led to the final decision bear less upon this than upon the question whether William should be king at all or not. We have before this date no record of any formal decision of this question. It had been doubtless tacitly understood by all; the crown was more or less openly the object of the expedition; but the time had now come when the question stood as a sharp issue before William and before his men and must be frankly met. If the Duke of the Normans was to be transformed into the King of the English, it could be done only with the loyal support of his Norman followers; nor is it at all likely that, in a state so thoroughly feudal as Normandy, the suzerain would have ventured to assume so great an increase of rank and probable power without the express consent of his vassals, in disregard of what was certainly the usual feudal practice. The decision of the council was favourable, and William accepted the crown. Immediately a force of men was sent forward to take military possession of the city and build, after the Norman fashion, some kind of defences there, and to make suitable preparation for the coming of the king who was to be. The interval William occupied in his favourite amusement of the chase, and his army in continuing to provide for their various wants from the surrounding country and that with no gentle hand.

Whatever may have prevented the coronation of Edgar, there was to be no unnecessary delay about William's. Christmas day, the nearest great festival of the Church, was fixed upon for the ceremony, which was to take place in the new abbey church of Westminster, where Harold had been crowned and where the body of Edward lay. The consecration was to be performed by Aldred, Archbishop of York. No Norman, least of all William, who had come with the special blessing of the rightful pope, could allow this sacred office to Stigand, whose way to the primacy had been opened by the outlawry of the Norman archbishop Robert, and whose paillium was the gift of a schismatic and excommunicated pope. With this slight defect, from which Harold's coronation also suffered, the ceremony was made as formal and stately as possible. Norman guards kept order about the place; a long procession of clergy moved into the church, with the duke and his supporting bishops at the end. Within, the old ritual of coronation was followed as nearly as we can judge. Englishmen and Frenchmen were asked in their own languages if they would have William to be king, and they shouted out their approval; William then took oath to defend the Church, to rule justly, to make and keep right law, and to prevent disorders, and at last he was anointed and crowned and became King of the English in title and in law. But all this had not taken place without some plain evidence of the unusual and violent character of the event. The Normans stationed without had mistaken the shouts of approval which came from within for shouts of anger and protest, and in true Norman fashion had at once fallen on whatever was at hand, people and buildings, slaying and setting fire, to create a diversion and to be sure of vengeance. In one point at least they were successful; the church was emptied of spectators and the ceremony was finished, king and bishops alike trembling with uncertain dread, in the light of burning buildings and amid the noise of the tumult.

At the time of his coronation William was not far from forty years of age. He was in the full tide of a vigorous physical life, in height and size, about the average, possibly a trifle above the average, of the men of his time, and praised for his unusual strength of arm. In mental gifts he stood higher above the general run of men than in physical. As a soldier and a statesman he was clear-headed, quick to see the right thing to do and the right time to do it; conscious of the ultimate end and of the combination of means, direct and indirect, slowly working out, which must be made to reach it. But the characteristic by which he is most distinguished from the other men of his time is one which he shares with many of the conquerors of history—a characteristic perhaps indispensable to that kind of success—an utterly relentless determination to succeed, if necessary without hesitation at the means employed, and without considering in the least the cost to others. His inflexible will greatly impressed his own time. The men who came in contact with him were afraid of him. His sternness and mercilessness in the enforcement of law, in the punishment of crime, and in the protection of what he thought to be his rights, were never relaxed. His laws were thought to be harsh, his money-getting oppressive, and his forest regulations cruel and unjust. And yet William intended to be, and he was, a good ruler. He gave his lands, what was in those days the best proof of good government, and to be had only of a strong king, internal peace. He was patient also, and did not often lose control of himself and yield to the terrible passion which could at last be roused. For thirty years, in name at least, he had ruled over Normandy, and he came to the throne of England with a long experience behind him of fighting against odds, of controlling a turbulent baronage, and of turning anarchy into good order.

William was at last crowned and consecrated king of the English. But the kingdom over which he could exercise any real rule embraced little more than the land through which he had actually passed; and yet this fact must not be understood to mean too much. He had really conquered England, and there was no avoiding the result. Notwithstanding all the difficulties which were still before him in getting possession of his kingdom, and the length of time before the last lingering resistance was subdued, there is no evidence anywhere of a truly national movement against him. Local revolts there were, some of which seemed for a moment to assume threatening proportions; attempts at foreign intervention with hopes of native aid, which always proved fallacious; long resistance by some leaders worthy of a better support, the best and bravest of whom became in the end faithful subjects of the new king: these things there were, but if we look over the whole period of the Conquest, we can only be astonished that a handful of foreign adventurers overcame so easily a strong nation. There is but one explanation to be found, the one to which such national overthrow is most often due, the lack of leadership.

The panegyrist of the new king, his chaplain, William of Poitiers, leads us to believe that very soon after the coronation William adopted somewhat extensive regulations for the settlement of his kingdom and for the restraint of disorders in his army. We may fairly insist upon some qualification of the unfailing wisdom and goodness which this semi-official historian attributes to his patron, but we can hardly do otherwise than consider his general order of events correct, and his account of what was actually done on the whole trustworthy. England had in form submitted, and this submission was a reality so far as all were concerned who came into contact with William or his army. And now the new government had to be set going at once. Men must know what law was to be enforced and under what conditions property was to be secure. The king's own followers, who had won his kingdom for him, must receive the rewards which they had expected; but the army was now a national and not an invading army, and it must be restrained from any further indiscriminate plunder or rioting. Two acts of William which we must assign to this time give some evidence that he did not feel as yet altogether sure of the temper of London. Soon after the ceremony at Westminster he retired to Barking, a few miles distant, and waited there while the fortification in the city was completed, which probably by degrees grew into the Tower. And apparently at this time, certainly not long afterwards, he issued to the bishop and the portreeve his famous charter for the city, probably drawn up originally in the English language, or if not, certainly with an English translation attached for immediate effect. In this charter the clearest assurance is given on two points about which a great commercial city, intimately concerned in such a revolution, would be most anxious,—the establishment of law and the security of property. The king pledges himself to introduce no foreign law and to make no arbitrary confiscations of property. To win the steady adhesion of that most influential body of men who were always at hand to bring the pressure of their public opinion to bear upon the leaders of the state, the inhabitants of London, this measure was as wise as was the building of the Tower for security against the sudden tumults so frequent in the medieval city, or even more dangerous insurrections.

At the same time strict regulations were made for the repression of disorders in the army. The leaders were exhorted to justice and to avoid any oppression of the conquered; the soldiers were forbidden all acts of violence, and the favourite vices of armies were prohibited,—too much drinking, we are told, lest it should lead to bloodshed. Judges were appointed to deal with the offences of the soldiers; the Norman members of the force were allowed no special privileges; and the control of law over the army, says the king's chaplain, proudly, was made as strict as the control of the army over the subject race. Attention was given also to the fiscal system of the country, to the punishment of criminals, and to the protection of commerce. Most of this we may well believe, though some details of fact as well as of motive may be too highly coloured, for our knowledge of William's attitude towards matters of this kind is not dependent on the words of any panegyrist.

While William waited at Barking, other English lords in addition to those who had already acknowledged him came in and made submission. The Norman authorities say that the earls Edwin and Morcar were the chief of these, and if not earlier, they must have submitted then. Two men, Siward and Eldred, are said to have been relatives of the last Saxon king, but in what way we do not know. Copsi, who had ruled Northumberland for a time under Tostig, the brother of Harold, impressed the Norman writers with his importance, and a Thurkill is also mentioned by name, while "many other nobles" are classed together without special mention. Another great name which should probably be added to this list is that of Waltheof, Earl of

Northampton and Huntingdon, of distinguished descent and destined later to an unhappy fate. All of these the king received most kindly. He accepted their oaths, restored to them all their possessions, and held them in great honour.

But certainly not in all cases did things go so easily for the English. Two bits of evidence, one in the Saxon Chronicle, that men bought their lands of the king, and one in Domesday Book, a statement of the condition of a piece of land "at the time when the English redeemed their lands," lead us to infer that William demanded of the English that they obtain from him in form a confirmation of their possessions for which they were obliged to pay a price. No statement is made of the reasons by which this demand was justified, but the temptation to regard it as an application of the principle of the feudal relief is almost irresistible; of the relief paid on the succession of a new lord, instead of the ordinary relief paid on the recognition of the heir to the fief. If the evidence were greater that this was a common practice in feudalism rather than an occasional one, as it seems only to have been, it would give us the simplest and most natural explanation of this act of William's. To consider that he regarded all the land of the kingdom as rightly confiscate, which has been suggested as an explanation, because of a resistance which in many cases never occurred, and in most had not at the time when this regulation must have been made, is a forced and unnatural theory, and not in harmony with William's usual methods. To suppose that he regarded this as an exceptional case, in which a relief on a change of lords could be collected, is a less violent supposition. Possibly it was an application more general than ordinary of the practice which was usual throughout the medieval world of obtaining at a price, from a new king, confirmations of the important grants of his predecessors. But any explanation of the ground of right on which the king demanded this general redemption of lands must remain from lack of evidence a mere conjecture. The fact itself seems beyond question, and is an indication of no little value of the views and intentions of the new king. The kingdom was his; all the land must be held of him and with his formal consent, but no uncalled-for disturbance of possession was to occur.

Beyond reasonable doubt at this time was begun that policy of actual confiscation, where reasons existed, which by degrees transformed the landed aristocracy from English into Norman. Those who had gained the crown for the new king must receive the minor rewards which they had had in view for themselves, and with no unnecessary delay. A new nobility must be endowed, and policy would dictate also that at the earliest moment the country should be garrisoned by faithful vassals of the king's own, supplied with means of defending themselves and having proportionately as much at stake in the country as himself. The lands and property of those who had fought against him or who were irreconcilable would be in his hands to dispose of, according to any theory of his position which William might hold. The crown lands of the old kings were of course his, and in spite of all the grants that were made during the reign, this domain was increased rather than diminished under William. The possessions of Harold's family and of all those who had fallen in the battle with him were at once confiscated, and these seem to have sufficed for present needs. Whatever may have been true later, we may accept the conclusion that "on the whole William at this stage of his reign warred rather against the memory of the dead than against the lives or fortunes of the living."

These confiscated lands the king bestowed on the chiefs of his army. We have little information of the way in which this change was carried out, but in many cases certainly the possessions held by a given Saxon thane in the days of Edward were turned over as a whole to a given Norman with no more accurate description than that the lands of A were now to be the lands of B. What lands had actually belonged to A, the old owner, was left to be determined by some sort of local inquiry, but with this the king did not concern himself beyond giving written orders that the change was to be made. Often this turning over to a Norman of the estate of a dispossessed Saxon resulted in unintended injustice and in legal quarrels which were unsettled years afterwards. Naturally the new owner considered himself the successor of the old one in all the rights which he possessed. If for some of his manors the Saxon was the tenant of a church or of an abbey, the Norman often seized upon these with the rest, as if all were rightfully confiscated together and all held by an equally clear title, and the Church was not always able, even after long litigation, to establish its rights. We have little direct evidence as to the relationship which such grants created between the recipient and the king, or as to the kind of tenure by which they were held, but the indirect evidence is constantly accumulating, and may be said to be now indeed conclusive, that the relation and the tenure made use of were the only ones with which the Normans were at this time familiar or which would be likely to seem to them possible, — the relationship of vassal and lord; and that with these first grants of land which the king made to his followers was introduced into England that side of the feudal system which Saxon England had never known, but which was, from this time on, for nearly two centuries, to be the ruling system in both public and private law.

In saying that the feudal system was introduced into England by these grants, we must guard against a misconception. The feudal system, if we use that name as we commonly do to cover the entire relations of the society of that age, had two sides to it, distinct in origin, character, and purpose.

To any clear understanding of the organization of feudal society, or of the change which its establishment made in English history, it is necessary, although it is not easy, to hold these two sides apart. There was in the practices and in the vocabulary of feudalism itself some confusion of the two in the borderland that lay between them, and the difficulty is made greater for us by the fact that both sides were primarily concerned with the holding of land, and especially by the fact that the same piece of land belonged at once to both sides and was held at the same time by two different men, by two different kinds of tenure, and under two different systems of law. The one side may be called from its ruling purpose economic and the other political. The one had for its object the income to be drawn from the land; the other regarded chiefly the political obligations joined to the land and the political or social rank and duties of the holders.

The economic side concerned the relations of the cultivators of the soil with the man who was, in relation to them, the owner of that soil; it regulated the tenures by which they held the little pieces which they cultivated, their rights over that land and its produce, their obligations to the owner of service in cultivating for him the lands which he reserved for his own use, and, in addition, of payments to him in kind and perhaps in money on a variety of occasions and occurrences throughout the year; it defined and practically limited, also, the owner's right of exaction from these cultivators. These regulations were purely customary; they had grown up slowly out of experience, and they were not written. But this was true also of almost all the law of that age, and this law of the cultivators was as valid in its place as the king's law, and was enforced in its own courts. It is true that most of these men who cultivated the soil were serfs, at least not entirely free; but that fact made no difference in this particular; they had their standing, their voice, and their rights in their lord's "customary" court, and the documents which describe to us these arrangements call them, as they do the highest barons of the realm, "peers," —that is, peers of these customary courts. Not all, indeed, were serfs; many freemen, small farmers, possibly it would not be wrong to say all who had formerly belonged to that class, had been forced by one necessity or another to enter into this system, to surrender the unqualified ownership of their lands, and to agree to hold them of some lord, though traces of their original full ownership may long have lingered about the land. When they did this, they were brought into very close relations with the unfree cultivators; they were parts of the same system and subject to some of the same regulations and services but their land was usually held on terms that were economically better than the serfs obtained, and they retained their personal freedom. They were members of the lords' courts, and there the serfs were their peers; but they were also members of the old national courts of hundred and shire, and there they were the peers of knights and barons.

This system, this economic side of feudalism, is what we know as the manorial system. Its unit was the manor, an estate of land larger or smaller, but large enough to admit of this characteristic organization, managed as a unit, usually from some well-defined centre, the manor house, and directed by a single responsible head, the lord's steward. The land which constituted the manor was divided into two clearly distinguished parts, the "domain" and the "tenures." The domain was the part of each manor that was reserved for the lord's own use, and cultivated for him by the labour of his tenants under the direction of the steward, as a part of the services by which they held their lands; that is, as a part of the rent paid for them. The returns from these domain lands formed a very large part, probably the largest part, of the income of the landlord class in feudal days. The "tenures" were the holdings of the cultivators, worked for themselves by their own labour, of varying sizes and held on terms of varying advantage, and usually scattered about the manor in small strips, a bit here and another there. Besides these cultivated lands there were also, in the typical manor, common pasture lands and common wood lands, in which the rights of each member of this little community were carefully regulated by the customary law of the manor. This whole arrangement was plainly economic in character and purpose it was not in the least political. Its object was to get the soil cultivated, to provide mankind with the necessary food and clothing, and the more fortunate members of the race with their incomes. This purpose it admirably served in an age when local protection was an ever present need, when the labouring man had often to look to the rich and strong man of the neighbourhood for the security which he could not get from the state. Whatever may have been the origin of this system, it was at any rate this need which perpetuated it for centuries from the fall of Rome to the later Middle Ages; and during this long time it was by this system that the western world was fed and all its activities sustained.

This economic side of feudalism, this manorial system, was not introduced into England by the Norman Conquest. It had grown up in the Saxon states, as it had on the continent, because of the prevalence there of the general social and economic conditions which favoured its growth. It was different from the continental system in some details; it used different terms for many things; but it was essentially the same system. It had its body of customary law and its private courts; and these courts, like their prototypes in the Frankish state, had in numerous cases usurped or had been granted the rights and functions of the local courts of the nation, and so had annexed a minor political function which did not naturally belong to the system. Indeed, this process had gone so far that we may believe that the stronger government of the state established by the Conqueror found it necessary to check it and to hold the operation of the private courts within stricter limits. This economic organization which the Normans found in England was so clearly parallel with that which they had always known that they made no change in it. They introduced their own vocabulary in many cases in place of the Saxon; they identified in some cases practices which looked alike but which were not strictly identical; and they had a very decided tendency to treat the free members of the manorial population, strongly intrenched as they were in the popular courts, as belonging at the same time to both sides of feudalism, the economic and the political: but the confusion of language and custom which they introduced in consequence is not sufficient to disguise from us the real relationships which existed. Nor should it be in the opposite process, which was equally easy, as when the Saxon chronicler, led by the superficial resemblance and overlooking the great institutional difference, called the curia of William by the Saxon name of witenagemot.

With the other side of feudalism, the political, the case was different. That had never grown up in the Saxon world. The starting-points in certain minor Roman institutions from which it had grown, seem to have disappeared with the Saxon occupation of Britain. The general conditions which favoured its development—the almost complete breakdown of the central government and the difficult and interrupted means of communication—existed in far less degree in the Saxon states than in the more extensive Frankish territories. Such rudimentary practices as seem parallel to early stages of feudal growth were more so in appearance than in reality, and we can hardly affirm with any confidence that political feudalism was even in process of formation in England before the Conquest, though it would undoubtedly have been introduced there by some process before very long.

The political feudal organization was as intimately bound up with the possession of land as the economic, but its primary object was different. It may be described as that form of organization in which the duties of the citizen to the state had been changed into a species of land rent. A set of legal arrangements and personal relationships which had grown up wholly in the field of private affairs, for the serving of private ends, had usurped the place of public law in the state. Duties of the citizen and functions of the government were translated into its terms and performed as incidents of a private obligation. The individual no longer served in the army because this service was a part of his obligation as a citizen, but because he had agreed by private contract to do so as a part of the rent he was to pay for the land he held of another man. The judicial organization was transformed in the same way. The national courts disappeared, and their place was taken by private courts made up of tenants. The king summoned at intervals the great men of Church and State to gather round him in his council, law court, and legislature, in so far as there was a legislature in that age, the curia regis, the mother institution of a numerous progeny; but he did not summon them, and they came no longer, because they were the great men of Church and State, the wise men of the land, but because they had entered into a private obligation with him to attend when called upon, as a return for lands which he had given them; or, in other words, as Henry II told the bishops in the Constitutions of Clarendon, because they were his vassals. Public taxation underwent the same change, and the money revenue of the feudal state which corresponds most nearly to the income of taxation, was made up of irregular payments due on the occurrence of specified events from those who held land of the king, and these in turn collected like payments of their tenants; the relief, for instance, on the succession of the heir to his father's holding, or the aids in three cases, on the knighting of the lord's eldest son, the marrying of his eldest daughter, and the ransom of his own person from imprisonment. The contact of the central government with the mass of the men of the state was broken off by the intervening series of lords who were political rulers each of the territory or group of lands immediately subject to himself, and exercised within those limits the functions which the general government should normally exercise for the whole state. The payments and services which the lord's vassals made to him, while they were of the nature of rent, were not rent in the economic sense; they were important to the suzerain less as matters of income than as defining his political power and marking his rank in this hierarchical organization. The state as a whole might retain its geographical outlines and the form of a common government, but it was really broken up into fragments of varying size, whose lords possessed in varying degrees of completeness the attributes of sovereignty.

This organization, however, never usurped the place of the state so completely as might be inferred. It had grown up within the limits of a state which was, during the whole period of its formation, nominally ruled over by a king who was served by a more or less centralized administrative system. This royal power never entirely disappeared. It survived as the conception of government. it survived in the exercise of some rights everywhere, and of many rights in some places, even in the most feudal of countries. Some feeling of public law and public duty still lingered. In the king's court, the curia regis, whether in England or in France, there was often present a small group of members, at first in a minor and subordinate capacity, who were there, not because they were the vassals of the king, but because they were the working members of a government machine. The military necessity of the state in all countries occasionally called out something like the old general levy. In the judicial department, in England at least, one important class of courts, the popular county courts, was never seriously affected by feudalism, either in their organization or in the law which they interpreted. Any complete description of the feudal organization must be understood to be a description of tendencies rather than of a realized system. It was the tendency of feudalism to transform the state into a series of principalities rising in tiers one above the other, and to get the business of the state done, not through a central constitutional machine, but through a series of graded duties corresponding to these successive stages and secured by private agreements between the landholders and by a customary law which was the outgrowth of such agreements.

, At the date of the Norman Conquest of England, this tendency was more nearly realized in France than anywhere else. Within the limits of that state a number of great feudal principalities had been formed, duchies and counties, round the administrative divisions of an earlier time as their starting-point, in many of which the sovereign of the state could exercise no powers of government. The extensive powers which the earlier system had intrusted to the duke or count as an administrative officer of the state he now exercised as a practically independent sovereign, and the state could expect from this portion of its territory only the feudal services of its ruler, perhaps ill-defined and difficult to enforce. In some cases, however, this process of breaking up the state into smaller units went no further. Normandy, with which we are particularly concerned, was an instance of this fact. The duke was practically the sole sovereign of that province. The king of France was entirely shut out. Even the Church was under the unlimited control of the duke. And with respect to his subjects his power was as great as with respect to his nominal sovereign. Very few great baronies existed in Normandy formed of contiguous territory and capable of development into independent principalities, and those that did exist were kept constantly in the hands of relatives of the ducal house and under strong control. Political feudalism existed in Normandy in even greater perfection and in a more logical completeness, if we regard the forms alone, its practices and customs, than was usual in the feudal world of that age; but it existed not as the means by which the state was broken into fragments, but as the machinery by which it was governed by the duke. It formed the bond of connexion between him and the great men of the state. It defined the services which he had the right to demand of them, and which they in turn might demand of their vassals. It formed the foundation of the army and of the judicial system. Every department of the state was influenced by its forms and principles. At the same time the Duke of Normandy was more than a feudal suzerain. He had saved on the whole, from the feudal deluge, more of the prerogatives of sovereignty than had the king of France. He had a considerable non-feudal administrative system, though it might not reach all parts of the duchy. The supreme judicial power had never been parted with, and the Norman barons were unable to exercise in its full extent the right of high justice. The oath of allegiance from all freemen, whosesoever vassals they might be, traces of which are to be found in many feudal lands and even under the Capetian kings, was retained in the duchy. Private war, baronial coinage, engagements with foreign princes to the injury of the duke,—these might occur in exceptional cases during a minority or under a weak duke, or in time of rebellion; but the strong dukes repressed them with an iron hand, and no Norman baron could claim any of them as a prescriptive right. Feudalism existed in Normardy as the organization of the state, and as the system which regulated the relations between the duke and the knights and the nobles of the land, but it did not exist at the expense of the sovereign rights of the duke.

This was the system which was introduced fully formed into England with the grants of land which the Conqueror made to his barons. It was the only system known to him by which to regulate their relations to himself and their duties to the state. To suppose a gradual introduction of feudalism into England, except in a geographical sense, as the confiscation spread over the land, is to misunderstand both feudalism itself and its history. This system gave to the baron opportunities which might be dangerous under a ruler who could not make himself obeyed, but there was nothing in it inconsistent with the practical absolutism exercised by the first of the Norman kings and by the more part of his immediate successors. Feudalism brought in with itself two ideas which exercised decisive influence on later English history. I do not mean to assert that these ideas were consciously held, or that they could have been formulated in words, though of the first at least this was very nearly true, but that they unconsciously controlled the facts of the time and their future development. One was the idea that all holders of land in the kingdom, except the king, were, strictly speaking, tenants rather than owners, which profoundly influenced the history of English law; the other was the idea that important public duties were really private obligations, created by a business contract, which as profoundly influenced the growth of the constitution. Taken together, the introduction of the feudal system was as momentous a change as any which followed the Norman Conquest, as decisive in its influence upon the future as the enrichment of race or of language; more decisive in one respect, since without the consequences in government and constitution, which were destined to follow from the feudalization of the English state, neither race nor language could have done the work in the world which they have already accomplished and are yet destined to perform in still larger measure.

But, however profound this change may have been, it affected but a small class, comparatively speaking. The whole number of military units, of knights due the king in service, seems to have been something less than five thousand.[3] For the great mass of the population, the working substratum, whose labours sustained the life of the nation, the Norman Conquest made but little change. The interior organization of the manor was not affected by it. Its work went on in the same way as before. There was a change of masters; there was a new set of ideas to interpret the old relationship; the upper grades of the manorial population suffered in some parts of England a serious depression. But in the main, as concerned the great mass of facts, there was no change of importance. Nor was there any, at first at least, which affected the position of the towns. The new system allowed as readily as the old the rights which they already possessed. In the end, the new ideas might be a serious matter for the towns in some particulars, but at present the conditions did not exist which were to raise these difficulties. At the time, to the mass of the nation, to everybody indeed, the Norman Conquest might easily seem but a change of sovereigns, a change of masters. It is because we can see the results of the changes which it really introduced that we are able to estimate their profound significance.

The spoiling of England for the benefit of the foreigner did not consist in the confiscation of lands alone. Besides the forced redemption of their lands, William seems to have laid a heavy tax on the nation, and the churches and monasteries whose lands were free from confiscation seem to have suffered heavy losses of their gold and silver and precious stuffs. The royal treasure and Harold's possessions would pass into William's hands, and much confiscated and plundered wealth besides. These things he distributed with a free hand, especially to the churches of the continent whose prayers and blessings he unquestionably regarded as a strong reinforcement of his arms. Harold's rich banner of the fighting man went to Rome, and valuable gifts besides, and the Norman ecclesiastical world had abundant cause to return thanks to heaven for the successes which had attended the efforts of the Norman military arm. If William despatched these gifts to the continent before his own return to Normandy, they did not exhaust his booty, for the wonder and admiration of the duchy is plainly expressed at the richness and beauty of the spoils which he brought home with him.

Having settled the matters which demanded immediate attention, the king proceeded to make a progress through those parts of his kingdom which were under his control. Just where he went we are not told, but he can hardly have gone far outside the counties of southern and eastern England which were directly influenced by his march on London. In such a progress he probably had chiefly in mind to take possession for himself and his men of confiscated estates and of strategic points. No opposition showed itself anywhere, but women with their children appeared along the way to beseech his mercy, and the favour which he showed to these suppliants was thought worthy of special remark. Winchester seems to have been visited, and secured by the beginning of a Norman castle within the walls, and the journey ended at Pevensey, where he had landed so short a time before in pursuit of the crown. William had decided that he could return to Normandy, and the decision that this could be safely done with so small a part of the kingdom actually in hand, with so few castles already built or garrisons established, is the clearest possible evidence of William's opinion of the situation. He would have been the last man to venture such a step if he had believed the risk to be great. And the event justified his judgment. The insurrectionary movements which called him back clearly appear to have been, not so much efforts of the nation to throw off a foreign yoke, as revolts excited by the oppression and bad government of those whom he had left in charge of the kingdom.

On the eve of his departure he confided the care of his new kingdom to two of his followers whom he believed the most devoted to himself, the south-east to his half brother Odo, and the north to William Fitz Osbern. Odo, Bishop of Bayeux, but less an ecclesiastic, according to the ideals of the Church, than a typically feudal bishop, was assigned the responsibility for the fortress of Dover, was given large estates in Kent and to the west of it, and was probably made earl of that county at this time. William Fitz Osbern was the son of the duke's guardian, who had been murdered for his fidelity during William's minority, and they had been boys together, as we are expressly told. He was appointed to be responsible for Winchester and to hold what might be called the marches, towards the unoccupied north and west. Very probably at this time also he was made Earl of Hereford? Some other of the leading nobles of the Conquest had been established in their possessions by this date, as we know on good evidence, like Hugh of Grantmesnil in Hampshire, but the chief dependence of the king was apparently upon these two, who are spoken of as having under their care the minor holders of the castles which had been already established.

No disorders in Normandy demanded the duke's return. Everything had been quiet there, under the control of Matilda and those who had been appointed to assist her. William's visit at this time looks less like a necessity than a parade to make an exhibition of the results of his venture. He took with him a splendid assortment of plunder and a long train of English nobles, among whom the young atheling Edgar, Stigand, Archbishop of Canterbury, Earls Edwin and Morcar, Waltheof, son of Siward, the Abbot of Glastonbury, and a thane of Kent, are mentioned by name. The favour and honour with which William treated these men did not disguise from them the fact that they were really held as hostages. No business of especial importance occupied William during his nine months' stay in Normandy. He was received with great rejoicing on every hand, especially in Rouen, where Matilda was staying, and his return and triumphal progress through the country reminded his panegyrist of the successes and glories of the great Roman commanders. He distributed with a free hand, to the churches and monasteries, the wealth which he had brought with him. A great assembly gathered to celebrate with him the Easter feast at the abbey of Fécamp. His presence was sought to add éclat to the dedication of new churches. But the event of the greatest importance which occurred during this visit to the duchy was the falling vacant of the primacy of Normandy by the death of Maurilius, Archbishop of Rouen. The universal choice for his successor was Lanfranc, the Italian, Abbot of St. Stephen's at Caen, who had already made evident to all the possession of those talents for government which he was to exercise in a larger field. But though William stood ready, in form at least, to grant his sanction, Lanfranc declined the election, which then fell upon John, Bishop of Avranches, a friend of his. Lanfranc was sent to Rome to obtain the pallium for the new archbishop, but his mission was in all probability one of information to the pope regarding larger interests than those of the archbishopric of Rouen.

In the meantime, affairs had not run smoothly in England. We may easily guess that William's lieutenants, especially his brother, had not failed on the side of too great gentleness in carrying out his directions to secure the land with garrisons and castles. In various places unconnected with one another troubles had broken out. In the north, where Copsi had been made Earl of Northumberland, an old local dynastic feud was still unsettled, and the mere appointment of an earl would not bring it to an end. Copsi was slain by his rival, Oswulf, who was himself soon afterward killed, but the Norman occupation had still to be begun. In the west a more interesting resistance to the Norman advance had developed near Hereford, led by Edric, called the Wild, descendant of a noble Saxon house. He had enlisted the support of the Welsh, and in retaliation for attacks upon himself had laid waste a large district in Herefordshire. Odo had had in his county an insurrection which threatened for a moment to have most serious consequences, but which had ended in a complete failure. The men of Kent, planning rebellion, had sent across the channel to Eustace, Count of Boulogne, who believed that he had causes of grievance against William, and had besought him to come to their aid in an attempt to seize the fortress of Dover. Eustace accepted the invitation and crossed over at the appointed time, but his allies had not all gathered when he arrived, and the unsteady character of the count wrecked the enterprise. He attacked in haste, and when he failed to carry the castle by storm, he retired in equal haste and abandoned the undertaking. William judged him too important a man to treat with severity, and restored him to his favour. Besides these signs which revealed the danger of an open outbreak, William undoubtedly knew that many of the English had left the country and had gone in various directions, seeking foreign aid. His absence could not be prolonged without serious consequences, and in December, 1067, he returned to England.

[1] William of Poitiers, in Migne's Patrologia Latina, cxlix, 1258, and see F. Baring, in Engl. Hist. Rev., xiii. 18 (1898).

[2] Orderic Vitalis, ii. 158 (ed. Le Prevost).

[3] Round, Feudal England, p. 292.

CHAPTER II.
THE SUBJUGATION OF LAND AND CHURCH

With William's return to England began the long and difficult task of bringing the country completely under his control. But this was not a task that called for military genius. Patience was the quality most demanded, and William's patience gave way but rarely. There was no army in the field against him. No large portion of the land was in insurrection. No formal campaign was necessary. Local revolts had to be put down one after another, or a district dealt with where rebellion was constantly renewed. The Scandinavian north and the Celtic west were the regions not yet subdued, and the seats of future trouble. Three years were filled with this work, and the fifteen years that follow were comparatively undisturbed. For the moment after his return, William was occupied with no hostilities. The Christmas of 1067 was celebrated in London with the land at peace, Normans and English meeting together to all appearance with cordial good-will. A native, Gospatric, was probably at this time made Earl of Northumberland, in place of Copsi, who had been killed, though this was an exercise of royal power in form rather than in reality, since William's authority did not yet reach so far. A Norman, Remigius, was made Bishop of Dorchester, in place of Wulfwig, who had died while the king was in Normandy, and William's caution in dealing with the matter of Church reform is shown in the fact that the new bishop received his consecration from Stigand. It is possible also that another heavy tax was imposed at this time.

But soon after Christmas, William felt himself obliged to take the field. He had learned that Exeter, the rich commercial city of the south-west, was making preparations to resist him. It was in a district where Harold and his family had had large possessions. His mother was in the city, and perhaps others of the family. At least some English of prominence seem to have rallied around them. The citizens had repaired and improved their already strong walls. They had impressed foreigners, merchants even, into their service, and were seeking allies in other towns. William's rule had never yet reached into that part of England, and Exeter evidently hoped to shut him out altogether. When the king heard of these preparations, he acted with his usual promptitude, but with no sacrifice of his diplomatic skill. The citizens should first be made to acknowledge their intentions. A message was sent to the city, demanding that the oath of allegiance to himself be taken. The citizens answered that they would take no oath, and would not admit him within the walls, but that they were willing to pay him the customary tribute. William at once replied that he was not accustomed to have subjects on such conditions, and at once began his march against the city. Orderic Vitalis thought it worthy of note, that in this army William was using Englishmen for the first time as soldiers.

When the hostile army drew near to the town, the courage of some of the leading men failed, and they went out to seek terms of peace. They promised to do whatever was commanded, and they gave hostages, but on their return they found their negotiations disavowed and the city determined to stand a siege. This lasted only eighteen days. Some decided advantage which the Normans gained—the undermining of the walls seems to be implied—induced the city to try again for terms. The clergy, with their sacred books and relics, accompanied the deputation, which obtained from the king better promises than had been hoped for. For some reason William departed from his usual custom of severity to those who resisted. He overlooked their evil conduct, ordered no confiscations, and even stationed guards in the gates to keep out the soldiers who would have helped themselves to the property of the citizens with some violence. But as usual he selected a site for a castle within the walls, and left a force of chosen knights under faithful command, to complete the fortification and to form the garrison. Harold's mother, Gytha, left the city before its surrender, and finally found a refuge in Saint Omer, in Flanders. Harold's sons also, if they were in Exeter, made their escape before its fall.

After subduing Exeter, William marched with his army into Cornwall, and put down without difficulty whatever resistance he found there. The confiscation of forfeited estates was no doubt one object of his march through the land, and the greater part of these were bestowed upon his own half brother, Robert, Count of Mortain, the beginning of what grew ultimately into the great earldom of Cornwall. In all, the grants which were made to Robert have been estimated at 797 manors, the largest made to any one as the result of the Conquest. Of these, 248 manors were in Cornwall, practically the whole shire; 75 in Dorset, and 49 in Devonshire. This was almost a principality in itself, and is alone nearly enough to disprove the policy attributed to William of scattering about the country the great estates which he granted. So powerful a possession was the earldom which was founded upon this grant that after a time the policy which had been followed in Normandy, in regard to the great counties, seemed the only wise one in this case also, and it was not allowed to pass out of the immediate family of the king until in the fourteenth century it was made into a provision for the king's eldest son, as it has ever since remained. These things done, William disbanded his army and returned to spend Easter at Winchester.

Once more for a moment the land seemed to be at peace, and William was justified in looking upon himself as now no longer merely the leader of a military adventure, seeking to conquer a foreign state, but as firmly established in a land where he had made a new home for his house. He could send for his wife; his children should be born here. It should be the native land of future generations for his family. Matilda came soon after Easter, with a distinguished train of ladies as well as lords, and with her Guy, Bishop of Amiens, who, Orderic tells us, had already written his poem on the war of William and Harold. At Whitsuntide, in Westminster, Matilda was crowned queen by Archbishop Aldred. Later in the summer Henry, the future King Henry I, was born, and the new royal family had completely identified itself with the new kingdom.

But a great task still lay before the king, the greatest perhaps that he had yet undertaken. The north was his only in name. Scarcely had any English king up to this time exercised there the sort of authority to which William was accustomed, and which he was determined to exercise everywhere. The question of the hour was, whether he could establish his authority there by degrees, as he seemed to be trying to do, or only after a sharp conflict. The answer to this question was known very soon after the coronation of Matilda. What seemed to the Normans a great conspiracy of the north and west was forming. The Welsh and English nobles were making common cause; the clergy and the common people joined their prayers; York was noted as especially enthusiastic in the cause, and many there took to living in tents as a kind of training for the conflict which was coming. The Normans understood at the time that there were two reasons for this determination to resist by force any further extension of William's rule. One was, the personal dissatisfaction of Earl Edwin. He had been given by William some undefined authority, and promoted above his brother, and he had even been promised a daughter of the king's as his wife. Clearly it had seemed at one time very necessary to conciliate him. But either that necessity had passed away, or William was reluctant to fulfil his promise; and Edwin, discontented with the delay, was ready to lead what was for him at least, after he had accepted so much from William, a rebellion. He was the natural leader of such an attempt; his family history made him that. Personal popularity and his wide connexions added to his strength, and if he had had in himself the gifts of leadership, it would not have been even then too late to dispute the possession of England on even terms. The second reason given us is one to which we must attach much greater force than to the personal influence of

Edwin. He in all probability merely embraced an opportunity. The other was the really moving cause. This is said to have been the discontent of the English and Welsh nobles under the Norman oppression, but we must phrase it a little differently. No direct oppression had as yet been felt, either in the north or west, but the severity of William in the south and east, the widespread confiscations there, were undoubtedly well known, and easily read as signs of what would follow in the north, and already the borders of Wales were threatened n with the pushing forward of the Norman lines, which went on so steadily and for so long a time.

Whether or not the efforts which had been making to obtain foreign help against William were to result finally in bringing in a reinforcement of Scots or Danes, the union of Welshmen and Englishmen was itself formidable and demanded instant attention. Early in the summer of 1068 the army began its march upon York, advancing along a line somewhat to the west of the centre of England, as the situation would naturally demand. As in William's earlier marches, so here again he encountered no resistance. Whatever may have been the extent of the conspiracy or the plans of the leaders, the entire movement collapsed before the Norman's firm determination to be master of the kingdom. Edwin and Morcar had collected an army and were in the field somewhere between Warwick and Northampton, but when the time came when the fight could no longer be postponed, they thought better of it, besought the king's favour again, and obtained at least the show of it. The boastful preparations at York brought forth no better result. The citizens went out to meet the king on his approach, and gave him the keys of the city and hostages from among them.

The present expedition went no further north, but its influence extended further. Ethelwin, the Bishop of Durham came in and made his submission. He bore inquiries also from Malcolm, the king of Scots, who had been listening to the appeals for aid from the enemies of William, and preparing himself to advance to their assistance. The Bishop of Durham was sent back to let him know what assurances would be acceptable to William, and he undoubtedly also informed him of the actual state of affairs south of his borders, of the progress which the invader had made, and of the hopelessness of resistance. The Normans at any rate believed that as a result of the bishop's mission Malcolm was glad to send down an embassy of his own which tendered to William an oath of obedience. It is not likely that William attached much weight to any profession of the Scottish king's. Already, probably as soon as the failure of this northern undertaking was apparent, some of the most prominent of the English, who seem to have taken part in it, had abandoned England and gone to the Scottish court. It is very possible that Edgar and his two sisters, Margaret and Christina, sought the protection of Malcolm at this time, together with Gospatric, who had shortly before been made Earl of Northumberland, and the sheriff Merleswegen. These men had earlier submitted to William, Merleswegen perhaps in the submission at Berkhampsted, with Edgar, and had been received with favour. Under what circumstances they turned against him we do not know, but they had very likely been attracted by the promise of strength in this effort at resistance, and were now less inclined than the unstable Edwin to profess so early a repentance. Margaret, whether she went to Scotland at this time or a little later, found there a permanent home, consenting against her will to become the bride of Malcolm instead of the bride of the Church as she had wished. As queen she gained, through teaching her wild subjects, by the example of gentle manners and noble life, a wider mission than the convent could have furnished her. The conditions which Malcolm accepted evidently contained no demand as to any English fugitives, nor any other to which he could seriously object. William was usually able to discern the times, and did not attempt the impracticable.

William intended this expedition of his to result in the permanent pacification of the country through which he had passed. There is no record of any special severity attending the march, but certainly no one was able to infer from it that the king was weak or to be trifled with. The important towns he secured with castles and garrisons, as he had in the south. Warwick and Northampton were occupied in this way as he advanced, with York at the north, and Lincoln, Huntingdon, and Cambridge along the east as he returned. A great wedge of fortified posts was thus driven far into that part of the land from which the greatest trouble was to be expected, and this, together with the general impression which his march had made, was the most which was gained from it. Sometime during this summer of 1068 another fruitless attempt had been made to disturb the Norman possession of England. Harold's sons had retired, perhaps after the fall of Exeter, to Ireland, where their father had formerly found refuge. There it was not difficult to stir up the love of plundering raids in the descendants of the Vikings, and they returned at this time, it is said with more than fifty ships, and sailed up the Bristol Channel. If any among them intended a serious invasion of the island, the result was disappointing. They laid waste the coast lands; attacked the city of Bristol, but were beaten off by the citizens; landed again further down in Somerset, and were defeated in a great battle by Ednoth, who had been Harold's staller, where many were killed on both sides, including Ednoth himself; and then returned with nothing gained but such plunder as they succeeded in carrying off. The next year they repeated the attempt in the same style, and were again defeated, even more disastrously, this time by one of the newcomers, Brian of Britanny. Such piratical descents were not dangerous to the Norman government, nor was a rally to beat them off any test of English loyalty to William.

Even the historian, Orderic Vitalis, half English by descent and wholly so by birth, but writing in Normandy for Normans and very favourable to William, or possibly the even more Norman William of Poitiers, whom he may have been following, was moved by the sufferings of the land under these repeated invasions, revolts, and harryings, and notes at the close of his account of this year how conquerors and conquered alike were involved in the evils of war, famine, and pestilence. He adds that the king, seeing the injuries which were inflicted on the country, gathered together the soldiers who were serving him for pay, and sent them home with rich rewards. We may regard this disbanding of his mercenary troops as another sign that William considered his position secure.

In truth, however, the year which was coming on, 1069, was another year of crisis in the history of the Conquest. The danger which had been threatening William from the beginning was this year to descend upon him, and to prove as unreal as all those he had faced since the great battle with Harold. For a long time efforts had been making to induce some foreign power to interfere in England and support the cause of the English against the invader. Two states seemed especially fitted for the mission, from close relationship with England in the past,—Scotland and Denmark. Fugitives, who preferred exile to submission, had early sought the one or the other of these courts, and urged intervention upon their kings. Scotland had for the moment formally accepted the Conquest. Denmark had not done so, and Denmark was the more directly interested in the result, not perhaps as a mere question of the independence of England, but for other possible reasons. If England was to be ruled by a foreign king, should not that king on historical grounds be a Dane rather than a Norman? Ought he not to be of the land that had already furnished kings to England? And if Sweyn dreamed of the possibility of extending his rule, at such a time, over this other member of the empire of his uncle, Canute the Great, he is certainly not to be blamed.

It is true that the best moment for such an intervention had been allowed to slip by, the time when no beginning of conquest had been made in the north, but the situation was not even yet unfavourable. William was to learn, when the new year had hardly begun, that he really held no more of the north than his garrisons commanded. Perhaps it was a rash attempt to try to establish a Norman earl of Northumberland in Durham before the land had been overawed by his own presence; but the post was important, the two experiments which had been made to secure the country through the appointment of English earls had failed, and the submission of the previous summer might prove to be real. In January Robert of Comines was made earl, and with rash confidence, against the advice of the bishop, he took possession of Durham with five hundred men or more. He expected, no doubt, to be very soon behind the walls of a new castle, but he was allowed no time. The very night of his arrival the enemy gathered and massacred him and all his men but two. Yorkshire took courage at this and cut up a Norman detachment. Then the exiles in Scotland believed the time had come for another attempt, and Edgar, Gospatric, and the others, with the men of Northumberland at their back, advanced to attack the castle in York. This put all the work of the previous summer in danger, and at the call of William Malet, who held the castle for him, the king advanced rapidly to his aid, fell unexpectedly on the insurgents, and scattered them with great slaughter. As a result the Norman hold on York was tightened by the building of a second castle, but Northumberland was still left to itself.

William may have thought, as he returned to celebrate Easter at Winchester, that the north had learned a lesson that would be sufficient for some time, but he must have heard soon after his arrival that the men of Yorkshire had again attacked his castles, though they had been beaten off without much difficulty. Nothing had been gained by any of these attempts, but they must have been indications to any abroad who were watching the situation, and to William as well, that an invasion of England in that quarter might hope for much local assistance. It was nearly the end of the summer before it came, and a summer that was on the whole quiet, disturbed only by the second raid of Harold's sons in the Bristol Channel.

Sweyn of Denmark had at last made up his mind, and had got ready an expedition, a somewhat miscellaneous force apparently, "sharked up" from all the Baltic lands, and not too numerous. His fleet sailed along the shores of the North Sea and first appeared off south-western England. A foolish attack on Dover was beaten off, and three other attempts to land on the east coast, where the country was securely held, were easily defeated. Finally, it would seem, off the Humber they fell in with some ships bearing the English leaders from Scotland, who had been waiting for them. There they landed and marched upon York, joined on the way by the men of the country of all ranks. And the mere news of their approach, the prospect of new horrors to be lived through with no chance of mitigating them, proved too much for the old archbishop, Aldred, and he died a few days before the storm broke. William was hunting in the forest of Dean, on the southern borders of Wales, when he heard that the invaders had landed, but his over-confident garrison in York reported that they could hold out for a year without aid, and he left them for the present to themselves. They planned to stand a siege, and in clearing a space about the castle they kindled a fire which destroyed the most of the city, including the cathedral church, but when the enemy appeared, they tried a battle in the open, and were killed or captured to a man.

The fall of York gave a serious aspect to the case, and called for William's presence. Soon after the capture of the city the Danes had gone back to the Humber, to the upper end of the estuary apparently, and there they succeeded in avoiding attack by crossing one river or another as the army of the king approached. In the meantime, in various places along the west of England, insurrections had broken out, encouraged probably by exaggerated reports of the successes of the rebels in the north. Only one of these, that in Staffordshire, required any attention from William, and in this case we do not know why. In all the other cases, in Devon, in Somerset, and at Shrewsbury, where the Welsh helped in the attack on the Norman castle, the garrisons and men of the locality unassisted, or assisted only by the forces of their neighbours, had defended themselves with success. If the Danish invasion be regarded as a test of the security of the Conquest in those parts of England which the Normans had really occupied, then certainly it must be regarded as complete.

Prom the west William returned to the north with little delay, and occupied York without opposition. Then followed the one act of the Conquest which is condemned by friend and foe alike. When William had first learned of the fate of his castles in York, he had burst out into ungovernable rage, and the mood had not passed away. He was determined to exact an awful vengeance for the repeated defiance of his power. War in its mildest form in those days was little regulated by any consideration for the conquered. From the point of view of a passionate soldier there was some provocation in this case. Norman garrisons had been massacred; detached parties had been cut off; repeated rebellion had followed every pacification. Plainly a danger existed here, grave in itself and inviting greater danger from abroad. Policy might dictate measures of unusual severity, but policy did not call for what was done, and clearly in this case the Conqueror gave way to a passion of rage which he usually held in check, and inflicted on the stubborn province a punishment which the standard of his own time did not justify.

Slowly he passed with his army through the country to the north of York, drawing a broad band of desolation between that city and Durham. Fugitives he sought out and put to the sword, but even so he was not satisfied. Innocent and guilty were involved in indiscriminate slaughter. Houses were destroyed, flocks and herds exterminated. Supplies of food and farm implements were heaped together and burned. With deliberate purpose, cruelly carried out, it was made impossible for men to live through a thousand square miles. Years afterwards the country was still a desert; it was generations before it had fully recovered. The Norman writer, Orderic Vitalis, perhaps following the king's chaplain and panegyrist William of Poitiers, while he confesses here that he gladly praised the king when he could, had only condemnation for this deed. He believed that William, responsible to no earthly tribunal, must one day answer for it to an infinite Judge before whom high and low are alike accountable.

Christmas was near at hand when William had finished this business, and he celebrated at York the nativity of the Prince of Peace, doubtless with no suspicion of inconsistency. Soon after Christmas, by a short but difficult expedition, William drove the Danes from a position on the coast which they had believed impregnable, and forced them to take to their ships, in which, after suffering greatly from lack of supplies, they drifted southward as if abandoning the land. During this expedition also, we are told, Gospatric, who had rebelled the year before, and Waltheof who had "gone out" on the coming of the Danes, made renewed submission and were again received into favour by the king. The hopes which the coming of foreign assistance had awakened were at an end.

One thing remained to be done. The men of the Welsh border must be taught the lesson which the men of the Scottish border had learned. The insurrection which had called William into Staffordshire the previous autumn seems still to have lingered in the region. The strong city of Chester, from which, or from whose neighbourhood at least, men had joined the attack on Shrewsbury, and which commanded the north-eastern parts of Wales, was still unsubdued. Soon after his return from the coast William determined upon a longer and still more difficult winter march, across the width of England, from York to Chester. It is no wonder that his army murmured and some at least asked to be dismissed. The country through which they must pass was still largely wilderness. Hills and forests, swollen streams and winter storms, must be encountered, and the strife with them was a test of endurance without the joy of combat. One expedition of the sort in a winter ought to be enough. But William treated the objectors with contempt. He pushed on as he had planned, leaving those to stay behind who would, and but few were ready for open mutiny. The hazardous march was made with success. What remained of the insurrection disappeared before the coming of the king; it has left to us at least no traces of any resistance. Chester was occupied without opposition. Fortified posts were established and garrisons left there and at Stafford. Some things make us suspect that a large district on this side of England was treated as northern Yorkshire had been, and homeless fugitives in crowds driven forth to die of hunger. The patience which pardoned the faithlessness of Edwin and Waltheof was not called for in dealing with smaller men.

From Chester William turned south. At Salisbury he dismissed with rich rewards the soldiers who had been faithful to him, and at Winchester he celebrated the Easter feast. There he found three legates who had been sent from the pope, and supported by their presence he at last took up the affairs of the English Church. The king had shown the greatest caution in dealing with this matter. It must have been understood, almost if not quite from the beginning of the Norman plan of invasion, that if the attempt were successful, one of its results should be the revolution of the English Church, the reform of the abuses which existed in it, as the continental churchman regarded them, and as indeed they were. During the past century a great reform movement, emanating from the monastery of Cluny, had transformed the Catholic world, but in this England had but little part. Starting as a monastic reformation, it had just succeeded in bringing the whole Church under monastic control. Henceforth the asceticism of the monk, his ideals in religion and worship, his type of thought and learning, were to be those of the official Church, from the papal throne to the country parsonage. It was for that age a true reformation. The combined influence of the two great temptations to which the churchmen of this period of the Middle Ages were exposed—ignorance so easy to yield to, so hard to overcome, and property, carrying with it rank and power and opening the way to ambition for oneself or one's posterity—was so great that a rule of strict asceticism, enforced by a powerful organization with fearful sanctions, and a controlling ideal of personal devotion, alone could overcome it. The monastic reformation had furnished these conditions, though severe conflicts were still to be fought out before they would be made to prevail in every part of western Europe. Shortly before the appointment of Stigand to the archbishopric of Canterbury, these new ideas had obtained possession of the papal throne in the person of Leo IX, and with them other ideas which had become closely and almost necessarily associated with them, of strict centralization under the pope, of a theocratic papal supremacy, in line certainly with the history of the Church, but more self-consciously held and logically worked out than ever before.

In this great movement England had had no permanent share. Cut off from easy contact with the currents of continental thought, not merely by the channel but by the lack of any common interests and natural incentives to common life, it stood in an earlier stage of development in ecclesiastical matters, as in legal and constitutional. In organization, in learning, and in conduct, ecclesiastical England at the eve of the Norman Conquest may be compared not unfairly to ecclesiastical Europe of the tenth century. There was the same loosening of the bonds of a common organization, the same tendency to separate into local units shut up to interest in themselves alone.

National councils had practically ceased to meet. The legislative machinery of the Church threatened to disappear in that of the State. An outside body, the witenagemot, seemed about to acquire the right of imposing rules and regulations upon the Church, and another outside power, the king, to acquire the right of appointing its officers. Quite as important in the eyes of the Church as the lack of legislative independence was the lack of judicial independence, which was also a defect of the English Church. The law of the Church as it bore upon the life of the citizen was declared and enforced in the hundred or shire court, and bishop and ealdorman sat together in the latter. Only over the ecclesiastical faults of his clergy did the bishop have exclusive jurisdiction, and this was probably a jurisdiction less well developed than on the continent. The power of the primate over his suffragans and of the bishop within his diocese was ill defined and vague, and questions of disputed authority or doubtful allegiance lingered long without exact decision, perhaps from lack of interest, perhaps from want of the means of decision.

In learning, the condition was even worse. The cloister schools had undergone a marked decline since the great days of Theodore and Alcuin. Not merely were the parish priests ignorant men, but even bishops and abbots. The universal language of learning and faith was neglected, and in England alone, of all countries, theological books were written in the local tongue, a sure sign of isolation and of the lack of interest in the common philosophical life of the world. In moral conduct, while the English clergy could not be held guilty of serious breaches of the general ethical code, they were far from coming up to the special standard which the canon law imposed upon the clergy, and which the monastic reformation was making the inflexible law of the time. Married priests abounded; there were said to be even married bishops. Simony was not infrequent. Every churchman of high rank was likely to be a pluralist, holding bishoprics and abbacies together, like Stigand, who held with the primacy the bishopric of Winchester and many abbeys. That such a man as Stigand, holding every ecclesiastical office that he could manage to keep, depriving monasteries of their landed endowments with no more right than the baron after him, refused recognition by every legally elected pope, and thought unworthy to crown a king, or even in most cases to consecrate a bishop, should have held his place for so many years as unquestioned primate in all but the most important functions, is evidence enough that the English Church had not yet been brought under the influence of the great religious reformation of the eleventh century.

This was the chief defect of the England of that time—a defect upon all sides of its life, which the Conquest remedied. It was an isolated land.

It stood in danger of becoming a Scandinavian land, not in blood merely, or in absorption in an actual Scandinavian empire, but in withdrawal from the real world, and in that tardy, almost reluctant, civilization which was possibly a necessity for Scandinavia proper, but which would have been for England a falling back from higher levels. It was the mission of the Norman Conquest—if we may speak of a mission for great historical events—to deliver England from this danger, and to bring her into the full current of the active and progressive life of Christendom.

It was more than three years after the coronation of William before the time was come for a thorough overhauling of the Church. So far as we know, William, up to that time, had given no sign of his intentions. The early adhesion of Stigand had been welcomed. The Normans seem to have believed that he enjoyed great consideration and influence among the Saxons, and he had been left undisturbed. He had even been allowed to consecrate the new Norman bishop of Dorchester, which looks like an act of deliberate policy. It had not seemed wise to alarm the Church so long as the military issue of the invasion could be considered in any sense doubtful, and not until the changes could be made with the powerful support of the head of the Church directly expressed. It is a natural guess, though we have no means of knowing, that Lanfranc's mission to Rome in 1067 had been to discuss this matter with the Roman authorities, quite as much as to get the pallium for the new Archbishop of Rouen. Now the time had come for action.

Three legates of the pope were at Winchester, and there a council was summoned to meet them. Two of the legates were cardinals, then a relatively less exalted rank in the Church than later, but making plain the direct support of the pope. The other was Ermenfrid, Bishop of Sion, or Sitten, in what is now the Swiss canton of the Vallais. He had already been in England eight years earlier as a papal legate, and he would bring to this council ideas derived from local observation, as well as tried diplomatic skill. Before the council met, the papal sanction of the Conquest was publicly proclaimed, when the cardinal legates placed the crown on the king's head at the Easter festival. On the octave of Easter, in 1070, the council met. Its first business was to deal with the case of Stigand. Something like a trial seems to have been held, but its result could never have been in doubt. He was deprived of the archbishopric, and, with that, of his other preferments, on three grounds: he had held Winchester along with the primacy; he had held the primacy while Robert was still the rightful archbishop according to the laws of the Church; and he had obtained his pallium and his only recognition from the antipope Benedict X. His brother, the Bishop of Elmham, was also deposed, and some abbots at the same time.

An English chronicler of a little later date, Florence of Worcester, doubtless representing the opinion of those contemporaries who were unfavourable to the Normans, believed that for many of these depositions there were no canonical grounds, but that they were due to the king's desire to have the help of the Church in holding and pacifying his new kingdom. We may admit the motive and its probable influence on the acts of the time, without overlooking the fact that there would be likely to be an honest difference in the interpretation of canonical rights and wrongs on the Norman and the English sides, and that the Normans were more likely to be right according to the prevailing standard of the Church. The same chronicler gives us interesting evidence of the contemporary native feeling about this council, and the way the rights of the English were likely to be treated by it, in recording the fact that it was thought to be a bold thing for the English bishop Wulfstan, of Worcester, to demand his rights in certain lands which Aldred had kept in his possession when he was transferred from the see of Worcester to the archbishopric of York. The case was postponed, until there should be an archbishop of York to defend the rights of his Church, but the brave bishop had nothing to lose by his boldness. The treatment of the Church throughout his reign is evidence of William's desire to act according to established law, though it is also evidence of his ruling belief that the new law was superior to the old, if ever a conflict arose between them.

Shortly after, at Whitsuntide, another council met at Windsor, and continued the work. The cardinals had returned to Rome, but Ermenfrid was still present. Further vacancies were made in the English Church in the same way as by the previous council—by the end of the year only two, or at most three, English bishops remained in office—but the main business at this time was to fill vacancies. A new Archbishop of York, Thomas, Canon of Bayeux, was appointed, and three bishops, Winchester, Selsey, and Elmham, all of these from the royal chapel. But the most important appointment of the time was that of Lanfranc, Abbot of St. Stephen's at Caen, to be Archbishop of Canterbury. With evident reluctance he accepted this responsible office, in which his work was destined to be almost as important in the history of England as William's own. Two papal legates crossing from England, Ermenfrid and a new one named Hubert, a synod of the Norman clergy, Queen Matilda, and her son Robert, all urged him to accept, and he yielded to their solicitation.

Lanfranc was at this time sixty-five years of age. An Italian by birth, he had made good use of the advantages which the schools of that land offered to laymen, but on the death of his father, while still a young man, he had abandoned the path of worldly promotion which lay open before him in the profession of the law, in which he had followed his father, and had gone to France to teach and finally to become a monk. By 1045 he was prior of the abbey of Bec, and within a few years he was famous throughout the whole Church as one of its ablest theologians. In the controversy with Berengar of Tours, on the nature of the Eucharist, he had argued with great skill in favour of transubstantiation. Still more important was the fact that his abilities and ideas were known to William, who had long relied upon his counsel in the government of the duchy, and that entire harmony of action was possible between them. He has been called William's "one friend," and while this perhaps unduly limits the number of the king's friends, he was, in the greatest affairs of his reign, his firm supporter and wise counsellor.

From the moment of his consecration, on August 29, 1070, the reformation of the English Church went steadily on, until it was as completely accomplished as was possible. The first question to be settled was perhaps the most important of all, the question of unity of national organization. The new Archbishop of York refused Lanfranc's demand that he should take the oath of obedience to Canterbury, and asserted his independence and coordinate position, and laid claim to three bordering bishoprics as belonging to his metropolitan see, — Worcester, Lichfield, and Dorchester. The dispute was referred to the king, who arranged a temporary compromise in favour of Lanfranc, and then carried to the pope, by whom it was again referred back to be decided by a council in England. This decision was reached at a council in Windsor at Whitsuntide in 1072, and was in favour of Lanfranc on all points, though it seems certain that the victory was obtained by an extensive series of forgeries of which the archbishop himself was probably the author.[4] It must be added, however, that the moral judgment of that age did not regard as ours does such forgeries in the interest of one's Church. If the decision was understood at the time to mean that henceforth all archbishops of York should promise canonical obedience to the Archbishop of Canterbury, it did not permanently secure that result. But the real point at issue in this dispute, at least for the time being, was no mere matter of rank or precedence; it was as necessary to the plans of Lanfranc and of the Church that his authority should be recognized throughout the whole kingdom as it was to those of William. Nor was the question without possible political significance. The political independence of the north — still uncertain in its allegiance — would be far easier to establish if it was, to begin with, ecclesiastically independent.

Hardly less important than the settlement of this matter was the establishment of the legislative independence of the Church. From the two legatine councils of 1070, at Winchester and Windsor, a series begins of great national synods, meeting at intervals to the end of the reign. Complete divorce from the State was not at first possible. The council was held at a meeting of the court, and was summoned by the king. He was present at the sessions, as were also lay magnates of the realm, but the questions proper to the council were discussed and decided by the churchmen alone, and were promulgated by the Church as its own laws. This was real legislative independence, even if the form of it was somewhat defective, and before very long, as the result of this beginning, the form came to correspond to the reality, and the process became as independent as the conclusion.

William's famous ordinance separating the spiritual and temporal courts decreed another extensive change necessary to complete the independence of the Church in its legal interests. The date of this edict is not certain, but it would seem from such evidence as we have to have been issued not very long after the meeting of the councils of 1070. It withdrew from the local popular courts, the courts of the hundred, all future enforcement of the ecclesiastical laws, subjected all offenders against these laws to trial in the bishop's court, and promised the support of the temporal authorities to the processes and decisions of the Church courts. This abolishing by edict of so important a prerogative of the old local courts, and annulling of so large a part of the old law, was the most violent and serious innovation made by the Conqueror in the Saxon judicial system; but it was fully justified, not merely by the more highly developed law which came into use as a result of the change, but by the necessity of a stricter enforcement of that law than would ever be possible through popular courts.

With these more striking changes went others, less revolutionary but equally necessary to complete the new ecclesiastical system. The Saxon bishops had many of them had their seats in unimportant places in their dioceses, tending to degrade the dignity almost to the level of a rural bishopric. The Norman prelates by degrees removed the sees to the chief towns, changing the names with the change of place. Dorchester was removed to Lincoln, Selsey to Chichester, Sherborne to Old Sarum, and Elmham by two removes to Norwich. The new cities were the centres of life and influence, and they were more suitable residences for barons of the king, as the Norman bishops were. The inner organization of these bishoprics was also improved. Cathedral chapters were reformed; in Rochester and Durham secular canons were replaced by monastic clergy under a more strict regime. New offices of law and administration were introduced. The country priests were brought under strict control, and earnest attempts were made to compel them to follow more closely the disciplinary requirements of the Church.

The monastic system as it existed at the time of the Conquest underwent the same reformation as the more secular side of the Church organization.

It was indeed regarded by the new ecclesiastical rulers as the source of the Church's strength and the centre of its life. English abbots were replaced by Norman, and the new abbots introduced a better discipline and improvement in the ritual. The rule was more strictly enforced. Worship, labour, and study became the constant occupations of the monks. Speedily the institution won a new influence in the life of the nation. The number of monks grew rapidly; new monasteries were everywhere established, of which the best remembered, the Conqueror's abbey of Battle, with the high altar of its church standing where Harold's standard had stood in the memorable fight, is only an example. Many of these new foundations were daughter-houses of great French monasteries, and it is a significant fact that by the end of the reign of William's son Henry, Cluny, the source of this monastic reformation for the world, had sent seventeen colonies into England. Wealth poured into these establishments from the gifts of king and barons and common men alike. Their buildings grew in number and in magnificence, and the poor and suffering of the realm received their share in the new order of things, through a wider and better organized charity.

With this new monastic life began a new era of learning. Schools were everywhere founded or renewed. The universal language of Christendom took once more its proper place as the literary language of the cloister, although the use of English lingered for a time here and there. England caught at last the theological eagerness of the continent in the age when the stimulus of the new dialectic method was beginning to be felt, and soon demanded to be heard in the settlement of the problems of the thinking world. Lanfranc continued to write as Archbishop of Canterbury.[5] Even something that may be called a literary spirit in an age of general barrenness was awakened. Poems were produced not unworthy of mention, and the generation of William's sons was not finished when such histories had been written as those of Eadmer and William of Malmesbury, superior in conception and execution to anything produced in England since the days of Bede. In another way the stimulus of these new influences showed itself in an age of building, and by degrees the land was covered with those vast monastic and cathedral churches which still excite our admiration and reveal to us the fact that the narrow minds of what we were once pleased to call the dark ages were capable, in one direction at least, of great and lofty conceptions. Norman ideals of massive strength speak to us as clearly from the arches of Winchester or the piers of Gloucester as from the firm hand and stern rule of William or Henry.

In general the Conquest incorporated England closely, as has already been said, with that organic whole of life and achievement which we call Christendom. This was not more true of the ecclesiastical side of things than of the political or constitutional. But the Church of the eleventh century included within itself relatively many more than the Church of to-day of those activities which quickly respond to a new stimulus and reveal a new life by increased production. The constitutional changes involved in the Conquest, and directly traceable to it through a long line of descent, though more slowly realized and for long in less striking forms, were in truth destined to produce results of greater permanence and a wider influence. The final result of the Norman Conquest was a constitutional creation, new in the history of the world. Nothing like this followed in the sphere of the Church. But for a generation or two the abundant vigour which flowed through the renewed religious life of Europe, and the radical changes which were necessary to bring England into full harmony with it, made the ecclesiastical revolution seem the most impressive and the most violent of the changes which took place in this age in English public organization and life. If we may trust a later chronicler, whose record is well supported by independent and earlier evidence, in the same year in which these legatine councils met, and in which the reformation of the Church was begun, there was introduced an innovation, so far as the Saxon Church is concerned, which would have seemed to the leaders of the reform party hostile to their cause had they not been so familiar with it elsewhere, or had they been conscious of the full meaning of their own demands. Matthew Paris, in the thirteenth century, records that, in 1070, the king decreed that all bishoprics and abbacies which were holding baronies, and which heretofore had been free from all secular obligations, should be liable to military service; and caused to be enrolled, according to his own will, the number of knights which should be due from each in time of war. Even if this statement were without support, it would be intrinsically probable at this or some near date. The endowment lands of bishopric and abbey, or rather a part of these lands in each case, would inevitably be regarded as a fief held of the crown, and as such liable to the regular feudal services. This was the case in every feudal land, and no one would suppose that there should be any exception in England. The amount of the service was arbitrarily fixed by the king in these ecclesiastical baronies, just as it was in the lay fiefs. The fact was important enough to attract the notice of the chroniclers because the military service, regulated in this way, would seem to be more of an innovation than the other services by which the fief was held, like the court service, for example, though it was not so in reality.

This transformation in life and culture was wrought in the English Church with the full sanction and support of the king. In Normandy, as well as in England, was this the case. The plans of the reform party had been carried out more fully in some particulars in these lands than the Church alone would have attempted at the time, because they had convinced the judgment of the sovereign and won his favour. At every step of the process where there was need, the power of the State had been at the command of the Church, to remove abuses or to secure the introduction of reforms. But with the theocratic ideas which went with these reforms in the teaching of the Church William had no sympathy. The leaders of the reformation might hold to the ideal supremacy of pope over king, and to the superior mission and higher power of the Church as compared with the State, but there could be no practical realization of these theories in any Norman land so long as the Conqueror lived. In no part of Europe had the sovereign exercised a greater or more direct power over the Church than in Normandy. All departments of its life were subject to his control, if there was reason to exert it. This had been true for so long a time that the Church was accustomed to the situation and accepted it without complaint. This power William had no intention of yielding. He proposed to exercise it in England as he had in Normandy,[6] and, even in this age of fierce conflict with its great temporal rival, the emperor, the papacy made no sharply drawn issue with him on these points. There could be no question of the headship of the world in his case, and on the vital moral point he was too nearly in harmony with the Church to make an issue easy. On the importance of obeying the monastic rule, the celibacy of the clergy, and the purchase of ecclesiastical office, he agreed in theory with the disciples of Cluny.[7] But, if he would not sell a bishopric, he was determined that the bishop should be his man; he stood ready to increase the power and independence of the Church, but always as an organ of the State, as a part of the machine through which the government was carried on.

It is quite within the limits of possibility that, in his negotiations with Rome before his invasion of England, William may have given the pope to understand, in some indefinite and informal way, that if he won the kingdom, he would hold it of St. Peter. In accepting the consecrated banner which the pope sent him, he could hardly fail to know that he might be understood to be acknowledging a feudal dependence. When the kingdom was won, however, he found himself unwilling to carry out such an arrangement, whether tacitly or openly promised. To Gregory VII's demand for his fealty he returned a respectful but firm refusal. The sovereignty of England was not to be diminished; he would hold the kingdom as freely as his predecessors had done. Peter's pence, which it belonged of right to England to pay, should be regularly collected and sent to Rome, but no right of rule, even theoretical, over king or kingdom, could be allowed the pope.

An ecclesiastical historian whose childhood and early youth fell in William's reign, and who was deeply impressed with the strong control under which he held the Church, has recorded three rules to govern the relation between Church and State, which he says were established by William.[8] These are: 1, that no one should be recognized as pope in England except at his command, nor any papal letters received without his permission; 2, that no acts of the national councils should be binding without his sanction; 3, that none of his barons or servants should be excommunicated, even for crimes committed, without his consent. Whether these were consciously formulated rules or merely generalizations from his conduct, they state correctly the principles of his action, and exhibit clearly in one most important sphere the unlimited power established by the Norman Conquest.

To this year, 1070, in which was begun the reformation of the Church, was assigned at a later time another work of constitutional interest. The unofficial compiler of a code of laws, the Leges Edwardi, written in the reign of Henry I, and drawn largely from the legislation of the Saxon kings, ascribed his work, after a fashion not unusual with writers of his kind, to the official act of an earlier king. He relates that a great national inquest was ordered by King William in this year, to ascertain and establish the laws of the English. Each county elected a jury of twelve men, who knew the laws, and these juries coming together in the presence of the king declared on oath what were the legal customs of the land. So runs the preface of the code which was given out as compiled from this testimony. Such a plan and procedure would not be out of harmony with what we know of William's methods and policy. The machinery of the jury, which was said to be employed, was certainly introduced into England by the first Norman king, and was used by him for the establishment of facts, both in national undertakings like the Domesday Book and very probably in local cases arising in the courts. We know also that he desired to leave the old laws undisturbed so far as possible, and the year 1070 is one in which an effort to define and settle the future legal code of the state would naturally fall. But the story must be rejected as unhistorical. An event of such importance as this inquisition must have been, if it took place, could hardly have occurred without leaving its traces in contemporary records of some sort, and an official code of this kind would have produced results in the history of English law of which we find no evidence. The Saxon law and the machinery of the local courts did survive the Conquest with little change, but no effort was made to reduce the customs of the land to systematic and written form until a later time, until a time indeed when the old law was beginning to give place to the new.

[4] See H. Bohmer, Die Falschungen Erzbischof Lanfranks van Canterbury (Leipzig, 1902).

[5] Böhmer, Kirche und Staat in England und in der Normandie, pp. 103-106.

[6] Eadmer, Historia Novorum, p. 9.

[7] Böhmer. Kirche und Staat, pp. 126 ff.

[8] Eadmer, Hist. Nov., p. 10.

CHAPTER III.
WILLIAM'S LATER YEARS

Political events had not waited for the reformation of the Church, and long before these reforms were completed, England had become a thoroughly settled state under the new king. The beginning of the year 1070 is a turning-point in the reign of William. The necessity for fighting was not over, but from this date onwards there was no more fighting for the actual possession of the land. The irreconcilables had still to be dealt with; in one small locality they retained even yet some resisting power; the danger of foreign invasion had again to be met: but not for one moment after William's return from the devastation of the north and west was there even the remotest possibility of undoing the Conquest.

The Danes had withdrawn from the region of the Humber, but they had not left the country. In the Isle of Ely, then more nearly an actual island than in modern times, was a bit of unsubdued England, and there they landed for a time. In this position, surrounded by fens and interlacing rivers, accessible at only a few points, occurred the last resistance which gave the Normans any trouble. The rich mythology which found its starting-point in this resistance, and especially in its leader, Hereward, we no longer mistake for history; but we should not forget that it embodies the popular attitude towards those who stubbornly resisted the Norman, as it was handed on by tradition, and that it reveals almost pathetically the dearth of heroic material in an age which should have produced it in abundance. Hereward was a tenant in a small way of the abbey of Peterborough. What led him into such a determined revolt we do not know, unless he was among those who were induced to join the Danes after their arrival, in the belief that their invasion would be successful. Nor do we know what collected in the Isle of Ely a band of men whom the Peterborough chronicler was probably not wrong, from any point of view, in calling outlaws. A force of desperate men could hope to maintain themselves for some time in the Isle of Ely; they could not hope for anything more than this. The coming of the Danes added little real strength, though the country about believed for the moment, as it had done north of the Humber, that the tide had turned. The first act of the allies was the plunder and destruction of the abbey and town of Peterborough shortly after the meeting of the council of Windsor. The English abbot Brand had died the previous autumn, and William had appointed in his place a Norman, Turold, distinguished as a good fighter and a hard ruler. These qualities had led the king to select him for this special post, and the plundering of the abbey, so far as it was not mere marauding, looks like an answering act of spite. The Danes seem to have been disposed at first to hold Peterborough, but Turold must have brought them proposals of peace from William, which induced them to withdraw at last from England with the secure possession of their plunder.

Hereward and his men accomplished nothing more that year, but others gradually gathered in to them, including some men of note. Edwin and Morcar had once more changed sides, or had fled from William's court to escape some danger there. Edwin had been killed in trying to make his way through to Scotland, but Morcar had joined the refugees in Ely. Bishop Ethelwin of Durham was also there, and a northern thane, Siward Barn. In 1074 William advanced in person against the "camp of refuge." A fleet was sent to blockade one side while the army attacked from the other. It was found necessary to build a long causeway for the approach of the army and around this work the fiercest fighting occurred; but its building could not be stopped, and just as it was finished the defenders of the Isle surrendered. The leaders were imprisoned, Morcar in Normandy for the rest of William's reign. The common men were mutilated and released. Hereward escaped to sea, but probably afterwards submitted to William and received his favour. Edric the Wild, who had long remained unsubdued on the Welsh borders, had also yielded before the surrender of the Isle of Ely, and the last resistance that can be called in any sense organized was at an end.

The comparatively easy pacification of the land, the early submission to their fate of so strong a nation, was in no small degree aided by the completeness with which the country was already occupied by Norman colonies, if we may call them so. Probably before the surrender of Ely every important town was under the immediate supervision of some Norman baron, with a force of his own. In all the strategically important places fortified posts had been built and regular garrisons stationed. Even the country districts had to a large extent been occupied in a similar way. It is hardly probable that as late as 1072 any considerable area in England had escaped extensive confiscations. Everywhere the Norman had appeared to take possession of his fief, to establish new tenants, or to bring the old ones into new relations with himself, to arrange for the administration of his manors, and to leave behind him the agents who were responsible to himself for the good conduct of affairs. If he made but little change in the economic organization of his property, and disturbed the labouring class but slightly or not at all, he would give to a wide district a vivid impression of the strength of the new order and of the hopelessness of any resistance.

Already Norman families, who were to make so much of the history of the coming centuries, were rooted in the land. Montfort and Mortimer; Percy, Beauchamp, and Mowbray; Ferrets and Lacy; Beaumont, Mandeville, and Grantmesnil; Clare, Bigod, and Bohun; and many others of equal or nearly equal name. All these were as yet of no higher than baronial rank, but if we could trust the chroniclers, we should be able to make out in addition a considerable list of earldoms which William had established by this date or soon afterwards, in many parts of England, and in these were other great names. According to this evidence, his two half brothers, the children of his mother by her marriage with Herlwin de Conteville, had been most richly provided for: Odo, Bishop of Bayeux, as Earl of Kent, and Robert, Count of Mortain, with a princely domain in the south-west as Earl of Cornwall. One of the earliest to be made an earl was his old friend and the son of his guardian, William Fitz Osbern, who had been created Earl of Hereford; he was now dead and was succeeded by his son Roger, soon very justly to lose title and land. Shrewsbury was held by Roger of Montgomery; Chester by Hugh of Avranches, the second earl; Surrey by William of Warenne; Berkshire by Walter Giffard. Alan Rufus of Britanny was Earl of Richmondshire; Odo of Champagne, Earl of Holderness; and Ralph of Guader, who was to share in the downfall of Roger Fitz Osbern, Earl of Norfolk. One Englishman, who with much less justice was to be involved in the fate which rightly befell these two Norman earls, was also earl at this time, Watheof, who had lately succeeded Gospatric in the troubled earldom of Northumberland, and who also held the earldoms of Northampton and Huntingdon. These men certainly held important lordships in the districts named, but whether so many earldoms, in form and law, had really been established by the Conqueror at this date, or were established by him at any later time, is exceedingly doubtful. The evidence of the chroniclers is easily shown to be untrustworthy in the matter of titles, and the more satisfactory evidence which we obtain from charters and the Domesday Book does not justify this extensive list. But the historian does not find it possible to decide with confidence in every individual case. Of the earldoms of this list it is nearly certain that we must drop out those of Cornwall, Holderness, Surrey, Berkshire, and Richmond, and almost or quite certain that we may allow to stand those of Waltheof and William Fitz Osbern, of Kent, Chester, and Shrewsbury.

Independently of the question of evidence, it is difficult to see what there was in the general situation in England which could have led the Conqueror to so wide a departure from the established practice of the Norman dukes as the creation of so many earls would be. In Normandy the title of count was practically unknown outside the ducal family. The feudal count as found in other French provinces, the sovereign of a little principality as independent of the feudal holder of the province as he himself was of the king, did not exist there. The four lordships which bore the title of count, Talou or Arques, Eu, Evreux, and Mortain, were reserved for younger branches of the ducal house, and carried with them no sovereign rights. The tradition of the Saxon earldom undoubtedly exercised by degrees a great influence on the royal practice in England, and by the middle of the twelfth century earls existed in considerable numbers; but the lack of conclusive evidence for the existence of many under William probably reflects the fact of his few creations. But in the cases which we can certainly trace to William, it was not the old Saxon earldom which was revived. The new earldom, with the possible exception of one or two earls who, like the old Frankish margrave, or the later palatine count, were given unusual powers to support unusual military responsibilities, was a title, not an office. It was not a government of provinces, but a mark of rank; and the danger involved in the older office, of the growth of independent powers within the state under local dynasties which would be, though existing under other forms, as difficult to control as the local dynasties of feudal France, was removed once for all by the introduction of the Norman centralization. That no serious trouble ever came from the so-called palatine earldoms is itself evidence of the powerful monarchy ruling in England.

This centralization was one of the great facts of the Conquest. In it resided the strength of the Norman monarchy, and it was of the utmost importance as well in its bearing on the future history of England. Delolme, one of the earliest of foreign writers on the English constitution, remarks that the explanation of English liberty is to be found in the absolute power of her early kings, and the most careful modern student can do no more than amplify this statement. That this centralization was the result of any deliberate policy on the part of William can hardly be maintained. A conscious modification of the feudal system as he introduced it into England, with a view to the preservation of his own power, has often been attributed to the Conqueror. But the political insight which would have enabled him to recognize the evil tendencies inherent in the only institutional system he had ever known, and to plan and apply remedies proper to counteract these tendencies but not inconsistent with the system itself, would indicate a higher quality of statesmanship than anything else in his career shows him to possess. More to the purpose is the fact that there is no evidence of any such modification, while the drift of evidence is against it. William was determined to be strong, not because of any theory which he had formed of the value of strength, or of the way to secure it, but because he was strong and had always been so since he recovered the full powers of a sovereign in the struggles which followed his minority. The concentration of all the functions of sovereignty in his own hands, and the reservation of the allegiance of all landholders to himself, which strengthened his position in England, had strengthened it first in Normandy.

Intentional weakening of the feudal barons has been seen in the fact that the manors which they held were scattered about in different parts of England, so that the formation of an independent principality, or a quick concentration of strength, would not be possible. That this was a fact characteristic of England is probably true. But it is sufficiently accounted for in part by the gradual spread of the Norman occupation, and of the consequent confiscations and re-grants, and in part by the fact that it had always been characteristic of England, so that when the holding of a given Saxon thane was transferred bodily to the Norman baron, he found his manors lying in no continuous whole. In any case, however, the divided character of the Norman baronies in England must not be pressed too far. The grants to his two half brothers, and the earldoms of Chester and Shrewsbury on the borders of Wales, are enough to show that William was not afraid of principalities within the state, and other instances on a somewhat smaller scale could be cited. Nor ought comparison to be made between English baronies, or earldoms even, and those feudal dominions on the continent which had been based on the counties of the earlier period. In these, sovereign rights over a large contiguous territory, originally delegated to an administrative officer, had been transformed into a practically independent power. The proper comparison is rather between the English baronies of whatever rank and those continental feudal dominions which were formed by natural process half economic and half political, without definite delegation of sovereign powers, within or alongside the provincial countships, and this comparison would show less difference.

If the Saxon earl did not survive the Conquest in the same position as before, the Saxon sheriff did. The office as the Normans found it in England was in so many ways similar to that of the viscount, vicecomes, which still survived in Normandy as an administrative office, that it was very easy to identify the two and to bring the Norman name into common use as an equivalent of the Saxon. The result of the new conditions was largely to increase the sheriff's importance and power. As the special representative of the king in the county, he shared in the increased power of his master, practically the whole administrative system of the state, as it affected its local divisions, was worked through him. Administrator of the royal domains, responsible for the most important revenues, vehicle of royal commands of all kinds, and retaining the judicial functions which had been associated with the office in Saxon times, he held a position, not merely of power but of opportunity. Evidence is abundant of great abuse of power by the sheriff at the expense of the conquered. Nor did the king always escape these abuses, for the office, like that of the Carolingian count, to which it was in many ways similar, contained a possibility of use for private and personal advantage which could be corrected, even by so strong a sovereign as the Anglo-Norman, only by violent intervention at intervals.

Some time after the Conquest, but at a date unknown, William set aside a considerable portion of Hampshire to form a hunting ground, the New Forest, near his residence at Winchester. The chroniclers of the next generation describe the formation of the Forest as the devastation of a large tract of country in which churches were destroyed, the inhabitants driven out, and the cultivated land thrown back into wilderness, and they record a contemporary belief that the violent deaths of so many members of William's house within the bounds of the Forest, including two of his sons, were acts of divine vengeance and proofs of the wickedness of the deed. While this tradition of the method of making the Forest is still generally accepted, it has been called in question for reasons that make it necessary, in my opinion, to pronounce it doubtful. It is hardly consistent with the general character of William. Such statements of chroniclers are too easily explained to warrant us in accepting them without qualification. The evidence of geology and of the history of agriculture indicates that probably the larger part of this tract was only thinly populated, and Domesday Book shows some portions of the Forest still occupied by cultivators.[9] The forest laws of the Norman kings were severe in the extreme. and weighed cruelly on beasts and men alike, and on men of rank as well as simple freemen. They excited a general and bitter hostility which lasted for generations, and prepared a natural soil for the rapid growth of a partially mythical explanation to account in a satisfactory way for the dramatic accidents which followed the family of the Conqueror in the Forest, by the direct and tangible wickedness which had attended the making of the hunting ground. It is probable also that individual acts of violence did accompany the making, and that some villages and churches were destroyed. But the likelihood is so strong against a general devastation that history should probably acquit William of the greater crime laid to his charge, and refuse to place any longer the devastation of Hampshire in the same class with that of Northumberland.

After the surrender of Ely, William's attention was next given to Scotland. In 1070 King Malcolm had invaded northern England, but without results beyond laying waste other portions of that afflicted country. It was easier to show the Scots than the Danes that William was capable of striking back, and in 1072, after a brief visit to Normandy, an army under the king's command advanced along the east coast with an accompanying fleet. No attempt was made to check this invasion in the field, and only when William had reached Abernethy did Malcolm come to meet him. What arrangement was made between them it is impossible to say, but it was one that was satisfactory to William at the time. Probably Malcolm became his vassal and gave him hostages for his good conduct, but if so, his allegiance did not bind him very securely. Norman feudalism was no more successful than the ordinary type, in dealing with a reigning sovereign who was in vassal relations.

The critical years of William's conquest of England had been undisturbed by any dangers threatening his continental possessions. Matilda, who spent most of the time in Normandy, with her councillors, had maintained peace and order with little difficulty; but in the year after his Scottish expedition he was called to Normandy by a revolt in his early conquest, the county of Maine, which it required a formidable campaign to subdue. William's plan to attach this important province to Normandy by a marriage between his son Robert and the youngest sister of the last count had failed through the death of the proposed heiress, and the county had risen in favour of her elder sister, the wife of the Italian Marquis Azo or of her son. Then a successful communal revolution had occurred in the city of Le Mans, anticipating an age of rebellion against the feudal powers, and the effort of the commune to bring the whole county into alliance with itself, though nearly successful for the moment at least, had really prepared the way for the restoration of the Norman power by dividing the party opposed to it. William crossed to Normandy in 1073, leading a considerable army composed in part of English. The campaign was a short one. Revolt was punished, as William sometimes punished it, by barbarously devastating the country. Le Mans did not venture to stand a siege, but surrendered on William's sworn promise to respect its ancient liberty. By a later treaty with Fulk of Anjou, Robert was recognized as Count of Maine, but as a vassal of Anjou and not of Normandy.

William probably returned to England after the settlement of these affairs, but of his doings there nothing is recorded, and for some time troubles in his continental dominions occupied more of his attention than the interests of the island. He was in Normandy, indeed, during the whole of that "most severe tempest," as a writer of the next generation called it, which broke upon a part of England in the year 1075; and the first feudal insurrection in English history was put down, as more serious ones were destined to be before the fall of feudalism, by the king's officers and the men of the land in the king's absence. To determine the causes of this insurrection, we need to read between the lines of the story as it is told us by the writers of that and the next age. Elaborate reasons for their hostility to William's government were put into the mouths of the conspirators by one of these writers, but these would mean nothing more than a general statement that the king was a very severe and stern ruler, if it were not for the more specific accusation that he had rewarded those who had fought for him very inadequately, and through avarice had afterward reduced the value even of these gifts.[10] A passage in a letter of Lanfranc's to one of the leaders of the rebellion, Roger, Earl of Hereford, written evidently after Roger's dissatisfaction had become known but before any open rebellion, gives us perhaps a key to the last part of this complaint.[11] He tells him that the king, revoking, we infer, former orders, has directed his sheriffs not to hold any more pleas in the earl's land until he can return and hear the case between him and the sheriffs. In a time when the profits of a law court were important to the lord who had the right to hold it, the entry of the king's officers into a "liberty" to hear cases there as the representative of the king, and to his profit, would naturally seem to the baron whose income was affected a diminution of the value of his fief, due to the king's avarice. Nothing could show us better the attitude natural to a strong king towards feudal immunities than the facts which these words of Lanfranc's imply, and though we know of no serious trouble arising from this reason for a century or more, it is clear that the royal view of the matter never changed, and finally like infringements on the baronial courts became one of the causes of the first great advance towards constitutional liberty, the Magna Carta.

This letter of Lanfranc's to Roger of Hereford is a most interesting illustration of his character and of his diplomatic skill, and it shows us clearly how great must have been his usefulness to William. Though it is perfectly evident to us that he suspects the loyalty of Roger to be seriously tempted, there is not a word of suspicion expressed in the letter, but the considerations most likely to keep him loyal are strongly urged. With the exception of the sentence about the sheriffs, and formal phrases at the beginning and end, the letter runs thus: "Our lord, the king of the English, salutes you and us all as faithful subjects of his in whom he has great confidence, and commands us that as much as we are able we should have care of his castles, lest, which God avert, they should be betrayed to his enemies; wherefore I ask you, as I ought to ask, most dear son, whom, as God is witness, I love with my whole heart and desire to serve, and whose father I loved as my soul, that you take such care of this matter and of all fidelity to our lord the king that you may have the praise of God, and of him, and of all good men. Hold always in your memory how your glorious father lived, and how faithfully he served his lord, and with how great energy he acquired many things and held them with great honour.... I should like to talk freely with you; if this is your will, let me know where we can meet and talk together of your affairs and of our lord the king's. I am ready to go to meet you wherever you direct."

The letter had no effect. Roger seems to have been a man of violent temper, and there was a woman in this case also, though we do not know that she herself influenced the course of events. The insurrection is said to have been determined upon, and the details of action planned, at the marriage of Roger's sister to Ralph Guader, Earl of Norfolk, a marriage which William had forbidden.

There was that bride-ale
That was many men's bale,

said the Saxon chronicler, and it was so indeed. The two chief conspirators persuaded Earl Waltheof to join them, at least for the moment, and their plan was to drive the king out of England and to divide the kingdom between them into three great principalities, "for we wish," the Norman historian Orderic makes them say, "to restore in all respects the kingdom of England as it was formerly in the time of King Edward," a most significant indication of the general opinion about the effect of the Conquest, even if the words are not theirs.

After the marriage the Earls of Norfolk and Hereford separated to raise their forces and bring them together, when they believed they would be too strong for any force which could be raised to act against them. They counted on the unpopularity of the Normans and on the king's difficulties abroad which would prevent his return to England. The king did not return, but their other hope proved fallacious. Bishop Wulfstan of Worcester and Abbot Ethelwy of Evesham, both English prelates, with some Norman help, cut off the line of communication in the west, and Earl Roger could not force his way through. The two justiciars, William of Warenne and Richard of Bienfaite, after summoning the earls to answer in the king's court, with the aid of Bishop Odo and the Bishop of Coutances, who was also a great English baron, raised an army of English as well as Normans, and went to meet Earl Ralph, who was marching westwards. Something like a battle took place, but the rebels were easily defeated. Ralph fled back to Norwich, but it did not seem to him wise to stop there. Leaving his wife to stand a siege in the castle, he sailed off to hasten the assistance which had already been asked for from the Danes. A Danish fleet indeed appeared off the coast, but it did nothing beyond making a plundering raid in Yorkshire. Emma, the new-made wife of Earl Ralph, seems to have been a good captain and to have had a good garrison. The utmost efforts of the king's forces could not take the castle, and she at last surrendered only on favourable terms. She was allowed to retire to the continent with her forces. The terms which were granted her, as they are made known in a letter from Lanfranc to William, are especially interesting as giving us one of the earliest glimpses we have of that extensive dividing out of land to under-vassals, the process of subinfeudation, which must already have taken place on the estates granted to the king's tenants in chief. A clear distinction was made between the men who were serving Ralph because they held land of him, and those who were merely mercenaries. Ralph's vassals, although they were in arms against Ralph's lord, the king, were thought to be entitled to better terms, and they secured them more easily than those who served him for money. Ralph and Emma eventually lived out the life of a generation of those days, on Ralph's Breton estates, and perished together in the first crusade.

Their fellow-rebels were less fortunate. Roger surrendered himself to be tried by the king's court, and was condemned "according to the Norman law," we are told, to the forfeiture of his estates and to imprisonment at the king's pleasure. From this he was never released. The family of William's devoted guardian, Osbern, and of his no less devoted friend, William Fitz Osbern, disappears from English history with the fall of this imprudent representative, but not from the country. It has been reserved for modern scholarship to prove the interesting fact of the continuance for generations of the male line of this house, though in minor rank and position, through the marriage of the son of Earl Roger, with the heiress of Abergavenny in Wales.[12] The fate of Waltheof was even more pathetic because less deserved. He had no part in the actual rebellion. Whatever he may have sworn to do, under the influence of the earls of stronger character, he speedily repented and made confession to Lanfranc as to his spiritual adviser. Lanfranc urged him to cross at once to Normandy and make his confession to the king himself. William received him kindly, showed no disposition to regard the fault as a serious one, and apparently promised him his forgiveness. Why, on his return to England, he should have arrested him, and after two trials before his court should have allowed him to be executed, "according to English law," we do not surely know. The hatred of his wife Judith, the king's niece, is plainly implied, but is hardly enough to account for so radical a departure from William's usual practice in this the only instance of a political execution in his reign. English sympathy plainly took the side of the earl. The monks of the abbey at Crowland, which he had favoured in his lifetime, were allowed the possession of his body. Soon miracles were wrought there, and he became, in the minds of monks and people, an unquestioned martyr and saint.

This was the end of William's troubles in England which have any real connexion with the Conquest. Malcolm of Scotland invaded Northumberland once more, and harried that long-suffering region, but without result; and an army of English barons, led by the king's son Robert, which returned the invasion soon after, was easily able to force the king of the Scots to renew his acknowledgment of subjection to England. The failure of Walcher, Bishop of Durham, to keep his own subordinates in order, led to a local riot, in which the bishop and many of his officers and clergy were murdered, and which was avenged in his usual pitiless style by the king's brother Odo. William himself invaded Wales with a large force; received submissions, and opened the way for the extension of the English settlements in that country. The great ambition of Bishop Odo, and the increase of wealth and power which had come to him through the generosity of his brother, led him to hope for still higher things, and he dreamed of becoming pope. This was not agreeable to William, and may even have seemed dangerous to him when the bishop began to collect his friends and vassals for an expedition to Italy. Archbishop Lanfranc, who had not found his brother prelate a comfortable neighbour in Kent, suggested to the king, we are told, the exercise of his feudal rights against him as his baron. The scene must have been a dramatic one, when in a session of the curia regis William ordered his brother's arrest, and when no one ventured to execute the order laid hands upon him himself, exclaiming that he arrested, not the Bishop of Bayeux, but the Earl of Kent. William must have had some strong reason for this action, for he refused to consent to the release of his brother as long as he lived. At one time what seemed like a great danger threatened from Denmark, in the plans of King Canute to invade England with a vast host and deliver the country from the foreigner. William brought over from Normandy a great army of mercenaries to meet this danger, and laid waste the country along the eastern coast that the enemy might find no supplies on landing; but this Danish threat amounted to even less than the earlier ones, for the fleet never so much as appeared off the coast. All these events are but the minor incidents which might occur in any reign; the Conquest had long been finished, and England had accepted in good faith her new dynasty.

Much more of the last ten years of William's life was spent in Normandy than in England. Revolts of unruly barons, attacks on border towns or castles, disputes with the king of France, were constantly occupying him with vexatious details, though with nothing of serious import. Most vexatious of all was the conduct of his son Robert. With the eldest son of William opens in English history a long line of the sons and brothers of kings, in a few cases of kings themselves, who are gifted with popular qualities, who make friends easily, but who are weak in character, who cannot control men or refuse favours, passionate and selfish, hardly strong enough to be violently wicked as others of the line are, but causes of constant evil to themselves and their friends, and sometimes to the state. And with him opens also the long series of quarrels in the royal family, of which the French kings were quick to take advantage, and from which they were in the end to gain so much. The ground of Robert's rebellion was the common one of dissatisfaction with his position and his father's refusal to part with any of his power in his favour. Robert was not able to excite any real insurrection in Normandy, but with the aid of his friends and of the French king he maintained a border war for some time, and defended castles with success against the king. He is said even, in one encounter, to have wounded and been on the point of slaying his father. For some time he wandered in exile in the Rhine valley, supported by gifts sent him by his mother, in spite of the prohibition of her husband. Once he was reconciled with his father, only to begin his rebellion again. When the end came, William left him Normandy, but people thought at least that he did it unwillingly, foreseeing the evil which his character was likely to bring on any land over which he ruled.

The year 1086 is remarkable for the formation of one of the most unique monuments of William's genius as a ruler, and one of the most instructive sources of information which we have of the condition of England during his reign. At the Christmas meeting of the court, in 1085, it was decided, apparently after much debate and probably with special reference to the general land-tax, called the Danegeld, to form by means of inquiries, officially made in each locality, a complete register of the occupied lands of the kingdom, of their holders, and of their values. The book in which the results of this survey of England were recorded was carefully preserved in the royal treasury, and soon came to be regarded as conclusive evidence in disputed questions which its entries would concern. Not very long after the record was made it came to be popularly known as the Domesday Book, and a hundred years later the writer on the English financial system of the twelfth century, the author of the "Dialogue concerning the Exchequer,"[13] explained the name as meaning that the sentences derived from it were final, and without appeal, like those of the last great day.

An especially interesting feature of this survey is the method which was employed to make it. Two institutions which were brought into England by the Conquest, the king's missi and the inquest, the forerunners of the circuit judge and of the jury, were set in motion for this work; and the organization of the survey is a very interesting foreshadowing of the organization which a century later William's great-grandson was to give to our judicial system in features which still characterize it, not merely in England but throughout great continents of which William never dreamed.

Royal commissioners, or missi, were sent into each county. No doubt the same body of commissioners went throughout a circuit of counties. In each the county court was summoned to meet the commissioners, just as later it was summoned to meet the king's justice on his circuit. The whole "county" was present to be appealed to on questions of particular importance or difficulty if it seemed necessary, but the business of the survey as a rule was not done by the county court. Each hundred was present by its sworn jury, exactly as in the later itinerant justice court, and it was this jury which answered on oath the questions submitted to it by the commissioners, exactly again as in the later practice. Their knowledge might be reinforced, or their report modified, by evidence of the men of the vill, or other smaller sub-division of the county, who probably attended as in the older county courts, and occasionally by the testimony of the whole shire; but in general the information on which the survey was made up was derived from the reports of the hundred juries. The questions which were submitted to these juries show both the object of the survey and its thorough character. They were required to tell the name of each manor and the name of its holder in the time of King Edward and at the time of the inquiry; the number of hides it contained; the number of ploughs employed in the cultivation of the lord's domain land, and the number so used on the lands held by the lord's men,—a rough way of determining the amount of land under cultivation. Then the population of the manor was to be given in classes: freemen and sokemen; villeins, cotters, and serfs; the amount of forest and meadow; the number of pastures, mills, and fish-ponds; and what the value of the manor was in the time of King Edward, at the date of its grant by King William, and at the time of the inquiry. In some cases evidently the jurors entered into such details of the live stock maintained by the manor as to justify the indignant words of the Saxon chronicler, that not "an ox nor a cow nor a swine was left that was not set down in his writing."

The object of all this is plain enough. It was an assessment of the property of the kingdom for purposes of taxation. The king wished to find out, as indeed we are told in what may be considered a copy or an abstract of the original writ directing the commissioners as to their inquiries, whether he could get more from the kingdom in taxes than he was then getting. But the record of this inquest has served far different purposes in later times. It is a storehouse of information on many sides of history, personal, family, geographical, and especially economic. It tells us much also of institutions, but less than we could wish, and less than it would have told us if its purpose had been less narrowly practical. Indeed, this limiting of the record to a single definite purpose, which was the controlling interest in making it, renders the information which it gives us upon all the subjects in which we are now most interested fragmentary and extremely tantalizing, and forces us to use it with great caution. It remains, however, even with this qualification, a most interesting collection of facts, unique in all the Middle Ages, and a monument to the practical genius of the monarch who devised it.

On August 1 of the same year in which the survey was completed, in a great assembly on Salisbury Plain, an oath of allegiance to the king was taken by all the land-holding men of England, no matter of whom they held. This has been represented as an act of new legislation of great institutional importance, but the view cannot be maintained. It is impossible to suppose that all land-owners were present or that such an oath had not been generally taken before; and the Salisbury instance was either a renewal of it such as was occasionally demanded by kings of this age, or possibly an emphatic enforcement of the principle in cases where it had been neglected or overlooked, now perhaps brought to light by the survey.

Already in 1083 Queen Matilda had died, to the lasting and sincere grief of her husband; and now William's life was about to end in events which were a fitting close to his stormy career. Border warfare along the French boundary was no unusual thing, but something about a raid of the garrison of Mantes, into Normandy, early in 1087, roused William's especial anger. He determined that plundering in that quarter should stop, and reviving old claims which had long been dormant he demanded the restoration to Normandy of the whole French Vexin, of which Mantes was the capital city. Philip treated his claims with contempt, and added a coarse jest on William's corpulence which roused his anger, as personal insults always did, to a white heat. The land around Mantes was cruelly laid waste by his orders, and by a sudden advance the city was carried and burnt down, churches and houses together. The heat and exertion of the attack, together with an injury which he received while riding through the streets of the city, by being thrown violently against the pummel of his saddle by the stumbling of his horse, proved too much for William in his physical condition, and he was carried back to Rouen to die after a few weeks.

A monastic chronicler of a little later date, Orderic Vitalis, gives us a detailed account of his death-bed repentance, but it was manifestly written rather for the edification of the believer than to record historical fact. It is interesting to note, however, that while William is made to express the deepest sorrow for the numerous acts of wrong which were committed in the process of the Conquest of England, there is no word which indicates any repentance for the Conquest itself or belief on William's part that he held England unjustly. He admits that it did not come to him from his fathers, but the same sentence which contains this admission affirms that he had gained it by the favour of God. It has been strongly argued from these words, and from others like them, which are put into the mouth of William later in this dying confession, when he comes to dispose of his realms and treasures, that William was conscious to himself that he did not possess any right to the kingdom of England which he could pass on hereditarily to his heirs. These words might without violence be made to yield this meaning, and yet it is impossible to interpret them in this way on any sound principle of criticism, certainly not as the foundation of any constitutional doctrine. There is not a particle of support for this interpretation from any other source; everything else shows that his son William succeeded him in England by the same right and in the same way that Robert did in Normandy. William speaks of himself in early charters, as holding England by hereditary right. He might be ready to acknowledge that it had not come to him by such right, but never that once having gained it he held it for himself and his family by any less right than this. The words assigned to William on his death-bed should certainly be interpreted by the words of the same chronicler, after he has finished the confession; and these indicate some doubt on William's part as to the effect of his death on the stability of his conquest in England, and his great desire to hasten his son William off to England with directions to Lanfranc as to his coronation before the news of his own death should be spread abroad. They imply that he is not sure who may actually become king in the tumults which may arise when it becomes known that his own strong rule is ended; that rests with God: but they express no doubt of the right of his heirs, nor of his own right to determine which one among them shall succeed him.

With reluctance, knowing his disposition, William conceded Normandy to Robert. The first-born son was coming to have special rights. More important in this case was the fact that Robert's right to Normandy had been formally recognized years before, and that recognition had never been withdrawn. The barons of the duchy had sworn fealty to him as his father's successor, and there was no time to put another heir in his place, or to deal with the opposition that would surely result from the attempt. William was his father's choice for England, and he was despatched in all haste to secure the crown with the aid of Lanfranc. To Henry was given only a sum of money, joined with a prophecy that he should eventually have all that the king had had, a prophecy which was certainly easy after the event, when it was written down, and which may not have been difficult to a father who had studied carefully the character of his sons. William was buried in the church of St. Stephen, which he had founded in Caen, and the manner in which such foundations were frequently made in those days was illustrated by the claim, loudly advanced in the midst of the funeral service, that the land on which the participants stood had been unjustly taken from its owners for the Conqueror's church. It was now legally purchased for William's burial place. The son, who was at the moment busy securing his kingdom in England, afterwards erected in it a magnificent tomb to the memory of his father.

[9] Round, Victoria History of Hampshire, i. 412-413. But See F. Baring in Engl. Hist. Rev. xvi. 427-438 (1901).

[10] Orderic Vitalis, ii. 260.

[11] Lanfranc, Opera (ed. Giles), i. 64.

[12] Round, Peerage Studies, pp. 181 ff.

[13] Dialogus de Scaccario, i. 16 (ed. Hughes, p. 108).

CHAPTER IV.
FEUDALISM AND A STRONG KING

William, the second son of the Conqueror, followed with no filial compunction his father's command that he should leave his death-bed and cross the channel at once to secure the kingdom of England. At the port of embarkation he learned that his father had died, but he did not turn back. Probably the news only hastened his journey, if this were possible. In England he went first to Winchester to get possession of his father's great treasure, and then to Canterbury with his letter to Lanfranc. Nowhere is there any sign of opposition to his succession, or of any movement in favour of Robert, or on Robert's part, at this moment. If the archbishop had any doubts, as a man of his good judgment might well have had, knowing the new king from his boyhood, they were soon quieted or he resolved to put them aside. He had, indeed, no alternative. There is nothing to indicate that the letter of his dying master allowed him any choice, nor was there any possible candidate who gave promise of a better reign, for Lanfranc must have known Robert as well as he knew William. Together they went up to London, and on September 26, 1087, hardly more than two weeks after he left his father's bedside, William was crowned king by Lanfranc. The archbishop took of him the customary oath to rule justly and to defend the peace and liberty of the Church, exacting a special promise always to be guided by his advice; but there is no evidence of any unusual assembly in London of magnates or people, of any negotiations to gain the support of persons of influence, or of any consent asked or given. The proceedings throughout were what we should expect in a kingdom held by hereditary right, as the chancery of the Conqueror often termed it, and by such a right descending to the heir. This appearance may possibly have been given to these events by haste and by the necessity of forestalling any opposition. Men may have found themselves with a new king crowned and consecrated as soon as they learned of the death of the old one; but no objection was ever made. Within a few months a serious insurrection broke out among those who hoped to make Robert king, but no one alleged that William's title was imperfect because he had not been elected. If the English crown was held by the people cf the time to be elective in any sense, it was not in the sense which we at present understand by the word "constitutional."

Immediately after the coronation, the new king went back to Winchester to fulfil a duty which he owed to his father. The great hoard which the Conqueror had collected in the ancient capital was distributed with a free hand to the churches of England. William II was as greedy of money as his father. His exactions pressed even more heavily on the kingdom, and the Church believed that it was peculiarly the victim of his financial tyranny, but he showed no disposition to begrudge these benefactions for the safety of his father's soul. Money was sent to each monastery and church in the kingdom, and to many rich gifts of other things, and to each county a hundred pounds for distribution to the poor.

Until the following spring the disposition of the kingdom which Lanfranc had made was unquestioned and undisturbed. William II wore his crown at the meeting of the court in London at Christmas time, and nothing during the winter called for any special exertion of royal authority on his part. But beneath the surface a great conspiracy was forming, for the purpose of overthrowing the new king and of putting his brother Robert in his place. During Lent the movers of this conspiracy were especially active, and immediately after Easter the insurrection broke out. It was an insurrection in which almost all the Norman barons of England took part, and their real object was the interest neither of king nor of kingdom, but only their own personal and selfish advantage. A purely feudal insurrection, inspired solely by those local and separatist tendencies which the feudal system cherished, it reveals, even more clearly than the insurrection of the Earls of Hereford and Norfolk under William I, the solid reserve of strength in the support of the nation which was the only thing that sustained the Norman kingship in England during the feudal age.

The writers upon whom we depend for our knowledge of these events represent the rebellious barons as moved by two chief motives. Of these that which is put forward as the leading motive is their opposition to the division of the Norman land into two separate realms, by the succession of the elder brother in Normandy and of the younger in England. The fact that these barons held fiefs in both countries, and under two different lords, certainly put them in an awkward position. but in one by no means uncommon throughout the feudal world. A suzerain of the Norman type, however, in the event of a quarrel between the king and the duke, could make things exceedingly uncomfortable for the vassals who held of both, and these men seem to have believed that their divided allegiance would endanger their possessions in one land or the other. They were in a fair way, they thought, to lose under the sons the increase of wealth and honours for which they had fought under the father. A second motive was found in the contrasted characters of the two brothers. Our authorities represent this as less influential than the first, but the circumstances of the case would lead us to believe that it had equal weight with the barons. William they considered a man of violence, who was likely to respect no right; Robert was "more tractable." That Robert was the elder son, that they had already sworn allegiance to him, while they owed nothing to William, which are suggested as among their motives, probably had no real influence in deciding their action. But the other two motives are so completely in accord with the facts of the situation that we must accept them as giving the reasons for the insurrection. The barons were opposed to the separation of the two countries, and they wished a manageable suzerain.

The insurrection was in appearance an exceedingly dangerous one. Almost every Norman baron in England revolted and carried his vassals with him. Odo, Bishop of Bayeux, the king's uncle, was the prime mover in the affair. He had been released from his prison by the Conqueror on his death-bed, and had been restored by William II to his earldom of Kent; but his hope of becoming the chief counsellor of the king, as he had become of Robert in Normandy, was disappointed. With him was his brother, Robert of Cornwall, Count of Mortain. The other great baron-bishop of the Conquest, Geoffrey of Coutances, was also in insurrection, and with him his nephew, Robert of Mowbray, Earl of Northumberland. Another leading rebel was Roger, Earl of Shrewsbury, with his three sons, the chief of whom, Robert of Bellême, was sent over from Normandy by Duke Robert, with Eustace of Boulogne, to aid the insurrection in England until he should himself be able to cross the channel. The treason of one man, William of St. Calais, Bishop of Durham, was regarded by the English writers as particularly heinous, if indeed we are right in referring their words to him and not to Bishop Odo; it is at least evident from the sequel that the king regarded his conduct in that light. The reason is not altogether clear, unless it be that the position of greatest influence in England, which Bishop Odo had desired in vain, had been given him by the king. Other familiar names must be added to these: William of Eu, Roger of Lacy, Ralph of Mortimer, Roger Bigod, Hugh of Grantmesnil. On the king's side there were few Norman names to equal these: Hugh of Avranches, Earl of Chester, William of Warenne, and of course the vassals of the great Archbishop Lanfranc. But the real strength of the king was not derived from the baronial elements. The castles in most of the great towns remained faithful, and so did nearly all the bishops and the Church as a whole. But the weight which turned the scale and gave the decision to the king, was the support of the great mass of the nation, of the English as opposed to the Norman.

For so great a show of strength, the insurrection was very short-lived, and it was put down with almost no fighting. The refusal of the barons to come to the Easter court, April 14, was their first overt act of rebellion, though it had been evident in March that the rebellion was coming, and before the close of the summer confiscation or amnesty had been measured out to the defeated rebels. We are told that the crown was offered to Robert and accepted by him, and great hopes were entertained of decisive aid which he was to send; but nothing came of it. Two sieges, of Pevensey castle and of Rochester castle, were the most important military events. There was considerable ravaging of the country by the rebels in the west, and some little fighting there. The Bishop of Coutances and his nephew seized Bristol and laid waste the country about, but were unsuccessful in their siege of Ilchester. Roger of Lacy and others collected a force at Hereford, and advanced to attack Worcester, but were beaten off by the Norman garrison and the men of Bishop Wulfstan. Minor incidents of the same kind occurred in Gloucestershire, Leicestershire, Norfolk, and the north. But the decisive events were in the south-east, in the operations of the king against his uncle Odo. At London William called round him his supporters, appealing especially to the English, and promising to grant good laws, to levy no unjust taxes, and to allow men the freedom of their woods and of hunting. With an army which did not seem large, he advanced against Rochester, where the Bishop of Bayeux was, to strike the heart of the insurrection.

Tunbridge castle, which was held for Odo, was first stormed, and on the news of this Odo thought it prudent to betake himself to Pevensey, where his brother, Robert of Mortain, was, and where reinforcements from Robert of Normandy would be likely to land. William at once turned from his march to Rochester and began the siege of Pevensey. The Norman reinforcements which Robert finally sent were driven back with great loss, and after some weeks Pevensey was compelled to surrender. Bishop Odo agreed to secure the surrender of Rochester, and then to retire from England, only to return if the king should send for him. But William unwisely sent him on to Rochester with a small advance detachment, to occupy the castle, while he himself followed more slowly with the main body. The castle refused to surrender. Odo's expression of face made known his real wishes, and was more convincing than his words. A sudden sally of the garrison overpowered his guards, and the bishop was carried into the castle to try the fortune of a siege once more. For this siege the king again appealed to the country and called for the help of all under the old Saxon penalty of the disgraceful name of "nithing." The defenders of the castle suffered greatly from the blockade, and were soon compelled to yield upon such terms as the king pleased, who was with difficulty persuaded to give up his first idea of sending them all to the gallows.

The monk Orderic Vitalis, who wrote an account of these events a generation after they occurred, was struck with one characteristic of this insurrection, which the careful observer of any time would hardly fail to notice. He says: "The rebels, although they were so many and abundantly furnished with arms and supplies, did not dare to join battle with the king in his kingdom." It was an age, to be sure, when wars were decided less by fighting in the open field than by the siege and defence of castles; and yet the collapse of so formidable an insurrection as this, after no resistance at all in proportion to its apparent fighting strength, is surely a significant fact. To notice here but one inference from it, it means that no one questioned the title of William Rufus to the throne while he was in possession. Though he might be a younger son, not elected, but appointed by his father, and put into the kingship by the act of the primate alone, he was, to the rebellious barons as to his own supporters, the rightful king of England till he could be overthrown.

The insurrection being put down, a general amnesty seems to have been extended to the rebels. The Bishop of Bayeux was exiled from England; some confiscations were made, and some rewards distributed; but almost without exception the leaders escaped punishment. The most notable exception, besides Odo, was William of St. Calais, the Bishop of Durham. For some reason, which does not clearly appear, the king found it difficult to pardon him. He was summoned before the king's court to answer for his conduct, and the account of the trial which followed in November of this year, preserved to us by a writer friendly to the bishop and present at the proceedings, is one of the most interesting and instructive documents which we have from this time. William of St. Calais, as the king's vassal for the temporalities of his bishopric, was summoned before the king's feudal court to answer for breach of his feudal obligations. William had shown, in one of the letters which he had sent to the king shortly before the trial, that he was fully aware of these obligations; and the impossibility of meeting the accusation was perfectly clear to his mind. With the greatest subtlety and skill, he sought to take advantage of his double position, as vassal and as bishop, and to transfer the whole process to different ground. With equal skill, and with an equally clear understanding of the principles involved, Lanfranc met every move which he made.[14]

From the beginning the accused insisted upon the privileges of his order. He would submit to a canonical trial only. He asked that the bishops should appear in their pontificals, which was a request that they judge him as bishops, and not as barons. Lanfranc answered him that they could judge him well enough clad as they were. William demanded that his bishopric should be restored to him before he was compelled to answer, referring to the seizing of his temporalities by the king. Lanfranc replied that he had not been deprived of his bishopric. He refused to plead, however, until the point had been formally decided, and on the decision of the court against him, he demanded the canonical grounds on which they had acted. Lanfranc replied that the decision was just, and that he ought to know that it was. He requested to be allowed to take counsel with the other bishops on his answer, and Lanfranc explained that the bishops were his judges and could not be his counsel, his answer resting on a principle of the law necessary in the courts of public assembly, one which gave rise to elaborate regulations in some feudal countries. Bishop William finally refused to accept the judgment of the court on several grounds, but especially because it was against the canons; and Lanfranc explained at greater length than before, that he had not been put on trial concerning his bishopric, but concerning his fief, as the Bishop of Bayeux had been tried under William I. But all argument was in vain. The bishop could not safely yield, and he insisted on his appeal to Rome. On his side the king insisted on the surrender of the bishop's castle, the last part of his fief which he still held, and was sustained by the court in this demand. The bishop demurred, but at last yielded the point to avoid arrest, and after considerable delay, he was allowed to cross over to the continent. There he was welcomed by Robert and employed in Normandy, but he never went any farther nor pushed his appeal to Rome, which in all probability he had never seriously intended, though there is evidence that the pope was disposed to take up his cause. Throughout the case the king was acting wholly within his right, regarding the bishop as his vassal; and Lanfranc's position in the trial was in strict accordance with the feudal law.

This was the end of serious rebellion against King William Rufus. Seven years later, in 1095, a conspiracy was formed by some of the barons who had been pardoned for their earlier rebellion, which might have resulted in a widespread insurrection but for the prompt action of William. Robert of Mowbray, Earl of Northumberland, who had inherited the 280 manors of his uncle, the Bishop of Coutances, and was now one of the most powerful barons of the kingdom, had been summoned to the king's court, probably because the conspiracy was suspected, since it was for a fault which would ordinarily have been passed over without remark, and he refused to appear. The king's hands were for the moment free, and he marched at once against the earl. By degrees the details of the conspiracy came out. From Nottingham, the Archbishop of Canterbury, who was accompanying the march, was sent back to Kent to hold himself in readiness at a moment's notice to defend that part of England against an expected landing from Normandy. This time it had been planned to make Stephen of Aumale, a nephew of the Conqueror, king in William's place; but no Norman invasion occurred. The war was begun and ended by the siege and surrender of Mowbray's two castles of Tynemouth and Bamborough. In the siege of the latter, Mowbray himself was captured by a trick, and his newly married wife was forced to surrender the castle by the threat of putting out his eyes. The earl was thrown into prison, where, according to one account, he was held for thirty years. Treachery among the traitors revealed the names of the leaders of the plot, and punishments were inflicted more generally than in 1088, but with no pretence of impartiality. A man of so high rank and birth as William of Eu was barbarously mutilated; one man of minor rank was hanged; banishment and fines were the penalties in other cases. William of St. Calais, who had been restored to his see, fell again under the suspicion of the king, and was summoned to stand another trial, but he was already ill when he went up to the court, and died before he could answer the charges against him. There were reasons enough in the heavy oppressions of the reign why men should wish to rebel against William, but he was so fixed in power, so resolute in action, and so pitiless towards the victims of his policy, that the forming of a dangerous combination against him was practically impossible.

The contemporary historians of his reign tell us much of William's personality, both in set descriptions and in occasional reference and anecdote. It is evident that he impressed in an unusual degree the men of his own time, but it is evident also that this impression was not so much made by his genius as a ruler or a soldier, by the possession of the gifts which a great king would desire, as by something in his spirit and attitude towards life which was new and strange, something out of the common in words and action, which startled or shocked men of the common level and seemed at times to verge upon the awful. In body he was shorter than his father, thick-set and heavy, and his red face gave him the name Rufus by which he was then and still is commonly known. Much of his father's political and military ability and strength of will had descended to him, but not his father's character and high purpose. Every king of those times thought chiefly of himself, and looked upon the state as his private property; but the second William more than most. The money which he wrung from churchman and layman he used in attempts to carry out his personal ambitions in Normandy, or scattered with a free hand among his favourites, particularly among the mercenary soldiers from the continent, with whom he especially loved to surround himself, and whose licensed plunderings added greatly to the burden and tyranny of his reign. But the ordinary doings of a tyrant were not the worst things about William Rufus.

Effeminate fashions, vices horrible and unheard-of in England, flourished at his court and threatened to corrupt the nation. The fearful profanity of the king, his open and blasphemous defiance of God, made men tremble, and those who were nearest to him testified "that he every morning got up a worse man than he lay down, and every evening lay down a worse man than he got up."

In the year after the suppression of the first attempt of the barons against the king, but before other events of political importance had occurred, on May 28, 1089, died Lanfranc, the great Archbishop of Canterbury, after nearly nineteen years of service in that office. Best of all the advisers of the first William, he was equally with him conqueror of England, in that conquest of laws and civilization which followed the mere conquest of arms. Not great, though famous as a theologian and writer, his powers were rather of a practical nature. He was skilful in the management of men; he had a keen appreciation of legal distinctions, and that comprehensive sight at the same time of ends and means which we call the organizing power. He was devoted to that great reformation in the religious and ecclesiastical world which occurred during his long life, but he was devoted to it in his own way, as his nature directed. He saw clearly, for one thing, that the success of that reformation in England depended on the maintenance of the strong government of the Norman kings; and from his loyalty to them he never swerved, serving them with wise counsel and with all the resources at his command. Less of a theologian and idealist than his successor Anselm, more of a lawyer and statesman, he could never have found himself, for another thing, in that attitude of opposition to the king which fills so much of his successor's pontificate.

As his life had been of constant service to England, his death was an immediate misfortune. We cannot doubt the opinion expressed by more than one of the writers of the next reign, that a great change for the worse took place in the actions of the king after the death of Lanfranc. The aged archbishop, who had been in authority since his childhood, who might seem to prolong in some degree the reign or the influence of his father, acted as a restraining force, and the true character of William expressed itself freely only when this was removed. In another way also the death of Lanfranc was a misfortune to England. It dates the rise to influence with the king of Ranulf Hambard, whose name is closely associated with the tyranny of Rufus; or if this may already have begun, it marks his very speedy attainment of what seems to have been the complete control of the administrative and judicial system of the kingdom. Of the early history of Ranulf Flambard we know but little with certainty. He was of low birth, probably the son of a priest, and he rose to his position of authority by the exercise of his own gifts, which were not small. A pleasing person, ingratiating manners, much quickness and ingenuity of mind, prodigality of flattery, and great economy of scruples,—these were traits which would attract the attention and win the favour of a man like William II. In Ranulf Flambard we have an instance of the constantly recurring historical fact, that the holders of absolute power are always able to find in the lower grades of society the ministers of their designs who serve them with a completeness of devotion and fidelity which the master rarely shows in his own interest, and often with a genius which he does not himself possess.

Our knowledge of the constitutional details of the reign either of William I or William II is very incomplete, and it is therefore difficult for us to understand the exact nature of the innovations made by Ranulf Flambard. The chroniclers leave us no doubt of the general opinion of contemporaries, that important changes had been made, especially in the treatment of the lands of the Church, and that these changes were all in the direction of oppressive exactions for the benefit of the king. The charter issued by Henry I at the beginning of his reign, promising the reform of various abuses of his brother's reign, confirms this opinion. But neither the charter nor the chroniclers enable us to say with confidence exactly in what the innovations consisted. The feudal system as a system of military tenures and of judicial organization had certainly been introduced by William the Conqueror, and applied to the great ecclesiastical estates of the kingdom very early in his reign. That all the logical deductions for the benefit of the crown which were possible from this system, especially those of a financial nature, had been made so early, is not so certain. In the end, and indeed before very long, the feudal system as it existed in England became more logical in details, more nearly an ideal feudalism, with reference to the rights of the crown, than anywhere else in Christendom. It is quite within the bounds of possibility that Ranulf Flambard, keen of mind, working under an absolute king, whose reign was followed by the longer reign of another absolute king, not easily forced to keep the promises of his coronation charter, may have had some share in the logical carrying out of feudal principles, or in their more complete application to the Church, which would be likely to escape feudal burdens under a king of the character of the first William. Indeed, such a complete application of the feudal rights of the crown to the Church, the development of the so-called regalian rights, was at this date incomplete in Europe as a whole, and according to the evidence which we now have, the Norman in England was a pioneer in that direction.

The loudest complaints of these oppressions have come down to us in regard to Canterbury and the other ecclesiastical baronies which fell vacant after the death of Lanfranc. This is what we should expect: the writers are monks. It seems from the evidence, also, that in most cases no exact division had as yet been made between those lands belonging to a monastic bishop or an abbot, which should be considered particularly to form the barony, and those which should be assigned to the support of the monastic body. Such a division was made in time, but where it had not been made before the occurrence of a vacancy, it was more than likely that the monks were placed on very short commons, and the right of the king to the revenues interpreted in the most ample sense. The charter of Henry I shows that in the case of lay fiefs the rights of the king, logically involved in the feudal system, had been stretched to their utmost limit, and even beyond. It would be very strange if this were not still more true in the case of ecclesiastical fiefs. The monks, we may be sure, had abundant grounds for their complaints. But we should notice that what they have in justice to complain of is the oppressive abuse of real rights. The system of Ranulf Flambard, so far as we can determine what it was, does not differ in its main features from that which was in operation without objection in the time of Henry II. The vacant ecclesiastical, like the vacant lay, fief fell back into the king's domain. It is difficult to determine just what its legal status was then considered to be, but it was perhaps regarded as a fief reverting on failure of heirs. Certainly it was sometimes treated as only an escheated or forfeited lay fief would be treated. Its revenues might be collected by the ordinary machinery, as they had been under the bishop, and turned into the king's treasury; or it might be farmed out as a whole to the highest bidder. There could be no valid objection to this. If the legal position which Lanfranc had so vigorously defended was correct, that a bishop might be tried as a baron by a lay court and a lay process, with no infringement of his ecclesiastical rights, then there could be no defence against this further extension of feudal principles. Relief, wardship, and escheat were perfectly legitimate feudal rights, and there was no reason which the state would consider valid why they should not be enforced in all fiefs alike. The case of the Bishop of Durham, in 1088, had already established a precedent for the forfeiture of an ecclesiastical barony for the treason of its holder, and in that case the king had granted fiefs within that barony to his own vassals. Still more clearly would such a fief return to the king's hands, if it were vacant. But if the right was clear, it might still be true that the enforcement of it was new and accompanied with great practical abuses. Of this much probably we must hold Ranulf Flambard guilty.

The extension and abuse of feudal law, however, do not fill up the measure of his guilt. Another important source of royal revenue, the judicial system, was put under his control, and was forced to contribute the utmost possible to the king's income. That the justiciarship was at this time as well defined an office, or as regularly recognized a part of the state machinery, as it came to be later, is hardly likely. But that some officer should be clothed with the royal authority for a special purpose, or in the absence of the king for general purposes, was not an uncommon practice. In some such way as this Ranulf Flambard had been given charge of the king's interests in the judicial system, and had much to do by his activities in that position with the development of the office of justiciar. Exactly what he did in this field is as uncertain as in that of feudal law, though the one specific instance which we have on record shows him acting in a capacity much like that of the later itinerant justice. However this may be, the recorded complaints of his oppressions as judge, though possibly less numerous and detailed than of his mistreatment of the Church, are equally bitter. He was the despoiler of the rich, the destroyer of the poor. Exactions already heavy and unjust he doubled. Money alone decided cases in the courts. Justice and the laws disappeared. The rope was loosened from the very neck of the robber if he had anything of value to promise the king; while the popular courts of shires and hundreds were forced to become engines of extortion, probably by the employment of the sheriffs, who were allowed to summon them, not according to the old practice, but when and where it suited their convenience. The machinery of the state and the interpretation of its laws were, in days like these, completely at the mercy of a tyrannous king and an unscrupulous minister. No system of checks on absolute power had as yet been devised; there were no means of expressing public discontent, nor any form of appeal but insurrection, and that was hopeless against a king so strong as Rufus. The land could only suffer and wait, and at last rejoice that the reign was no longer. In the meantime, from the beginning of Robert's rule in the duchy across the channel, the condition of things there had been a standing invitation to his brother to interfere. Robert is a fair example of the worst type of men of the Norman-Angevin blood. Not bad in intention, and not without abilities, he was weak with that weakness most fatal of all in times when the will of the ruler gave its only force to law, the inability to say no, the lack of firm resisting power. The whole eleventh century had been nourishing the growth, in the favouring soil of feudalism, of the manners and morals of chivalry. The generation to which William and Robert belonged was more strongly influenced in its standards of conduct by the ideals of chivalry than by any other ethical code, and both these princes are examples of the superior power of these ideals. In the age of chivalry no princely virtue was held of higher worth than that of "largesse," the royal generosity which scattered gifts on all classes with unstinted hand; but Robert's prodigality of gifts was greater than the judgment of his own time approved, and, combined with the inability to make himself respected or obeyed, which often goes with such generosity, it was the source of most of his difficulties. His ideal seemed to be that every man should have what he wanted, and soon it was apparent that he had retained very little for himself.

The castles of Normandy were always open to the duke, and William the Conqueror had maintained garrisons of his own in the most important of them, to insure the obedience of their holders. The first move that was made by the barons of Normandy, on the news of William's death, was to expel these garrisons and to substitute others of their own. The example was set by Robert of Bellême, the holder of a powerful composite lordship on the south-west border and partly outside the duchy. On his way to William's court, he heard of the duke's death, and he instantly turned about, not merely to expel the ducal garrisons from the castles of his own fiefs, but to seize the castles of his neighbours which he had reason to desire, and some of these he destroyed and some he held for himself. This action is typical of the influence of Robert's character on government in Normandy. Contempt for the authority of the duke meant not merely that things which belonged to him would be seized upon and his rights denied, but also that the property and rights of the weak, and even of those who were only a little weaker than their neighbours, were at the mercy of the stronger.

Duke Robert's squandering of his resources soon brought him to a want of ready money intolerable to a prince of his nature, and his mind turned at once with desire to the large sum in cash which his father had left to Henry. But Henry was not at all of the stamp of Robert. He was perfectly clear headed, and he had no foolish notions about the virtue of generosity. He preferred to buy rather than to give away. A bargain was struck between them, hardly six months after their father's death, and the transaction is characteristic of the two brothers. For three thousand pounds of silver, Henry purchased what people of the time regarded as a third of Robert's inheritance, the lordship of the Cotentin, with its important castles, towns, and vassals. The chroniclers call him now Count of the Cotentin, and he there practised the art of government for a time, and, in sharp contrast to Robert, maintained order with a strong hand. During the same summer of 1088, Henry crossed over to England to get possession of the lands of his mother Matilda, which she had bequeathed to him on her death. This inheritance he does not seem to have obtained, at least not permanently; but there was no quarrel between him and William at that time. In the autumn he returned to Normandy, taking with him Robert of Bellême. Robert had been forgiven his rebellion by the king, and so clear was the evidence that Henry and Robert of Bellême had entered into some kind of an arrangement with King William to assist his designs on Normandy, or so clear was it made to seem to Duke Robert, that on their landing he caused them both to be arrested and thrown into prison. On the news of this the Earl of Shrewsbury, the father of Robert of Bellême, crossed over from England to the aid of his son, and a short civil war followed, in the early part of the next year, in which the military operations were favourable to the duke, but his inconstancy and weakness of character were shown in his releasing Robert of Bellême at the close of the war as if he had himself been beaten. Henry also was soon released, and took up again his government of the Cotentin.

William may have felt that Robert's willingness to accept the crown of England from the rebel barons gave him the right to take what he could get in Normandy, though probably he was not particularly troubled by the question of any moral justification of his conduct. Opportunity would be for him the main consideration, and the growing anarchy in the duchy furnished this. Private war was carried on without restraint in more than one place, and though the reign of a weak suzerain was to the advantage of the rapacious feudal baron, many of the class preferred a stronger rule. The arguments also in favour of a union of the kingdom and the duchy, which had led to the rebellion against William, would now, since that attempt had failed, be equally strong against Robert. For William no motive need be sought but that of ambition, nor have we much right to say that in such an age the ambition was improper. The temptation which the Norman duchy presented to a Norman king of England was natural and irresistible, and we need only note that with William II begins that determination of the English kings to rule also in continental dominions which influences so profoundly their own history, and hardly less profoundly the history of their island kingdom, for centuries to come. To William the Conqueror no such question could ever present itself, but the moment that the kingdom and the duchy were separated in different hands it must have arisen in the mind of the king.

But if William did not himself care for any moral justification of his plans, he must make sure of the support of his English vassals in such an undertaking; and the policy of war against Robert was resolved upon in a meeting of the court, probably the Easter meeting of 1090. But open war did not begin at once. William contented himself for some months with sending over troops to occupy castles in the north-eastern portion of Normandy, which were opened to him by barons who were favourable to his cause or whose support was purchased. The alarm of Robert was soon excited by these defections, and he appealed to his suzerain, King Philip I of France, for aid. If the policy of ruling in Normandy was natural for the English king, that of keeping kingdom and duchy in different hands was an equally natural policy for the French king. It is hardly so early as this, however, that we can date the beginning of this which comes in the end to be a ruling motive of the Capetian house. Philip responded to his vassal's call with a considerable army, but the money of the king of England quickly brought him to a different mind, and he retired from the field, where he had accomplished nothing.

In the following winter, early in February of 1091, William crossed over into Normandy to look after his interests in person. The money which he was wringing from England by the ingenuity of Ranulf Flambard he scattered in Normandy with a free hand, to win himself adherents, and with success. Robert could not command forces enough to meet him in the field, and was compelled to enter into a treaty with him, in which, in return for some promises from William, he not merely accepted his occupation of the eastern side of the duchy, which was already accomplished, but agreed to a similar occupation by William of the north-western corner.

Cherbourg and Mont-Saint-Michel, two of the newly ceded places, belonged to the dominions which "Count" Herry had purchased of his brother, and must be taken from him by force. William and Robert marched together against him, besieged him in his castle of Mont-Saint-Michel, and stripped him of his lordship. Robert received the lion's share of the conquest, but William obtained what he wished. Henry was once more reduced to the condition of a landless prince, but when William returned to England in August of this year both his brothers returned with him, and remained there for some time.

William had been recalled to England by the news that King Malcolm of Scotland had invaded England during his absence and harried Northumberland almost to Durham. Malcolm had already refused to fulfil his feudal obligations to the new king of England, and William marched against him immediately on his return, taking his two brothers with him. At Durham Bishop William of St. Calais, who had found means to reconcile himself with the king, was restored to his rights after an exile of three years. The expedition to Scotland led to no fighting. William advanced with his army to the Firth of Forth. Malcolm met him there with an army of his own, but negotiations were begun and conducted for William by his brother Robert, and for Malcolm by the atheling Edgar, whose expulsion from Normandy had been one of the conditions of the peace between William and Robert. Malcolm at last agreed to acknowledge himself the man of William II, with the same obligations by which he had been bound to his father, and the king returned to England, as he had gone, by way of Durham. Very likely something in this expedition suggested to William that the north-western frontier of England needed rectification and defence. At any rate, early in the spring of the next year, 1092, he marched against Carlisle, expelled Dolphin, son of the Gospatric of William the Conqueror's time, who was holding it under Malcolm of Scotland, built and garrisoned a castle there, and after his return to the south sent a colony of English families to occupy the adjacent country. This enlargement of the area of England was practically a conquest from the king of Scotland, and it may have been, in violation of the pledge which William had just given, to restore to Malcolm all his former possessions. Something, at least, led to immediate complaints from Malcolm, which were without avail, and a journey that he made by invitation the next year, to confer with William at Gloucester, resulted only in what he regarded as further humiliating treatment. On his return to Scotland he immediately took arms, and again invaded Northumberland. This, however, was destined to be the last of his incursions, for he was killed, together with his eldest son, Edward, near Alnwick, on the eastern coast. The news of the death of her husband and son at once proved fatal to Queen Margaret. A reaction followed against English influence in the state, which she had supported, and a conflict of parties and a disputed succession gave to William an opportunity to interfere in favour of candidates of his own, though with little real success. At least the north of England was relieved of the danger of invasion. This year was also marked by important advances in the conquest of South Wales by the Norman barons of the country.

[14] Dugdale, Monasticon, ed. 1846, 1.244 ff—and Symeon of Durham, Deinjusta Vexations (Rolls series), i. 170 ff.

CHAPTER V.
WILLIAM RUFUS AND ANSELM

In following the history of Malcolm of Scotland we have passed by events of greater importance which make the year 1093 a turning-point in the reign of William Rufus. The appointment of Anselm to the archbishopric of Canterbury divides the reign into two natural divisions. In the first period William secures his hold on power, develops his tyrannous administrative system and his financial extortions, begins his policy of conquest in Normandy, forces Scotland to recognize his supremacy, and rounds off his kingdom towards the north-west. The second period is more simple in character, but its events are of greater importance. Apart from the abortive rebellion of Robert of Mowbray, which has already been narrated, William's authority is unquestioned. Flambard's machine appears to run smoothly. Monks record their groans and give voice to their horror, but the peace of the state is not disturbed, nor are precautions necessary against any foreign enemy. Two series of events fill up the history of the period, both of great and lasting interest. One is the long quarrel between the king and the archbishop, which involve the whole question of the relation between Church and State in the feudal age; and the other is the king's effort to gain possession of Normandy, the introductory chapter of a long history.

Early in Lent, 1093, or a little earlier, King William fell sick at a royal manor near to Gloucester, and was carried in haste into that city. There he lay during the rest of Lent, so ill that his death was expected at any moment, and it was even reported that he had died. Brought face to face with death, the terrors of the world to come seized hold of him. The medieval sinner who outraged the moral sentiment of his time, as William did, was sustained by no philosophical doubt of the existence of God or belief in the evolutionary origin of ethics. His life was a reckless defiance or a careless disregard of an almighty power, whose determination and ability to punish him, if not bought off, he did not question. The torments of a physical hell were vividly portrayed on all occasions, and accepted by the highest as well as the lowest as an essential part of the divine revelation. William was no exception to this rule. He became even more shockingly defiant of God after his recovery than he had been before. God, he declared to the Bishop of

Rochester, should never have in him a good man because of the evil which He had done him. And God let him have what he wished, adds the pious historian, according to the idea of good which he had formed. And yet, if he had been allowed time for a death-bed repentance at the end of his life, he would have yielded undoubtedly to the same vague terrors, and have made a hasty bid for safety with gifts and promises. At any rate now, when the nobles and bishops who came to visit him suggested that it was time for him to make atonement for his evil deeds, he eagerly seized upon the chance. He promised to reform his life, to protect the churches, and not put them up any more for sale, to annul bad laws, and to decree good ones; and bishops were sent to lay these promises on the altar. Some of his good resolutions could only be carried out by virtue of a royal writ, and an order was drawn up and sealed, commanding the release of prisoners, the remission of debts due the crown, and the forgiving of offences. Great was the rejoicing at these signs of reformation, and prayers were, everywhere offered for so good a king, but when he had once recovered, his promises were as quickly forgotten as the very similar ones which he had made in the crisis of the rebellion of loss. William probably still believed, when he found himself restored to health, that nobody can keep all his promises, as he had answered when Lanfranc remonstrated with him on the violation of his coronation pledges. Before his recovery, however, he took one step in the way of reformation from which he did not draw back. He appointed a new Archbishop of Canterbury. It was the fear of death alone which wrung this concession from the king, and it shows a clear consciousness on his part of the guilt of retaining the archbishopric in his hands. Only a few weeks earlier, at the meeting of the Christmas court, when the members had petitioned that he would be graciously pleased to allow prayers to be offered that he might be led to see the wrong which he was doing, he had answered with contempt, "Pray as much as you like; I shall do what I please. Nobody's praying is going to change my mind." Now, however, he was praying himself, and anxious to get rid of this guilt. The man whom all England with one voice declared to be the ideal archbishop was at hand, and the king besought him most earnestly to accept the appointment, and so to aid him in his endeavour to save his soul.

This man was Anselm, now abbot of the famous monastery of Bec, where Lanfranc had been at one time prior. Born sixty years before, at Aosta, in the kingdom of Burgundy, in the later Piedmont, he had crossed into France, like Lanfranc, led by the desire of learning and the religious life. Finally he had become a monk at Bec, and had devoted himself to study and to theological writing. Only with great reluctance, and always imperfectly, did he attend to the administrative duties which fell to him as he was made first prior and then abbot of the monastery. His cast of mind was wholly metaphysical, his spirit entirely of the cloister and the school. The monastic life, free from the responsibilities of office, exactly suited him, and he was made for it. When all England was importuning him to accept the primacy, he shrank back from it with a reluctance which was wholly genuine, and an obstinacy which belonged also to his nature. He felt himself unfitted for the place, and he foresaw the result. He likened his future relation with the king to that of a weak old sheep yoked with an untamed bull. In all this he was perfectly right. That harmony which had existed between Lanfranc and the Conqueror, because each understood the other's position and rights and was interested in his work, was never for a moment possible between Anselm and William Rufus; and this was only partly due to the character of the king. So wholly did the archbishop belong to another world than the king's that he never appreciated the double position in which his office placed him. One side of it only, the ecclesiastical, with its duties and rights and all their logical consequences, he clearly saw. At the beginning of his primacy, he seemed to understand, and he certainly accepted, the feudal relationship in which he was placed to the king, but the natural results of this position he never admitted. His mind was too completely taken up with the other side of things; and with his fixedness of purpose, almost obstinacy of character, and the king's wilfulness, conflict was inevitable.

It was only with great difficulty that Anselm was brought to accept the appointment. Being in England on a visit to Hugh, Earl of Chester, he had been brought to the king's bedside when he fell sick, as the man best able to give him the most certain spiritual comfort; and when William had been persuaded of his guilt in keeping the primacy so long vacant, Anselm was dragged protesting to the presence of the sick man, and his fingers were partially forced open to receive the pastoral staff which William extended to him. Then he was carried off, still protesting, to a church near by, where the religious ceremonies usual on the appointment of a bishop were performed. Still Anselm refused to yield to this friendly violence. He returned immediately to the king, predicted his recovery, and declared that he had not accepted the primacy, and did not accept it, in spite of all that had been done. For some reason, however, William adhered to this much of his reformation. He gave order for the immediate transfer to his appointee of all that pertained to the archbishopric, and sent to Normandy for the consent of the secular and ecclesiastical superiors of Anselm, the duke and the Archbishop of Rouen, and of the monks of his abbey. At length Anselm yielded, not because his judgment had been changed as to the wisdom of the appointment, but sacrificing himself rather, in the monastic spirit, to the call of Heaven.

It was near the end of September, however, before the new archbishop was enthroned. Several matters had first to be arranged to the satisfaction of Anselm, and among these were three conditions which he presented to be agreed to by the king. William was probably ready to agree without hesitation that he would take the archbishop as his guide and director in religious matters, and equally ready to pay no attention to the promise afterward. A more difficult condition was, that all the lands which had belonged to the church of Canterbury at Lanfranc's death should be restored, including, evidently, certain lands which William had granted to his own men. This condition would show that the king had treated the archbishopric as a forfeited fief, and that its lands had been alienated on terms unfavourable to the Church. William hesitated long on this condition, and tried to persuade Anselm to waive it; but the letters of the future archbishop show that his conscience was deeply engaged and would not permit him to agree to anything that would impoverish his see, and the king must have yielded in the end. The third condition was, that Anselm should be allowed to continue in the obedience of Pope Urban II, whom he had already acknowledged in Normandy. This must also have been a disagreeable condition to the king. The divided state of Christendom, into which it had been thrown by the conflict between the pope and the emperor on the question of investitures, was favourable to that autocratic control of the Church which William Rufus desired to maintain. He had no wish to decide between the rival popes, nor was he willing to modify his father's rule that no pope should be recognized by the English Church without the king's consent. We are not told that in this particular he made anything more than a vague promise to do what he ought to do, but very likely Anselm may have regarded this point more as a warning to the king of his own future action than as a necessary condition of his acceptance of the archbishopric.

All these preliminaries being settled in some form satisfactory to Anselm, he yielded to the universal desire, and was enthroned on September 25. The rejoicing of this day at Canterbury was not allowed to go on, however, without interruption by the king. Ranulf Flambard appeared in person and served a writ on the new archbishop, summoning him to answer in some suit in the king's court. The assurance of Anselm's friend and biographer, Eadmer, that this action concerned a matter wholly within the province of the Church, we can hardly accept as conclusive evidence of the fact; but Anselm was certainly right in regarding such an act on this day as foreboding greater troubles to come. On December 4, Anselm was consecrated at an assembly of almost all the bishops of England, including Thomas, Archbishop of York. The occasion is noteworthy because the Archbishop of York interrupted the proceedings to object to the term "metropolitan of all Britain," applied to the church of Canterbury, calling attention to the fact that the church of York was known to be metropolitan also. The term primate was at once substituted for that of metropolitan, since the archbishops of Canterbury did not claim the right to exercise an administrative authority within the see of York.

It is interesting to notice, in view of the conflict on investitures which was before long to begin in England, and which had already been for years so bitterly fought upon the continent, that all these events happened without the slightest questioning on the part of any one of the king's sole right to dispose of the highest see of the realm as he pleased. There was no suggestion of the right of election, no objection to lay investiture, no protest from any one. Anselm accepted investiture with the staff from the hand of the king without remark. He acknowledged his feudal relation to him, swore fealty to him as a vassal,[15] and was ready to perform his obligations of feudal service, at least upon his own interpretation of their extent. A little later, in 1095, after the first serious conflict between himself and the king, when the papal legate in England took of him his oath of fealty to the pope, the oath contained the usual Norman clause reserving his fealty to the king. A clause in the bishop's oath to the pope so unusual as this could not have passed in that age without notice. It occasioned instant criticism from strict ecclesiastics on the continent, and it must have been consciously inserted by Anselm and consciously accepted by the legate. Such facts as these, combined with the uncompromising character of Anselm, are more striking evidence of the absolutism of the Norman monarchy than anything which occurred in the political world during this period.

Within a few days after his consecration, Anselm set out from Canterbury to attend the Christmas meeting of the king's court at Gloucester. There he was well received by the king, but the most important business before the court was destined to lead to the first breach between them. Robert of Normandy had grown tired of his brother's long delay in keeping the promises which he had made in the treaty of Caen. Now there appeared at Gloucester a formal embassy from him, authorized to declare William forsworn and faithless, and to renounce all peace and agreement with him unless he held to the treaty or exculpated himself in due form. There could be no hesitation about an answer to this demand. It is more than likely that William himself, within a short time, would have sought for some excuse to begin again his conquest of Normandy, if Robert had not furnished him this one. War was at once resolved upon, and preparations made for an immediate campaign. The most important preliminary question, both for William and for England, was that of money, and on this question the scruples of Anselm and the will of the king first came into collision. Voluntary aids, donations of money for the special undertakings or necessities of the king, were a feature of William's financial management, though their voluntary character seems often to have been more a matter of theory than of reality. If the sum offered was not so large as the king expected, he refused to accept it and withdrew his favour from the delinquent until he received the amount he thought proper. Anselm was persuaded by his friends to conform to this custom, and hoping that he might in this way secure the favour and support of the king in his ecclesiastical plans, he offered him five hundred pounds of silver. At first William was pleased with the gift and accepted it, but his counsellors advised him that it was too small, and Anselm was informed that it would not be received. The archbishop's attempt to persuade William to take the money only called out an angry answer. "Keep your own to yourself," the king said, "I have enough of mine;" and Anselm went away rejoicing that now evil-minded men would have no occasion to say that he had bought his office, and he promised the money to the poor. The archbishop was acting here entirely within his legal rights, but it was not an auspicious beginning of his pontificate. Within a few weeks the prelates and nobles of England were summoned to meet again—at Hastings, from which port the king intended to cross to Normandy. The weather was for some weeks unfavourable, and during the delay the church of the new abbey of Battle was dedicated; Robert Bloet, who had been appointed Bishop of Lincoln while the king was in fear of death, was consecrated, though Anselm himself had not as yet received his pallium from the pope; and Herbert Losinga, Bishop of Thetford, who had bought his bishopric from the king and afterwards, apparently in repentance, had personally sought the confirmation of the pope, was suspended from his office because he had left the realm without the permission of the king and had sought from the unacknowledged Pope Urban the bishopric which the king asserted his full right to confer. He afterwards recovered William's favour and removed his see to Norwich. At Hastings, in a personal interview with the king, Anselm sought permission to hold a synod of the kingdom, which had not up to this time been allowed during the reign, and remonstrated with him in the plainest language for keeping so many monasteries without abbots while he used their revenues for wars and other secular purposes. In both respects William bluntly refused to change his conduct, and when Anselm sought through the bishops the restoration of his favour, refused that also "because," he said, "I do not know why I should grant it." When it was explained to Anselm that this was a formula of the king's which meant that his favour was to be bought, he refused on grounds of policy as well as of principle to increase, or even to renew, his former offer. This seemed like a final breach with the king. William's anger was great when he heard of Anselm's decision. He declared that he would hate him constantly more and more, and never would hold him for his spiritual father or a bishop. "Let him go home as soon as he likes," he cried, "he need not wait any longer to give his blessings to my crossing over" and Anselm departed at once from Hastings.

On March 19, 1094, William at last crossed to Normandy. The campaign which followed was without decisive results. He was no nearer the conquest of the duchy at the end than at the beginning. Indeed, we can hardly say that the campaign had an end. It died away by degrees, but no formal peace was made, and the duchy came finally into the hands of William, not by conquest, but by other means. On William's landing an attempt was made to renew the peace at an interview between him and Robert, but without avail. Then those who had signed the treaty of Caen as guarantors, twelve barons for Robert and twelve for William, were called upon to say who was acting in violation of the treaty. They decided, apparently without disagreement, against William, but he refused to be bound by their verdict. The war which followed was a typical feudal war, the siege of castles, the capture of men and towns. Robert called in once more his suzerain, Philip of France, to his aid, and captured two important castles, that of Argentan towards the south, and that of La Houlme in the north-west. William then took a step which illustrates again the extent of his power and his arbitrary use of it. He ordered a levy of ten thousand men from England to be sent him in Normandy, and when they had assembled at Hastings, Ranulf Flambard, by the king's orders we are told, took from them the ten shillings which each man had been furnished for his expenses, and sent them home. Robert and Philip were now marching against William at Eu, and it was probably by the liberal use of this money that "the king of France was turned back by craft and all the expedition dispersed." About the same time William sent for his brother Henry to join him. Henry had reappeared in western Normandy not long before, and had begun the reconstruction of his power there. Invited by the inhabitants of Domfront to protect them against Robert of Bellême, he had made that place a starting-point from which he had recovered a considerable part of his earlier possessions. Now William sent ships to bring him by sea to Eu, probably wishing to use his military skill against their common enemy. For some reason, however, the ships departed from their course, and on the last day of October he landed at Southampton, where he stayed some weeks. On December 28, William also returned to England, and in the spring, Henry was sent back to Normandy with supplies of money to keep up the war against Robert.

The year 1094 had been a hard one for both England and Normandy. The duchy had suffered more from the private wars which prevailed everywhere, and which the duke made no effort to check, than from the invasion of William. England in general had had peace, under the strong hand of the king, but so heavy had been the burden of the taxation which the war in Normandy had entailed that agriculture declined, we are told, and famine and pestilence followed. In the west the Welsh had risen against the Norman lords, and had invaded and laid waste parts of the English border counties. In Scotland William's ally, Duncan, had been murdered, and his uncle, Donald, who represented the Scottish national party, had been made king in his place. William found difficulties enough in England to occupy him for some time, particularly when, as was told above, the refusal of Robert of Mowbray to appear at court in March revealed the plans of the barons for another insurrection.

Before he could attempt to deal with any of these difficulties, however, another question, more troublesome still, was forced upon the king. A few weeks after his landing Anselm came to him and asked leave to go to Rome to get his pallium from the pope. "From which pope?" asked the king. Anselm had already given warning of the answer which he must make, and at once replied, "From Urban." Here was joined an inevitable issue between the king and the archbishop; inevitable, not because of the character of the question but because of the character of the two men. No conflict need have arisen upon this question. When Anselm had remonstrated with the king on the eve of his Norman expedition, about the vacant abbeys that were in his hands, William in anger had replied that Lanfranc would never have dared to use such language to his father. We may be sure for one thing, that Lanfranc would have dared to oppose the first William with all his might, if he had thought the reason sufficient, but also that his more practical mind would never have allowed him to regard this question as important enough to warrant the evils that would follow in the train of an open quarrel between king and primate. During the last years of Lanfranc's life, at least from 1084, no pope had been formally recognized in England. To Anselm's mind, however, the question was one of vital importance, where delay would be the sacrifice of principle to expediency. On the other hand, it seems clear to us, looking back on these events, that William, from the strength of his position in England, could have safely overlooked Anselm's personal recognition of Urban, and could have tacitly allowed him even to get his pallium from the pope without surrendering anything of his own practical control of the Church. William, however, refused to take this course. Perhaps he had come to see that a conflict with Anselm could not be avoided, and chose not to allow him any, even merely formal, advantages. The student of this crisis is tempted to believe, from the facts of this case, from the king's taking away "the staff" from the Bishop of Thetford, if the words used refer to anything more than a confiscation of his fief, and especially from his steady refusal to allow the meeting of a national council, that William had conceived the idea of an independent Church under his supreme control in all that pertained to its government, and that he was determined to be rid of an Archbishop of Canterbury, who would never consent to such a plan.

Of the dispute which followed we have a single interesting and detailed account, written by Eadmer who was in personal attendance on Anselm through it all, but it is the account of a devoted partisan of the archbishop which, it is clear, we cannot trust for legal distinctions, and which is not entirely consistent with itself. According to this narrative, William asserted that Anselm's request, as amounting to an official recognition of one of the two popes, was an attack upon his sovereignty as king. This Anselm denied,—he could not well appreciate the point,—and he affirmed that he could at the same time be true to the pope whom he had recognized and to the king whose man he was. This was perfectly true from Anselm's point of view, but the other was equally true from William's. The fundamental assumptions of the two men were irreconcilable. The position of the bishop in a powerful feudal monarchy was an impossible one without some such practical compromise of tacit concessions from both sides, as existed between Lanfranc and William I. Anselm desired that this question, whether he could not at the same time preserve his fidelity to both pope and king, be submitted to the decision of the king's court, and that body was summoned to meet at Rockingham castle at an early date. The details of the case we cannot follow. The king appears to have been desirous of getting a condemnation of Anselm which would have at least the practical effect of vacating the archbishopric, but he met with failure in his purpose, whatever it was, and this it seems less from the resistance of the bishops to his will than from the explicit refusal of the lay barons to regard Anselm as no longer archbishop. The outcome of the case makes it clear that there was in Anselm's position no technical violation of his feudal obligations to the king. At last the actual decision of the question was postponed to a meeting to be held on the octave of Whitsuntide, but in the meantime the king had put into operation another plan which had been devised for accomplishing his wish. He secretly despatched two clerks of his chapel to Italy, hoping, so at least Anselm's biographer believed, to obtain, as the price of his recognition of Urban, the deposition of Anselm by the authority of the pope for whom he was contending. The opportunity was eagerly embraced at Rome. A skilful and not over-scrupulous diplomatist, Walter, Cardinal-Bishop of Albano, was immediately sent back to England with the messengers of Rufus, doubtless with instructions to get as much as possible from the king without yielding the real principle involved in Anselm's case. In the main point Walter was entirely successful. The man of violent temper is not often fitted for the personal conflicts of diplomacy; at least in the strife with the papal legate the king came off second best. It is more to be wondered at that a man of so acute a mind as William of St. Calais, who was now one of the king's most intimate advisers, did not demand better guarantees.

Cardinal Walter carefully abstained at first from any communication with Anselm. He passed through Canterbury without the archbishop's knowledge; he seemed to acquiesce in the king's view of the case. William believed that everything was going as he wished, and public proclamation was made that Urban was to be obeyed throughout his dominions. But when he pressed for a deposition of Anselm, he found that this had not been included in the bargain; nor could he gain, either from the legate or from Anselm, the privilege of bestowing the pallium himself. He was obliged to yield in everything which he had most desired; to reconcile himself publicly with the archbishop, and to content himself with certain not unimportant concessions, which the cardinal wisely yielded, but which brought upon him the censure of the extreme Church party. Anselm promised to observe faithfully the laws and customs of the kingdom; at this time also was sworn his oath of fidelity to the pope, with the clause reserving his fealty to the king; and Cardinal Walter formally agreed that legates should be sent to England only with the consent of the king. But in the most important points which concerned the conflict with the archbishop the king had been defeated. Urban was officially recognized as pope, and the legate entered Canterbury in solemn procession, bearing the pallium, and placed it on the altar of the cathedral, from which Anselm took it as if he had received it from the hands of the pope.

Inferences of a constitutional sort are hardly warranted by the character of our evidence regarding this quarrel, but the facts which we know seem to imply that even so powerful and arbitrary a king as William Rufus could not carry out a matter on which his heart was so set as this without some pretence of legal right to support him, at least in the case of so high a subject as the Archbishop of Canterbury; and that the barons of the kingdom, with the law on their side, were able to hold the king's will in check. Certainly the different attitude of the barons in the quarrel of 1097, where Anselm was clearly in the wrong, is very suggestive.

Already before the close of this business the disobedience of Robert of Mowbray had revealed to the king the plot against him, and a considerable part of the summer of 1095 was occupied in the reduction of the strongholds of the Earl of Northumberland. In October the king invaded Wales in person, but found it impossible to reach the enemy, and retired before the coming on of winter. In this year died the aged Wulfstan, Bishop of Worcester, the last of the English bishops who survived the Conquest. His bishopric fell into the hands of Flambard, and furnishes us one of the best examples we have of his treatment of these fiefs. On the first day of the next year died also William of St. Calais, Bishop of Durham, who had once more fallen under the king's displeasure for some reason, and who had been compelled to come up to the Christmas court, though too ill to travel. He left incomplete his new cathedral of Durham, which he had begun on a splendid scale soon after his return from exile early in the reign, beginning also a new period in Norman architecture of lighter and better-proportioned forms, with no sacrifice of the impression of solid strength.

This year of 1096, which thus began for England with the death of one of the ablest of her prelates, is the date of the beginning for Europe as a whole of one of the most profound movements of medieval times. The crusades had long been in preparation, but it was the resolution and eloquence of Pope Urban which turned into a definite channel the strong ascetic feeling and rapidly growing chivalric passion of the west, and opened this great era. The Council of Clermont, at which had occurred Urban's famous appeal and the enthusiastic vow of the crusaders, had been held in November, 1095, and the impulse had spread rapidly to all parts of France. The English nation had no share in this first crusade, and but little in the movement as a whole; but its history was from the beginning greatly influenced by it. Robert of Normandy was a man of exactly the type to be swept away by such a wave of enthusiasm, and not to feel the strength of the motives which should have kept him at home. His duty as sovereign of Normandy, to recover the castles held by his brother, and to protect his subjects from internal war, were to him as nothing when compared with his duty to protect pious pilgrims to the tomb of Christ, and to deliver the Holy Land from the rule of the infidel. William Rufus, on the other hand, was a man to whom the motives of the crusader would never appeal, but who stood ready to turn to his own advantage every opportunity which the folly of his brother might offer. Robert's most pressing need in such an undertaking was for money, and so much more important did this enterprise seem to him than his own proper business that he stood ready to deliver the duchy into the hands of his brother, with whom he was even then in form at war for its possession, if he could in that way obtain the necessary resources for his crusade. William was as eager to get the duchy as Robert was to get the money, and a bargain was soon struck between them. William carried over to Normandy 10,000 marks—the mark was two-thirds of a pound—and received from Robert, as a pledge for the payment of the loan, the possession of the duchy for a period of at least three years, and for how much longer we cannot now determine with certainty, but for a period which was probably intended to cover Robert's absence. The duke then set off at once on his crusade, satisfied with the consciousness that he was following the plain path of duty. With him went his uncle, Odo, Bishop of Bayeux, to die in Sicily in the next winter.

William had bought the possession of Normandy at a bargain, but he did not propose to pay for it at his own cost. The money which he had spent, and probably more than that, he recovered by an extraordinary tax in England, which excited the bitter complaints of the ecclesiastical writers. If we may trust our interpretation of the scanty accounts which have reached us, this money was raised in two ways, by a general land-tax and by additional personal payments from the king's own vassals. By grant of the barons of England a Danegeld of four shillings on the hide, double the usual tax, was collected, and this even from the domain lands of the Church, which it was asserted, though with doubtful truth, had always been exempt. The clergy paid this tax, but entered formal protest against it, probably in order to prevent, if possible, the establishment of a precedent against their liberties. The additional payment suggested by some of the chroniclers is to be seen in detail in the case of Anselm, who regarded this as a reasonable demand on the part of the king, and who, besides passing over to the treasury what he collected from his men, made on advice a personal payment of 200 marks, which he borrowed from the Canterbury monks on the security of one of his domain manors. Not all the churches were so fortunate as to have the ready money in the treasury, and in many cases ornaments and sacred utensils were sacrificed, while the lay lords undoubtedly recovered their payments by like personal auxilia from their men, until the second tax really rested like the first upon the land. The whole formed a burden likely to cripple seriously the primitive agriculture of the time, as we are told that it did.

Having taken possession of Normandy, William returned to England at Easter in 1097. The Welsh had been making trouble again, and the king once more marched against them in person; but a country like Wales was easily defended against a feudal army, and the expedition accomplished little and suffered much, especially in the loss of horses. William returned probably in no very amiable mood, and at once sent off a letter to Anselm complaining that the contingent of knights which he had sent to meet his obligation of service in the campaign was badly furnished and not fit for its duties, and ordered him to be ready to do him right according to the sentence of the king's court whenever he should bring suit against him. To this letter Anselm paid no attention, and he resolved to let the suit against him go by default, on the ground that everything was determined in the court by the will of the king, and that he could get no justice there. In taking this position, the archbishop was putting himself in the wrong, for the king was acting clearly within his legal rights; but this fact Anselm probably did not understand. He could not enter into the king's position nor his own in relation to him, but he might have remembered that two years before, for once at least, the king had failed to carry through his will in his court.

The case came on for trial at the Whitsuntide court at Windsor, but before anything was determined Anselm sent by certain barons to ask the king's leave to go to Rome, which was at once refused. This action was evidently not intended by Anselm as an appeal of the case to Rome, nor was it so understood by the king; but for some reason the suits against him were now dropped. Anselm's desire to visit Rome apparently arose from the general condition of things in the kingdom, from his inability to hold synods, to get important ecclesiastical offices filled, or to reform the evils of government and morals which prevailed under William. In other words, he found himself nominally primate of England and metropolitan of the great province of Canterbury, but in reality with neither power nor influence. Such a condition of things was intolerable to a man of Anselm's conscientiousness, and he had evidently been for some time coming to the conclusion that he must personally seek the advice of the head of the Church as to his conduct in such a difficult situation. He had now definitely made up his mind, and as the Bishop of Winchester told him at this time, he was not easy to be moved from a thing he had once undertaken. He repeated his request in August, and again in October of the same year. On the last occasion William lost his temper and threatened him with another suit in the court for his vexatious refusal to abide by the king's decision. Anselm insisted on his right to go. William pointed out to him, that if he was determined to go, the result would be the confiscation of the archbishopric,—that is, of the barony. Anselm was not moved by this. Then the bishops attempted to show him the error of his ways, but there was so little in common between their somewhat worldly position as good vassals of the king, and his entire other-worldliness, that nothing was gained in this way. Finally, William informed him that if he chose he might go, on the conditions which had been explained to him,—that is, of the loss of all that he held of the king. This was permission enough for Anselm, and he at once departed, having given his blessing to the king.

No case could be more typical than this of the irreconcilable conflict between Church and State in that age, irreconcilable except by mutual concessions and compromise, and the willingness of either to stand partly in the position of the other. If we look at the matter from the political side, regarding the bishop as a public officer, as a baron in a feudally organized state, the king was entirely right in this case, and fully justified in what he did. Looking at the Church as a religious institution, charged with a spiritual mission and the work of moral reformation, we must consider Anselm's conduct justified, as the only means by which he could hope to obtain freedom of action. Both were in a very real sense right in this quarrel, and both were wrong. Not often during the feudal period did this latent contradiction of rights come to so open and plain an issue as this. That it did so here was due in part to the character of the king, but in the main to the character of the archbishop. Whether Lanfranc could have continued to rule the Church in harmony with William Rufus is an interesting question, but one which we cannot answer. He certainly would not have put himself legally in the wrong, as Anselm did, and he would have considered carefully whether the good to be gained for the cause of the Church from a quarrel with the king would outweigh the evil. Anselm, however, was a man of the idealistic type of mind, who believed that if he accepted as the conditions of his work the evils with which he was surrounded, and consented to use the tools that he found ready to his hand, he had made, as another reformer of somewhat the same type once said of the constitution of the United States in the matter of slavery, "a covenant with death and an agreement with hell."

Anselm left England early in November, 1097, not to return during the lifetime of William. If he had hoped, through the intervention of the pope, to weaken the hold of the king on the Church of England, and to be put in a position where he could carry out the reforms on which his heart was set, he was doomed to disappointment. After a stay of some months at Lyons, with his friend Archbishop Hugh, he went on to Rome, where he was treated with great ceremonial honour by the pope, but where he learned that the type of lofty and uncompromising independence which he himself represented was as rare in the capital of the Christian world as he had found it among the bishops of England. There, however, he learned a stricter doctrine on the subject of lay investitures, of appointments to ecclesiastical office by kings and princes, than he had yet held, so that when he finally returned to England he brought with him the germs of another bitter controversy with a king, with whom but for this he might have lived in peace.

In the same month with Anselm, William also crossed to Normandy, but about very different business. Hardly had he obtained possession of the duchy when he began to push the claims of the duke to bordering lands, to the French Vexin, and to the county of Maine, claims about which his brother had never seriously concerned himself and which, in one case, even his father had allowed to slumber for years. Robert had, indeed, asserted his claim to Maine after the death of his father, and had been accepted by the county; but a revolt had followed in 1190, the Norman rule had been thrown off, and after a few months Elias of La Fleche, a baron of Maine and a descendant of the old counts, had made himself count. He was a man of character and ability, and the peace which he established was practically undisturbed by Robert; but the second William had no mind to give up anything to which he could lay a claim. He demarded of the French king the surrender of the Vexin, and warned Elias, who had taken the cross, that the holy errand of the crusade would not protect his lands during his absence. War followed in both cases, simultaneous wars, full of the usual incidents, of the besieging of castles, the burning of towns, the laying waste of the open country; wars in which the ruin of his peasantry was almost the only way of coercing the lord. William's operations were almost all successful, but he died without accomplishing all that he had hoped for in either direction. In the Vexin he captured a series of castles, which brought him almost to Paris; in Maine he captured Le Mans, lost it agair, and finally recovered its possession, but the southern part of the county and the castles of Elias there he never secured.

In the year 1098 Magnus, king of Norway, had appeared for a moment with a hostile fleet off the island of Anglesey. Some reason not certainly known had brought him round Scotland, perhaps to make an attack on Ireland. He was the grandson of the King Harold of Norway, who had invaded England on the eve of the Norman Conquest and perished in the battle of Stamford Bridge, and he had with him, it is said, a son of Harold of England: to him the idea of a new invasion of England would not seem strange. At any rate, after taking possession of the Isle of Man, he came to the help of the Welsh against the earls, Hugh of Chester and Hugh of Shrewsbury, who were beginning the conquest of Anglesey. The incident is noteworthy because, in the brief fighting which occurred, the Earl of Shrewsbury was slain. His death opened the way for the succession of his brother, Robert of Bellême, to the great English possessions of their father in Wales, Shropshire, and Surrey, to which he soon added by inheritance the large holdings of Roger of Bully in Yorkshire and elsewhere. These inheritances, when added to the lands, almost a principality in themselves, which he possessed in southern Normandy and just over the border in France, made him the most powerful vassal of the English king. In character he had inherited far more from his tyrannous and cruel mother, Mabel, daughter of William Talvas of Bellême, than from his more high-minded father, Roger of Montgomery, the companion of the Conqueror. As a vassal he was utterly untrustworthy, and he had become too powerful for his own safety or for that of the king.

Some minor events of these years should be recounted. In 1097 William had sent Edgar the atheling to Scotland with an army, King Donald had been overthrown, and Edgar's nephew, himself named Edgar, with the support of the English king, had been made king. In 1099 Ranulf Flambard received the reward of his faithful services, and was made Bishop of Durham, in some respects the most desirable bishopric in England. Greater prospects still of power and dominion were opened to William a few months before his death, by the proposition of the Duke of Aquitaine to pledge him his great duchy for a sum of money to pay the expenses of a crusade. To add to the lands he already ruled those between the Loire and the Garonne would be almost to create a new monarchy in France and to threaten more dangerously at this moment the future of the Capetian kingdom than did two generations later the actual union of these territories and more under the king of England.

But William was now rapidly approaching the term of his life. The monastic chronicles, written within a generation or two later, record many visions and portents of the time foreshadowing the doom which was approaching, but these are to us less records of actual facts than evidences of the impression which the character and government of the king had made, especially upon the members of the Church. On August 2, 1100, William rode out to hunt in the New Forest, as was his frequent custom. In some way, how we do not know, but probably by accident, he was himself shot with an arrow by one of his company, and died almost instantly. Men believed, not merely that he was justly cut off in his sins with no opportunity for the final offices of the Church, but that his violent death was an instance, the third already, of the doom which followed his father's house because of the evil that was done in the making of the Forest. The king's body was brought to Winchester, where it was buried in the old minster, but without the ordinary funeral rites. One of his companions that day, Walter Tirel, a French baron who had been attracted to the service of the king by the prospect of rich reward which it offered, was thought to have been responsible for his death, and he fled in haste and escaped to his home; but he afterwards solemnly declared, when there would have been no danger to himself in confession, that it was not his arrow that slew the king, and whose it was will never be known.

[15] Eadmer, Hist. Nov., p. 41.

CHAPTER VI.
THE STRUGGLE FOR POWER

In the hunting party which William Rufus led out on August 2, 1100, to his mysterious death in the New Forest, was the king's younger brother, Henry. When the cry rang through the Forest that the king was dead, Henry seized the instant with the quick insight and strong decision which were marked elements of his genius. He rode at once for Winchester. We do not even know that he delayed long enough to make sure of the news by going to the spot where his brother's body lay. He rode at full speed to Winchester, and demanded the keys of the royal treasury, "as true heir," says Ordesic Vitalis, one of the best historians of Henry's reign, recording rather, it is probable, his own opinion than the words of the prince. Men's ideas were still so vague, not yet fixed and precise as later, on the subject of rightful heirship, that such a demand as Henry's—a clear usurpation according to the law as it was finally to be—could find some ground on which to justify itself; at least this, which his historian suggests and which still meant much to English minds, that he was born in the purple, the son of a crowned king.

But not every one was ready to admit the claim of Henry. Between him and the door of the treasury William of Breteuil, who also had been of the hunting party and who was the responsible keeper of the hoard, took his stand. Against the demand of Henry he set the claim of Robert, the better claim according even to the law of that day, though the law which he urged was less that which would protect the right of the eldest born than the feudal law regarding homage done and fealty sworn. "If we are going to act legally," he said to Henry, "we ought to remember the fealty which we have promised to Duke Robert, your brother. He is, too, the eldest born son of King William, and you and I, my Lord Henry, have done him homage. We ought to keep faith to him absent in all respects as if he were present." He followed his law by an appeal to feeling, referring to Robert's crusade. "He has been labouring now a long time in the service of God, and God has restored to him, without conflict, his duchy, which as a pilgrim he laid aside for love of Him." Then a strife arose, and a crowd of men ran together to the spot. We can imagine they were not merely men of the city, but also many of the king's train who must have ridden after Henry from the Forest. Whoever they were, they supported Henry, for we are told that as the crowd collected the courage of the "heir who was demanding his right" increased. Henry drew his sword and declared he would permit no "frivolous delay." His insistence and the support of his friends prevailed, and castle and treasury were turned over to him.[16]

This it was which really determined who should be king. Not that the question was fully settled then, but the popular determination which showed itself in the crowd that gathered around the disputants in Winchester probably showed itself, in the days that followed, to be the determination of England in general, and thus held in check those who would have supported Robert, while Henry rapidly pushed events to a conclusion and so became king. There is some evidence that, after the burial of William, further discussion took place among the barons who were present, as to whether they would support Henry or not, and that this was decided in his favour largely by the influence of Henry of Beaumont, Earl of Warwick, son of his father's friend and counsellor, the Count of Meulan. But we ought not to allow the use of the word witan in this connexion, by the Saxon chronicler, or of "election" by other historians or by Henry himself, to impose upon us the belief in a constitutional right of election in the modern sense, which could no more have existed at that time than a definite law of inheritance. In every case of disputed succession the question was, whether that one of the claimants who was on the spot could secure quickly enough a degree of support which would enable him to hold the opposition in check until he became a crowned king. A certain amount of such support was indispensable to success. Henry secured this in one way, Stephen in another, and John again in a third. In each case, the actual events show clearly that a small number of men determined the result, not by exercising a constitutional right of which they were conscious, but by deciding for themselves which one of the claimants they would individually support. Some were led by one motive, and some by another. In Henry's case we cannot doubt that the current of feeling which had shown itself in Winchester on the evening of the king's death had a decisive influence on the result, at least as decisive as the early stand of London was afterwards in Stephen's case.

Immediately, before leaving Winchester, Henry performed one royal act of great importance to his cause, and skilfully chosen as a declaration of principles. He appointed William Giffard, who had been his brother's chancellor, Bishop of Winchester. This see had been vacant for nearly three years and subject to the dealings of Ranulf Flambard. The immediate appointment of a bishop was equivalent to a proclamation that these dealings should now cease, that bishoprics should no longer be kept vacant for the benefit of the king, and it was addressed to the Church, the party directly interested and one of the most powerful influences in the state in deciding the question of succession. The speed with which Henry's coronation was carried through shows that the Church accepted his assurances.

There was no delay in Winchester. William was killed on the afternoon of Thursday, August 2; on Sunday, Henry was crowned in Westminster, by Maurice, Bishop of London. Unhesitating determination and rapid action must have filled the interval. Only a small part of England could have learned of William's death when Henry was crowned, and he must have known at the moment that the risk of failure was still great. But everything indicates that Henry had in mind a clearly formed policy which he believed would lead to success, and he was not the man to be afraid of failure. The Archbishop of Canterbury was still in exile; the Archbishop of York was far away and ill; the Bishop of London readily performed the ceremony, which followed the old ritual. In the coronation oath of the old Saxon formula, Henry swore, with more intention of remembering it than many kings, that the Church of God and all Christian people he would keep in true peace, that he would forbid violence and iniquity to all men, and that in all judgments he would enjoin both justice and mercy.

The man who thus came to the throne of England was one of her ablest kings. We know far less of the details of his reign than we could wish. Particularly scanty is our evidence of the growth in institutions which went on during these thirty-five years, and which would be of especial value in illustrating the character and abilities of the king. But we know enough to warrant us in placing Henry beyond question in the not long list of statesmen kings. Not without some trace of the passions which raged in the blood of the Norman and Angevin princes, he exceeded them all in the strength of his self-control. This is the one most marked trait which constantly recurs throughout the events of his long reign. Always calm, we are sometimes tempted to say even cold, he never lost command of himself in the most trying circumstances. Perfectly clear-headed, he saw plainly the end to be reached from the distant beginning, and the way to reach it, and though he would turn aside from the direct road for policy's sake, he reached the goal in time. He knew how to wait, to allow circumstances to work for him, to let men work out their own destruction, but he was quick to act when the moment for action came. Less of a military genius than his father, he was a greater diplomatist. And yet perhaps we call him less of a military genius than his father because he disliked war and gave himself no opportunities which he could avoid; but he was a skilful tactician when he was forced to fight a battle. But diplomacy was his chosen weapon, and by its means he won battles which most kings would have sought to win by the sword.

With justice William of Malmesbury applied to him the words of Scipio Africanus: "My mother brought me forth a general, not a mere soldier."

These were the gifts of nature. But when he came to the throne, he was a man already disciplined in a severe school. Ever since the death of his father, thirteen years before, when he was not yet twenty, the events which had befallen him, the opportunities which had come to him, the inferences which he could not have failed to make from the methods of his brothers, had been training him for the business of his life. It was not as a novice, but as a man experienced in government, that he began to reign. And government was to him a business. It is clear that Henry had always far less delight in the ordinary or possible glories of the kingship than in the business of managing well a great state; and a name by which he has been called, "The Lion of Justice," records a judgment of his success. Physically Henry followed the type of his house. He was short and thick-set, with a tendency to corpulence. He was not "the Red"; the mass of his black hair and his eyes clear and serene struck the observer. Naturally of a pleasant disposition and agreeable to those about him, he was quick to see the humorous side of things and carried easily the great weight of business which fell to him. He was called "Beauclerc," but he was never so commonly known by this name as William by his of "Rufus." But he had, it would seem with some justice, the reputation of being a learned king. Some doubtful evidence has been interpreted to mean that he could both speak and read English. Certainly he cherished a love of books and reading remarkable, at that time, in a man of the world, and he seems to have deserved his reputation of a ready, and even eloquent, speaker.

It was no doubt partly due to Henry's love of business that we may date from his reign the beginning of a growth in institutions after the Conquest. The machinery of good government interested him. Efforts to improve it had his support. The men who had in hand its daily working in curia regis and exchequer and chancery were certain of his favour, when they strove to devise better ways of doing things and more efficient means of controlling subordinates. But the reign was also one of advance in institutions because England was ready for it. In the thirty-five years since the Conquest, the nation which was forming in the island had passed through two preparatory experiences. In the first the Norman, with his institutions, had been introduced violently and artificially, and planted alongside of the native English. It had been the policy of the Conqueror to preserve as much as possible of the old while introducing the new. This was the wisest possible policy, but it could produce as yet no real union. That could only be the work of time. A new nation and a new constitution were foreshadowed but not yet realized. The elements from which they should be made had been brought into the presence of each other, but not more than this was possible. Then followed the reign of William II. In this second period England had had an experience of one side, of the Norman side, carried to the extreme. The principles of feudalism in favour of the suzerain were logically carried out for the benefit of the king, and relentlessly applied to the Church as to the lay society. That portion of the old English machinery which the Conqueror had preserved fell into disorder, and was misused for royal, and worse still, for private advantage. This second period had brought a vivid experience of the abuses which would result from the exaggeration of one of the elements of which the new state was to be composed at the expense of the other. One of its most important results was the reaction which seems instantly to have shown itself on the death of William Rufus, the reaction of which Henry was quick to avail himself, and which gives us the key to an understanding of his reign.

It is not possible to cite evidence from which we may infer beyond the chance of question, either a popular reaction against the tyranny of William Rufus, or a deliberate policy on the part of the new king to make his hold upon the throne secure by taking advantage of such a reaction. It is perhaps the duty of the careful historian to state his belief in these facts, in less dogmatic form. And yet, when we combine together the few indications which the chroniclers give us with the actual events of the first two years of Henry's reign, it is hardly possible to avoid such a conclusion. Henry seems certainly to have believed that he had much to gain by pledging himself in the most binding way to correct the abuses which his brother had introduced, and also that he could safely trust his cause to an English, or rather to a national, party against the element in the state which seemed unassimilable, the purely Norman element.

On the day of his coronation, or at least within a few days of that event, Henry issued, in form of a charter, — that is, in the form of a legally binding royal grant, — his promise to undo his brother's misdeeds; and a copy of this charter, separately addressed, was sent to every county in England. Considered both in itself as issued in the year 1100, and in its historical consequences, this charter is one of the most important of historical documents. It opens a long list of similar constitutional documents which very possibly is not yet complete, and it is in form and spirit worthy of the best of its descendants. Considering the generally unformulated character of feudal law at this date, it is neither vague nor general. It is to be noticed also, that the practical character of the Anglo-Saxon race rules in this first charter of its liberties. It is as business-like and clean cut as the Bill of Rights, or as the American Declaration of Independence when this last gets to the business in hand.

The charter opens with an announcement of Henry's coronation. In true medieval order of precedence, it promises first to the Church freedom from unjust exactions. The temporalities of the Church shall not be sold nor put to farm, nor shall anything be taken from its domain land nor from its men during a vacancy. Then follows a promise to do away with all evil customs, and a statement that these in part will be enumerated. Thus by direct statement here and elsewhere in the charter, its provisions are immediately connected with the abuses which William II had introduced, and the charter made a formal pledge to do away with them. The first promises to the lay barons have to do with extortionate reliefs and the abuse of the rights of wardship and marriage. The provision inserted in both these cases, that the barons themselves shall be bound by the same limitations in regard to their men, leads us to infer that William's abuses had been copied by his barons, and suggests that Henry was looking for the support of the lower ranks of the feudal order. Other promises concern the coinage, fines, and debts due the late king, the right to dispose by will of personal property, excessive fines, and the punishment of murder. The forests Henry announces he will hold as his father held them. To knights freedom of taxation is promised in the domain lands proper of the estates which they hold by military service. The law of King Edward is to be restored with those changes which the Conqueror had made, and finally any property of the crown or of any individual which has been seized upon since the death of William is to be restored under threat of heavy penalty.

So completely does this charter cover the ground of probable abuses in both general and local government, when its provisions are interpreted as they would be understood by the men to whom it was addressed, that it is not strange if men thought that all evils of government were at an end. Nor is it strange in turn, that Henry was in truth more severe upon the tyranny of his brother while he was yet uncertain of his hold upon the crown, than in the practice of his later years. As a matter of fact, not all the promises of the charter were kept. England suffered much from heavy financial exactions during his reign, and the feudal abuses which had weighed most heavily on lay and ecclesiastical barons reappeared in their essential features. They became, in fact, recognized rights of the crown. Henry was too strong to be forced to keep such promises as he chose to forget, and it was reserved for a later descendant of his, weaker both in character and in might of hand, to renew his charter at a time when the more exact conception, both of rights and of abuses, which had developed in the interval, enabled men not merely to enlarge its provisions but to make them in some particulars the foundation of a new type of government. Events rapidly followed the issue of the charter which were equally emphatic declarations of Henry's purpose of reform, and some of which at least would seem like steps in actual fulfilment of the promises of the charter. Ranulf Flambard was arrested and thrown into the Tower; on what charge or under what pretence of right we do not know, but even if by some exercise of arbitrary power, it must have been a very popular act. Several important abbacies which had been held vacant were at once filled. Most important of all, a letter was despatched to Archbishop Anselm, making excuses for the coronation of the king in his absence, and requesting his immediate return to England. Anselm was at the abbey of La Chaise Dieu, having just come from Lyons, where he had spent a large part of his exile, when the news came to him of the death of his royal adversary. He at once started for England, and was on his way when he was met at Cluny by Henry's letter. Landing on September 23, he went almost immediately to the king, who was at Salisbury. There two questions of great importance at once arose, in one of which Anselm was able to assist Henry, while the other gave rise to long-continued differences between them.

The question most easily settled was that of Henry's marriage. According to the historians of his reign, affection led Henry to a marriage which was certainly most directly in line with the policy which he was carrying out. Soon after his coronation, he proposed to marry Edith, daughter of Malcolm, king of Scotland, and of Margaret, sister of the atheling Edgar. She had spent almost the whole of her life in English monasteries, a good part of it at Romsey, where her aunt Christina was abbess. Immediately the question was raised, whether she had not herself taken the veil, which she was known to have worn, and therefore whether the marriage was possible. This was the question now referred to Anselm, and he made a most careful examination of the case, and decision was finally pronounced in a council of the English Church. The testimony of the young woman herself was admitted and was conclusive against any binding vow. She had been forced by her aunt to wear the veil against her will as a means of protection in those turbulent times, but she had always rejected it with indignation when she had been able to do so, nor had it been her father's intention that she should be a nun. Independent testimony confirmed her assertion, and it was formally declared that she was free to marry. The marriage took place on November 11, and was celebrated by Anselm, who also crowned the new queen under the Norman name of Matilda, which she assumed.

No act which Henry could perform would be more pleasing to the nation as a whole than this marriage, or would seem to them clearer proof of his intention to rule in the interest of the whole nation and not of himself alone, or of the small body of foreign oppressors. It would seem like the expression of a wish on Henry's part to unite his line with that of the old

English kings, and to reign as their representative as well as his father's, and it was so understood, both by the party opposed to Henry and by his own supporters. Whatever we may think of the dying prophecy attributed to Edward the Confessor, that the troubles which he foresaw for England should end when the green tree—the English dynasty—cut off from its root and removed for the space of three acres' breadth—three foreign reigns—should without human help be joined to it again and bring forth leaves and fruit, the fact that it was thought, in Henry's reign, to have been fulfilled by his marriage with Matilda and by the birth of their children, shows plainly enough the general feeling regarding the marriage and that for which it stood. The Norman sneer, in which the king and his wife are referred to as Godric and Godgifu, is as plain an indication of the feeling of that party. Such a taunt as this could not have been called out by the mere marriage, and would never have been spoken if the policy of the king, in spite of the marriage, had been one in sympathy with the wishes of the extreme Norman element.

But if it was Henry's policy to win the support of the nation as a whole, and to make it clear that he intended to undo the abuses of his brother, he had no intention of abandoning any of the real rights of the crown. The second question which arose on the first meeting of Anselm and Henry involved a point of this kind. The temporalities of the Archbishop of Canterbury were still in the king's hands, as seized by William Rufus on Anselm's departure. Henry demanded that Anselm should do homage for this fief, as would any baron of the king, and receive it from his hand. To the astonishment of every one, Anselm flatly refused. In answer to inquiries, he explained the position of the pope on the subject of lay investiture, declared that he must stand by that position, and that if Henry also would not obey the pope, he must leave England again. Here was a sharp issue, drawn with the greatest definiteness, and one which it was very difficult for the king to meet. He could not possibly afford to renew the quarrel with Anselm and to drive him into exile again at this moment, but it was equally impossible for him to abandon this right of the crown, so long unquestioned and one on which so much of the state organization rested. He proposed a truce until Easter, that the question might be referred to the pope, in the hope that he would consent to modify his decrees in view of the customary usages of the kingdom, and agreeing that the archbishop should, in the meantime, enjoy the revenues of his see. To this delay Anselm consented, though he declared that it would be useless.

According to the archbishop's devoted friend and biographer, Eadmer, who was in attendance on him at this meeting at Salisbury, Anselm virtually admitted that this was a new position for him to take. He had learned these things at Rome, was the explanation which was given; and this was certainly true, though his stay at Lyons, under the influence of his friend, Archbishop Hugh, a strong partisan of the papal cause, was equally decisive in his change of views.[17] He had accepted investiture originally from the hand of William Rufus without scruple; he had never objected to it with regard to any of that king's later appointments. In the controversy which followed with Henry, there is nothing which shows that his own conscience was in the least degree involved in the question. He opposed the king with his usual unyielding determination, not because he believed himself that lay investiture was a sin, but because pope and council had decided against it, and it was his duty to maintain their decision.

This was a new position for Anselm to take; it was also raising a new question in the government of England. For more than a quarter of a century the papacy had been fighting this battle against lay investiture with all the weapons at its disposal, against its nearest rival, the emperor, and with less of open conflict and more of immediate success in most of the other lands of Europe. But in the dominions of the Norman princes the question had never become a living issue. This was not because the papacy had failed to demand the authority there which it was striving to secure elsewhere. Gregory VII had laid claim to an even more complete authority over England than this. But these demands had met with no success. Even as regards the more subordinate features of the Hildebrandine reformation, simony and the celibacy of the clergy, the response of the Norman and English churches to the demand for reformation had been incomplete and half-hearted, and not even the beginning of a papal party had shown itself in either country. This exceptional position is to be accounted for by the great strength of the crown, and also by the fact that the sovereign in his dealings with the Church was following in both states the policy marked out by a long tradition. Something must also be attributed, and probably in Normandy as well as in England, to the clearness with which Lanfranc perceived the double position of the bishop in the feudal state. The Church was an important part of the machinery of government, and as such its officers were appointed by the king, and held accountable to him for a large part at least of their official action. This was the theory of the Norman state, and this theory had been up to this time unquestioned. It is hardly too much to call the Norman and English churches, from the coronation of William I on to this time, practically independent national churches, with some relationship to the pope, but with one so external in its character that no serious inconvenience would have been experienced in their own government had some sudden catastrophe swept the papacy out of existence.

It was, however, in truth impossible for England to keep itself free from the issue which had been raised by the war upon lay investiture. The real question involved in this controversy was one far deeper than the question of the appointment of bishops by the sovereign of the state. That was a point of detail, a means to the end; very important and essential as a means, but not the end itself. Slowly through centuries of time the Church had become conscious of itself. Accumulated precedents of the successful exercise of power, observation of the might of organization, and equally instructive experience of the weakness of disorganization and of the danger of self-seeking, personal or political, in the head of the Christian world, had brought the thinking party in the Church to understand the dominant position which it might hold in the world if it could be controlled as a single organization and animated by a single purpose. It was the vision of the imperial Church, free from all distracting influence of family or of state, closely bound together into one organic whole, an independent, world-embracing power: more than this even, a power above all other powers, the representative of God, on earth, to which all temporal sovereigns should be held accountable.

That the Church failed to gain the whole of that for which it strove was not the fault of its leaders. A large part of the history of the world in the eleventh and twelfth centuries is filled with the struggle to create, in ideal completeness, this imperial Church. The reformation of Cluny had this for its ultimate object. From the beginning made by that movement, the political genius of Hildebrand sketched the finished structure and pointed out the means to be employed in its completion. That the emperor was first and most fiercely attacked was not due to the fact that he was a sinner above all others in the matter of lay investiture or simony. It was the most urgent necessity of the case that the papacy should make itself independent of that power which in the past had exercised the most direct sovereignty over the popes, and before the conflict should end be able to take its seat beside the empire as an equal, or even a superior, world power. But if the empire must be first overcome, no state could be left out of this plan, and in England as elsewhere the issue must sooner or later be joined.

It must not be understood that mere ambition was at the bottom of this effort of the Church. Of ambition in the ordinary sense it is more than probable that no leader of this movement was conscious. The cause of the Church was the cause of God and of righteousness. The spiritual power ought justly to be superior to the temporal, because the spiritual interests of men so far outweigh their temporal. If the spiritual power is supreme, and holds in check the temporal, and calls the sovereign to account for his wrong-doing, the way of salvation will be easier for all men, and the cause of righteousness promoted. If this kind of a Church is to be organized, and this power established in the world, it is essential that so important an officer in the system as the bishop should be chosen by the Church alone, and with reference alone to the spiritual interests which he is to guard, and the spiritual duties he must perform. Selection by the state, accountability to the state, would make too serious a flaw in the practical operation of this system to be permitted. The argument of the Church against the practice of lay investiture was entirely sound.

On the other hand, the argument of the feudal state was not less sound. It is difficult for us to get a clear mental picture of the organization of the feudal state, because the institutions of that state have left few traces in modern forms of government. The complete transformation of the feudal baronage into a modern nobility, and the rise on the ruins of the feudal state of clearly defined, legislative, judicial, and administrative systems have obscured the line of direct descent. But the feudal baron was very different from a modern noble, and there was no bureaucracy and no civil service in the feudal state beyond their mere beginnings in the personal servants of the king. No function of government was the professional business of any one, but legislative, judicial, administrative, financial, and military operations were all incidental to something else. This may not seem true of the sheriff; but that he had escaped transformation, after the feudalization of England, into something more than an administrative officer makes the Norman state somewhat exceptional at that time, and the history of this office, even under the most powerful of kings, shows the strength of the tendency toward development in the direction of a private possession. Even while remaining administrative, the office was known to the Normans by a name which to some extent in their own home, and generally elsewhere, had come to be an hereditary feudal title, — the viscount. In this system of government, the baron was the most essential feature. Every kind of government business was performed in the main through him, and as incidental to his position as a baron. The assembly of the barons, the curia regis, whether the great assembly of all the barons of the kingdom, meeting on occasions by special summons, or the smaller assembly in constant attendance on the king, was the primitive and undifferentiated machine by which government was carried on. If the baronage was faithful to the crown, or if the crown held the baronage under a strong control, the realm enjoyed good government and the nation bore with comparatively little suffering the burdens which were always heavy. If the baronage was out of control, government fell to pieces, and anarchy and oppression took its place.

In this feudal state, however, a bishop was a baron. The lands which formed the endowment of his office — and in those days endowment could take no other form—constituted a barony. The necessity of a large income and the generosity of the faithful made of his endowment a great fief. It is important to realize how impossible any other conception than this was to the political half of the world. In public position, influence upon affairs, wealth, and popular estimation, the bishop stood in the same class with the baron. The manors which were set aside from the general property of the Church to furnish his official income would, in many cases, provide for an earldom. In fitness to perform the manifold functions of government which fell to him, the bishop far exceeded the ordinary baron. The state could not regard him as other than a baron; it certainly could not dispense with his assistance. It was a matter of vital importance to the king to be able to determine what kind of men should hold these great fiefs and occupy these influential positions in the state, and to be able to hold them to strict accountability. The argument of the state in favour of lay investiture was as sound as the argument of the Church against it.

Here was a conflict of interests in which no real compromise was possible. Incidental features of the conflict might be found upon which the form of a compromise could be arranged. But upon the one essential point, the right of selecting the man, one or the other of the parties whose interests were involved must give way. It is not strange that in the main, except where the temporary or permanent weakness of the sovereign made an exception, that interest which seemed to the general run of men of most immediate and pressing importance gained the day, and the spiritual gave way to the temporal. But in England the conflict was now first begun, and the time of compromise had not yet come. Henry's proposal to Anselm of delay and of a new appeal to the pope was chiefly a move to gain time until the situation of affairs in England should turn more decidedly in his favour. He especially feared, Eadmer tells us, lest Anselm should seek out his brother Robert and persuade him—as he easily could—to admit the papal claims, and then make him king of England.

Robert had returned to Normandy from the Holy Land before the arrival of Anselm in England. He had won much glory on the crusade, and in the rush of events and in the constant fighting, where responsibility for the management of affairs did not rest upon him alone, he had shown himself a man of energy and power. But he came back unchanged in character. Even during the crusade he had relapsed at times into his more indolent and careless mood, from which he had been roused with difficulty. In southern Italy, where he had stopped among the Normans on his return, he had married Sibyl, daughter of Geoffrey of Conversana, a nephew of Robert Guiscard, but the dowry which he received with her had rapidly melted away in his hands. He was, however, now under no obligation to redeem Normandy. The loan for which he had pledged the duchy was regarded as a personal debt to William Rufus, not a debt to the English crown, and Henry laid no claim to it. Robert took possession of Normandy without opposition from any quarter. It is probable that if Robert had been left to himself, he would have been satisfied with Normandy, and that his easy-going disposition would have led him to leave Henry in undisturbed possession of England. But he was not left to himself. The events which had occurred soon after the accession of William Rufus repeated themselves soon after Henry's. No Norman baron could expect to gain any more of the freedom which he desired under Henry than he had had under William. The two states would also be separated once more if Henry remained king of England. Almost all the Normans accordingly applied to Robert, as they had done before, and offered to support a new attempt to gain the crown. Robert was also urged forward by the advice of Ranulf Flambard, who escaped from the Tower in February, 1101, and found a refuge and new influence in Normandy. Natural ambition was not wanting to Robert, and in the summer of 1101 he collected his forces for an invasion of England.

Though the great Norman barons stood aloof from him—Robert of Bellême and his two brothers Roger and Arnulf, William of Warenne, Walter Giffard. and Ivo of Grantmesnil, with others—Henry was stronger in England than Robert. No word had yet been received from Rome in answer to the application which he had made to the pope on the subject of the investiture; and in this crisis the king was liberal with promises to the archbishop, and Anselm was strongly on his side with the Church as a whole. His faithful friends, Robert, Count of Meulan, and his brother Henry, Earl of Warwick, were among the few whom he could trust. But his most important support he found, as his brother William had found it in similar circumstances, in the mass of the nation which would now be even more ready to take the side of the king against the Norman party.

Henry expected the invaders to land at Pevensey, but apparently, with the help of some part of the sailors who had been sent against him, Robert landed without opposition at Portsmouth, towards the end of July, 1101. Thence he advanced towards London, and Henry went to meet him. The two armies came together near Alton, but no battle was fought. In a conflict of diplomacy, Henry was pretty sure of victory, and to this he preferred to trust. A meeting of the brothers was arranged, and as a result Robert surrendered all the real advantages which he had crossed the channel to win, and received in place of them gains which might seem attractive to him, but which must have seemed to Henry, when taken all together, a cheap purchase of the crown. Robert gave up his claim to the throne and released Henry, as being a king, from the homage by which he had formerly been bound. Henry on his side promised his brother an annual payment of three thousand marks sterling, and gave up to him all that he possessed in Normandy, except the town of Domfront, which he had expressly promised not to abandon. It was also agreed, as formerly between Robert and William Rufus, that the survivor should inherit the dominions of the other if he died without heirs. A further provision concerned the adherents of each of the brothers during this strife. Possessions in England of barons of Normandy, which had been seized by Henry because of their fidelity to Robert, should be restored, and also the Norman estates of English barons seized by Robert, but each should be free to deal with the barons of his own land who had proved unfaithful. This stipulation would be of especial value to Henry, who had probably not found it prudent to deal with the traitors of his land before the decision of the contest; but some counter-intrigues in Normandy in favour of Henry were probably not unknown to Robert.

Robert sent home at once a part of his army, but he himself remained in England long enough to witness in some cases the execution by his brother of the provision of the treaty concerning traitors. He took with him, on his return to Normandy, Orderic Vitalis says, William of Warenne and many others disinherited for his sake. Upon others the king took vengeance one at a time, on one pretext or another, and these included at least Robert of Lacy, Robert Malet, and Ivo of Grantmesnil. The possessions of Ivo in Leicestershire passed into the hands of the faithful Robert, Count of Meulan—faithful to Henry if not to the rebel who sought his help—and somewhat later became the foundation of the earldom of Leicester.

Against the most powerful and most dangerous of the traitors, Robert of Bellême, Henry felt strong enough to take steps in the spring of 1102. In a court in that year Henry brought accusation against Robert on forty-five counts, of things done or said against himself or against his brother Robert. The evidence to justify these accusations Henry had been carefully and secretly collecting for a year. When Robert heard this indictment, he knew that his turn had come, and that no legal defence was possible, and he took advantage of a technical plea to make his escape. He asked leave to retire from the court and take counsel with his men. As this was a regular custom leave was granted, but Robert took horse at once and fled from the court. Summoned again to court, Robert refused to come, and began to fortify his castles. Henry on his side collected an army, and laid siege first of all to the castle of Arundel. The record of the siege gives us an incident characteristic of the times. Robert's men, finding that they could not defend the place, asked for a truce that they might send to their lord and obtain leave to surrender. The request was granted, the messengers were sent, and Robert with grief "absolved them from their promised faith and granted them leave to make concord with the king." Henry then turned against Robert's castles in the north. Against Blyth he marched himself, but on his approach he was met by the townsmen who received him as their "natural lord." To the Bishop of Lincoln he gave orders to besiege Tickhill castle, while he advanced towards the west, where lay Robert's chief possessions and greatest strength.

In his Shrewsbury earldom Robert had been preparing himself for the final struggle with the king ever since he had escaped his trial in the court. He counted upon the help of his two brothers, whose possessions were also in those parts, Arnulf of Pembroke, and Roger called the Poitevin, who had possession of Lancaster. The Welsh princes also stood ready, as their countrymen stood for centuries afterwards, to combine with any party of rebellious barons in England, and their assistance proved of as little real value then as later. With these allies and the help of Arnulf he laid waste a part of Staffordshire before Henry's arrival, the Welsh carrying off their plunder, including some prisoners. Robert's chief dependence, however, must have been upon his two very strong castles of Bridgenorth and Shrewsbury, both of which had been strengthened and provisioned with care for a stubborn resistance.

Henry's first attack with what seems to have been a large force was on Bridgenorth castle. Robert had himself chosen to await the king's attack in Shrewsbury, and had left three of his vassals in charge of Bridgenorth, with a body of mercenaries, who often proved, notwithstanding the oaths of vassals, the most faithful troops of feudal days. He had hoped that his Welsh friends would be able to interfere seriously with Henry's siege operations, but in this he was disappointed. The king's offers proved larger than his, at least to one of the princes, and no help came from that quarter. One striking incident of this siege, though recorded by Orderic Vitalis only, is so characteristic of the situation in England, at least of that which had just preceded the rebellion of Robert, and bears so great an appearance of truth, that it deserves notice. The barons of England who were with the king began to fear that if he were allowed to drive so powerful an earl as Robert of Bellême to his ruin the rest of their order would be henceforth at his mercy, and no more than weak "maid-servants" in his sight. Accordingly, after consulting among themselves, they made a formal attempt to induce the king to grant terms to Robert. In the midst of an argument which the king seems to have been obliged to treat with consideration, the shouts of 3000 country soldiers stationed on a hill near by made themselves heard, warning Henry not to trust to "these traitors," and promising him their faithful assistance. Encouraged by this support, the king rejected the advice of the barons.

The siege of Bridgenorth lasted three weeks. At the end of that time, Henry threatened to hang all whom he should capture, unless the castle were surrendered in three days; and despite the resistance of Robert's mercenaries, the terms he offered were accepted. Henry immediately sent out his forces to clear the difficult way to Shrewsbury, where Robert, having learned of the fall of Bridgenorth, was awaiting the issue, uncertain what to do. One attempt he made to obtain for himself conditions of submission, but met with a flat refusal. Unconditional surrender was all that Henry would listen to. Finally, as the king approached, he went out to meet him, confessed himself a traitor and beaten, and gave up the keys of the town. Henry used his victory to the uttermost. Personal safety was granted to the earl, and he was allowed to depart to his Norman possessions with horses and arms, but this was all that was allowed him. His vast possessions in England were wholly confiscated; not a manor was left him. His brothers soon afterwards fell under the same fate, and the most powerful and most dangerous Norman house in England was utterly ruined. For the king this result was not merely the fall of an enemy who might well be feared, and the acquisition of great estates with which to reward his friends; it was a lesson of the greatest value to the Norman baronage. Orderic Vitalis, who gives us the fullest details of these events states this result in words which cannot be improved upon: "And so, after Robert's flight, the kingdom of Albion was quiet in peace, and King Henry reigned prosperously three and thirty years, during which no man in England dared to rebel or to hold any castle against him."

From these and other forfeitures Henry endowed a new nobility, men of minor families, or of those that had hitherto played no part in the history of the land. Many of them were men who had had their training and attracted the king's attention in the administrative system which he did so much to develop, and their promotion was the reward of faithful service. These "new men" were settled in some numbers in the north, and scholars have thought they could trace the influence of their administrative training and of their attitude towards the older and more purely feudal nobility in the events of a century later in the struggle for the Great Charter.

These events, growing directly out of Robert's attempt upon England, have carried us to the autumn of 1102; but in the meantime the equally important conflict with Anselm on the subject of investitures had been advanced some stages further. The answer of Pope Paschal II to the request which had been made of him, to suspend in favour of England the law of the Church against lay investitures, had been received at least soon after the treaty with Robert. The answer was a flat refusal, written with priestly subtlety, arguing throughout as if what Henry had demanded was the spiritual consecration of the bishops, though it must be admitted that in the eyes of men who saw only the side of the Church the difference could not have been great. So far as we know, Henry said nothing of this answer. He summoned Anselm to court, apparently while his brother was still in England, and peremptorily demanded of him that he should become his man and consecrate the bishops and abbots whom he had appointed, as his predecessors had done, or else immediately leave the country. It is uncertain whether the influence of Robert had anything to do with this demand, as Eadmer supposed, but the recent victory which the king had gained, and the greater security which he must have felt, doubtless affected its peremptory character. Anselm again based his refusal of homage on his former position, on the doctrine which he had learned at Rome. Of this Henry would hear nothing; he insisted upon the customary rights of English kings. The other alternative, however, which he offered the archbishop, or with which he threatened him, of departure from England, Anselm also declined to accept, and he returned to Canterbury to carry on his work quietly and to await the issue.

This act of Anselm's was a virtual challenge to the king to use violence against him if he dared, and such a challenge Henry was as yet in no condition to take up. Not long after his return to Canterbury, Anselm received a friendly letter from the king, inviting him to come to Westminster, to consider the business anew. Here, with the consent of the assembled court, a new truce was arranged, and a new embassy to Rome determined on. This was to be sent by both parties and to consist of ecclesiastics of higher rank than those of the former embassy, who were to explain clearly to the pope the situation in England, and to convince him that some modification of the decrees on the subject would be necessary if he wished to retain the country in his obedience. Anselm's representatives were two monks, Baldwin of Bee and Alexander of Canterbury; the king's were three bishops, Gerard of Hereford, lately made Archbishop of York by the king, Herbert of Norwich, and Robert of Coventry.

The embassy reached Rome; the case was argued before the pope; he indignantly refused to modify the decrees; and the ambassadors returned to England, bringing letters to this effect to the king and to the archbishop. Soon after their return, which was probably towards the end of the summer, 1102, Anselm was summoned to a meeting of the court at London, and again required to perform homage or to cease to exercise his office. He of course continued to refuse, and appealed to the pope's letters for justification. Henry declined to make known the letter he had received, and declared that he would not be bound by them. His position was supported by the three bishops whom he had sent to Rome, who on the reading of the letter to Anselm declared that privately the pope had informed them that so long as the king appointed suitable men he would not be interfered with, and they explained that this could not be stated in the letters lest the news should be carried to other princes and lead them to usurp the rights of the Church. Anselm's representatives protested that they had heard nothing of all this, but it is evident that the solemn assertion of the three bishops had considerable weight, and that even Anselm was not sure but that they were telling the truth.

On a renewed demand of homage by the king, supported by the bishops and barons of the kingdom, Anselm answered that if the letters had corresponded to the words of the bishops, very likely he would have done what was demanded as the case stood, he proposed a new embassy to Rome to reconcile the contradiction, and in the meantime, though he would not consecrate the king's nominees, he agreed not to regard them as excommunicate. This proposal was at once accepted by Henry, who regarded it as so nearly an admission of his claim that he immediately appointed two new bishops: his chancellor, Roger, to Salisbury, and his larderer, also Roger, to Hereford.

Perhaps in the same spirit, regarding the main point as settled, Henry now allowed Anselm to hold the council of the English Church which William Rufus had so long refused him. The council met at Westminster and adopted a series of canons, whose chief object was the complete carrying out of the Gregorian reformation in the English Church. The most important of them concerned the celibacy of the priesthood, and enacted the strictest demands of the reform party, without regard to existing conditions. No clerics of any grade from subdeacon upward, were to be allowed to marry, nor might holy orders be received hereafter without a previous vow of celibacy. Those already married must put away their wives, and if any neglected to do so, they were no longer to be considered legal priests, nor be allowed to celebrate mass. One canon, which reveals one of the dangers against which the Church sought to guard by these regulations, forbade the sons of priests to inherit their father's benefices. It is very evident from these canons, that this part of the new reformation had made but little, if any, more headway in England than that which concerned investiture, and we know from other sources that the marriage of secular clergy was almost the rule, and that the sons of priests in clerical office were very numerous. Less is said of the other article of the reform programme, the extinction of the sin of simony, but three abbots of important monasteries, recently appointed by the king, were deposed on this ground without objection. This legislation, so thorough-going and so regardless of circumstances, is an interesting illustration of the uncompromising character of Anselm, though it must be noticed that later experience raised the question in his mind whether some modifications of these canons ought not to be made.

That Henry on his side had no intention of surrendering anything of his rights in the matter of investiture is clearly shown, about the same time, by his effort to get the bishops whom he had appointed to accept consecration from his very useful and willing minister, Gerard, Archbishop of York. Roger the larderer, appointed to Hereford, had died without consecration, and in his place Reinelm, the queen's chancellor, had been appointed. When the question of consecration by York was raised, rather than accept it he voluntarily surrendered his bishopric to the king. The other two persons appointed, William Giffard of Winchester, and Roger of Salisbury, seemed willing to concede the point, but at the last moment William drew back and the plan came to nothing. The bishops, however, seem to have refused consecration from the Archbishop of York less from objection to royal investiture than out of regard to the claims of Canterbury. William Giffard was deprived of his see, it would seem by judicial sentence, and sent from the kingdom.

About the middle of Lent of the next year, 1103, Henry made a new attempt to obtain his demands of Anselm. On his way to Dover he stopped three days in Canterbury and required the archbishop to submit. What followed is a repetition of what had occurred so often before. Anselm offered to be guided by the letters from Rome, in answer to the last reference thither, which had been received but not yet read. This Henry refused. He said he had nothing to do with the pope. He demanded the rights of his predecessors. Anselm on his side declared that he could consent to a modification of the papal decrees only by the authority which had made them. It would seem as if no device remained to be tried to postpone a complete breach between the two almost co-equal powers of the medieval state; but Henry's patience was not yet exhausted, or his practical wisdom led him to wish to get Anselm out of the kingdom before the breach became complete. He begged Anselm to go himself to Rome and attempt what others had failed to effect. Anselm suspected the king's object in the proposal, and asked for a delay until Easter, that he might take the advice of the king's court. This was unanimous in favour of the attempt, and on April 27, 1103, he landed at Wissant, not an exile, but with his attendants, "invested with the king's peace."

Four years longer this conflict lasted before it was finally settled by the concordat of August, 1107; but these later stages of it, though not less important considered in themselves, were less the pressing question of the moment for Henry than the earlier had been. They were rather incidents affecting his gradually unfolding foreign policy, and in turn greatly affected by it. From the fall of Robert of Bellême to the end of Henry's reign, the domestic history of England is almost a blank. If we put aside two series of events, the ecclesiastical politics of the time, of which interested clerks have given us full details, and the changes in institutions which were going on, but which they did not think posterity would be so anxious to understand, we know of little to say of this long period in the life of the English people. The history which has survived is the history of the king, and the king was in the main occupied upon the continent. But in the case of Henry I, this is not improperly English history. It was upon no career of foreign conquest, no seeking after personal glory, that Henry embarked in his Norman expeditions. It was to protect the rights of his subjects in England that he began, and it was because he could accomplish this in no other way that he ended with the conquest of the duchy and the lifelong imprisonment of his brother. There were so many close bonds of connexion between the two states that England suffered keenly in the disorders of Normandy, and the turbulence and disobedience of the barons under Robert threatened the stability of Henry's rule at home.

[16] Ordetic Vitalis, iv. 87 f.

[17] Liebermami, Anselm und Hugo van Lyon, in Aufsätze dem Andenken an Georg Waitz gewidmet.

CHAPTER VII.
CONFLICT WITH THE CHURCH

Robert of Belême had lost too much in England to rest satisfied with the position into which he had been forced. He was of too stormy a disposition himself to settle down to a quiet life on his Norman lands. Duke Robert had attacked one of his castles, while Henry was making war upon him in England, but, as was usual in his case, totally failed; but it was easy to take vengeance upon the duke, and he was the first to suffer for the misfortunes of the lord of Belême. All that part of Normandy within reach of Robert was laid waste; churches and monasteries even, in which men had taken refuge, were burned with the fugitives. Almost all Normandy joined in planning resistance. The historian, Orderic, living in the duchy, speaks almost as if general government had disappeared, and the country were a confederation of local states. But all plans were in vain, because a "sane head" was lacking. Duke Robert was totally defeated, and obliged to make important concessions to Robert of Belême. At last Henry, moved by the complaints which continued to come to him from churchmen and barons of Normandy, some of whom came over to England in person, as well as from his own subjects, whose Norman lands could not be protected, resolved himself to cross to Normandy. This he did in the autumn of 1104, and visited Domfront and other towns which belonged to him. There he was joined by almost all the leading barons of Normandy, who were, indeed, his vassals in England, but who meant more than this by coming to him at this time.

The expedition, however, was not an invasion. Henry did not intend to make war upon his brother or upon Robert of Belême. It was his intention rather to serve notice on all parties that he was deeply interested in the affairs of Normandy and that anarchy must end. To his brother Robert he read a long lecture, filled with many counts of his misconduct, both to himself personally and in the government of the duchy. Robert feared worse things than this, and that he might turn away his brother's wrath, ceded to him the county of Evreux, with the homage of its count, William, one of the most important possessions and barons of the duchy. Already in the year before Robert had been forced to surrender the pension Henry had promised him in the treaty which they had made after Robert's invasion.

This was because of a rash visit he had paid to England without permission, at the request of William of Warenne, to intercede for the restoration of his earldom of Surrey. By these arrangements Robert was left almost without the means of living, but he was satisfied to escape so easily, for he feared above all to be deprived of the name of duke and the semblance of power. Before winter came on the king returned to England.

In this same year, following out what seems to have been the deliberate purpose of Henry to crush the great Norman houses, another of the most powerful barons of England was sent over to Normandy, to furnish in the end a strong reinforcement to Robert of Bellême, a man of the same stamp as himself, namely William of Mortain, Earl of Cornwall, the king's own cousin. At the time of Henry's earliest troubles with his brother Robert, William had demanded the inheritance of their uncle Odo, the earldom of Kent. The king had delayed his answer until the danger was over, had then refused the request, and shortly after had begun to attack the earl by suits at law. This drove him to Normandy and into the party of the king's open enemies. On Henry's departure, Robert with the help of William began again his ravaging of the land of his enemies, with all the former horrors of fire and slaughter. The peasants suffered with the rest, and many of them fled the country with their wives and children.

If order was to be restored in Normandy and property again to become secure, it was clear that more thorough-going measures than those of Henry's first expedition must be adopted. These he was now determined to take, and in the last week of Lent, 1105, he landed at Barfleur, and within a few days stormed and destroyed Bayeux, which had refused to surrender, and forced Caen to open its gates. Though this formed the extent of his military operations in this campaign, a much larger portion of Normandy virtually became subject to him through the voluntary action of the barons. And in a quite different way his visit to Normandy was of decisive influence in the history of Henry and of England. As the necessity of taking complete possession of the duchy, in order to secure peace, became clear to Henry, or perhaps we should say as the vision of Normandy entirely occupied and subject to his rule rose before his mind, the conflict with Anselm in which he was involved began to assume a new aspect. As an incident in the government of a kingdom of which he was completely master, it was one thing; as having a possible bearing on the success with which he could conquer and incorporate with his dominions another state, it was quite another.

Anselm had gone to Rome toward the end of the summer of 1103. There he had found everything as he had anticipated. The argument of Henry's representative that England would be lost to the papacy if this concession were not granted, was of no avail. The pope stood firmly by the decrees against investiture. But Henry's ambassador was charged with a mission to Anselm, as well as to the pope; and at Lyons, on the journey back, the archbishop was told that his return to England would be very welcome to the king when he was ready to perform all duties to the king as other archbishops of Canterbury had done them. The meaning of this message was clear. By this stroke of policy, Henry had exiled Anselm, with none of the excitement or outcry which would have been occasioned by his violent expulsion from the kingdom.

On the return of his embassy from Rome, probably in December, 1103, Henry completed the legal breach between himself and Anselm by seizing the revenues of the archbishopric into his own hands. This, from his interpretation of the facts, he had a perfect right to do, but there is very good ground to suppose that he might not have done it even now, if his object had been merely to punish a vassal who refused to perform his customary services. Henry was already looking forward to intervention in Normandy. His first expedition was not made until the next summer, but it must by this time have been foreseen, and the cost must have been counted. The revenues of Canterbury doubtless seemed quite worth having. Already, in 1104, we begin to get complaints of the heavy taxation from which England was suffering. In the year of the second expedition, 1105, these were still more frequent and piteous. Ecclesiastics and Church lands bore these burdens with the rest of the kingdom, and before the close of this year we are told that many of the evils which had existed under William Rufus had reappeared.[18]

True to his temporizing policy, when complaints became loud, as early as 1104, Henry professed his great desire for the return of Anselm, provided always he was willing to observe the customs of the kingdom, and he despatched another embassy to Rome to persuade the pope to some concession. This was the fifth embassy which he had sent with this request, and he could not possibly have expected any other answer than that which he had already received. Soon a party began to form among the higher clergy of England, primarily in opposition to the king, and, more for this reason probably than from devotion to the reformation, in support of Anselm, though it soon began to show a disposition to adopt the Gregorian ideas for which Anselm stood. This disposition was less due to any change of heart on their part than to the knowledge which they had acquired of their helplessness in the hands of an absolute king, and of the great advantage to be gained from the independence which the Gregorian reformation would secure them. Even Gerard of York early showed some tendency to draw toward Anselm, as may be seen from a letter which he despatched to him in the early summer of 1105, with some precautions, suppressing names and expressions by which the writer might be identified.[19] Toward the end of the year he joined with five other bishops, including William Giffard, appointed by Henry to Winchester, in a more open appeal to Anselm, with promise of support. How early Henry became aware of this movement of opposition is not certain, but we may be sure that his department of secret service was well organized. We shall not be far wrong if we assign to a knowledge of the attitude of powerful churchmen in England some weight among the complex influences which led the king to the step which he took in July of this year.

In March, 1105, Pope Paschal II, whose conduct throughout this controversy implies that he was not more anxious to drive matters to open warfare than was Henry, advanced so far as to proclaim the excommunication of the Count of Meulan and the other counsellors of the king, and also of those who had received investiture at his hand. This might look as if the pope were about to take up the case in earnest and would proceed shortly to excommunicate the king himself. But Anselm evidently interpreted it as the utmost which he could expect in the way of aid from Rome, and immediately determined to act for himself. He left Lyons to go to Reims, but learning on the way of the illness of the Countess of Blois, Henry's sister Adela, he went to Blois instead, and then with the countess, who had recovered, to Chartres. This brought together three persons deeply interested in this conflict and of much influence in England and with the king Anselm, who was directly concerned; the Countess Adela, a favourite with her brother and on intimate terms with him and Bishop Ivo of Chartres, who had written much and wisely on the investiture controversy. And here it seems likely were suggested, probably by Bishop Ivo, and talked over among the three, the terms of the famous compromise by which the conflict was at last ended.

Anselm had made no secret of his intention of proceeding shortly to the excommunication of Henry. The prospect excited the liveliest apprehension in the mind of the religiously disposed Countess Adela, and she bestirred herself to find some means of averting so dread a fate from her brother. Henry himself had heard of the probability with some apprehension, though of a different sort from his sister's. The respect which Anselm enjoyed throughout Normandy and northern France was so great that, as Henry looked forward to an early conquest of the duchy, he could not afford to disregard the effect upon the general feeling of an open declaration of war by the archbishop. The invitation of the king of France to Anselm, to accept an asylum within his borders, was a plain foreshadowing of what might follow.[20] Considerations of home and foreign politics alike disposed

Henry to meet halfway the advances which the other side was willing to make under the lead of his sister.

With the countess, Anselm entered Normandy and met Henry at Laigle on July 21, 1105. Here the terms of the compromise, which were more than two years later adopted as binding law, were agreed upon between themselves, in their private capacity. Neither was willing at the moment to be officially bound. Anselm, while personally willing, would not formally agree to the concessions expected of him, until he had the authority of the pope to do so. Subsequent events lead us to suspect that once more Henry was temporizing. Anselm was not in good health. He was shortly after seriously ill. It is in harmony with Henry's policy throughout, and with his action in the following months, to suppose that he believed the approaching death of the archbishop would relieve him from even the slight concessions to which he professed himself willing to agree. It is not the place here to state the terms and effect of this agreement, but in substance Henry consented to abandon investiture with the ring and staff, symbols of the spiritual office; and Anselm agreed that the officers of the Church should not be excommunicated nor denied consecration if they received investiture of their actual fiefs from the hand of the king. Henry promised that an embassy should be at once despatched to Rome, to obtain the pope's consent to this arrangement, in order that Anselm, to whom the temporalities of his see were now restored, might be present at his Christmas court in England.

Delay Henry certainly gained by this move. The forms of friendly intercourse were restored between himself and Anselm. The excommunication was not pronounced. The party of the king's open enemies in Normandy, or of those who would have been glad to be his open enemies in France, if circumstances had been favourable, was deprived of support from any popular feeling of horror against an outcast of the Church. But he made no change in his conduct or plans. By the end of summer he was back in England, leaving things well under way in Normandy. Severer exactions followed in England, to raise money for new campaigns. One invention of some skilful servant of the king's seemed to the ecclesiastical historians more intolerable and dangerous than anything before. The king's justices began to draw the married clergy before the secular courts, and to fine them for their violation of the canons. By implication this would mean a legal toleration of the marriage, on payment of fines to the king, and thus it would cut into the rights of the Church in two directions. It was the trial of a spiritual offence in a secular court, and it was the virtual suspension of the law of the Church by the authority of the State. Still no embassy went to Rome. Christmas came and it had not gone. Robert of Bellême, alarmed at the plans of Henry, which were becoming evident, came over from

Normandy to try to make some peaceable arrangement with the king, but was refused all terms. In January, 1106, Robert of Normandy himself came over, to get, if possible, the return of what he had lost at home; but he also could obtain nothing. All things were in Henry's hands. He could afford to refuse favours, to forget his engagements, and to encourage his servants in the invention of ingenious exactions.

But Anselm was growing impatient. New appeals to action were constantly reaching him from England. The letter of the six bishops was sent toward the close of 1105. He himself began again to hint at extreme measures, and to write menacing letters to the king's ministers. Finally, early in 1106, the embassy was actually sent to Rome. Towards the end of March the Roman curia took action on the proposal, and Anselm was informed, in a letter from the pope, that the required concessions would be allowed. The pope was disposed to give thanks that God had inclined the king's heart to obedience; yet the proposal was approved of, not as an accepted principle, but rather as a temporary expedient, until the king should be converted by the preaching of the archbishop, to respect the rights of the Church in full. But Anselm did not yet return to England. Before the envoys came back from Rome, Henry had written to him of his expectation of early crossing into Normandy. On learning that the compromise would be accepted by the pope, Henry had sent to invite him at once to England, but Anselm was then too ill to travel, and he continued so for some time. It was nearly August before Henry's third expedition actually landed in Normandy, and on the 15th of that month the king and the archbishop met at the Abbey of Bec, and the full reconciliation between them took place. Anselm could now agree to the compromise. Henry promised to make reformation in the particulars of his recent treatment of the Church, of which the archbishop complained. Then Anselm crossed to Dover, and was received with great rejoicing.

The campaign upon which Henry embarked in August ended by the close of September in a success greater than he could have anticipated. He first attacked the castle of Tinchebrai, belonging to William of Mortain, and left a fortified post there to hold it in check. As soon as the king had retired, William came to the relief of his castle, reprovisioned it, and shut up the king's men in their defences. Then Henry advanced in turn with his own forces and his allies, and began a regular siege of the castle. The next move was William's, and he summoned to his aid Duke Robert and Robert of Bellême, and all the friends they had left in Normandy. The whole of the opposing forces were thus face to face, and the fate of Normandy likely to be settled by a single conflict. Orderic, the historian of the war, notes that Henry preferred to fight rather than to withdraw, as commanded by his brother, being willing to enter upon this "more than civil war for the sake of future peace."

In the meantime, the men of religion who were present began to exert themselves to prevent so fratricidal a collision of these armies, between whose opposing ranks so many families were divided. Henry yielded to their wishes, and offered to his brother terms of reconciliation which reveal not merely his belief in the strength of his position in the country and his confidence of success, but something also of his general motive. The ardour of religious zeal which the historian makes Henry profess we may perhaps set aside, but the actual terms offered speak for themselves. Robert was to surrender to Henry all the castles and the jurisdiction and administration of the whole duchy. This being done, Henry would turn over to him, without any exertion on his part, the revenues of half the duchy to enjoy freely in the kind of life that best pleased him. If Robert had been a different sort of man, we should commend his rejection of these terms. Possibly he recalled Henry's earlier promise of a pension, and had little confidence in the certainty of revenues from this source. But Henry, knowing the men whose advice Robert would ask before answering, had probably not expected his terms to be accepted.

The battle was fought on September 28, and it was fiercely fought, the hardest fight and with the largest forces of any in which Normans or Englishmen had been engaged for forty years. The main body of both armies fought on foot. The Count of Mortain, in command of Robert's first division, charged Henry's front, but was met with a resistance which he could not overcome. In the midst of this struggle Robert's flank was charged by Henry's mounted allies, under Count Elias of Maine, and his position was cut in two. Robert of Bellême, who commanded the rear division, seeing the battle going against the duke, took to flight and left the rest of the army to its fate. This was apparently to surrender in a body. Henry reports the number of common soldiers whom he had taken as ten thousand, too large a figure, no doubt, but implying the capture of Robert's whole force. His prisoners of name comprised all the leaders of his brother's side except Robert of Bellême, including the duke himself, Edgar the English atheling, who was soon released, and William of Mortain. The victory at once made Henry master of Normandy. There could be no further question of this, and it is of interest to note that the historian, William of Malmesbury, who in his own person typifies the union of English and Norman, both in blood and in spirit, records the fact that the day was the same as that on which the Conqueror had landed forty years earlier, and regards the result as reversing that event, and as making Normandy subject to England. This was not far from its real historical meaning.

Robert clearly recognized the completeness of Henry's success. By his orders Falaise was surrendered, and the castle of Rouen; and he formally absolved the towns of Normandy in general from their allegiance to himself. At Falaise Robert's young son William, known afterwards as William Clito, was captured and brought before Henry. Not wishing himself to be held responsible for his safety, Henry turned him over to the guardianship of Elias of Saint-Saens, who had married a natural daughter of Robert's. One unsought-for result of the conquest of Normandy was that Ranulf Flambard, who was in charge of the bishopric of Lisieux, succeeded in making his peace with the king and obtained his restoration to Durham, but he never again became a king's minister. Only Robert of Bellême thought of further fighting. As a vassal of Elias, Count of Maine, he applied to him for help, and promised a long resistance with his thirty-four strong castles. Elias refused his aid, pointed out the unwisdom of such an attempt, defended Henry's motives, and advised submission, promising his good influences with Henry. This advice Robert concluded to accept. Henry, on his side, very likely had some regard to the thirty-four castles, and decided to bide his time. Peace, for the present, was made between them.

Some measures which Henry considered necessary for the security of Normandy, he did not think it wise to carry out by his own unsupported action. In the middle of October a great council of Norman barons was called to meet at Lisieux. Here it was decreed that all possessions which had been wrongfully taken from churches or other legitimate holders during the confusion of the years since the death of William the Conqueror should be restored, and all grants from the ducal domain to unworthy persons, or usurpations which Robert had not been able to prevent, were ordered to be resumed. It is of especial interest that the worst men of the prisoners taken at Tinchebrai were here condemned to perpetual imprisonment. The name of Robert is not mentioned among those included in this judgment, and later Henry justifies his conduct toward his brother on the ground of political necessity, not of legal right. The result of all these measures—we may believe it would have been the result of the conquest alone—was to put an end at once to the disorder, private warfare, and open robbery from which the duchy had so long suffered. War enough there was in Normandy, in the later years of Henry's reign, but it was regular warfare. The license of anarchy was at an end. Robert was carried over to England, to a fate for which there could be little warrant in strict law, but which was abundantly deserved and fully supported by the public opinion of the time. He was kept in prison in one royal castle or another until his death twenty-eight years later. If Henry's profession was true, as it probably was, that he kept him as a royal prisoner should be kept, and supplied him with the luxuries he enjoyed so much, the result was, it is possible, not altogether disagreeable to Robert himself. Some time later, when the pope remonstrated with Henry on his conduct, and demanded the release of Robert, the king's defence of his action was so complete that the pope had no reply to make. Political expediency, the impossibility of otherwise maintaining peace, was the burden of his answer, and this, if not actual justice, must still be Henry's defence for his treatment of his brother.

Henry returned to England in time for the Easter meeting of his court, but the legalization of the compromise with Anselm was deferred to Whitsuntide because the pope was about to hold a council in France, from which some action affecting the question might be expected. At Whitsuntide Anselm was ill, and another postponement was necessary. At last, early in August, at a great council held in the king's palace in London, the agreement was ratified. No formal statement of the terms of this compromise has been given us by any contemporary authority, but such accounts of it as we have, and such inferences as seem almost equally direct, probably leave no important point unknown. Of all his claims, Henry surrendered only the right of investiture with ring and staff. These were spiritual symbols, typical of the bishop's relation to his Church and of his pastoral duties. To the ecclesiastical mind the conferring of them would seem more than any other part of the procedure the actual granting of the religious office, though they had been used by the kings merely as symbols of the fief granted. Some things would seem to indicate that the forms of canonical election were more respected after this compromise than they had been before, but this is true of forms only, and if we may judge from a sentence in a letter to the pope, in which Anselm tells him of the final settlement, this was not one of the terms of the formal agreement, and William of Malmesbury says distinctly that it was not. In all else the Church gave way to the king. He made choice of the person to be elected, with such advice and counsel as he chose to take, and his choice was final. He received the homage and conferred investiture of the temporalities of the office of the new prelate as his father and brother had done. Only when this was completed to the king's satisfaction, and his permission to proceed received, was the bishop elect consecrated to his spiritual office.

To us it seems clear that the king had yielded only what was a mere form, and that he had retained all the real substance of his former power, and probably this was also the judgment of the practical mind of Henry and of his chief adviser, the Count of Meulan. We must not forget, however, that the Church seemed to believe that it had gained something real, and that a strong party of the king's supporters long and vigorously resisted these concessions in his court. The Church had indeed set an example, for itself at least, of successful attack on the absolute monarchy, and had shown that the strongest of kings could be forced to yield a point against his will. Before the century was closed, in a struggle even more bitterly fought and against a stronger king, the warriors of the Church looked back to this example and drew strength from this success. It is possible, also, that these cases of concession forced from reluctant kings served as suggestion and model at the beginning of a political struggle which was to have more permanent results. All this, however, lay yet in the future, and could not be suspected by either party to this earliest conflict.

The agreement ratified in 1107 was the permanent settlement of the investiture controversy for England, and under it developed the practice on ecclesiastical vacancies which we may say has continued to the present time, interrupted under some sovereigns by vacillating practice or by a more or less theoretical concession of freedom of election to the Church. Henry's grandson, Henry II, describes this practice as it existed in his day, in one of the clauses of the Constitutions of Clarendon. The clause shows that some at least of the inventions of Ranulf Flambard had not been discarded, and there is abundant evidence to show that the king was really stating in it, as he said he was, the customs of his grandfather's time. The clause reads: "When an archbishopric or bishopric or abbey or priory of the king's domain has fallen vacant, it ought to be in the king's hands, and he shall take thence all the returns and revenues as domain revenues, and when the time has come to provide for the Church, the king shall call for the chief persons of the Church [that is, summon a representation of the Church to himself], and in the king's chapel the election shall be made with the assent of the king and with the counsel of those ecclesiastics of the kingdom whom he shall have summoned for this purpose, and there the elect shall do homage and fealty to the king, as to his liege lord, of his life and limb and earthly honour, saving his order, before he shall be consecrated."

This long controversy having reached a settlement which Anselm was at least willing to accept, he was ready to resume the long-interrupted duties of primate of Britain. On August 11, assisted by an imposing assembly of his suffragan bishops, and by the Archbishop of York, he consecrated in Canterbury five bishops at once, three of these of long-standing appointment,—William Giffard of Winchester, Roger of Salisbury, and Reinelm of Hereford; the other two, William of Exeter and Urban of Landaff, recently chosen. The renewed activity of Anselm as head of the English Church, which thus began, was not for long. His health had been destroyed. His illness returned at frequent intervals, and in less than two years his life and work were finished. These months, however, were filled with considerable activity, not all of it of the kind we should prefer to associate with the name of Anselm. Were we shut up to the history of this time for our knowledge of his character, we should be likely to describe it in different terms from those we usually employ. The earlier Anselm, of gentle character, shrinking from the turmoil of strife and longing only for the quiet of the abbey library, had apparently disappeared. The experiences of the past few years had been, indeed, no school in gentleness, and the lessons which he had learned at Rome were not those of submission to the claims of others. In the great council which ratified the compromise, Anselm had renewed his demand for the obedience of the Archbishop of York, and this demand he continued to push with extreme vigour until his death, first against Gerard, who died early in 1108, and then against his successor, Thomas, son of Bishop Samson of Worcester, appointed by Henry. A plan for the division of the large diocese of Lincoln, by the creation of a new diocese of Ely, though by common consent likely to improve greatly the administration of the Church, he refused to approve until the consent of the pope had been obtained. He insisted, against the will of the monks and the request of the king, upon the right of the archbishop to consecrate the abbot of St. Augustine's, Canterbury, in whatever church he pleased, and again, in spite of the king's request, he maintained the same right in the consecration of the bishop of London. The canon law of the Church regarding marriage, lay or priestly, he enforced with unsparing rigour. Almost his last act, it would seem, before his death, was to send a violent letter to Archbishop Thomas of York, suspending him from his office and forbidding all bishops of his obedience, under penalty of "perpetual anathema," to consecrate him or to communicate with him if consecrated by any one outside of England. On April 21, 1109, this stormy episcopate closed, a notable instance of a man of noble character, and in some respects of remarkable genius, forced by circumstances out of the natural current of his life into a career for which he was not fitted.

For Henry these months since the conquest of Normandy and, the settlement of the dispute with Anselm had been uneventful. Normandy had settled into order as if the mere change of ruler had been all it needed, and in England, which now occupied Henry's attention only at intervals, there was no occasion of anxiety. Events were taking place across the border of Normandy which were to affect the latter years of Henry and the future destinies of England in important ways. In the summer of 1108, the long reign of Philip I of France had closed, and the reign, nearly as long, of his son, Louis VI, had begun, the first of the great Capetian kings, in whose reign begins a definite policy of aggrandizement for the dynasty directed in great part against their rivals, the English kings Just before the death of Anselm occurred that of Fulk Rechin, Count of Anjou, and the succession of his son Fulk V. He was married to the heiress of Maine, and a year later this inheritance, the overlordship of which the Norman dukes had so long claimed, fell in to him. Of Henry's marriage with Matilda two children had been born who survived infancy,—Matilda, the future empress, early in 1102, and William in the late summer or early autumn of 1103. The queen herself, who had for a time accompanied the movements of her husband, now resided mostly at Westminster, where she gained the fame of liberality to foreign artists and of devotion to pious works.

It was during a stay of Henry's in England, shortly after the death of Anselm, that he issued one of the very few documents of his reign which give us glimpses into the changes in institutions which were then taking place. This is a writ, which we have in two slightly varying forms, one of them addressed to Bishop Samson of Worcester, dealing with the local judicial system. From it we infer that the old Saxon system of local justice, the hundred and county courts, had indeed never fallen into disuse since the days of the Conquest, but that they had been subjected to many irregularities of time and place, and that the sheriffs had often obliged them to meet when and where it suited their convenience; and we are led to suspect that they had been used as engines of extortion for the advantage both of the local officer and of the king. All this Henry now orders to cease. The courts are to meet at the same times and places as in the days of King Edward, and if they need to be summoned to special sessions for any royal business, due notice shall be given.

Even more important is the evidence which we get from this document of a royal system of local justice acting in conjunction with the old system of shire courts. The last half of the writ implies that there had arisen thus early the questions of disputed jurisdiction, of methods of trial, and of attendance at courts, with which we are familiar a few generations later in the history of English law. Distinctly implied is a conflict between a royal jurisdiction on one side and a private baronial jurisdiction on the other, which is settled in favour of the lord's court, if the suit is between two of his own vassals; but if the disputants are vassals of two different lords, it is decided in favour of the king's,—that is, of the court held by the king's justice in the county, who may, indeed, be no more than the sheriff acting in this capacity. This would be in strict harmony with the ruling feudal law of the time. But when the suit comes on for trial in the county court, it is not to be tried by the old county court forms. It is not a case in the sheriffs county court, the people's county court, but one before the king's justice, and the royal, that is, Norman method of trial by duel is to be adopted. Finally, at the close of the writ, appears an effort to defend this local court system against the liberties and immunities of the feudal system, an attempt which easily succeeded in so far as it concerned the king's county courts, but failed in the case of the purely local courts.[21]

If this interpretation is correct, this writ is typical of a process of the greatest interest, which we know from other sources was characteristic of the reign, a process which gave their peculiar form to the institutions of England and continued for more than a century. By this process the local law and institutions of Saxon England, and the royal law and central institutions of the Normans, were wrought into a single and harmonious whole. This process of union which was long and slow, guided by no intention beyond the convenience of the moment, advances in two stages. In the first, the Norman administration, royal and centralized, is carried down into the counties and there united, for the greater ease of accomplishing certain desired ends of administration, with the local Saxon system. This resulted in several very important features of our judicial organization. The second stage was somewhat the reverse of this. In it, certain features which had developed in the local machinery, the jury and election, are adopted by the central government and applied to new uses. This was the origin of the English parliamentary system. It is of the first of these stages only that we get a glimpse, in this document, and from other sources of the reign of Henry, and these bits of evidence only allow us to say that those judicial arrangements which were put into organized form in his grandson's reign had their beginning, as occasional practices, in his own. Not long after the date of this charter, a series of law books, one of the interesting features of the reign, began to appear. Their object was to state the old laws of England, or these in connexion with the laws then current in the courts, or with the legislation of the first of the Norman kings. Private compilations, or at most the work of persons whose position in the service of the state could give no official authority to their codes, their object was mainly practical; but they reveal not merely a general interest in the legal arrangements existing at the moment, but a clear consciousness that these rested upon a solid substratum of ancient law, dating from a time before the Conquest. Towards this ancient law the nation had lately turned, and had been answered by the promise in Henry's coronation charter. Worn with the tyranny of William Rufus, men had looked back with longing to the better conditions of an earlier age, and had demanded the laws of Edward or of Canute, as, under the latter, men had looked back to the laws of Edgar, demanding laws, not in the sense of the legislation of a certain famous king, but of the whole legal and constitutional situation of earlier times, thought of as a golden age from which the recent tyranny had departed. What they really desired was never granted them. The Saxon law still survived, and was very likely renewed in particulars by Henry I, but it survived as local law and as the law of the minor affairs of life. The law of public affairs and of all great interests, the law of the tyranny from which men suffered, was new. It made much use of the local machinery which it found but in a new way, and it was destined to be modified in some points by the old law, but it was new as the foundation on which was to be built the later constitution of the state. The demand for the laws of an earlier time did not affect the process of this building, and the effort to put the ancient law into accessible form, which may have had this demand as one of its causes, is of interest to the student of general history chiefly for the evidence it gives of the great work of union which was then going on, of Saxon and Norman, in law as in blood, into a new nation.

It was during the same stay in England that an opportunity was offered to Henry to form an alliance on the continent which promised him great advantages in case of an open conflict with the king of France. At Henry's Whitsuntide court, in 1109, appeared an embassy from Henry V of Germany, to ask for the hand of his daughter, then less than eight years old. This request Henry would not be slow to grant. Conflicting policies would never be likely to disturb such an alliance, and the probable interest which the sovereign of Germany would have in common with himself in limiting the expansion of France, or even in detaching lands from her allegiance, would make the alliance seem of good promise for the future. On the part of Henry of Germany, such a proposal must have come from policy alone, but the advantage which he hoped to gain from it is not so easy to discover as in the case of Henry of England. If he entertained any idea of a common policy against France, this was soon dropped, and his purpose must in all probability be sought in plans within the empire. Henry's recent accession to the throne of Germany had been followed by—a change of policy. During the later years of his unfortunate father, whose stormy reign had closed in the triumph of the two enemies whom he had been obliged to face at once, the Church of Gregory VII, contending with the empire for equality and even for supremacy, and the princes of Germany, grasping in their local dominions the rights of sovereignty, the ambitious prince had fought against the king, his father. But when he had at last become king himself, his point of view was changed. The conflict in which his father had failed he was ready to renew with vigour and with hope of success. That he should have believed, as he evidently did, that a marriage with the young English princess was the most useful one he could make in this crisis of his affairs is interesting evidence, not merely of the world's opinion of Henry I, but also of the rank of the English monarchy among the states of Europe.

Just as she was completing her eighth year, Matilda was sent over to Germany to learn the language and the ways of her new country. A stately embassy and a rich dower went with her, for which her father had provided by taking the regular feudal aid to marry the lord's eldest daughter, at the rate of three shillings per hide throughout England. On April 10, 1110, she was formally betrothed to the emperor-elect at Utrecht. On July 25, she was crowned Queen of Germany at Mainz. Then she was committed to the care of the Archbishop of Trier, who was to superintend her education. On January 7,1114, just before Matilda had completed her twelfth year, the marriage was celebrated at Mainz, in the presence of a great assembly. All things had been going well with Henry. In Germany and in Italy he had overcome the princes and nobles who had ventured to oppose him. The clergy of Germany seemed united on his side in the still unsettled investiture conflict with the papacy. The brilliant assembly of princes of the empire and foreign ambassadors which gathered in the city for this marriage was in celebration as well of the triumph of the emperor. On this great occasion, and in spite of her youth, Matilda bore herself as a queen, and impressed those who saw her as worthy of the position, highest in rank in the world, to which she had been called. To the end of her stay in Germany she retained the respect and she won the hearts of her German subjects.

By August, 1111, King Henry's stay in England was over, and he crossed again to Normandy. What circumstances called him to the continent we do not know, but probably events growing out of a renewal of war with Louis VI, which seems to have been first begun early in 1109.[22] However this may be, he soon found himself in open conflict all along his southern border with the king of France and the Count of Anjou, with Robert of Bellême and other barons of the border to aid them. Possibly Henry feared a movement in Normandy itself in favour of young William Clito, or learned of some expression of a wish not infrequent among the Norman barons in times a little later, that he might succeed to his father's place. At any rate, at this time, Henry ordered Robert of Beauchamp to seize the boy in the castle of Elias of Saint-Saens, to whom he had committed him five years before. The attempt failed. William was hastily carried off to France by friendly hands, in the absence of his guardian. Elias joined him soon after, shared his long exile, and suffered confiscation of his fief in consequence. It would not be strange if Henry was occasionally troubled, in that age of early but full-grown chivalry, by the sympathy of the Norman barons with the wanderings and friendless poverty of their rightful lord; but Henry was too strong and too severe in his punishment of any treason for sympathy ever to pass into action on any scale likely to assist the exiled prince, unless in combination with some strong enemy of the king's from without.

Henry would appear at first sight greatly superior to Louis VI of France in the military power and resources of which he had immediate command, as he certainly was in diplomatic skill. The Capetian king, master only of the narrow domains of the Isle of France, and hardly of those until the constant fighting of Louis's reign had subdued the turbulent barons of the province; hemmed in by the dominions, each as extensive as his own, of the great barons nominally his vassals but sending to his wars as scanty levies as possible, or appearing openly in the ranks of his enemies as their own interests dictated; threatened by foreign foes, the kings of England and of Germany, who would detach even these loosely held provinces from his kingdom,—the Capetian king could hardly have defended himself at this epoch from a neighbour so able as Henry I, wielding the united strength of England and Normandy, and determined upon conquest. The safety of the Capetian house was secured by the absence of both these conditions. Henry was not ambitious of conquest; and as his troubles with France increased so did dissensions in Normandy, which crippled his resources and divided his efforts. The net result at the close of Henry's reign was that the king of England was no stronger than in 1110, unless we count the uncertain prospect of the Angevin succession; while the king of France was master of larger resources and a growing power.

It seems most likely that it was in the spring of 1109 that the rivalry of the two kings first led to an open breach. This was regarding the fortress of Gisors, on the Epte, which William Rufus had built against the French Vexin. Louis summoned Henry either to surrender or to demolish it, but Henry refused either alternative, and occupied it with his troops. The French army opposed him on the other side of the river, but there was no fighting. Louis, who greatly enjoyed the physical pleasure of battle, proposed to Henry that they should meet on the bridge which crossed the river at this point, in sight of the two armies, and decide their quarrel by a duel. Henry, the diplomatist and not the fighter, laughed at the proposition. In Louis's army were two men, one of whom had lately been, and the other of whom was soon to be, in alliance with Henry, Robert of Jerusalem, Count of Flanders, and Theobald, Count of Blois, eldest son of Henry's sister and brother of his successor as king, Stephen of England. Possibly a truce had soon closed this first war, but if so, it had begun again in the year of Henry's crossing, 1111; and the Count of Blois was now in the field against his sovereign and defeated Louis in a battle in which the Count of Flanders was killed. The war with Louis ran its course for a year and a half longer without battles. Against Anjou Henry built or strengthened certain fortresses along the border and waited the course of events.

On November 4, 1112, an advantage fell to Henry which may have gone far to secure him the remarkable terms of peace with which the war was closed. He arrested Robert of Bellême, his constant enemy and the enemy of all good men, "incomparable in all forms of evil since the beginning of

Christian days." He had come to meet the king at Bonneville, to bring a message from Louis, thinking that Henry would be obliged to respect his character as an envoy. Probably the king took the ground that by his conduct Robert had forfeited all rights, and was to be treated practically as a common outlaw. At any rate, he ordered his arrest and trial. On three specific counts—that he had acted unjustly toward his lord, that summoned three times to appear in court for trial he had not come, and that as the king's viscount he had failed to render account of the revenues he had collected—he was condemned and sentenced to imprisonment. On Henry's return to England he was carried over and kept in Wareham castle, where he was still alive in 1130. The Norman historian Orderic records that this action of Henry's met with universal approval and was greeted with general rejoicing.

During Lent of the next year, 1113, Henry made formal peace with both his enemies, the king of France and the Count of Anjou. The peace with the latter was first concluded. It was very possibly Fulk's refusal to recognize Henry's overlordship of Maine that occasioned the war. To this he now assented. He did homage for the county, and received investiture of it from the hand of the king. He also promised the hand of his daughter Matilda to Henry's son William. Henry, on his side, restored to favour the Norman allies of Fulk. A few days later a treaty was made at Gisors, with the king of France. Louis formally conceded to Henry the overlordship of Bellême, which had not before depended upon the duchy of Normandy, and that of Maine, and Britanny. In the case of Maine and of Britanny this was the recognition of long-standing claims and of accomplished facts, for Count Alan Fergant of Britanny, as well as Fulk of Anjou, had already become the vassal of Henry, and had obtained the hand of a natural daughter of the king for his son Conan, who in this year became count. But the important lordship of Bellême was a new cession. It was not yet in Henry's hands, nor had it been reckoned as a part of Normandy, though the lords of Bellême had been also Norman barons. Concessions such as these, forming with Normandy the area of many a kingdom, were made by a king like Louis VI, only under the compulsion of necessity. They mark the triumph of Henry's skill, of his vigorous determination, and of his ready disregard of the legal rights of others, if they would not conform to his ideas of proper conduct or fit into his system of government. The occupation of Bellême required a campaign. William Talvas, the son of Robert, while himself going to defend his mother's inheritance of Ponthieu, had left directions with the vassals of Bellême for its defence, but the campaign was a short one. Henry, assisted by his new vassal, the Count of Anjou, and by his nephew, Theobald of Blois, speedily reduced city and lordship to submission.

Orderic Vitalis, who was living in Normandy at this time, in the monastery of St. Evroul, declares that following this peace, made in the spring of 1113, for five years, Henry governed his kingdom and his duchy on the two sides of the sea with great tranquillity. These years, to the great insurrection of the Norman barons in 1118, were not entirely undisturbed, but as compared with the period which goes before, or with that which follows, they deserve the historian's description. One great army was led into Wales in 1114, and the Welsh princes were forced to renew their submission. Henry was apparently interested in the slow incorporation of Wales in England which was going forward, but prudently recognized the difficulties of attempting to hasten the process by violence. He was ready to use the Church, that frequent medieval engine of conquest, and attempted with success, both before this date and later, to introduce English bishops into old Welsh sees. From the early part of this reign also dates the great Flemish settlement in Pembrokeshire, which was of momentous influence on all that part of Wales.

These years were also fully occupied with controversies in the Church, whose importance for the state Henry clearly recognized. Out of the conflict over investitures, regarded from the practical side, the Norman monarchy had emerged, as we have seen, in triumph, making but one slight concession, and that largely a matter of form. From the struggle with the empire on the same issue, which was at this date still unsettled, the Church was destined to gain but little more, perhaps an added point of form, depending for its real value on the spirit with which the final agreement was administered. In the matter of investitures, the Church could claim but little more than a drawn battle on any field; and yet, in that great conflict with the monarchies of Europe into which the papacy had been led by the genius of Hildebrand, it had gained a real and great victory in all that was of the most vital importance. The pope was no longer the creature and servant of the emperor; he was not even a bishop of the empire. In the estimation of all Christendom, he occupied an equal throne, exercised a co-ordinate power, and appeared even more directly as the representative of the divine government of the world. Under his rule was an empire far more extensive than that which the emperor controlled, coming now to be closely centralized with all the machinery of government, legal, judicial, and administrative, highly organized and pervaded from the highest to the lowest ranks with a uniform theory of the absolute right of the ruler and of the duty of unquestioning obedience which the most perfect secular absolutism would strive in vain to secure. To have transformed the Church, which the emperor Henry III had begun to reform in 1046, into that which survived the last year of his dynasty, was a work of political genius as great as history records.

It was not before the demand of the pope in the matter of investiture that the Norman absolute government of the Church went down. It fell because the Norman theory of the national Church, closely under the control of the state in every field of its activity, a part of the state machinery, and a valuable assistant in the government of the nation, was undermined and destroyed by a higher, and for that age a more useful, conception. When the idea of the Church as a world-wide unity, more closely bound to its theocratic head than to any temporal sovereign, and with a mission and responsibility distinct from those of the state, took possession of the body of the clergy, as it began to do in the reign of Henry, it was impossible to maintain any longer the separateness of the Norman Church. But the incorporation of the Norman and English churches in the papal monarchy meant the slipping from the king's hands of power in many individual cases, which the first two Norman kings had exercised without question, and which even the third had continued to exercise.

The struggle of York to free itself from the promise of obedience to Canterbury was only one of the many channels through which these new ideas entered the kingdom. A new tide of monasticism had arisen on the continent, which did not spend itself even with the northern borders of England. The new orders and the new spirit found many abiding places in the kingdom, and drew laity as well as clergy under their strong influence. This was especially, though not alone, true of the Augustinian canons, who possessed some fifty houses in England at the close of Henry's reign, and in the later years of his life, of the Cistercians, with whose founding an English saint, Stephen Harding, had had much to do, and some of whose monasteries founded in this period, Tintern, Rievaulx, Furness, and Fountains, are still familiar names, famous for the beauty of their ruins. This new monasticism had been founded wholly in the ideas of the new ecclesiastical monarchy, and was an expression of them. The monasteries it created were organized, not as parts of the state in which they were situated, but as parts of a great order, international in its character, free from local control, and, though its houses were situated in many lands, forming almost an independent state under the direct sovereignty of the pope. The new monarchical papacy, which emerged from the conflicts of this period, occupied Christendom with its garrisons in these monastic houses, and every house was a source from which its ruling ideas spread widely abroad.

A new education was also beginning in this same period, and was growing in definiteness of content and of organization, in response to a demand which was becoming eager. At many centres in Europe groups of scholars were giving formal lectures on the knowledge of the day, and were attracting larger and larger numbers of students by the fame of their eloquence, or by the stimulus of their new method. The beginnings of Oxford as a place of teachers, as well as of Paris, reach back into this time. The ambitious young man, who looked forward to a career in the Church, began to feel the necessity of getting the training which these new schools could impart. The number of students whom we can name, who went from England to Paris or elsewhere to study, is large for the time; but if we possessed a list of all the English students, at home or abroad, of this reign, we should doubtless estimate the force of this influence more highly, even in the period of its beginning. For the ideas which now reigned in the Church pervaded the new education as they did the new monasticism. There was hardly a source, indeed, from which the student could learn any other doctrine, as there has remained none in the learning of the Roman Church to the present day. The entire literature of the Church, its rapidly forming new philosophy and theology, its already greatly developed canon law, breathed only the spirit of a divinely inspired centralization. And the student who returned, very likely to rapid promotion in the English Church, did not bring back these ideas for himself alone. He set the fashion of thinking for his less fortunate fellows.

It was by influences like these that the gradual and silent transformation was wrought which made of the English Church a very different thing at the end of these thirty-five years from what it had been at the beginning of the reign. The first two Norman kings had reigned over a Church which knew no other system than strict royal control. Henry I continued to exercise to the end of his reign, with only slight modification and the faint beginnings of change, the same prerogatives, but it was over a Church whose officers had been trained in an opposing system, and now profoundly disbelieved in his rights. How long would it avail the Norman monarchy anything to have triumphed in the struggle of investitures, when it could no longer find the bishop to appoint who was not thoroughly devoted to the highest papal claims? The answer suggested, in its extreme form, is too strong a statement for the exact truth; for in whatever age, or under whatever circumstances, a strong king can maintain himself, there he can always find subservient tools. But the interested service of individuals is a very different foundation of power from the traditional and unquestioning obedience of a class. The history of the next age shows that the way had been prepared for rapid changes, when political conditions would permit; and the grandson of the first Henry found himself obliged to yield, in part at least, to demands of the Church entirely logical in themselves, but unheard of in his grandfather's time.

[18] Eadmer, p. 172.

[19] Liebermann, Quadripartitus, p. 155.

[20] Anselm, Epist. iv. 50, 51; Luchaire, Louis VI, Annales, No. 31.

[21] See American Historical Review, viii, 478.

[22] Luchaire, Louis VI, Annales, p. cxv.

CHAPTER VIII.
THE KING'S FOREIGN INTERESTS

We need not enter into the details of the long struggle between Canterbury and York. The archbishopric of Canterbury was vacant for five years after the death of Anselm; its revenues went to support the various undertakings of the king. In April, 1114, Ralph of Escures, Bishop of Rochester, was chosen Anselm's successor. The archbishopric of York had been vacant only a few months, when it was filled, later in the summer, by the appointment of Thurstan, one of the king's chaplains. The question of the obligation of the recently elected Archbishop of York to bind himself to obedience to the primate of Britain, whether settled as a principle or as a special case, by an English council or by the king or under papal authority, arose anew with every new appointment. In the period which follows the appointment of Thurstan, a new element of interest was added to the dispute by the more deliberate policy of the pope to make use of it to gain a footing for his authority in England, and to weaken the unity and independence of the English Church. This attempt led to a natural alliance of parties, in which, while the issue was at bottom really the same, the lines of the earlier investiture conflict were somewhat rearranged. The pope supported the claim of York, while the king defended the right of Canterbury as bound up with his own.

At an important meeting of the great council at Salisbury, in March, 1116, the king forced upon Thurstan the alternative of submission to Canterbury or resignation. The barons and prelates of the realm had been brought together to make formal recognition of the right to the succession of Henry's son William, now fourteen years of age. Already in the previous summer this had been done in Normandy, the barons doing homage and swearing fealty to the prince. Now the English barons followed the example, and, by the same ceremony, the strongest tie known to the feudal world, bound themselves to accept the son as their lord on the death of his father. The prelates, for their part, took oath that if they should survive Henry, they would recognize William as king, and then do homage to him in good faith. The incident is interesting less as an example of this characteristic feudal method of securing the succession, for this had been employed since the Conquest both in Normandy and in England, than because we are told that on this occasion the oath was demanded, not merely of all tenants in chief, but of all inferior vassals. If this statement may be accepted, and there is no reason to doubt it, we may conclude that the practice established by the Conqueror at an earlier Salisbury assembly had been continued by his sons. This was a moment when Henry was justified in expressing his will, even on a matter of Church government, in peremptory command, and when no one was likely to offer resistance. Thurstan chose to surrender the archbishopric, and promised to make no attempt to recover it; but apparently the renunciation was not long regarded as final on either side. He was soon after this with the king in Normandy, but he was refused the desired permission to go to Rome, a journey which Archbishop Ralph soon undertook, that he might try the influence of his presence there in favour of the cause of Canterbury and against other pretensions of the pope.

From the date of this visit to Normandy, in the spring of 1116, Henry's continental interests mix themselves with those of the absolute ruler of the English Church, and he was more than once forced to choose upon which side he would make some slight concession or waive some right for the moment. Slowly the sides were forming themselves and the opposing interests growing clear, of a great conflict for the dominion of northern France, a conflict forced upon the English king by the necessity of defending the position he had gained, rather than sought by him in the spirit of conquest, even when he seemed the aggressor; a conflict in which he was to gain the victory in the field and in diplomacy, but to be overcome by the might of events directed by no human hand and not to be resisted by any.

The peace between Henry and Louis, made in the spring of 1113, was broken by Henry's coming to the aid of his nephew, Theobald of Blois. Theobald had seized the Count of Nevers on his return from assisting Louis in a campaign in the duchy of France in 1115. The cause was bad, but Henry could not afford to see so important an ally as his nephew crushed by his enemies, especially as his dominions were of peculiar strategical value in any war with the king of France. To Louis's side gathered, as the war developed, those who had reason from their position to fear what looked like the policy of expansion of this new English power in north-western France, especially the Counts of Flanders and of Anjou. The marriage of Henry's son William with Fulk's daughter had not yet taken place, and the Count of Anjou might well believe—particularly from the close alliance of Henry with the rival power of Blois—that he had more to fear than to hope for from the spread of the Norman influence. At the same time the division began to show itself among the Norman barons, of those who were faithful to Henry and those who preferred the succession of Robert's son William; and it grew more pronounced as the war went on, for Louis took up the cause of William as the rightful heir of Normandy. In doing this he began the policy which the French kings followed for so many years, and on the whole with so little advantage, of fomenting the quarrels in the English royal house and of separating if possible the continental possessions from the English.

On Henry's side were a majority of the Norman barons and the counts of Britanny and of Blois. For the first time, also, appeared upon the stage of history in this war Henry's other nephew, Stephen, who was destined to do so much evil to England and to Henry's plans before his death. His uncle had already made him Count of Mortain. The lordship of Bellême, which Henry had given to Theobald, had been by him transferred to Stephen in the division of their inheritance. It was probably not long after this that Henry procured for him the hand of Matilda, heiress of the county of Boulogne, and thus extended his own influence over that important territory on the borders of Flanders. France, Flanders, and Anjou certainly had abundant reason to fear the possible combination into one power of Normandy, Britanny, Maine, Blois, and Boulogne, and that a power which, however pacific in disposition, showed so much tendency to expansion. For France, at least, the cause of this war was not the disobedience of a vassal, nor was it to be settled by the siege and capture of border castles.

The war which followed was once more not a war of battles. Armies, large for the time, were collected, but they did little more than make threatening marches into the enemy's country. In 1118 the revolt of the Norman barons, headed by Amaury of Montfort, who now claimed the county of Evreux, assumed proportions which occasioned the king many difficulties. This was a year of misfortunes for him. The Count of Anjou, the king of France, the Count of Flanders, each in turn invaded some part of Normandy, and gained advantages which Henry could not prevent. Baldwin of Flanders, however, returned home with a wound from an arrow, of which he shortly died. In the spring of this year Queen Matilda died, praised by the monastic chroniclers to the last for her good deeds. A month later Henry's wisest counsellor, Robert of Meulan, died also, after a long life spent in the service of the Conqueror and of his sons. The close of the year saw no turn of the tide in favour of Henry. Evreux was captured in October by Amaury of Montfort, and afterwards Alençon by the Count of Anjou.

The year 1119, which was destined to close in triumph for Henry, opened no more favourably. The important castle of Les Andelys, commanding the Norman Vexin, was seized by Louis, aided by treachery. But before the middle of the year, Henry had gained his first great success. He induced the Count of Anjou, by what means we do not know,—by money it was thought by some at the time,—to make peace with him, and to carry out the agreement for the marriage of his daughter with the king's son. The county of Maine was settled on the young pair, virtually its transfer to Henry. At the same time, Henry granted to William Talvas, perhaps as one of the conditions of the treaty, the Norman possessions which had belonged to his father, Robert of Bellême. In the same month, June, 1119, Baldwin of Flanders died of the wound which he had received in Normandy, and was succeeded by his nephew, Charles the Good, who reversed Baldwin's policy and renewed the older relations with England. The sieges of castles, the raiding and counter-raiding of the year, amounted to little until, on August 20, while each was engaged in raiding, the opposing armies commanded by the two kings in person unexpectedly found themselves in the presence of one another. The battle of Bremule, the only encounter of the war which can be called a battle, followed. Henry and his men again fought on foot, as at Tinchebrai, with a small reserve on horseback. The result was a complete victory for Henry. The French army was completely routed, and a large number of prisoners was taken, though the character which a feudal battle often assumed from this time on is attributed to this one, in the fact reported that in the fighting and pursuit only three men were killed.

A diplomatic victory not less important followed the battle of Bremule by a few weeks. The pope was now in France. His predecessor, Gelasius II, had been compelled to flee from Italy by the successes of the Emperor Henry V, and had died at Cluny in January, 1119, on his way to the north. The cardinals who had accompanied him elected in his stead the Archbishop of Vienne, who took the name of Calixtus II. Gelasius in his short and unfortunate reign had attempted to interfere with vigour in the dispute between York and Canterbury, and had summoned both parties to appear before him for the decision of the case. This was in Henry's year of misfortunes, 1118, and he was obliged to temporize. The early death of Gelasius interrupted his plan, but only until Calixtus II was ready to go on with it. He called a council of the Church to meet at Reims in October, to which he summoned the English bishops, and where he proposed to decide the question of the obedience of York to Canterbury. Henry granted a reluctant consent to the English bishops to attend this council, but only on condition that they would allow no innovations in the government of the English Church. To Thurstan of York, to whom he had restored the temporalities of his see, under the pressure of circumstances nearly two years before, he granted permission to attend on condition that he would not accept consecration as archbishop from the pope. This condition was at once violated, and Thurstan was consecrated by the pope on October 19. Henry immediately ordered that he should not be allowed to return to any of the lands subject to his rule.

At this council King Louis of France, defeated in the field and now without allies, appealed in person to the pope for the condemnation of the king of England. He is said, by Orderic Vitalis who was probably present at the council and heard him speak, to have recited the evil deeds of Henry, from the imprisonment of Robert to the causes of the present war. The pope himself was in a situation where he needed to proceed with diplomatic caution, but he promised to seek an interview with Henry and to endeavour to bring about peace. This interview took place in November, at Gisors, and ended in the complete discomfiture of the pope. Henry was now in a far stronger position than he had been at the beginning of the year, and to the requests of Calixtus he returned definite refusals or vague and general answers of which nothing was to be made. The pope was even compelled to recognize the right of the English king to decide when papal legates should be received in the kingdom. Henry was, however, quite willing to make peace. He had won over Louis's allies, defeated his attempt to gain the assistance of the pope, and finally overcome the revolted Norman barons. He might reasonably have demanded new advantages in addition to those which had been granted him in the peace of 1113, but all that marks this treaty is the legal recognition of his position in Normandy. Homage was done to Louis for Normandy, not by Henry himself, for he was a king, but by his son William for him. It is probable that at no previous date would this ceremony have been acceptable, either to Louis or to Henry. On Louis's part it was not merely a recognition of Henry's right to the duchy of Normandy, but it was also a formal abandonment of William Clito, and an acceptance of William, Henry's son, as the heir of his father. This act was accompanied by a renewal of the homage of the Norman barons to William, whether made necessary by the numerous rebellions of the past two years, or desirable to perfect the legal chain, now that William had been recognized as heir by his suzerain, a motive that would apply to all the barons.

This peace was made sometime during the course of the year 1120. In November Henry was ready to return to England, and on the 25th he set sail from Barfleur, with a great following. Then suddenly came upon him, not the loss of any of the advantages he had lately gained nor any immediate weakening of his power, but the complete collapse of all that he had looked forward to as the ultimate end of his policy. His son William embarked a little later than his father in the White Ship, with a brilliant company of young relatives and nobles. They were in a very hilarious mood, and celebrated the occasion by making the crew drunk. Probably they were none too sober themselves; certainly Stephen of Blois was saved to be king of England in his cousin's place, by withdrawing to another vessel when he saw the condition of affairs on the White Ship. It was night and probably dark. About a mile and a half from Barfleur the ship struck a rock, and quickly filled and sank. It was said that William would have escaped if he had not turned back at the cries of his sister, Henry's natural daughter, the Countess of Perche. All on board were drowned except a butcher of Rouen. Never perished in any similar calamity so large a number of persons of rank. Another child of Henry's, his natural son Richard, his niece Matilda, sister of Theobald and Stephen, a nephew of the Emperor Henry V, Richard, Earl of Chester, and his brother, the end of the male line of Hugh of Avranches, and a crowd of others of only lesser rank. Orderic Vitalis records that he had heard that eighteen ladies perished, who were the daughters, sisters, nieces, or wives of kings or earls. Henry is said to have fallen to the ground in a faint when the news was told him, and never to have been the same man again.

But if Henry could no longer look forward to the permanence in the second generation of the empire which he had created, he was not the man to surrender even to the blows of fate. The succession to his dominions of Robert's son William, who had been so recently used by his enemies against him, but who was now the sole male heir of William the Conqueror, was an intolerable idea. In barely more than a month after the death of his son, the king took counsel with the magnates of the realm, at a great council in London, in regard to his remarriage. In less than another month the marriage was celebrated. Henry's second wife was Adelaide, daughter of Geoffrey, Duke of Lower Lorraine, a vassal of his son-in-law, the emperor, and his devoted supporter, as well as a prince whose alliance might be of great use in any future troubles with France or Flanders. This marriage was made chiefly in hope of a legitimate heir, but it was a childless marriage, and Henry's hope was disappointed.

For something more than two years after this fateful return of the king to England, his dominions enjoyed peace scarcely broken by a brief campaign in Wales in 1121. At the end of 1120, Archbishop Thurstan, for whose sake the pope was threatening excommunication and interdict, was allowed to return to his see, where he was received with great rejoicing. But the dispute with Canterbury was not yet settled. Indeed, he had scarcely returned to York when he was served with notice that he must profess, for himself at least, obedience to Canterbury, as his predecessors had done. This he succeeded in avoiding for a time, and at the beginning of October, in 1122, Archbishop Ralph of Canterbury died, not having gained his case. An attempt of Calixtus II to send a legate to England, contrary to the promise he had made to Henry at Giscrs, was met and defeated by the king with his usual diplomatic skill, so far as the exercise of any legatine powers is concerned, though the legate was admitted to England and remained there for a time. In the selection of a successor to Ralph of

Canterbury a conflict arose between the monastic chapter of Christ church and the bishops of the province, and was decided undoubtedly according to the king's mind in favour of the latter, by the election of William of Corbeil, a canon regular. Another episcopal appointment of these years illustrates the growing importance in the kingdom of the great administrative bishop, Roger of Salisbury, who seems to have been the king's justiciar, or chief representative, during his long absences in Normandy. The long pontificate of Robert Bloet, the brilliant and worldly Bishop of Lincoln, closed at the beginning of 1123 by a sudden stroke as he was riding with the king, and in his place was appointed Roger's nephew, Alexander.

During this period also, probably within a year after the death of his son William, Henry took measures to establish the position of one of his illegitimate sons, very likely with a view to the influence which he might have upon the succession when the question should arise. Robert of Caen, so called from the place of his birth, was created Earl of Gloucester, and was married to Mabel, heiress of the large possessions of Robert Fitz Hamon in Gloucester, Wales, and Normandy. Robert of Gloucester, as he came to be known, was the eldest of Henry's illegitimate sons, born before his father's accession to the throne, and he was now in the vigour of young manhood. He was also, of all Henry's children of whom we know anything, the most nearly like himself, of more than average abilities, patient and resourceful, hardly inheriting in full his father's diplomatic skill but not without gifts of the kind, and earning the reputation of a lover of books and a patron of writers. A hundred years earlier there would have been no serious question, in the circumstances which had arisen, of his right to succeed his father, at least in the duchy of Normandy. That the possibility of such a succession was present in men's minds is shown by a contemporary record that the suggestion was made to him on the death of Henry, and rejected at once through his loyalty to his sister's son. Whether this record is to be believed or not, it shows that the event was thought possible.[23]

Certainly there was no real movement, not even the slightest, in his favour, and this fact reveals the change which had taken place in men's ideas of the succession in a century. The necessity of legitimate birth was coming to be recognized as indisputable, though it had not been by the early Teutonic peoples. Of the causes of this change, the teachings of the Church were no doubt the most effective, becoming of more force with its increasing influence, and especially since, as a part of the Hildebrandine reformation, it had insisted with so much emphasis on the fact that the son of a married priest could have no right of succession to his father's benefice, being of illegitimate birth; but the teachings of the sacredness of the marriage tie, of the sinfulness of illicit relations, and of the nullity of marriage within the prohibited degrees, were of influence in the change of ideas. It is also true that men's notions of the right of succession to property in general were becoming more strict and definite, and very possibly the importance of the succession involved in this particular case had its effect. One may almost regret that this change of ideas, which was certainly an advance in morals, as well as in law, was not delayed for another generation; for if Robert of Gloucester could have succeeded on the death of Henry without dispute, England would have been saved weary years of strife and suffering.

The death of the young William was a signal to set Henry's enemies in motion again. But they did not begin at once. Henry's position was still unweakened. Very likely his speedy marriage was a notice to the world that he did not propose to modify in the least his earlier plans. Probably also the absence of Fulk of Anjou, who had gone on a pilgrimage to Jerusalem soon after his treaty of 1119 with Henry, was a cause of delay, for the natural first move would be for him to demand a return of his daughter and her dowry. Fulk's stay was not long in the land of which he was in a few years to be king, and on his return he at once sent for his daughter, probably in 1121. She returned home, but as late as December, 1122, there was still trouble between him and Henry in regard to her dowry, which Henry no doubt was reluctant to surrender.

About the same time, Henry's old enemy, Amaury of Montfort, disliking the strictness of Henry's rule and the frequency of his demands for money, began to work among the barons of Normandy and with his nephew, the Count of Anjou, in favour of William Clito. It was already clear that Henry's hope of another heir was likely to be disappointed, and Normandy would naturally be more easily attracted to the son of Robert than England The first step was one which did not violate any engagement with Henry, but which was, nevertheless, a decided recognition of the claims of his nephew, and an open attack on his plans. Fulk gave his second daughter, Sibyl, in marriage to William Clito, and with her the county of Maine, which had been a part of Matilda's dower on her marriage with Henry's son William. Under the circumstances, this was equivalent to an announcement that he expected William Clito to be the Duke of Normandy. Early in 1123, Henry sent over troops to Normandy, and in June of that year he crossed himself, to be on the spot if the revolt and war which were threatening should break out. In September the discontented barons agreed together to take arms. It is of interest that among these was Waleran of Meulan, the son of the king's faithful counsellor, Count Robert. Waleran had inherited his father's Norman possessions while his brother Robert had become Earl of Leicester in England.

In all this the hand of Louis, king of France, was not openly seen. Undoubtedly, however, the movement had his encouragement from the beginning, and very likely his promise of open support when the time should come. The death of the male heir to England and Normandy would naturally draw Henry's daughter Matilda, and her husband the emperor, nearer to him; and of this, while Henry was still in England, some evidence has come down to us though not of the most satisfactory kind. Any evidence at the time that this alliance was likely to become more close would excite the fear of the king of France and make him ready to support any movement against the English king. Flanders would feel the danger as keenly, and in these troubles Charles the Good abandoned his English alliance and supported the cause of France.

The contest which followed between the king and his revolted barons is hardly to be dignified with the name of war. The forced surrender of a few strongholds, the long siege of seven weeks, long for those days, of Waleran of Meulan's castle, of Pont Audemer and its capture, and the occupation of Amaury of Montfort's city of Evreux, filled the remainder of the year 1123, and in March of 1124 the battle of Bourgtheroulde, in which Ralph, Earl of Chester, defeated Amaury and Waleran and captured a large number of prisoners, virtually ended the conflict. Upon the leaders whom he had captured Henry inflicted his customary punishment of long imprisonment, or the worse fate of blinding. The Norman barons had taken arms, and had failed without the help from abroad which they undoubtedly expected. We do not know in full detail the steps which had been taken to bring about this result, but it was attributed to the diplomacy of Henry, that neither Fulk of Anjou nor Louis of France was able to attack him.

Henry probably had little difficulty in moving his son-in-law, the emperor Henry V, to attack Louis of France. Besides the general reason which would influence him, of willingness to support Matilda's father at this time, and of standing unfriendliness with France, he was especially ready to punish the state in which successive popes had found refuge and support when driven from Italy by his successes. The policy of an attack on Louis was not popular with the German princes, and the army with which the Emperor crossed the border was not a large one. To oppose him, Louis advanced with a great and enthusiastic host. Taking in solemn ceremony from the altar of St Denis the oriflamme, the banner of the holy defender of the land, he aroused the patriotism of northern France as against a hereditary enemy. Even Henry's nephew, Theobald of Blois, led out his forces to aid the king. The news of the army advancing against them did not increase the ardour of the German forces; and hearing of an insurrection in Worms, the

Emperor turned back, having accomplished nothing more than to secure a free hand for Henry of England against the Norman rebels.

Against Fulk of Anjou Henry seems to have found his ally in the pope. The marriage of William Clito with Sibyl, with all that it might carry with it, was too threatening a danger to be allowed to stand, if in any way it could be avoided. The convenient plea of relationship, convenient to be remembered or forgotten according to the circumstances, was urged upon the pope. The Clito and his bride were related in no nearer degree than the tenth, according to the reckoning of the canon law, which prohibited marriage between parties related in the seventh degree, and Henry's own children, William in his earlier, and Matilda in her later marriage, with the sister and brother of Sibyl, were equally subject to censure. But this was a different case. Henry's arguments at Rome—Orderic tells us that threats, prayers, and money were combined—were effective, and the marriage was ordered dissolved. Excommunication and interdict were necessary to enforce this decision; but at last, in the spring of 1125, Fulk was obliged to yield, and William Clito began his wanderings once more, followed everywhere by the "long arm" of his uncle.

At Easter time in 1125, probably a few days before the date of the papal bull of interdict which compelled the dissolution of the marriage of William and Sibyl, a papal legate, John of Crema, landed in England. Possibly this departure from Henry's practice down to this time was a part of the price which the papal decision cost. The legate made a complete visitation of England, had a meeting with the king of Scots, and presided at a council of the English Church held in September, where the canons of Anselm were renewed in somewhat milder form. On his return to Rome in October, he was accompanied by the Archbishops of Canterbury and York, who went there about the still unsettled question of the obedience of the latter. Not even now was this question settled on its merits, but William of Corbeil made application, supported by the king, to be appointed the standing papal legate in Britain. This request was granted, and formed a precedent which was followed by successive popes and archbishops. This appointment is usually considered a lowering of the pretensions of the Archbishop of Canterbury, and an infringement of the independence of the English Church, and to a considerable extent this is true. Under a king as strong as Henry I, with an archbishop no stronger than William of Corbeil, or, indeed, with one not exceptionally strong, the papal authority gained very little from the arrangement. But it was a perpetual opportunity; it was a recognition of papal right. Under it the number of appeals to Rome increased; it marks in a legal way the advance of papal authority and of a consciousness of unity in the Church since the accession of the king, and it must have been so regarded at Rome. The appointment gave to Canterbury at once undoubted supremacy over York, but not on the old grounds, and that question was passed on to the future still unsettled.

In the spring of 1125 also occurred an event which again changed the direction of Henry's plans. On May 23, the emperor Henry V died, without children by his marriage to Matilda. The widowed Empress, as she was henceforth called by the English though she had never received the imperial crown, obeyed her father's summons to return to him in Normandy with great reluctance. She had been in Germany since her early childhood, and she was now twenty-three years of age. She could have few recollections of any other home. She loved the German people, and was beloved by them. We are told even that some of them desired her to reign in her husband's stead, and came to ask her return of Henry. But the death of her husband had rendered her succession to the English throne a matter of less difficulty, and Henry had no mind to sacrifice his own plans for the benefit of a foreign people. In September, 1126, he returned with Matilda to England, and in January following, at a great council in London, he demanded and obtained of the baronage, lay and spiritual, an oath to accept Matilda as sovereign if he should die without a male heir. The inference is natural from the account William of Malmesbury gives of this event, that in the argument before the council much was made of the fact that Matilda was a descendant of the old Saxon, as well as of the Norman, line. It is evident, also, that there was hesitation on the part of the barons, and that they yielded reluctantly to the king's demand.

The feudalism of France and England clearly recognized the right of women to succeed to baronies, even of the first importance, though with some irregularities of practice and the feudal right of marriage which the English kings considered so important rested, in the case of female heirs, on this principle. The king's son, Robert of Gloucester, and his nephew Stephen, now Count of Boulogne, who disputed with one another the right to take this oath to Matilda's succession next after her uncle, David, king of Scots, had both been provided for by Henry in this way. Still, even in these cases, a difference was likely to be felt between succession to the barony itself, and to the title and political authority which went with it, and the difference would be greater in the case of the highest of titles, of the throne of such a dominion as Henry had brought together. Public law in the Spanish peninsula had already, in one case, recognized the right of a woman to reign, but there had been as yet no case in northern Europe. The dread of such a succession was natural, in days when feudal turbulence was held in check only by the reigning king, and when even this could be accomplished only by a king of determined force. The natural feeling in such cases is undoubtedly indicated by the form of the historian's statement referred to above, that Robert of Gloucester declined the suggestion that he should be king out of loyalty to "his sister's son." It was the feeling that the female heir could pass the title on to her son, rather than that she could hold it herself.

William of Malmesbury states, in his account of these events, that he had often heard Bishop Roger of Salisbury say that he considered himself released from this oath to Matilda because it had been taken on condition that she should not be married out of the kingdom except with the counsel of the barons.[24] The writer takes pains at the same time to say that he records this fact rather from his sense of duty as a historian than because he believes the statement. It has, however, a certain amount of inherent probability. To consult with his vassals on such a question was so frequently the practice of the lord, and it was so entirely in line with feudal usage, that the barons would have had some slight ground on which to consider themselves released from this oath, even if such a specific promise had not been made, nor is it likely that Henry would hesitate to make it if he thought it desired. It is indeed quite possible that Henry had not yet determined upon the plan which he afterwards carried out, though it may very likely have been in his mind, and that he was led to this by events which were taking place at this very time in France.

Matilda's return to her father, and Henry's evident intention to make her the heir of his dominions, of Normandy as well as of England, seem to have moved King Louis to some immediate action in opposition. The separation of the duchy from the kingdom, so important for the interests of the Capetian house, could not be hoped for unless this plan was defeated. The natural policy of opposition was the support of William Clito. At a great council of his kingdom, meeting at the same time with Henry's court in which Matilda's heirship was recognized, the French king bespoke the sympathy and support of his barons for "William of Normandy." The response was favourable, and Louis made him a grant of the French Vexin, a point of observation and of easy approach to Normandy. At the same time, a wife was given William in the person of Jeanne, half sister of Louis's queen, and daughter of the Marquis of Montferrat. A few weeks later William advanced with an armed force to Gisors, and made formal claim to Normandy.

It was hardly these events, though they were equivalent to a formal notification of the future policy of the king of France, which brought Henry to a decision as to his daughter's marriage. On March 2, the Count of Flanders, Charles the Good, was foully murdered in the Church of St. Donatian at Bruges. He was without children or near relatives, and several claimants for the vacant countship at once appeared. Even Henry I is said to have presented his claim, which he would derive from his mother, but he seems never seriously to have prosecuted it. Louis, on the contrary, gave his whole support to the claim of William Clito, and succeeded with little difficulty in getting him recognized by most of the barons and towns as count. This was a new and most serious danger to Henry's plans, and he began at once to stir up troubles for the new count among his vassals, by the support of rival claimants, and in alliance with neighbouring princes. But the situation demanded measures of direct defence, and Henry was led to take the decisive step, so eventful for all the future history of England, of marrying Matilda a second time. Immediately after Whitsuntide of 1127, Matilda was sent over to Normandy, attended by Robert of Gloucester and Brian Fitz Count, and at Rouen was formally betrothed by the archbishop of that city to Geoffrey, son of Fulk of Anjou. The marriage did not take place till two years later.

For this marriage no consent of English or Norman barons was asked, and none was granted. Indeed, we are led to suspect that Henry considered it unlikely that he could obtain consent, and deemed it wiser not to let his plans be known until they were so far accomplished as to make opposition useless. The natural rivalry and hostility between Normandy and Anjou had been so many times passed on from father to son that such a marriage as this could seem to the Norman barons nothing but a humiliation, and to the Angevins hardly less than a triumph. The opposition, however, spent itself in murmurs. The king was too strong. Probably also the political advantages were too obvious to warrant any attempt to defeat the scheme. Matilda herself is said to have been much opposed to the marriage, and this we can easily believe. Geoffrey was more than ten years her junior, and still a mere boy. She had but recently occupied the position of highest rank in the world to which a woman could attain. She was naturally of a proud and haughty spirit. We are told nothing of the arguments which induced her to consent; but in this case again the political advantage, the necessity of the marriage to the security of her succession, must have been the controlling motive.

That these considerations were valid, that Henry was fully justified in taking this step in the circumstances which had arisen, is open to no question, if the matter is regarded as one of cold policy alone. To leave Matilda's succession to the sole protection of the few barons of England, who were likely to be faithful, however powerful they might be, would have been madness under the new conditions. With William Clito likely to be in possession of the resources of a strong feudal state, heartily supported by the king of France, felt by the great mass of Norman barons to be the rightful heir, and himself of considerable energy of character, the odds would be decidedly in favour of his succession. The balance could be restored only by bringing forward in support of Matilda's claim a power equal to William's and certain not to abandon her cause. Henry could feel that he had accomplished this by the marriage with Geoffrey, and he had every reason to believe that he had converted at the same time one of the probable enemies of his policy into its most interested defender. Could he have foreseen the early death of William, he might have had reason to hesitate and to question whether some other marriage might not lead to a more sure success. That this plan failed in the end is only a proof of Henry's foresight in providing, against an almost inevitable failure, the best defence which ingenuity could devise.

William Clito's tenure of his countship was of but little more than a year, and a year filled with fighting. Boulogne was a vassal county of Flanders; but the new count, Stephen, undoubtedly carrying out the directions of his uncle, refused him homage, and William endeavoured to compel his obedience by force. Insurrections broke out behind him, due in part to his own severity of rule; and the progress of one of his rivals who was destined to succeed him, Dietrich of Elsass, was alarming. Louis attempted to come to his help, but was checked by a forward move of Henry with a Norman army. The tide seemed about to turn in Henry's favour once more, when it was suddenly impelled that way by the death of William. Wounded in the hand by a spear, in a fight at Alost, he died a few days later. His father was still alive in an English prison, and was informed in a dream, we are told, of this final blow of fortune. But for Henry this opportune death not merely removed from the field the most dangerous rival for Matilda's succession, but it also re-established the English influence in Flanders. Dietrich of Elsass became count, with the consent of Louis, and renewed the bond with England. Not long afterwards by the influence of Henry he obtained as wife, Geoffrey of Anjou's sister Sibyl, who had been taken from William Clito.

Geoffrey and Matilda were married at Le Mans, on June g, 1129, by the Bishop of Avranches, in the presence of a brilliant assembly of nobles and prelates, and with the appearance of great popular rejoicing. After a stay there of three weeks, Henry returned to Normandy, and Matilda, with her husband and father-in-law, went to Angers. The jubilation with which the bridal party was there received was no doubt entirely genuine. Already before this marriage an embassy from the kingdom of Jerusalem had sought out Fulk, asking him to come to the aid of the Christian state, and offering him the hand of the heiress of the kingdom with her crown. This offer he now accepted and left the young pair in possession of Anjou. But this happy outcome of Henry's policy, which promised to settle so many difficulties, was almost at the outset threatened with disaster against which even he could not provide. Matilda was not of gentle disposition. She never made it easy for her friends to live with her, and it is altogether probable that she took no pains to conceal her scorn of this marriage and her contempt for the Angevins, including very likely her youthful husband. At any rate, a few days after Henry's return to England, July 7,1129, he was followed by the news that Geoffrey had repudiated and cast off his wife, and that Matilda had returned to Rouen with few attendants. Henry did not, however, at once return to Normandy, and it was two full years before Matilda came back to England.

The disagreement between Geoffrey and Matilda ran its course as a family quarrel. It might endanger the future of Henry's plans, but it caused him no present difficulty. His continental position was now, indeed, secure and was threatened during the short remainder of his life by none of his enemies, though his troubles with his son-in-law were not yet over. The defeat of Robert and the crushing of the most powerful nobles had taught the barons a lesson which did not need to be repeated, and England was not easily accessible to the foreign enemies of the king. In Normandy the case was different, and despite Henry's constant successes and his merciless severity, no victory had been final so long as any claimant lived who could be put forward to dispute his possession. Now followed some years of peace, in which the history of Normandy is as barren as the history of England had long been, until the marriage of Matilda raised up a new claimant to disturb the last months of her father's life. During Henry's last stay in Normandy death had removed one who had once filled a large place in history, but who had since passed long years in obscurity. Ranulf Flambard died in 1128, having spent the last part of his life in doing what he could to redeem the earlier, by his work on the cathedral of Durham, where in worthy style he carried on the work of his predecessor, William of St. Calais. Soon after died William Giffard, the bishop whom Henry had appointed before he was himself crowned, and in his place the king appointed his nephew, Henry of Blois, brother of Count Stephen, who was to play so great a part in the troubles that were soon to begin. About the same time we get evidence that Henry had not abandoned his practice of taking fines from the married clergy, and of allowing them to retain their wives.

The year 1130, which Henry spent in England, is made memorable by a valuable and unique record giving us a sight of the activities of his reign on a side where we have little other evidence. The Pipe Roll of that year has come down to us.[25] The Pipe Rolls, so called apparently from the shape in which they were filed for preservation, are the records of the accounting of the Exchequer Court with the sheriffs for the revenues which they had collected from their counties, and which they were bound to hand over to the treasury. From a point in the reign of Henry's grandson, these rolls become almost continuous, and reveal to us in detail many features of the financial system of these later times. This one record from the reign of the first Henry is a slender foundation for our knowledge of the financial organization of the kingdom, but from it we know with certainly that this organization had already begun as it was afterward developed.

It has already been said that the single organ of the feudal state, by which government in all its branches was carried on, was the curia regis. We shall find it difficult to realize a fact like this, or to understand how so crude a system of government operated in practice, unless we first have clearly in mind the fact that the men of that time did not reason much about their government. They did not distinguish one function of the state from another, nor had they yet begun to think that each function should have its distinct machinery in the governmental system. All that came later, as the result of experience, or more accurately, of the pressure of business. As yet, business and machinery both were undeveloped and undifferentiated. In a single session of the court advice might be given to the king on some question of foreign policy and on the making or revising of a law; and a suit between two of the king's vassals might be heard and decided: and no one would feel that work of different and somewhat inconsistent types had been done. One seemed as properly the function of the assembly as the other. In the composition of the court, and in the practice as to time and place of meeting, there was something of the same indefiniteness. The court was the king's. It was his personal machine for managing the business of his great property, the state. As such it met when and where the king pleased, certain meetings being annually expected; and it was composed of any persons who stood in immediate relations with the king, and whose presence he saw fit to call for by special or general summons, his vassals and the officers of his household or government. If a vassal of the king had a complaint against another, and needed the assistance of the king to enforce his view of the case, he might look upon his standing in the curia regis as a right; but in general it was a burden, a service, which could be demanded of him because of some estate or office which he held.

In the reign of the first Henry we can indeed trace the beginnings of differentiation in the machinery of government, but the process was as yet wholly unconscious. We find in this reign evidence of a large curia regis and of a small curia regis. The difference had probably existed in the two preceding reigns, but it now becomes more apparent because the increasing business of the state makes it more prominent. More frequent meetings of the curia regis were necessary, but the barons of the kingdom could not be in constant attendance at the court and occupied with its business. The large court was the assembly of all the barons, meeting on occasions only, and on special summons. The small court was permanently in session, or practically so, and was composed of the king's household officers and of such barons or bishops as might be in attendance on the king or present at the time. The distinction thus beginning was destined to lead to most important results, plainly to be seen in the constitution of to-day, but it was wholly unnoticed at the time. To the men of that time there was no distinction, no division. The small curia regis was the same as the larger; the larger was no more than the smaller. Who attended at a given date was a matter of convenience, or of precedent on the three great annual feasts, or of the desire of the king for a larger body of advisers about some difficult question of policy; but the assembly was always the same, with the same powers and functions, and doing the same business. Cases were brought to the smaller body for trial, and its decision was that of the curia regis. The king asked advice of it, and its answer was that of the council. The smaller was not a committee of the larger. It did not act by delegated powers. It was the curia regis itself. In reality differentiation of old institutions into new ones had begun, but the beginning was unperceived.

It was by a process similar to this that the financial business of the state began to be set off from the legislative and judicial, though it was long before it was entirely dissociated from the latter, and only gradually that the Exchequer Court was distinguished from the curia regis. The sheriffs, as the officers who collected the revenues of the king, each in his own county, were responsible to the curia regis. probably from early times the mechanical labour of examining and recording the accounts had been performed by subordinate officials; but any question of difficulty which arose, any disputed point, whether between the sheriff and the state or between the sheriff and the taxpayer, must have been decided by the court itself, though probably by the smaller rather than by the larger body. Certainly it is the small curia regis which has supervision of the matter when we get our first glimpse of the working of this machinery. Already at this date a procedure had developed for examining and checking the sheriff's accounts, which is evidently somewhat advanced, but which is interesting to us because still so primitive. Twice a year, at Easter and at Michaelmas, the court met for the purpose, under an organization peculiar to this work, and with some persons especially assigned to it; and it was then known as the Exchequer. The name was derived from the fact that the method of balancing accounts reminded one of the game of chess. Court and sheriff sat about a table of which the cloth was divided into squares, seven columns being made across the width of the cloth, and these divided by lines running through the middle along the length of the table, thus forming squares. Each perpendicular column of squares stood for a fixed denomination of money, pence, shillings, pounds, scores of pounds, hundreds of pounds, etc. The squares on the upper side of the table stood for the sum for which the sheriff was responsible, and when this was determined the proper counters were placed on their squares to set out the sum in visible form, as on an abacus. The squares of the lower side of the table were those of the sheriffs credits, and in them counters were placed to represent the sum for which the sheriff could submit evidence of payments already made. Such payments the sheriff was constantly making throughout the year, for fixed expenses of the state or on special orders of the king for supplies for the court, for transport, for the keeping of prisoners, for public works, and for various other purposes. The different items of debt and credit were noted down by clerks for the permanent record. When the account was over, a simple process of subtracting the counters standing in the credit squares from those in the debit showed the account balanced, or the amount due from the sheriff, or the credit standing in his favour, as the case might be.

At the Easter session of the court the accounts for the whole year were not balanced, the payment then made by the sheriff being an instalment on account, of about one-half the whole sum due for the year. For this he received a tally stick as a receipt, in which notches of different positions and sizes stood for the sum he had paid. A stick exactly corresponding was kept by the court, split off, indeed, from his, and the matching of the two at the Michaelmas session, when the year's account was finally closed, was the sheriff's proof of his former payment. The revenue of which the sheriff gave account in this way consisted of a variety of items. The most important was the firma comitatus, the farm or annual sum which the sheriff paid for his county as the farmer of its revenue. This was made up of the estimated returns from two sources, the rents from the king's lands in the county, and the share of the fines which went to the king from cases tried in the old popular courts of shire and hundred. The administration of justice was a valuable source of income in feudal days, whether to the king or to the lord who had his own court. But the fines which helped to make up the ferm of the county were not the only ones for which the sheriff accounted. He had also to collect, or at least in a general way to be responsible for, the fines inflicted in the king's courts as held in his county by the king's justices on circuits, and these were frequent in Henry's time. If a Danegeld or an aid was taken during the year, this must also be accounted for, together with such of the peculiarly feudal sources of income, ward-ships, marriages, escheats, etc., as were in the sheriffs hands. On the roll appear also numerous entries of fees paid by private persons to have their cases tried in the king's courts, or to have the king's processes or officers for the enforcement of their rights.

Altogether the items were almost as numerous as in a modern budget, but one chief source of present revenue, the customs duties, is conspicuously absent, and the general aspect of the system is far more that of income from property than in a modern state, even fines and fees having a personal rather than a political character. A careful estimate of all the revenue accounted for in this Pipe Roll of 1130 shows that Henry's annual income probably fell a little short of 30,000 English pounds in the money of that day, which should be equal in purchasing power, in money of our time, to a million and a half or two million pounds.[26] This was a large revenue for the age. Henry knew the value of money for the ends he wished to accomplish, and though he accumulated large store of it, he spent it unsparingly when the proper time came. England groaned constantly under the heavy burden of his taxes, and the Pipe Roll shows us that there was ground for these complaints. The Danegeld, the direct land-tax, had been taken for some years before this date, with the regularity of a modern tax, and as it was taken at a rate which would make it in any age a heavy burden, we can well believe that it was found hard to bear in a time when the returns of agriculture were more uncertain than now, and when the frequently occurring bad seasons were a more serious calamity. Economically, however, England was well-to-do. She had enjoyed during Henry's reign a long age of comparative quiet. For nearly a generation and a half, as the lives of men then averaged, there had been no war, public or private, to lay waste any part of the land. In fact, since early in the reign of Henry's father, England had been almost without experience of the barbarous devastation that went with war in feudal days. Excessive taxation and licensed oppression had seemed at times a serious burden. Bad harvests and the hunger and disease against which the medieval man could not protect himself had checked the growth of wealth and population. Yet on the whole the nation had gained greatly in three generations.

Especially is this to be seen in the development of the towns, in the growth of a rich burgher class containing many foreign elements, Norman, Flemish, and Jewish, and living with many signs of comfort and luxury, as well as in the indications of an active and diversified commercial life. The progress of this portion of the nation, the larger portion in numbers but making little show in the annals of barons and bishops whose more dramatic activities it supported is marked in an interesting way by a charter granted by Henry to London, in the last years of his reign.[27] His father had put into legal form a grant to the city, but it was not, strictly speaking, a city charter. It was no more than a promise that law and property should be undisturbed. Henry's charter goes much beyond this, though it tells us no more of the internal government of the city. In return for a rent of L300 a year, the king abandoned to the city all his revenues from Middlesex, and because he would have no longer any interest in the collection of these revenues the city might choose its own sheriff, and presumably collect them for itself. The king's pleas were surrendered, the city was to have its own justiciar, and to make this concession a real one, no citizen need plead in any suit outside the city walls. Danegeld and murder fines were also given up, and the local courts of the city were to have their regular sittings. Behind a grant like this must lie some considerable experience of self-government, a developed and conscious capacity in the citizens to organize and handle the machinery of administration. But of this there is no hint in the charter, nor do we know much of the inner government of London till some time later. Of the wealth and power of the city the charter speaks still more plainly, and of this there was to be abundant evidence in the period which follows the close of Henry's reign.

Henry's stay in England at this time was not long. Towards the end of the summer he returned to Normandy, though with what he was occupied there we have little knowledge. A disputed election to the papacy had taken place, and the pope of the reform party, Innocent II, had come to France, where that party was strong. The great St. Bernard, the most influential churchman of his time, had declared for him, and through his influence Henry, who met Innocent in January, 1131, recognized him as the rightful pope. In the following summer he returned to England, and brought back with him Matilda, who had now been two full years separated from her husband; but about this time Geoffrey thought better of his conduct, or determined to try the experiment of living with his wife again, and sent a request that Matilda be sent back to him. What answer should be given him was considered in a meeting of the great council at Northampton, September 8, almost as if her relationship with Geoffrey were a new proposition; and it was decided that she should go. A single chronicler records that Henry took advantage of this coming together of the barons at the meeting of the court to demand fealty to Matilda, both from those who had formerly sworn it and from those who had not.[28] Such a fact hardly seems consistent with the same chronicler's record of the excuse of Roger, Bishop of Salisbury, for violating his oath; but if it occurred, as this repetition of the fealty was after Matilda's marriage with Geoffrey and immediately after a decision of the baronage that she should return to him, it would make the bishop's argument a mere subterfuge or, at best, an exception applying to himself alone. Matilda immediately went over to Anjou, where she was received with great honour.

Few things remain to be recorded of the brief period of life left to the king. He had been interested, as his brother had been, in the extension of

English influence in Cumberland, and now he erected that county into a new bishopric of Carlisle, in the obedience of the Archbishop of York. On March 25, 1133, was born Matilda's eldest son, the future Henry II; and early in August the king of England crossed the channel for the last time, undoubtedly to see his grandson. On June 1, of the next year, his second grandson, Geoffrey, was born. A short time before, the long imprisonment of Robert of Normandy closed with his death, and the future for which Henry had so long worked must have seemed to him secure. But his troubles were not over. The medieval heir was usually in a hurry to enter into his inheritance, and Geoffrey of Anjou, who probably felt his position greatly strengthened by the birth of his son, was no exception to the rule. He demanded possessions in Normandy. He made little wars on his own account. Matilda, who seems now to have identified herself with her husband's interests, upheld his demands. Some of the Norman barons, who were glad of any pretext to escape from the yoke of Henry, added their support, especially William Talvas, the son of Robert of Bellême, who might easily believe that he had a long account to settle with the king. But Henry was still equal to the occasion. A campaign of three months, in 1135, drove William Talvas out of the country and brought everything again under the king's control, though peace was not yet made with his belligerent son-in-law. Then came the end suddenly. On November 25, Henry, still apparently in full health and vigour, planning a hunt for the next day, ate too heartily of eels, a favourite dish but always harmful to him, and died a week later, December 1, of the illness which resulted. Asked on his death-bed what disposition should be made of the succession, he declared again that all should go to Matilda, but made no mention of Geoffrey.

Henry was born in 1068, and was now past the end of his sixty-seventh year. His reign of a little more than thirty-five years was a long one, not merely for the middle ages, when the average of human life was short, but for any period of history. He was a man of unusual physical vigour. He had been very little troubled with illness. His health and strength were still unaffected by the labours of his life. He might reasonably have looked forward to seeing his grandson, who was now nearing the end of his third year, if not of an age to rule, at least of an age to be accepted as king with a strong regency under the leadership of Robert of Gloucester. A few years more of life for King Henry might have saved England from a generation that laboured to undo his work.

With the death of Henry I a great reign in English history closed. Considered as a single period, it does not form an epoch by itself. It is rather an introductory age, an age of beginnings, which, interrupted by a generation of anarchy, were taken up and completed by others. We are tempted to suspect that these others receive more credit for the completed result than they really deserve, because we know their work so well and Henry's so imperfectly. Certainly, we may well note this fact, that every new bit of evidence which the scholar from time to time rescues from neglect tends to show that the special creations for which we have distinguished the reign of Henry's grandson, reach further back in time than we had supposed. To this we may add the fact that, wherever we can follow in detail the action of the king, we find it the action of a man of political genius. Did we know as much of Henry's activity in government and administration as we do of the carrying out of his foreign policy, it is more than probable that we should find in it the clear marks of creative statesmanship. Not the least important of Henry's achievements of which we are sure was the peace which he secured and maintained for England with a strong and unsparing hand. More than thirty years of undisturbed quiet was a long period for any land in the middle ages, and during that time the vital process of union, the growing together in blood and laws and feeling of the two great races which occupied the land, was going rapidly forward.

[23] Gesta Stephani (Rolls Series), p. 10.

[24] William of Malmesbury, Gesta Regum sec. 452.

[25] Edited by Joseph Hunter and published by the Record Commission in 1833.

[26] Ramsay, Foundations of England, ii, 328.

[27] Round, Geoffrey de Mandeville, 347 ff.

[28] W. Malm., Historia Novella, sec. 455, and cf. sec. 452.

CHAPTER IX.
BARGAINING FOR THE CROWN

Earls and barons, whom the rumour of his illness had drawn together, surrounded the death-bed of Henry I and awaited the result. Among them was his natural son Robert of Gloucester; but his legal heiress, the daughter for whom he had done so much and risked so much, was not there. The recent attempt of her husband, Geoffrey of Anjou, to gain by force the footing in Normandy which Henry had denied him, had drawn her away from her father, and she was still in Anjou. It was afterward declared that Henry on his death-bed disinherited her and made Stephen of Boulogne heir in her place; but this is not probable, and it is met by the statement which we may believe was derived directly from Robert of Gloucester, that the dying king declared his will to be still in her favour. However this may be, no steps were taken by any one in Normandy to put Matilda in possession of the duchy, or formally to recognize her right of succession. Why her brother Robert did nothing and allowed the opportunity to slip, we cannot say. Possibly he did not anticipate a hostile attempt. At Rouen, whither Henry's body was first taken, the barons adopted measures to preserve order and to guard the frontiers, which show that they took counsel on the situation; but nothing was done about the succession.

In the meantime, another person, as deeply interested in the result, did not wait for events to shape themselves. Stephen of Boulogne had been a favourite nephew of Henry I and a favourite at his uncle's court, and he had been richly provided for. The county of Mortain, usually held by some member of the ducal house, had been given him; he had shared in the confiscated lands of the house of Bellême; and he had been married to the heiress of the practically independent county of Boulogne, which carried with it a rich inheritance in England. Henry might very well believe that gratitude would secure from Stephen as faithful a support of his daughter's cause as he expected from her brother Robert. But in this he was mistaken. Stephen acted so promptly on the news of his uncle's death that he must already have decided what his action would be.

When he heard that his uncle had died, Stephen crossed at once to England. Dover and Canterbury were held by garrisons of Earl Robert's and refused him admittance, but he pushed on by them to London. There he was received with welcome by the citizens. London was in a situation to hail the coming of any one who promised to re-establish order and security, and this was clearly the motive on which the Londoners acted in all that followed. A reign of disorder had begun as soon as it was known that the king was dead, as frequently happened in the medieval state, for the power that enforced the law, or perhaps that gave validity even to the law and to the commissions of those who executed it, was suspended while the throne was vacant. A great commercial city, such as London had grown to be during the long reign of Henry, would suffer in all its interests from such a state of things. Indeed, it appears that a body of plunderers, under one who had been a servant of the late king's, had established themselves not far from the city, and were by their operations manufacturing pressing arguments in favour of the immediate re-establishment of order. It is not necessary to seek for any further explanation of the welcome which London extended to Stephen. Immediately on his arrival a council was held in the city, probably the governing body of the city, the municipal council if we may so call it, which determined what should be done. Negotiations were not difficult between parties thus situated, and an agreement was speedily reached. The city bound itself to recognize Stephen as king, and he promised to put down disorder and maintain security. Plainly from the account we have of this arrangement, it was a bargain, a kind of business contract; and Stephen proceeded at once to show that he intended to keep his side of it by dispersing the robber band which was annoying the city and hanging its captain.

It is unnecessary to take seriously the claim of a special right to fill the throne when it was vacant, which the citizens of London advanced for themselves according to a contemporary historian of these events. [29] This is surely less a claim of the citizens than one invented for them by a partisan who wishes to make Stephen's position appear as strong as possible; and no one at the time paid any attention to it. Having secured the support of London, after what can have been only a few days' stay, Stephen went immediately to Winchester. Before he could really believe himself king, he had to secure the royal treasures and more support than he had yet gained. Stephen's own brother Henry, who owed his promotion in the Church, as Stephen did his in the State, to his uncle, was at this time Bishop of Winchester; and it was due to him, as a contemporary declares, that the plan of Stephen succeeded, and the real decision of the question was made, not at London, but at Winchester.[30] Henry went out with the citizens of Winchester to meet his brother on his approach, and he was welcomed as he had been at London. Present there or coming in soon after, were the Archbishop William of Canterbury, Roger, Bishop of Salisbury, the head of King Henry's administrative system, and seemingly a few, but not many, barons. On the question of making Stephen king, the good, though not strong, Archbishop of Canterbury, was greatly troubled by the oath which had been sworn in the interest of Matilda. "There are not enough of us here," his words seem to mean, "to decide upon so important a step as recognizing this man as king, when we are bound by oath to recognize another."[31]

Though our evidence is derived from clerical writers, who might exaggerate the importance of the point, it seems clear from a number of reasons that this oath to Matilda was really the greatest difficulty in Stephen's way. That it troubled the conscience of the lay world very much does not appear, nor that it was regarded either in Normandy or England as settling the succession. If the Norman barons had been bound by this oath as well as the English, as is altogether probable, they certainly acted as if they considered the field clear for other candidates. But it is evident that the oath was the first and greatest difficulty to be overcome in securing for Stephen the support of the Church, and this was indispensable to his success. The active condemnation of the breaking of this oath survived for a long time in the Church, and with characteristic medieval logic the fate of those few who violated their oaths and met some evil end was pointed to as a direct vengeance of God, while that of the fortunate majority of the faithless is passed over in silence, including the chief traitor Hugh Bigod, who, as Robert of Gloucester afterwards declared, had twice sworn falsely, and made of perjury an elegant accomplishment.[32]

If the scruples of the archbishop were to be overcome, it could not be done by increasing the number of those who were present to agree to the accession of Stephen. No material increase of the party of his adherents could be expected before the ceremony of coronation had made him actual king. It seems extremely probable that it was at this crisis of affairs, that the scheme was invented to meet the hesitation of the archbishop; and it was the only way in which it could have been overcome at the moment. Certain men stepped forward and declared that at the last Henry repented of having forced his barons to take this oath, and that he released them from it. It is hardly possible to avoid the accumulated force of the evidence which points to Hugh Bigod as the peculiarly guilty person, or to doubt it was here that he committed the perjury of which so many accused him. He is said to have sworn that Henry cut off Matilda from the succession and appointed Stephen his heir; but he probably swore to no more than is stated above.[33] That Matilda was excluded would be an almost necessary inference from it, and that Stephen was appointed heir in her place natural embroidery upon it. Nor can there be any reasonable doubt, I think, that his oath was deliberately false. Who should be made to bear the guilt of this scheme, if such it was, cannot be said. It is hardly likely that Henry of Winchester had any share in it. Whether true or false, the statement removed the scruples of the archbishop and secured his consent to Stephen's accession.

With this declaration of Hugh Bigod's, however, was coupled another matter more of the nature of a positive inducement to the Church. Bishop Henry seems to have argued with much skill, and very likely to have believed himself, that if they should agree to make his brother king, he would restore to the Church that freedom from the control of the State for which it had been contending since the beginning of the reign of Henry I, and which was now represented as having been the practice in the time of their grandfather, William the Conqueror. Stephen agreed at once to the demand. He was obliged to pay whatever price was set upon the crown by those who had the disposal of it; but of all the promises which he made to secure it, this is the one which he came the nearest to keeping. He swore to "restore liberty to the Church and to preserve it," and his brother pledged himself that the oath would be kept. Besides the adhesion of the Church, Stephen secured at Winchester the royal treasure which had been accumulated by his uncle and which was not small, and the obedience of the head of the administrative system, Roger of Salisbury, who seems to have made no serious difficulty, but who excused his violation of his oath to Matilda by another pretext, as has already been mentioned, than the one furnished by Hugh Bigod.

With the new adherents whom he had gained, Stephen at once returned from Winchester to London for his formal coronation. This took place at Westminster, probably on December 22, certainly within a very few days of that date. His supporters were still a very small party in the state. Very few of the lay barons had as yet declared for him. His chief dependence must have been upon the two cities of London and Winchester, and upon the three bishops who had come to his coronation with him, and who certainly held positions of influence and power in Church and State far beyond that of the ordinary bishop. At his coronation Stephen renewed his oath to respect the liberty of the Church, and he issued a brief charter to the nation at large which is drawn up in very general terms, confirming the liberties and good laws of Henry, king of the English, and the good laws and good customs of King Edward, but this can hardly be regarded as anything more than a proclamation that he intended to make no changes, a general confirmation of existing rights at the beginning of a new reign. The Christmas festival Stephen is said to have celebrated at London with great display. His party had not yet materially grown in strength, but he was now a consecrated king, and this fait accompli, as it has been called, was undoubtedly a decided argument with many in the next few weeks.

Throughout the three weeks that had elapsed since he had learned of his uncle's death, Stephen had acted with great energy, rapidity, and courage. Nor is there anything in the course of his reign to show that he was at any time lacking in these qualities. The period of English history upon which we enter with the coronation of Stephen is not merely a dreary period, with no triumphs abroad to be recorded, nor progress at home, with much loss of what had already been gained, temporary, indeed, but threatening to be permanent. It is also one of active feudal strife and anarchy, lasting almost a generation, of the loosening of the bonds of government, and of suffering by the mass of the nation, the like of which never recurs in the whole of that history. But this misery fell upon the country in Stephen's time, not because he failed to understand the duty of a king, nor because he lacked the energy or courage which a king must have. The great defect of Stephen's character for the time in which he lived was that he yielded too easily to persuasion. Gifted with the popular qualities which win personal favour among men, he had also the weakness which so often goes with them; he could not long resist the pressure of those about him. He could not impress men with the fact that he must be obeyed. His life after his coronation was a laborious one, and he did not spare himself in his efforts to keep order and to put down rebellion; but the situation passed irrecoverably beyond his control as soon as men realized that his will was not inflexible, and that swift and certain punishment of disobedience need not be feared. Stephen was at this time towards forty years old, an age which promised mature judgment and vigorous rule. His wife, who bore the name of Matilda, so common in the Norman house, was a woman of unusual spirit and energy, and devotedly attached to him. She stood through her mother, daughter of Malcolm and Margaret of Scotland, in the same relationship to the empress Matilda that her husband did, and her descendants would therefore be equally near akin to the old Saxon dynasty as those of the Empress.

If Stephen had seized the earliest opportunity, his cousin Matilda had been scarcely less prompt, but she had acted with less decision and with less discernment of the strategic importance of England. As soon as she learned of her father's death, she entered Normandy from the south, near Domfront, and was admitted to that town and to Argentan and Exmes without opposition by the viscount of that region, who was one of King Henry's "new men" in Normandy, and who recognized her claims at once. In a few days she was followed by her husband, Geoffrey, who entered the duchy a little farther to the east, in alliance with William Talvas, who opened to him Sees and other fortified places of his fief. So far all seemed going well, though as compared with the rapidity of Stephen's progress during those same days, such successes would count but little. Then, for some unaccountable reason, Geoffrey allowed his troops to plunder the Normans and to ravage cruelly the lands which had received him as a friend. The inborn fierceness of the Normans burst out at such treatment, and the Angevins were swept out of the country with as great cruelties as they had themselves exercised. Whether this incident had any influence on the action of the Norman barons it is not possible to say, but it must have been about the same time that they met at Neubourg to decide the question of the succession. We have no account of what they did or of what motives influenced their first decision. Theobald, Count of Blois and of Champagne, Stephen's elder brother, was present apparently to urge his own claim, and him they decided, or were on the point of deciding, to recognize as duke. At this moment a messenger from Stephen arrived and announced that all the English had accepted Stephen and agreed that he should be king. This news at once settled the question for the Norman barons. The reason which we have seen acting so strongly on earlier occasions—the fear of the consequences if they should try to hold their lands of two different suzerains—was once more the controlling motive, and they determined to accept Stephen. Theobald acquiesced in this decision, though unwillingly, and retired to his own dominions, to show but little interest in the long strife which these events began.

In England the effect of Stephen's coronation soon made itself felt. Immediately after the Christmas festivities in London he went with his court to Reading, whither the body of King Henry had now been brought from Normandy. There it was interred with becoming pomp, in the presence of the new king, in the abbey which Henry had founded and richly endowed. There Stephen issued a charter which is of especial historical value. It records a grant to Miles of Gloucester, and is signed among others by Payne Fitz-John. Both these were among Henry's "new men." Miles of Gloucester especially had received large gifts from the late king, and had held important office under him. Such men would naturally support Matilda. They might be expected certainly to hesitate until her cause was hopeless. Their presence with Stephen, accepting him as king so soon after his coronation, is evidence of great value as to the drift of opinion in England about the chance of his success. The charter is evidence also of one of the difficulties in Stephen's way, and of the necessity he was under of buying support, which we have seen already and which played so great a part in the later events of his reign. The charter confirms Miles in the possession of all the grants which had been made him in the late reign, and binds the king not to bring suit against him for anything which he held at the death of Henry. The question whether a new king, especially one who was not the direct heir of his predecessor, would respect his grants was a question of great importance to men in the position of Miles of Gloucester.

At Reading, or perhaps at Oxford, where Stephen may have gone from the burial of Henry, news came to him that David, king of Scotland, had crossed the border and was taking possession of the north of England, from Carlisle to Newcastle. David professed to be acting in behalf of his niece, Matilda, and out of respect to the oath he had sworn to support her cause, and he was holding the plundering habits of his army well in check. We are told that it was with a great army that Stephen marched against him. He had certainly force enough to make it seem wise to David, who was on his way to Durham, to fall back and negotiate. Terms were quickly arranged. David would not conform to the usual rule and become Stephen's man; and Stephen, still yielding minor matters to secure the greater, did not insist. But David's son Henry did homage to Stephen, and received the earldom of Huntingdon, with a vague promise that he might be given at some later time the other part of the possessions of his grandfather, Waltheof, the earldom of Northumberland, and with the more substantial present grant of Carlisle and Doncaster. The other places which David had occupied were given up.

From the north Stephen returned to London to hold his Easter court. He was now, he might well believe, king without question, and he intended to have the Easter assembly make this plain. Special writs of summons were sent throughout England to all the magnates of Church and State; and a large and brilliant court came together in response. Charters issued at this date, when taken together, give us the names of three archbishops—one, the Archbishop of Rouen—and thirteen bishops, four being Norman, and thirty-nine barons and officers of the court who were present, including King David's son Henry, who had come with Stephen from the north. At this assembly Stephen's queen, Matilda, was crowned, and so brilliant was the display and so lavish the expenditure that England was struck with the contrast to the last reign, whose economies had in part at least accumulated the treasure which Stephen might now scatter with a free hand to secure his position. The difficulties of his task are illustrated by an incident which occurred at this court. Mindful of the necessity of conciliating Scotland, he gave to young Henry, at the Easter feast, the seat of honour at his right hand; whereupon, the Archbishop of Canterbury, offended because his claims of precedence had been set aside, left the court; and Ralph, Earl of Chester, angered because Carlisle, to which he asserted claims of hereditary right, had been made over to Henry, cried out upon the young man, and with other barons insulted him so grievously that his father David was very angry in his turn.

Immediately after the Easter festivities, the court as a body removed to Oxford. Just after Easter Robert of Gloucester, the Empress's brother, had landed in England. Stephen had been importuning him for some time to give up his sister's cause and acknowledge him as king. So far as we know, Robert had done nothing up to this time to stem the current of events, and these events were probably a stronger argument with him than Stephen's inducements. All England and practically all Normandy had accepted Stephen. The king of Scotland had abandoned the opposition. Geoffrey and Matilda had accomplished nothing, and seemed to be planning nothing. The only course that lay plainly open was to make the best terms possible with the successful usurper, and to await the further course of events. William of Malmesbury, who looked upon Earl Robert as his patron and who wrote almost as his panegyrist, thinking, perhaps, dissimulation a smaller fault than disregard of his oath, accounted for his submission to Stephen by his desire to gain an opportunity to persuade the English barons to saner counsels. This statement can hardly be taken as evidence of Robert's intention, but at any rate he now joined the court at Oxford and made his bargain with Stephen. He did him homage, and promised to be his man so long as the king should maintain him in his position and keep faith with him.

At this Oxford meeting another bargain, even more important to Stephen than his bargain with the Earl of Gloucester, was put into a form which may be not improperly called a definitive treaty. This was the bargain with the Church, to the terms of which Stephen had twice before consented. The document in which this treaty was embodied is commonly known as Stephen's second charter; and, witnessed by nearly all those who witnessed the London charters already referred to, and by the Earl of Gloucester in addition, it had the force of a royal grant confirmed by the curia regis. Nothing could prove to us more clearly than this charter how conscious Stephen was of the desperate character of the undertaking on which he had ventured, and of the vital necessity of the support of the Church. The grant is of the most sweeping sort. All that the Church had demanded in the conflict between Anselm and Henry I is freely yielded, and more. All simony shall cease, vacancies shall be canonically filled; the possessions of the Church shall be administered by its own men during a vacancy,—that is, the feudal rights which had been exercised by the last two kings are given up; jurisdiction over all ecclesiastical persons and property is abandoned to the Church; ecclesiastics shall have full power to dispose of their personal property by will; all unjust exactions, by whomsoever brought in,— including among these, no doubt, as Henry of Huntingdon expressly says, the Danegeld, which the Church had insisted ought not to be paid by its domain lands,—are to be given up. "These all I concede and confirm," the charter closes, "saving my royal and due dignity." Dignity in the modern sense might be left the king, but not much real power over the Church if this charter was to determine future law and custom. The English Church would have reached at a stroke a nearer realization of the full programme of the Hildebrandine reform than all the struggles of nearly a century had yet secured in any other land, if the king kept his promises. As a matter of fact, he did not do so entirely, though the Church made more permanent gain from the weakness of this reign than any other of the contending and rival parties.

One phrase at the beginning of this charter strikes us with surprise. In declaring how he had become king, Stephen adds to choice by clergy and people, and consecration by the archbishop, the confirmation of the pope. Since when had England, recognized the right of the pope to confirm its sovereigns or to decide cases of disputed succession? Or is the papacy securing here, from the necessities of Stephen, a greater concession than any other in the charter, a practical recognition of the claim which once Gregory VII had made of the Conqueror only to have it firmly rejected, and which the Church had not succeeded in establishing in any European land? In reality England had recognized no claim of papal overlordship, nor was any such claim in the future based upon this confirmation. The reference to the pope had been practically forced upon Stephen, whether he would have taken the step himself or not, and the circumstances made it of the highest importance to him to proclaim publicly the papal sanction of his accession. Probably immediately on hearing the news of Stephen's usurpation, Matilda had despatched to Pope Innocent II,—then residing at Pisa because Rome was in possession of his rival, Anacletus II,—an embassy headed by the Bishop of Angers, to appeal to the pope against the wicked deeds of Stephen, in that he had defrauded her of her rights and broken his oath, as William of Normandy had once appealed to the pope against the similar acts of Harold.[34] At Pisa this embassy was opposed by another of Stephen's, whose spokesman was the archdeacon of Sees. It must have started at about the same time as Matilda's, and it brought to the pope the official account of the bishops who had taken part in the coronation of Stephen.

In the presence of Innocent something like a formal trial occurred. The case was argued by the champions of the two sides, on questions which it belonged to the Church to decide, or which at least the Church claimed the right to decide, the usurpation of an inheritance, and the violation of an oath. Against Matilda's claim were advanced the arguments which had already been used with effect in England, that the oath had been extorted from the barons by force, and that on his death-bed Henry had released them from it; but more than this, Stephen's advocates suddenly sprang on their opponents a new and most disconcerting argument, one which would have had great weight in any Church court, and which attacked both their claims at once. Matilda could not be the rightful heir, and so the oath itself could not be binding, because she was of illegitimate birth, being the daughter of a nun. One account of this debate represents Matilda's side as nonplussed by this argument and unable to answer it. And they might well be, for during the long generation since Henry's marriage, no question of its validity had ever been publicly raised. The sudden advancing of the doubt at this time shows, however, that it had lingered on in the minds of some in the Church. It is not likely that the point would have been in the end dangerous to Matilda's cause, for it would not have been possible to produce evidence sufficient to warrant the Church in reversing the decision which Archbishop Anselm had carefully made at the time. But the pope did not allow the case to come to a decision. He broke off the debate, and announced that he would not decide the question nor permit it to be taken up again. His caution was no doubt due to the difficult position in which Innocent was then placed, with a rival in possession of the capital of Christendom, the issue uncertain, and the support of all parties necessary to his cause. Privately, but not as an official decision, he wrote to Stephen recognizing him as king of England. The letter reveals a reason in Stephen's favour which probably availed more with the pope than all the arguments of the English embassy, the pressure of the king of France. The separation of Anjou at least, if not of Normandy also, from England, was important to the plans of France, and the support of the king was essential to the pope.

To Stephen the reasons for the pope's letter were less important than the fact that such decision as there was was in his favour. He could not do otherwise than make this public. The letter probably arrived in England just before, or at the time of, the Easter council in London. To the Church of England, in regard to the troublesome matter of the oath, it would be decisive. There could be no reason why Stephen should not be accepted as king if the pope, with full understanding of the facts, had accepted him. And so the Church was ready to enter into that formal treaty with the king which is embodied in Stephen's second charter, which is a virtual though conditional recognition of him, and which naturally, as an essential consideration, recites the papal recognition and calls it not unnaturally a confirmation, though this word may be nothing more than the mere repetition of an ecclesiastical formula set down by a clerical hand, without especial significance.

Stephen might now believe himself firmly fixed in the possession of power. His bold stroke for the crown had proved as successful as Henry I's, and everything seemed to promise as secure and prosperous a reign. The all-influential Church had declared for him, and its most influential leader was his brother Henry of Winchester, who had staked his own honour in his support. The barons of the kingdom had accepted him, and had attended his Easter court in unusual numbers as compared with anything we know of the immediately preceding reigns. Those who should have been the leaders of his rival's cause had all submitted, — her brother, Robert of Gloucester, Brian Fitz Count, Miles of Gloucester, Payne Fitz John, the Bishop of Salisbury, and his great ministerial family. The powerful house of Beaumont, the earls of Warwick and of Leicester, who held almost a kingdom in middle England, promised to be as faithful to the new sovereign as it had been to earlier ones. Even Matilda herself and her husband Geoffrey seemed to have abandoned effort, having met with no better success in their appeal to the pope than in their attack on Normandy. For more than two years nothing occurs which shakes the security of Stephen's power or which seriously threatens it with the coming of any disaster.

And yet Stephen, like Henry I, had put himself into a position which only the highest gifts of statesmanship and character could maintain, and in these he was fatally lacking. The element of weakness, which is more apparent in his case, though perhaps not more real, than in Henry's, that he was a king by "contract," as the result of various bargains, and that he might be renounced by the other parties to these bargains if he violated their terms, was only one element in a general situation which could be dominated by a strong will and by that alone. These bargains served as excuses for rebellion, — unusually good, to be sure, from a legal point of view, — but excuses are always easy to find, or are often thought unnecessary, for resistance to a king whom one may defy with impunity. The king's uncle had plainly marked out a policy which a ruler in his situation should follow at the beginning of his reign — to destroy the power of the most dangerous barons, one by one, and to raise up on their ruins a body of less powerful new men devoted to himself; but this policy Stephen had not the insight nor the strength of purpose to follow. His defect was not the lack of courage. He was conscious of his duty and unsparing of himself, but he lacked the clear sight and the fixed purpose, the inflexible determination which the position in which he had placed himself demanded. To understand the real reason for the period of anarchy which follows, to know why Stephen, with as fair a start, failed to rule as Henry I had done, one must see as clearly as possible how, in the months when his power seemed in no danger of falling, he undermined it himself through his lack of quick perception and his unsteadiness of will.

It would not be profitable to discuss here the question whether or not Stephen was a usurper. Such a discussion is an attempt to measure the acts of that time by a standard not then in use. As we now judge of such things he was a usurper; in the forum of morals he must be declared a usurper, but no one at the time accused him of any wrong-doing beyond the breaking of his oath.[35] Of no king before or after is so much said, in chronicles and formal documents, of "election" as is said of Stephen; but of anything which may be called a formal or constitutional election there is no trace. The facts recorded indeed illustrate more clearly than in any other case the process by which, in such circumstances, a king came to the throne. It was clearly a process of securing the adhesion and consent, one after another, of influential men or groups of men. In this case it was plainly bargaining. In every case there was probably something of that—as much as might be necessary to secure the weight of support that would turn the scale.

Within a few days of this brilliant assembly at the Easter festival, the series of events began which was to test Stephen's character and to reveal its weakness to those who were eager in every reign of feudal times to profit by such a revelation. A rumour was in some way started that the king was dead. Instantly Hugh Bigod, who had been present at the Oxford meeting, and who had shown his own character by his willingness to take on his soul the guilt of perjury in Stephen's cause, seized Norwich castle. The incident shows what was likely always to happen on the death of the king,—the seizure of royal domains or of the possessions of weaker neighbours, by barons who hoped to gain something when the time of settlement came. Hugh Bigod had large possessions in East Anglia, and was ambitious of a greater position still. He became, indeed, in the end, earl, but without the possession of Norwich. Now he was not disposed to yield his prey, even if the king were still alive; he did so only when Stephen came against him in person, and then very unwillingly. That he received any punishment for his revolt we are not told.

Immediately after this Stephen was called to the opposite side of the kingdom by news of the local depredations of Robert of Bampton, a minor baron of Devonshire. His castle was speedily captured, and he was sent into exile. But greater difficulties were at hand in that region. A baron of higher rank, Baldwin of Redvers, whose father before him, and himself in succession, had been faithful adherents of Henry I from the adventurous and landless days of that prince, seized the castle of Exeter and attempted to excite a revolt, presumably in the interests of Matilda. The inhabitants of Exeter refused to join him, and sent at once to Stephen for aid, which was hurriedly despatched and arrived just in time to prevent the sacking of the town by the angry rebel. Here was a more important matter than either of the other two with which the king had had to deal, and he sat down to the determined siege of the castle. It was strongly situated on a mass of rock, and resisted the king's earlier attacks until, after three months, the garrison was brought to the point of yielding by want of water. At first Stephen, by the advice of his brother Henry, insisted upon unconditional surrender, even though Baldwin's wife came to him in person and in great distress to move his pity. But now, as in Henry I's attack on Robert of Bellême at the beginning of his reign, another influence made itself felt. The barons in Stephen's camp began to put pressure on the king to induce him to grant favourable terms. We know too little of the actual circumstances to be able to say to what extent Stephen was really forced to yield. In the more famous incident at Bridgenorth Henry had the support of the English common soldiers in his army. Here nothing is said of them, or of any support to the king. But with or without support, he yielded. The garrison of the castle were allowed to go free with all their personal property. Whether this was a concession which in the circumstances Stephen could not well refuse, or an instance of his easy yielding to pressure, of which there are many later, the effect was the same. Contemporary opinion declared it to be bad policy, and dated from it more general resistance to the king. It certainly seems clear from these cases, especially from the last, that Stephen had virtually given notice at the beginning of his reign that rebellion against him was not likely to be visited with the extreme penalty. Baldwin of Redvers did not give up the struggle with the surrender of Exeter castle. He had possessions in the Isle of Wight, and he fortified himself there, got together some ships, and began to prey on the commerce of the channel. Stephen followed him up, and was about to invade the island when he appeared and submitted. This time he was exiled, and crossing over to Normandy he took refuge at the court of Geoffrey and Matilda, where he was received with a warm welcome.

For the present these events were not followed by anything further of a disquieting nature. To all appearances Stephen's power had not been in the least affected. From the coast he went north to Brampton near Huntingdon, to amuse himself with hunting. There he gave evidence of how strong he felt himself to be, for he held a forest assize and tried certain barons for forest offences. In his Oxford charter he had promised to give up the forests which Henry had added to those of the two preceding kings, but he had not promised to hold no forest assizes, and he could not well surrender them. There was something, however, about his action at Brampton which was regarded as violating his "promise to God and to the people"; and we may regard it, considering the bitterness of feeling against the forest customs, especially on the part of the Church, as evidence that he felt himself very secure, and more important still as leading to the belief that he would not be bound by his promises.

A somewhat similar impression must have been made at about this time, the impression at least that the king was trying to make himself strong enough to be independent of his pledges, if he wished, by the fact that he was collecting about him a large force of foreign mercenaries, especially men from Britanny and Flanders. From the date of the Conquest itself, the paid soldier, the mercenary drawn from outside the dominions of the sovereign, had been constantly in use in England, not merely in the armies of the king, but sometimes in the forces of the greater barons, and had often been a main support in both cases. When kept under a strong control, the presence of mercenaries had given rise to no complaints; indeed, it is probable that in the later part of reigns like those of William I and Henry I their number had been comparatively insignificant. But in a reign in which the king was dependent on their aid and obliged to purchase their support by allowing them liberties, as when William II proposed to play the tyrant, or in the time of Stephen from the weakness of the king, complaints are frequent of their cruelties and oppressions, and the defenceless must have suffered whatever they chose to inflict. The contrast of the reign of Stephen, in the conduct and character of the foreigners in England, with that of Henry, was noted at the time. In the commander of his mercenaries, William of Ypres, who had been one of the unsuccessful pretenders to the countship of Flanders some years before, Stephen secured one of his most faithful and ablest adherents.

In the meantime a series of events in Wales during this same year was revealing another side of Stephen's character, his lack of clear political vision, his failure to grasp the real importance of a situation. At the very beginning of the year, the Welsh had revolted in South Wales, and won a signal victory. From thence the movement spread toward the west and north, growing in success as it extended. Battles were won in the field, castles and towns were taken, leaders among the Norman baronage were slain, and the country was overrun. It looked as if the tide which had set so steadily against the Welsh had turned at last, at least in the south-west, and as if the Norman or Flemish colonists might be driven out. But Stephen did not consider the matter important enough to demand his personal attention, even after he was relieved of his trouble with Baldwin of Redvers, though earlier kings had thought less threatening revolts sufficiently serious to call for great exertions on their part. He sent some of his mercenaries, but they accomplished nothing; and he gave some aid to the attempts of interested barons to recover what had been lost, with no better result. Finally, we are told by the writer most favourable to Stephen's reputation, he resolved to expend no more money or effort on the useless attempt, but to leave the Welsh to weaken themselves by their quarrels among themselves.[36] The writer declares the policy successful, but we can hardly believe it was so regarded by those who suffered from it in the disasters of this and the following year, or by the barons of England in general.

It might well be the case that Stephen's funds were running low. The heavy taxes and good management of his uncle had left him a full treasury with which to begin, but the demands upon it had been great. Much support had undoubtedly been purchased outright by gifts of money. The brilliant Easter court had been deliberately made a time of lavish display; mercenary troops could have been collected only at considerable cost; and the siege of Exeter castle had been expensive as well as troublesome. Stephen's own possessions in England were very extensive, and the royal domains were in his hands; but the time was rapidly coming when he must alienate these permanent sources of supply, lands and revenues, to win and hold support. It was very likely this lack of ready money which led Stephen to the second violation of his promises, if the natural interpretation of the single reference to the fact is correct.[37] In November of this year, 1136, died William of Corbeil, who had been Archbishop of Canterbury for thirteen years and legate of the pope in England for nearly as long. Officers of the king took possession of his personal property, which Stephen had promised the Church should dispose of, and found hidden away too large a store of coin for the archbishop's reputation as a perfect pastor, for he should have distributed it in his lifetime and then it would have gone to the poor and to his own credit.

Whatever opinion about Stephen might be forming in England during this first year of his reign, from his violation of his pledges, or his determination to surround himself with foreign troops, or his selfish sacrificing of national interests, or his too easy dealing with revolt, there was as yet no further movement against him. Nobody seemed disposed to question his right to reign or to withhold obedience, and he could, without fear of the consequences, turn his attention to Normandy to secure as firm possession of the duchy as he now had of the kingdom. About the middle of Lent, 1137, Stephen crossed to Normandy, and remained there till Christmas of the same year. Normandy had accepted him the year before, as soon as it knew the decision of England, but there had been no generally recognized authority to represent the sovereign, and some parts of the duchy had suffered severely from private war. In the south-east, the house of Beaumont, Waleran of Meulan and Robert of Leicester, were carrying on a fierce conflict with Roger of Tosny. In September, 1136, central

Normandy was the scene of another useless and savage raid of Geoffrey of Anjou, accompanied by William, the last duke of Aquitaine, William Talvas, and others. They penetrated the country as far as Lisieux, treating the churches and servants of God, says Orderic Vitalis, after the manner of the heathen, but were obliged to retreat; and finally, though he had been joined by Matilda, Geoffrey, badly wounded, abandoned this attempt also and returned to Anjou.

The general population of the duchy warmly welcomed the coming of Stephen, from whom they hoped good things and especially order; but the barons seem to have been less enthusiastic. They resented his use of Flemish soldiers and the influence of William of Ypres, and they showed themselves as disposed as in England to prevent the king from gaining any decisive success. Still, however, there was no strong party against him, and Stephen seemed to be in acknowledged control of the duchy, even if it was not a strong control. In May he had an interview with Louis VI of France, and was recognized by him as duke, on the same terms as Henry I had been, his son Eustace doing homage in his stead. This arrangement with France shows the strength of Stephen's position, though the acknowledgment was no doubt dictated as well by the policy of Louis, but events of the same month showed Stephen's real weakness. In May Geoffrey attempted a new invasion with four hundred knights, this time intending the capture of Caen. But Stephen's army, the Flemings under William of Ypres, and the forces of some of the Norman barons, blocked the way. William was anxious to fight, but the Normans refused, and William with his Flemings left them in disgust and joined Stephen. Geoffrey, however, gave up his attempt on Caen and drew back to Argentan. In June, on Stephen's collecting an army to attack Geoffrey, the jealousies between the Normans and the hired soldiers broke out in open fighting, many were slain, and the Norman barons withdrew from the army. Geoffrey and Stephen were now both ready for peace. Geoffrey, it is said, despaired of accomplishing anything against Stephen, so great was his power and wealth; and Stephen, on the contrary, must have been influenced by the weakness which recent events had revealed. In July a truce for two years was agreed to between them.

Closely connected with these events, but in exactly what way we do not know, were others which show us something of the relations between the king and the Earl of Gloucester, and which seem to indicate the growth of suspicion on both sides. Robert had not come to Normandy with Stephen, but on his departure he had followed him, crossing at Easter. What he had been doing in England since he had made his treaty with the king at Oxford, or what he did in Normandy, where he had extensive possessions, we do not know; but the period closes with an arrangement between him and Stephen which looks less like a renewal of their treaty than a truce. In the troubles in the king's army during the summer campaign against Geoffrey, Robert was suspected of treason. At one time William of Ypres set some kind of a trap for him, in which he hoped to take him at a disadvantage, but failed. The outcome of whatever happened was, evidently that Stephen found himself placed in a wrong and somewhat dangerous position, and was obliged to take an oath that he would attempt nothing further against the earl, and to pledge his faith in the hand of the Archbishop of Rouen. Robert accepted the new engagements of the king in form, and took no open steps against him for the present; but it is clear that the relation between them was one of scarcely disguised suspicion. It was a situation with which a king like Henry I would have known how to deal, but a king like Henry I would have occupied by this time a stronger position from which to move than Stephen did, because his character would have made a far different impression.

While these events were taking place in Normandy, across the border in France other events were occurring, to be in the end of as great interest in the history of England as in that of France. When William, Duke of Aquitaine, returned from his expedition with Geoffrey, he seems to have been troubled in his conscience by his heathenish deeds in Normandy, and he made a pilgrimage to St. James of Compostella to seek the pardon of heaven. In this he seemed to be successful, and he died there before the altar of the apostle, with all the comforts of religion. When he knew that his end was approaching, he besought his barons to carry out the plan which he had formed of conveying the duchy to the king of France, with the hand of his daughter and heiress Eleanor for his son Louis. The proposition was gladly accepted, the marriage took place in July at Bordeaux, and the young sovereign received the homage of the vassals of a territory more than twice his father's in area, which was thus united with the crown. Before the bridal pair could return to Paris, the reign of Louis VI had ended, and Louis the Young had become king as Louis VII. He was at this time about seventeen years old. His wife was two years younger, and Henry of Anjou, the son of Matilda, whose life was to be even more closely associated with hers, had not yet finished his fifth year.

During Stephen's absence in Normandy there had been nothing to disturb the peace of England. Soon after his departure the king of Scotland had threatened to invade the north, but Thurstan, the aged Archbishop of York, went to meet him, and persuaded him to agree to a truce until the return of King Stephen from Normandy. This occurred not long before Christmas. Most of the barons of Normandy crossed over with him, but Robert of Gloucester again took his own course and remained behind. There was business for Stephen in England at once. An embassy from David of

Scotland waited on him and declared the truce at an end unless he were prepared to confer the half-promised earldom of Northumberland on Henry without further delay. Another matter, typical of Stephen and of the times, demanded even earlier attention. Stephen owed much, as had all the Norman kings, to the house of Beaumont, and he now attempted to make some return. Simon of Beauchamp, who held the barony of Bedford and the custody of the king's castle in that town, had died shortly before, leaving a daughter only. In the true style of the strong kings, his predecessors, Stephen proposed, without consulting the wishes of the family, to bestow the hand and inheritance of the heiress on Hugh, known as "the Poor," because he was yet unprovided for, brother of Robert of Leicester and Waleran of Meulan, and to give him the earldom of Bedford. The castle had been occupied with his consent by Miles of Beauchamp, Simon's nephew, and to him Stephen sent orders to hand the castle over to Hugh and to do homage to the new Earl of Bedford for whatever he held of the king. It was to this last command apparently that Miles especially objected, and he refused to surrender the castle unless his own inheritance was secured to him. In great anger, Stephen collected a large army and began the siege of the castle, perhaps on Christmas day itself. The castle was stoutly defended. The siege had to be turned into a blockade. Before it ended the king was obliged to go away to defend the north against the Scots. After a siege of five weeks the castle was surrendered to Bishop Henry of Winchester, who seems for some reason to have opposed his brother's action in the case from the beginning.

[29] Gesta Stephani, 5.

[30] W. Malm., Hist. Nov., sec. 460.

[31] Gesta Stefhani, 8.

[32] Henry of Huntingdon, 270.

[33] See Round, G. de Mandeville, 6.

[34] Round, Geoffrey de Mandeville, 250-261; and Böhmer, Kirche und Staat, 333-335.

[35] Freeman, Norman Conquest, Vol. V, App. DD., is right in calling attention to the fact but wrong in the use he makes of it.

[36] Gesta Stephani, 14.

[37] Ibid., 7.

CHAPTER X.
FEUDALISM UNDER A WEAK KING

The year 1138, which began with the siege of Bedford castle, has to be reckoned as belonging to the time when Stephen's power was still to all appearance unshaken. But it is the beginning of the long period of continuous civil warfare which ended only a few months before his death. Judgment had already been passed upon him as a king. It is clear that certain opinions about him, of the utmost importance as bearing on the future, had by this time fixed themselves in the minds of those most interested—that severe punishment for rebellion was not to be feared from him; that he was not able to carry through his will against strong opposition, or to force obedience; and that lavish grants of money and lands were to be extorted from him as a condition of support. The attractive qualities of Stephen's personality were not obscured by his faults or overlooked in passing this judgment upon him, for chroniclers unfavourable to him show the influence of them in recording their opinion of his weakness; but the general verdict is plainly that which was stated by the Saxon Chronicle under the year 1137, in saying that "he was a mild man, and soft, and good, and did no justice." Such traits of character in the sovereign created conditions which the feudal barons of any land would be quick to use to their own advantage.

The period which follows must not be looked upon as merely the strife between two parties for the possession of the crown. It was so to the candidates themselves; it was so to the most faithful of their supporters. But to a large number of the barons most favourably situated, or of those who were most unprincipled in pursuit of their own gain, it was a time when almost anything they saw fit to demand might be won from one side or the other, or from both alternately by well-timed treason. It was the time in the history of England when the continental feudal principality most nearly came into existence,—the only time after the Conquest when several great dominions within the state, firmly united round a local chief, obtained a virtual, or even it may be a formal, independence of the sovereign's control. These facts are quite as characteristic of the age as the struggle for the crown, and they account for the continuance of the conflict more than does the natural balance of the parties. No triumph for either side was possible, and the war ended only when the two parties agreed to unite and to make common cause against those who in reality belonged to neither of them.

From the siege of Bedford castle, Stephen had been called to march to the north by the Scottish invasion, which early in January followed the failure of David's embassy. All Scottish armies were mixed bodies, but those of this period were so not merely because the population of Scotland was mixed, but because of the presence of foreign soldiers and English exiles, and many of them were practically impossible to control. Portions of Northumberland down to the Tyne were ravaged with the usual barbarities of Scottish warfare before the arrival of Stephen. On his coming David fell back across the border, and Stephen made reprisals on a small district of southern Scotland. But his army would not support him in a vigorous pushing of the campaign. The barons did not want to fight in Lent, it seemed. Evidences of more open treason appear also to have been discovered, and Stephen, angry but helpless, was obliged to abandon further operations.

Shortly after Easter David began a new invasion, and at about the same time rebellion broke out in the south-west of England, in a way that makes the suspicion natural that the two events were parts of a concerted movement in favour of Matilda. This second Scottish invasion was hardly more than a border foray, though it penetrated further into the country than the first, and laid waste parts of Durham and Yorkshire. Lack of discipline in the Scottish army prevented any wider success. The movement in the south-west, however, proved more serious, and from it may be dated the beginning of continuous civil war. Geoffrey Talbot, who had accepted Stephen two years before, revolted and held Hereford castle against him. From Gloucester, where he was well received, the king advanced against Hereford about the middle of May, and took the castle after a month's blockade, letting the garrison off without punishment, Talbot himself having escaped the siege. But by the time this success had been gained, or soon after, the rebellion had spread much wider.

Whether the insurrection in the south and west had become somewhat general before, or was encouraged by it to begin, the chief event connected with it was the formal notice which Robert of Gloucester served on the king, by messengers from Normandy, who reached Stephen about the middle of June, that his allegiance was broken off. A beginning of rebellion, at least, as in England, had occurred somewhat earlier across the channel. In May Count Waleran of Meulan and William of Ypres had gone back to Normandy to put down the disturbances there. In June, Geoffrey of Anjou entered the duchy again with an armed force, and is said to have persuaded Robert to take the side of his sister. Probably Robert had quite as much as Geoffrey to do with the concerted action which seems to have been adopted, and himself saw that the time had come for an open stand. He had been taking counsel of the Church on the ethics of the case. Numerous churchmen had informed him that he was endangering his chances of eternal life by not keeping his original oath. He had even applied to the pope, and had been told, in a written and formal reply, that he was under obligation to keep the oath which he had sworn in the presence of his father. Whether Innocent II was deciding an abstract question of morals in this answer, or was moved by some temporary change of policy, it is impossible to say. Robert's conscience was not troubled by the oath he had taken to Stephen except because it was in violation of the earlier one. That had been a conditional oath, and Robert declared that Stephen had not kept the terms of the agreement; besides he had no right to be king and therefore no right to demand allegiance. Robert's possessions in England were so wide, including the strong castles of Bristol and Dover, and his influence over the baronage was so great, that his defection, though Stephen must have known for some time that it was probable, was a challenge to a struggle for the crown more desperate than the king had yet experienced.

It is natural to suppose that the many barons who now declared against the king, and fortified their castles, were influenced by a knowledge of Robert's action, or at least by a knowledge that it was coming. No one of these was of the rank of earl. William Peverel, Ralph Lovel, and Robert of Lincoln, William Fitz John, William of Mohun, Ralph Paganel, and William Fitz Alan, are mentioned by name as holding castles against the king, besides a son of Robert's and Geoffrey Talbot who were at Bristol, and Walkelin Maminot who held Dover. The movement was confined to the southwest, but as a beginning it was not to be neglected. Stephen acted with energy. He seized Robert's lands and destroyed his castles wherever he could get at them. A large military force was summoned. The queen was sent to besiege Dover castle, and she drew from her county of Boulogne a number of ships sufficient to keep up the blockade of the harbour. The king himself advanced from London, where he had apparently gone from Hereford to collect his army and arrange his plans, against Bristol which was the headquarters of Robert's party.

Bristol was strong by nature, protected by two rivers and open to the sea, and it had been strongly fortified and prepared for resistance. There collected the main force of the rebels, vassals of Robert, or men who, like Geoffrey Talbot, had been dispossessed by Stephen, and many mercenaries and adventurers. Their resources were evidently much less than their numbers, and probably to supply their needs as well as to weaken their enemies they began the ravaging of the country and those cruel barbarities quickly imitated by the other side, and by many barons who rejoiced in the dissolution of public authority—the plundering of the weak by all parties—from which England suffered so much during the war. The lands of the king and of his supporters were systematically laid waste. Cattle were driven off, movable property carried away, and men subjected to ingenious tortures to force them to give up the valuables they had concealed. Robert's son, Philip Gai, acquired the reputation of a skilful inventor of new cruelties. These plundering raids were carried to a distance from the city, and men of wealth were decoyed or kidnapped into Bristol and forced to give up their property. The one attempt of these marauders which was more of the nature of regular warfare, before the king's approach, illustrates their methods as well. Geoffrey Talbot led an attack on Bath, hoping to capture the city, but was himself taken and held a prisoner. On the news of this a plot was formed in Bristol for his release. A party was sent to Bath, who besought the bishop to come out and negotiate with them, promising under oath his safe return; but when he complied they seized him and threatened to hang him unless Geoffrey were released. To this the bishop, in terror of his life, at last agreed. Stephen shortly after came to Bath on his march against Bristol, and was with difficulty persuaded not to punish the bishop by depriving him of his office.

Stephen found a difficult task before him at Bristol. Its capture by assault was impracticable. A siege would have to be a blockade, and this it would be very hard to make effective because of the difficulty of cutting off the water communication. Stephen's failure to command the hearty and honest support of his own barons is also evident here as in almost every other important undertaking of his life. All sorts of conflicting advice were given him, some of it intentionally misleading we are told.[38] Finally he was persuaded that it would be better policy to give up the attempt on Bristol for the present, and to capture as many as possible of the smaller castles held by the rebels. In this he was fairly successful. He took Castle Gary and Harptree, and, after somewhat more prolonged resistance, Shrewsbury, which was held by William Fitz Alan, whose wife was Earl Robert's niece. In this last case Stephen departed from his usual practice and hanged the garrison and its commander. The effect of this severity was seen at once. Many surrenders and submissions took place, including, probably at this time, the important landing places of Dover and Wareham.

In the meantime, at almost exactly the date of the surrender of Shrewsbury, affairs in the north had turned even more decidedly in the king's favour. About the end of July, King David of Scotland, very likely as a part of the general plan of attack on Stephen, had crossed the borders into England, for the third time this year, with a large army gathered from all his dominions and even from beyond. Treason to Stephen, which had before been suspected, now in one case at least openly declared itself. Eustace Fitz John, brother of Payne Fitz John, and like him one of Henry I's new men who had been given important trusts in the north, but who had earlier in the year been deprived by Stephen of the custody of Bamborough Castle on suspicion, joined King David with his forces, and arranged to give up his other castles to him. David with his motley host came on through Northumberland and Durham, laying waste the land and attacking the strongholds in his usual manner. On their side the barons of the north gathered in York at the news of this invasion, the greatest danger of the summer, but found themselves almost in despair at the prospect. Stephen, occupied with the insurrection in the south, could give them no aid, and their own forces seemed unequal to the task. Again the aged Archbishop Thurstan came forward as the real leader in the crisis. He pictured the sacred duty of defence, and under his influence barons and common men alike were roused to a holy enthusiasm, and the war became a crusade. He promised the levies of the parishes under the parish priests, and was with difficulty dissuaded, though he was ill, from encouraging in person the warriors on the battlefield itself. A sacred banner was given them under which to fight—the standard from which this most famous battle of Stephen's reign gets its name—a mast erected on a wagon, carrying the banners of St. Peter of York, St. John of Beverly, and St. Wilfrid of Ripon, and with a pyx at the top containing the Host, that, "present in his body with them, Christ might be their leader in the battle." The army was full of priests and higher clergy, who moved through the ranks before the fighting began, stimulating the high religious spirit with which all were filled.

The list of the barons who gathered to resist this invasion contains an unusual number of names famous in the later history of England. The leader, from his age and experience and the general respect in which he was held, was Walter Espec; the highest in rank was William of Aumale. Others were Robert of Bruce, William of Percy, Ilbert of Lacy, Richard of Courcy, Robert of Stuteville, William Fossard, Walter of Ghent, and Roger of Mowbray, who was too young, men thought, to be in battle. Stephen had sent a small reinforcement under Bernard of Balliol, and Robert of Ferrers was there from Derbyshire, and William Peverel even, though his castles were at the time defying the king in the further south. As the armies were drawing near each other, Bruce and Balliol went together to remind the Scottish king of all that his family owed to the kings of England, and to persuade him to turn back, but they were hailed as traitors because they owed a partial allegiance to Scotland, and their mission came to nothing.

The battle was fought early in the day on August 22 near Northallerton. The English were drawn up in a dense mass round their standard, all on foot, with a line of the best-armed men on the outside, standing "shield to shield and shoulder to shoulder," locked together in a solid ring, and behind them the archers and parish levies. Against this "wedge" King David would have sent his men-at-arms, but the half-naked men of Galloway demanded their right to lead the attack. "No one of these in armour will go further to-day than I will," cried a chieftain of the highlands, and the king yielded. But their fierce attack was in vain against the "iron wall"; they only shattered themselves. David's son Henry made a gallant though badly executed attempt to turn the fortunes of the day, but this failed also, and the Scottish army was obliged to withdraw defeated to Carlisle. There was little pursuit, but the Scottish loss was heavy, and great spoil of baggage and armour abandoned in their hasty retreat was gathered by the English. David did not at once give up the war, but the capture of Wark and a few border forays of subordinates were of no influence on the result. The great danger of a Scottish conquest of the north or invasion of central England was for the present over.

In a general balance of the whole year we must say that the outcome was in favour of Stephen. The rebellion had not been entirely subdued. Bristol still remained a threatening source of future danger. Stephen himself had given the impression of restless but inefficient energy, of rushing about with great vigour from one place to another, to besiege one castle or another, but of accomplishing very little. As compared with the beginning of the year he was not so strong or so secure as he had been; yet still there was no serious falling off of power. There was nothing in the situation which threatened his fall, or which would hold out to his enemies any good hope of success. In Normandy the result of the year was but little less satisfactory. Geoffrey's invasion in June had been checked and driven back by Count Waleran and William of Ypres. In the autumn the attempt was renewed, and with no better result, though Argentan remained in Geoffrey's hands. The people of the duchy had suffered as much as those of England from private war and unlicensed pillage, but while such things indicated the weakness of authority they accomplished little towards its overthrow.

During this year, 1138, Stephen adopted a method of strengthening himself which was imitated by his rival and by later kings, and which had a most important influence on the social and constitutional history of England. We have noticed already his habit of lavish gifts. Now he began to include the title of earl among the things to be given away to secure fidelity. Down to this time the policy of William the Conqueror had been followed by his successors, and the title had been very sparingly granted. Stephen's first creation was the one already mentioned, that of Hugh "the Poor," of Beaumont, as Earl of Bedford, probably just at the end of 1137. In the midst of the insurrection of the south-west, Gilbert of Clare, husband of the sister of the three Beaumont earls, was made Earl of Pembroke. As a reward for their services in defeating King David at the battle of the standard, Robert of Ferrers was made Earl of Derby, and William of Aumale Earl of Yorkshire. Here were four creations in less than a year, only a trifle fewer than the whole number of earls in England in the last years of Henry I. In the end Stephen created nine earls. Matilda followed him with six others, and most of these new titles survived the period in the families on which they were conferred. It is from Stephen's action that we may date the entry of this title into English history as a mark of rank in the baronage, more and more freely bestowed, a title of honour to which a family of great possessions or influence might confidently aspire. But it must be remembered that the earldoms thus created are quite different from those of the Anglo-Saxon state or from the countships of France. They carried with them increase of social consideration and rank, usually some increase of wealth in grants from crown domains accompanying the creation, and very probably increased influence in state and local affairs, but they did not of themselves, without special grant, carry political functions or power, or any independence of position. They meant rank and title simply, not office.

Just at the close of the year the archbishopric of Canterbury was filled, after being a twelvemonth in the king's hands. During the vacancy the pope had sent the Bishop of Ostia as legate to England. He had been received without objection, had made a visitation of England, and at Carlisle had been received by the Scottish king as if that city were a part of his kingdom. The ambition of Henry of Winchester to become primate of Britain was disappointed. He had made sure of the succession, and seems actually to have exercised some metropolitan authority; perhaps he had even been elected to the see during the time when his brother's position was in danger. But now Stephen declared himself firmly against his preferment, and the necessary papal sanction for his translation from one see to another was not granted. Theobald, Abbot of Bec, was elected by a process which was in exact accordance with that afterwards described in the Constitutions of Clarendon, following probably the lines of the compromise between Henry and Anselm;[39] and he departed with the legate to receive his pallium, and to attend with other bishops from England the council which had been called by the pope. If Stephen's refusal to allow his brother's advancement had been a part of a systematic policy, carefully planned and firmly executed, of weakening and finally overthrowing the great ecclesiastics and barons of England who were so strong as to be dangerous to the crown, it would have been a wise act and a step towards final success. But an isolated case of the sort, or two or three, badly connected and not plainly parts of a progressive policy, could only be exasperating and in truth weakening to himself. We are told that Henry's anger inclined him to favour the Empress against his brother, and though it may not have been an actual moving cause, the incident was probably not forgotten when the question of supporting Matilda became a pressing one.

The year 1139, which was destined to see the king destroy by his own act all prospect of a secure and complete possession of the throne, opened and ran one-half its course with no change of importance in the situation. In April, Queen Matilda, who was in character and abilities better fitted to rule over England than her husband, succeeded in making peace with King David of Scotland, who stood in the same relation to her as to the other Matilda, the Empress, since she was the daughter of his sister Mary. The earldom of Northumberland was at last granted to Henry, except the two strong castles of Newcastle and Barnborough, and under certain restrictions, and the Scots gave hostages for the keeping of the peace. At the same date, in the great Lateran council at Rome, to which the English bishops had gone with the legate, the pope seems to have put his earlier decision in favour of Stephen into formal and public shape. In Stephen's mind this favour of the pope's was very likely balanced by another act of his which had just preceded it, by which Henry of Winchester had been created papal legate in England. By this appointment he was given supreme power over the English Church, and gained nearly all that he had hoped to get by becoming Archbishop of Canterbury. Personally Stephen was occupied during the early months of the year, as he had been the year before, in attacking the castles which were held against him; but in the most important case, the siege of Ludlow castle, he met with no success.

At the end of June the great council of the kingdom came together at Oxford, and there it was that Stephen committed the fatal mistake which turned the tide of affairs against him. Of all the men who had been raised to power in the service of Henry I, none occupied so commanding a position as Roger, Bishop of Salisbury. As a priest he had attracted the attention of Henry before he became king by the quickness with which he got through the morning mass; he was taken into his service, and steadily rose higher and higher until he became the head of the whole administrative system, standing next to the king when he was in England, and exercising the royal authority, as justiciar, when he was absent. In his rise he had carried his family with him. His nephew Alexander was Bishop of Lincoln. Another nephew Nigel was Bishop of Ely. His son Roger was chancellor of the kingdom. The administrative and financial system was still in the hands of the family. The opportunities which they had enjoyed for so many years to enrich themselves from the public revenues, very likely as a tacitly recognized part of the payment of their services, they had not neglected. But they had gone further than this. Evidently with some ulterior object in view, but with precisely what we can only guess, they had been strengthening royal castles in their hands, and even building new ones. That bishops should fortify castles of their own, like barons, was not in accordance with the theory of the Church, nor was it in accordance with the custom in England and Normandy. The example had been followed apparently by Henry of Winchester, who had under his control half a dozen strongholds. The situation would in itself, and in any circumstances, be a dangerous one. In the present circumstances the suspicion would be natural that a family which owed so much to King Henry was secretly preparing to aid his daughter in an attempt to gain the throne, and this suspicion was generally held by the king's party. To this may be added the fact that, in the blow which he now struck, we very possibly have an attempt on Stephen's part to carry further the policy of weakening, in the interest of the crown, the too strong ecclesiastical and baronial element in the state, which he had begun in refusing the archbishopric of Canterbury to his brother. The wealth of the family may have been an additional incentive, and intrigues against these bishops by the powerful house of Beaumont are mentioned. There is no reason to suppose, however, that the Beaumonts were not acting, as they had so often done, in the real interests of the king, which plainly demanded the breaking up of this threatening power. There was nothing to indicate that the present was not a favourable time to undertake it, and the best accounts of these events give us the impression that Stephen was acting throughout with much confidence and a feeling of strength and security.

Whatever may have been his motive, Stephen's first move at the beginning of the Oxford meeting was the extreme one of ordering the arrest of bishops Roger and Alexander. The pretext for this was a street brawl between some of their men and followers of the Beaumonts, and their subsequent refusal to surrender to the king the keys of their castles. A step of this kind would need clear reasons to justify it and much real strength to make it in the end successful. Taken on what looked like a mere pretext arranged for the purpose, it was certain to excite the alarm and opposition of the Church. Stephen himself hesitated, as perhaps he would have in any circumstances. The historian most in sympathy with his cause expresses his disapproval.[40] The familiar point was urged that the bishops were arrested, not as bishops, but as the king's ministers; and this would have been sufficient under a king like the first two Williams. But the arrest was not all. The bishops were treated with much indignity, and were compelled to deliver up their castles by fear of something worse. In Roger's splendid castle of Devizes were his nephew, the Bishop of Ely, who had escaped arrest at Oxford, and Maud of Ramsbury, the mother of his son Roger the Chancellor. William of Ypres forced its surrender by making ready to hang the younger Roger before the walls, and Newark castle was driven to yield by threatening to starve Bishop Alexander.

The indignation of the clergy is expressed by every writer of the time. It was probably especially bitter because Stephen was so deeply indebted to them for his success and had recently made them such extensive promises. Henry of Winchester, who may have had personal reasons for alarm, was not disposed to play the part of Lanfranc and defend the king for arresting bishops. He evidently believed that the king was not strong enough to carry through his purpose, and that the Church was in a position to force the issue upon him. Acting for the first time under his commission as legate which he had received in the spring of the year, he called a council to meet at Winchester, and summoned his brother to answer before it for his conduct. The council met on August 30. The Church was well represented. The legate's commission was read, and he then opened the subject in a Latin speech in which he denounced his brother's acts. The king was represented by Aubrey de Vere and the Archbishop of Rouen, the baron defending the king's action point by point, and the ecclesiastic denying the right of the bishops to hold castles, and maintaining the right of the king to call for them. The attempt of Henry did not succeed. His demand that the castles should be given back to the bishops until the question should be settled was refused, and the bishops were threatened with exile if they carried the case to Rome. The council ended without taking any action against the king. Some general decrees were adopted against those who laid hands on the clergy or seized their goods, but it was also declared, if we are right in attributing the action to this body, that the castles of the kingdom belonged to the king and to his barons to hold, and that the duties of the clergy lay in another direction. Stephen retained the bishops' castles and the treasures which he had found in them; and when Bishop Roger died, three months later, his personal property was seized into the king's hands.

While these events were going on, the Empress and her brother had decided that the time was favourable for a descent on England. In advance of their coming, Baldwin of Redvers landed with some force at Wareham and intrenched himself in Corfe castle against the king. Matilda and Robert landed at Arundel on the last day of September with only one hundred and forty men. Stephen had abandoned the siege of Corfe castle on the news that they were about to cross, and had taken measures to prevent their landing; but he had again turned away to something else, and their landing was unopposed. Arundel castle was in possession of Adelaide, the widowed queen of Henry I, now the wife of William of Albini. It is not possible to suppose that this place was selected for the invasion without a previous understanding; and there, in the keeping of her stepmother, Robert left his sister and set out immediately on his landing for Bristol, taking with him only twelve men. On hearing of this Stephen pursued, but failed to overtake him, and turned back to besiege Arundel castle. Then occurred one of the most astonishing events of Stephen's career — astonishing alike to his contemporaries and to us, but typical in a peculiar degree of the man.

Queen Adelaide became alarmed on the approach of Stephen, and began to take thought of what she had to lose if the king should prove successful, as there was every reason to suppose he would; and she proposed to abandon Matilda's cause and to hand her over at once to Stephen. Here was an opportunity to gain a most decided advantage — perhaps to end the whole strife. With Matilda in his hands, Stephen would have been master of the situation. He could have sent her back to Normandy and so have ended the attempt at invasion. He could have kept her in royal captivity, or have demanded the surrender of her claims as the price of her release. Instead of seizing the occasion, as a Henry or a William would certainly have done, he was filled with chivalrous pity for his cousin's strait, and sent her with an escort under Henry of Winchester and Waleran of Meulan to join her brother at Bristol. The writers of the time explain his conduct by his own chivalrous spirit, and by the treasonable persuasions of his brother Henry, who, we may believe, had now reasons for disloyalty. The chivalrous ideals of the age certainly had great power over Stephen, as they would have over any one with his popular traits of mind and manners; and his strange throwing away of this advantage was undoubtedly due to this fact, together with the readiness with which he yielded to the persuasions of a stronger spirit. The judgment of Orderic Vitalis, who was still writing in Normandy, is the final judgment of history on the act: "Surely in this permission is to be seen the great simplicity of the king or his great stupidity, and he is to be pitied by all prudent men because he was unmindful of his own safety and of the security of his kingdom."

This was the turning-point in Stephen's history. Within the brief space of two months, by two acts surprisingly ill-judged and even of folly, he had turned a position of great strength, which might easily have been made permanently secure, into one of great weakness; and so long as the struggle lasted he was never able to recover what he had lost. By his treatment of the bishops he had turned against himself the party in the state whose support had once been indispensable, and whose power to injure him he was soon to feel. By allowing Matilda and her brother to enter Bristol, he had given to all the diverse elements of opposition in England the only thing they still needed; a natural leadership, and from an impregnable position. Either of these mistakes alone might not have been fatal. Their coming together as they did made then irretrievable blunders.

No sudden falling off of strength marks the beginning of Stephen's decline. Two barons of the west who had been very closely connected with Henry I and with Robert, but who had both accepted Stephen, declared now for Matilda, Brian Fitz Count of Wallingford, and Miles of Gloucester. Other minor accessions in the neighbourhood seem to have followed. About the middle of October the Empress went on to Gloucester, where her followers terrorized city and country as they had at Bristol. Stephen conducted his counter-campaign in his usual manner, attacking place after place without waiting to finish any enterprise. The recovery of Malmesbury castle, which he had lost in October, was his only success, and this was won by persuasion rather than by arms. Hereford and Worcester suffered severely from attacks of Matilda's forces, and Hereford was captured. The occupation of Gloucester and Hereford was the most important success of the Empress's party, and with Bristol they mark the boundaries of the territory she may be said to have gained, with some outlying points like Wallingford, which the king had not been able to recover. On December 11, Bishop Roger of Salisbury died, probably never having recovered from the blow struck by Stephen in August. He had occupied a great place in the history of England, but it had been in political and constitutional, not in religious history. It may very likely have seemed to him, in the last three months of his life, that the work to which he had given himself, in the organization of the administrative and financial machinery of the government, was about to be destroyed in the ruin of his family and the anarchy of civil war; but such forebodings, if he felt them, did not prove entirely true.

The year 1140 is one of the most dreary in the slow and wearing conflict which had now begun. No event of special interest tempts us to linger upon details. The year opens with a successful attack by the king on Nigel, Bishop of Ely, who had escaped at the time of his uncle's arrest, and who was now preparing for revolt in his bishopric. Again the bishop himself escaped, and joined Matilda's party, but Stephen took possession of the Isle of Ely. An effort to add Cornwall to the revolted districts was equally unsuccessful. Reginald of Dunstanville, a natural son of Henry I, appeared there in the interest of his sister, who, imitating the methods of Stephen, created him, at this time or a little later, Earl of Cornwall; but his rule was unwise, and Stephen advancing in person had no difficulty in recovering the country. The character which the war was rapidly assuming is shown by the attempt of Robert Fitz Hubert, a Flemish mercenary, to hold the strong castle of Devizes, which he had seized by surprise, in his own interest and in despite of both parties. He fell a victim to his own methods employed against himself, and was hanged by Robert of Gloucester. In the spring a decided difference of opinion arose between the king and his brother Henry about the appointment of a successor to Roger of Salisbury, which ended in the rejection of both their candidates and a long vacancy in the bishopric. Henry of Winchester was, however, not yet ready openly to abandon the cause of his brother, and he busied himself later in the year with efforts to bring about an understanding between the opposing parties, which proved unavailing. A meeting of representatives of both sides near Bath led to no result, and a journey of Henry's to France, perhaps to bring the influence of his brother Theobald and of the king of France to bear in favour of peace, was also fruitless. During the summer Stephen gained an advantage in securing the hand of Constance, the sister of Louis VII of France, for his son Eustace, it was believed at the time by a liberal use of the treasures of Bishop Roger.

At Whitsuntide and again in August the restlessness of Hugh Bigod in East Anglia had forced Stephen to march against him. Perhaps he felt that he had not received a large enough reward for the doubtful oath which he had sworn to secure the king his crown. Stephen at any rate was now in a situation where he could not withhold rewards, or even refuse demands in critical cases; and it was probably at this time, certainly not long after, that, following the policy he had now definitely adopted, he created Hugh Earl of Norfolk. A still more important and typical case, which probably occurred in the same year, is that of Geoffrey de Mandeville. Grandson of a baron of the Conquest, he was in succession to his father, constable of the Tower in London, and so held a position of great strategic importance in turbulent times. Early in the strife for the crown he seems to have seen very clearly the opportunity for self-aggrandizement which was offered by the uncertainty of Stephen's power, and to have resolved to make the most of it for his own gain without scruple of conscience. His demand was for the earldom of Essex, and this was granted him by the king. Apparently about the same time occurred a third case of the sort which completes the evidence that the weakness of Stephen's character was generally recognized, and that in the resulting attitude of many of the greater barons we have the key to his reign. One of the virtually independent feudal principalities created in England by the Conqueror and surviving to this time was the palatine earldom of Chester. The then earl was Ralph II, in succession to his father Ralph Meschin, who had succeeded on the death of Earl Richard in the sinking of the White Ship. It had been a grievance of the first Ralph that he had been obliged by King Henry to give up his lordship of Carlisle on taking the earldom, and this grievance had been made more bitter for the second Ralph when the lordship had been transferred to the Scots. There was trouble also about the inheritance of his mother Lucy, in Lincolnshire, in which another son of hers, Ralph's half-brother, William of Roumare, was interested. We infer that toward the end of the year 1140 their attitude seemed threatening to the king, for he seems to have visited them and purchased their adherence with large gifts, granting to William the earldom of Lincoln.

Then follows rapidly the series of events which led to the crisis of the war. The brothers evidently were not yet satisfied. Stephen had retained in his hands the castle of Lincoln and this Ralph and William seized by a stratagem. Stephen, informed of what had happened by a messenger from the citizens, acted with his characteristic energy at the beginning of any enterprise, broke up his Christmas court at London, and suddenly, to the great surprise of the earls, appeared in Lincoln with a besieging army. Ralph managed to escape to raise in Chester a relieving army, and at once took a step which becomes from this time not infrequent among the barons of his stamp. He applied for help to Robert of Gloucester, whose son-in-law he was, and offered to go over to Matilda with all that he held. He was received, of course, with a warm welcome. Robert recognized the opportunity which the circumstances probably offered to strike a decisive blow, and, gathering the strongest force he could, he advanced from Gloucester against the king. On the way he was joined by the Earl of Chester, whose forces included many Welsh ready to fight in an English quarrel but badly armed. The attacking army skirted Lincoln and appeared on the high road leading to it from the north, where was the best prospect of forcing an entrance to the city.

The approach of the enemy led, as usual in Stephen's armies, to divided counsels. Some were in favour of retreating and collecting a larger army, others of fighting at once. To fight at once would be Stephen's natural inclination, and he determined to risk a battle, which he must have known would have decisive consequences. His army he drew up in three bodies across the way of approach. Six earls were with the king, reckoning the Count of Meulan, but they had not brought strong forces and there were few horsemen. Five of these earls formed the first line. The second was under William of Ypres and William of Aumale, and was probably made up of the king's foreign troops. Stephen himself, with a strong band of men all on foot, was posted in the rear. The enemy's formation was similar. The Earl of Chester claimed the right to lead the attack, because the quarrel was his, but the men upon whom Robert most depended were the "disinherited," of whom he had collected many,—men raised up by Matilda's father and cast down by Stephen, and now ready to stake all on the hope of revenge and of restoration; and these he placed in the first line. Earl Ralph led the second, and himself the third. The battle was soon over, except the struggle round the king. His first and second lines were quickly swept away by the determined charge of Robert's men and took to flight, but Stephen and his men beat off several attacks before he was finally overpowered and forced to yield. He surrendered to Robert of Gloucester. Many minor barons were taken prisoners with him, but the six earls all escaped. The citizens of Lincoln were punished for their adhesion to the king's side by a sacking of the city, in which many of them were slain. Stephen was taken to Gloucester by Robert, and then sent to imprisonment in the castle of Bristol, the most secure place which Matilda possessed.

[38] Gesta Stephani, 42.

[39] Gervase of Canterbury, i. 109. But see Ralph de Diceto, i. 252, n. 2, and Böhmer, Kirche und Staat, 375.

[40] Gesta Stephani, 47.

CHAPTER XI.
THE LAST STAGE OF THE CIVIL WAR

The victory at Lincoln changed the situation of affairs at a blow. From holding a little oval of territory about the mouth of the Severn as the utmost she had gained, with small immediate prospect of enlarging it, Matilda found the way to the throne directly open before her with no obstacle in sight not easily overcome. She set out at once for Winchester. On his side, Bishop Henry was in no mood to stake his position and influence on the cause of his brother. Stephen's attitude towards him and towards the Church had smoothed the way for Matilda at the point where she might expect the first and most serious check. The negotiations were not difficult, but the result shows as clearly as in the case of Stephen the disadvantage of the crown at such a crisis, and the opportunity offered to the vassal, whether baron or bishop, who held a position of independent strength and was determined to use it in his own interests. The arrangement was called at the time a pactus—a treaty. The Empress took oath to the bishop that all the more important business of England, especially the filling of bishoprics and abbacies, should be done according to his desire, and her oath was supported by those of her brother and of the leading barons with her. The bishop in turn received her as "Lady of England," and swore fealty to her as long as she should keep this pact. The next day, March 3, she entered the city, took possession of the small sum of money which had been left in the treasury by Stephen and of the royal crown which was there, entered the cathedral in solemn procession, supported by Henry and the Bishop of St. David's, with four other bishops and several abbots present, and had herself proclaimed at once "lady and queen of England," whatever the double title may mean. Certainly she intended to be and believed herself nothing less than reigning queen.[41] Without waiting for any ceremony of coronation, she appointed a bishop, created earls, and spoke in a formal document of her kingdom and her crown.

Directly after these events Henry of Winchester had summoned a council, to learn, very likely to guide, the decision of the Church as to a change of allegiance. The council met in Winchester on April 7. On that day the legate met separately, in secret session, the different orders of the clergy, and apparently obtained from them the decision which he wished. The next day in a speech to the council, he recited the misgovernment of his brother, who, he declared, had, almost immediately after his accession to power, destroyed the peace of the kingdom; and without any allusion to his deposition, except to the battle of Lincoln as a judgment of God, and with no formal action of the council as a whole, he announced the choice of the Church in favour of Matilda. The day following, a request of the Londoners and of the barons who had joined them for the release of Stephen, and one of his queen's to the same effect, was refused. The Empress was not present at the council. She spent Easter at Oxford, receiving reports, no doubt, of the constant successes her party was now gaining in different parts of England. It was not, however, till the middle of June that London, naturally devoted to Stephen, was ready to receive her.

Her reception in London marks the height of her success. She bought the support of the powerful Geoffrey de Mandeville by confirming to him the price which he had extorted from Stephen, the earldom of Essex, and by bidding higher than her rival with gifts of lands, revenues, and privileges which started him on the road to independence of the crown, which he well knew how to follow. Preparations were no doubt at once begun for her coronation. Her uncle King David came down from Scotland to lend it dignity, but it was destined never to occur. Her fall was as rapid as her rise, and was due, even more clearly than Stephen's, to her own inability to rule. The violent and tyrannical blood of her uncle, William Rufus, showed itself in her as plainly as the irresolute blood of Robert Curthose in her cousin, but she did not wait to gain her uncle's security of position to make violence and tyranny possible. Already, before she came up to London, she had offended her followers by the arrogance and harshness of her conduct. Now these traits of character proved fatal to her cause. She greatly offended the legate, to whom she was as deeply indebted as Stephen had been, and whose power to injure her she might easily understand, by refusing to promise that Eustace might hold his father's continental counties of Boulogne and Mortain. Equally unwise was her attitude towards London. She demanded a large subsidy. The request of the citizens for a confirmation of the laws of King Edward, because her father's were too heavy for them, she sternly refused. Queen Matilda, "acting the part of a man," advanced with her forces to the neighbourhood of the city and brought home to the burghers the evils of civil war. They were easily moved. A sudden uprising of the city forced the Empress to "ignominious" flight, leaving her baggage behind. She retreated to Oxford, and Matilda the queen entered the recovered city. Geoffrey de Mandeville at once brought his allegiance to the new market and obtained, it is probable, another advance of price and Henry of

Winchester was easily persuaded to return to his brother's side. "Behold," says the historian of the Empress's party, "while she was thinking that she could immediately possess all England, everything changed." He adds that the change was her own fault, and in this he was right.[42]

But Matilda was not ready to accept calmly so decided a reverse, nor to allow Winchester to remain in undisturbed possession of her enemies, and her brother Robert was not. They had been driven from London on June 24. At the end of July, with a strong force, they attacked the older capital city, took possession of a part of it, forced the bishop to flee, and began the siege of his castle. At once the leaders of Stephen's cause, encouraged by recent events, gathered against them. While the Empress besieged the bishop's men from within, she was herself besieged from without by superior forces. At last the danger of being cut off from all supplies forced her to retreat, and in the retreat Robert of Gloucester, protecting his sister's flight, was himself captured. This was a great stroke of fortune, because it balanced for practical purposes the capture of Stephen at the battle of Lincoln, and it at once suggested an even exchange. Negotiations were not altogether easy. Robert modestly insisted that he was not equal to a king, but the arrangement was too obvious to admit of failure, and the exchange was effected at the beginning of November.

Since the middle of June the course of affairs had turned rapidly in favour of the king, but he was still far from having recovered the position of strength which he occupied before the landing of Matilda. Oxford was still in her hands, and so was a large part of the west of England. The Earl of Chester was still on her side, though he had signified his willingness to change sides if he were properly received. Stephen had yet before him a hard task in recovering his kingdom, and he never accomplished it. The war dragged on its slow length for more than ten years. Its dramatic period, however, was now ended. Only the story of Matilda's flight from Oxford enlivens the later narrative. Siege and skirmish, treason and counter-treason, fill up the passing months, but bring the end no nearer, until the entry of the young Henry on the scene lends a new element of interest and decision to the dull movement of events.

At first after his release Stephen carried on the work of restoration rapidly and without interruption. London received him with joy. At Christmas time he wore his crown at Canterbury; he was probably, indeed, re-crowned by the archbishop, to make good any defect which his imprisonment might imply. Already, on December 7, a new council, assembling in Westminster, had reversed the decisions of the council of Winchester, and, supported by a new declaration of the pope in a letter to the legate, had restored the allegiance of the Church to Stephen. At the Christmas assembly Geoffrey de

Mandeville secured from the king the reward of his latest shift of sides, in a new charter which increased a power already dangerous and made him an almost independent prince. In the creation of two new earls a short time before, William of Albini as Earl of Sussex or Arundel, and Gilbert of Clare as Earl of Hertford, Stephen sought to confirm a doubtful, and to reward a steady, support. No event of importance marks the opening months of 1142. Lent was spent in a royal progress through eastern England, where as yet the Empress had obtained no footing, to York. On the way, at Stamford, he seems to have recovered the allegiance of the Earl of Chester and of his brother, the Earl of Lincoln, a sure sign of the change which had taken place since the battle in which they had overcome him so disastrously a year before.

In the summer Stephen again assumed the offensive and pushed the attack on his enemies with energy and skill. After a series of minor successes he advanced against the Empress herself at Oxford, where she had made her headquarters since the loss of London. Her brother Robert, who was the real head of her party, was now in Normandy, whither he had gone to persuade Geoffrey to lend the support of his personal presence to his wife's cause in England, but he had made sure, as he believed, of his sister's safety before going. The fortifications of Oxford had been strengthened. The barons had pledged themselves to guard Matilda, and hostages had been exacted from some as a check on the fashion of free desertion. It seems to have been felt, however, that Stephen would not venture to attack Oxford, and there had been no special concentration of strength in the city; so that when he suddenly appeared on the south, having advanced down the river from the west, he was easily able to disperse the burghers who attempted to dispute his passage of the river, and to enter one of the gates with them in their flight. The town was sacked, and the king then sat down to a siege of the castle. The siege became a blockade, which lasted from the end of September to near Christmas time, though it was pushed with all the artillery of the age, and a blockade in which the castle was carefully watched day and night. Stephen seems to have changed his mind since the time when he had besieged Matilda in Arundel castle, and to have been now determined to take his rival prisoner. The barons who had promised to protect the Empress gathered at Wallingford, but did not venture to attempt a direct raising of the siege. Robert of Gloucester returned from Normandy about December 1, but Stephen allowed him to win a small success or two, and kept steadily to his purpose.

As it drew near to Christmas provisions became low in the castle, and the necessity of surrender unpleasantly clear. Finally Matilda determined to attempt a bold escape. It was a severe winter and the ground was entirely covered with snow. With only a few attendants—three and five are both mentioned—she was let down with ropes from a tower, and, clad all in white, stole through the lines of the besiegers, detected only by a sentry, who raised no alarm. With determined spirit and endurance she fled on foot through the winter night and over difficult ways to Abingdon, six miles away. There she obtained horses and rode on to Wallingford, where she was safe. The castle of Oxford immediately surrendered to Stephen, but the great advantage for which he had striven had escaped him when almost in his hands. Robert of Gloucester, who was preparing to attempt the raising of the siege, at once joined his sister at Wallingford, and brought with him her son, the future Henry II, sent over in place of his father, on his first visit to England. Henry was now in his tenth year, and for four years and more he remained in England in the inaccessible stronghold of Bristol, studying with a tutor under the guardianship of his uncle. Robert's mission of the previous summer, to get help for Matilda in England, proved more useful to Geoffrey than to his wife. During a rapid campaign the conquest of the duchy had at last been really begun, and in the two following years it was carried to a successful conclusion. On January 20, 1144, the city of Rouen surrendered to the Count of Anjou, though the castle held out for some time longer. Even Waleran of Meulan recognized the new situation of affairs, and gave his aid to the cause of Anjou, and before the close of the year Louis VII formally invested Geoffrey with the duchy. This much of the plan of Henry I was now realized; Stephen never recovered possession of Normandy. But without England, it was realized in a way which destroyed the plan itself, and England was still far from any union with the Angevin dominions.

By the time the conquest of Normandy was completed, events of equal interest had taken place in England, involving the fall of the powerful and shifty Earl of Essex, Geoffrey de Mandeville. Soon after Easter, 1142, he had found an opportunity for another prudent and profitable change of sides. The king had fallen ill on his return from the north, and, once more, as at the beginning of his reign, the report of his death was spread abroad. Geoffrey seems to have hurried at once to the Empress, as a probable source of future favours, and to have carried with him a small crowd of his friends and relatives, including the equally unscrupulous Hugh Bigod, Earl of Norfolk. Matilda, who was then at Oxford, and had no prospect of any immediate advance, was again ready to give him all he asked. Her fortunes were at too low an ebb to warrant her counting the cost, and in any case what she was buying was of great value if she could make sure that the sellers would keep faith. Geoffrey, with his friends, and Nigel, Bishop of Ely, who was already on her side, controlling Essex, Hertford, Norfolk, Suffolk, and Cambridge, could give her possession of as large a territory on the east of England as she now held on the west, and this would very likely carry with it the occupation of London once more, and would threaten to cut the kingdom of Stephen into two detached fragments. Geoffrey was in a position to drive a good bargain, and he did so. New lands and revenues, new rights and privileges, were added to those he had already extorted from both sides; the Empress promised to make no peace without his consent with his "mortal enemies," the burghers of London, towards whom she probably had herself just then no great love. Geoffrey's friends were admitted to share with him in the results of his careful study of the conditions of the market, especially his brother-in-law, Aubrey de Vere, who was made Earl by his own choice of Cambridge, but in the end of Oxford, probably because Matilda's cousin, Henry of Scotland, considered that Cambridge was included in his earldom of Huntingdon. What price was offered to Hugh Bigod, or to Gilbert Clare, Earl of Pembroke, who seems to have been of the number, we do not know.

As a matter of fact, neither Geoffrey nor the Empress gained anything from this bargaining. Stephen was not dead, and his vigorous campaign of the summer of 1142 evidently made it seem prudent to Geoffrey to hold his intended treason in reserve for a more promising opportunity. It is probable that Stephen soon learned the facts, before very long they became common talk, but he awaited on his side a better opportunity to strike. The earl had grown too powerful to be dealt with without considering ways and means. Contemporary writers call him the most powerful man in England, and they regard his abilities with as much respect as his possessions and power. Stephen took his opportunity in the autumn of 1143, at a court held at St. Albans. The time was not wisely chosen. Things had not been going well with him during the summer. At Wilton he had been badly defeated by the Earl of Gloucester, and nearly half of England was in Matilda's possession or independent of his own control. But he yielded to the pressure of Geoffrey's enemies at the court, and ordered and secured his arrest on a charge of treason. The stroke succeeded no better than such measures usually did with Stephen, for he was always satisfied with a partial success. A threat of hanging forced the earl to surrender his castles, including the Tower of London, and then he was released. Geoffrey was not the man to submit to such a sudden overthrow without a trial of strength. With some of his friends he instantly appealed to arms, took possession of the Isle of Ely, where he was sure of a friendly reception, seized Ramsey Abbey, and turning out the monks made a fortress of it, and kept his forces in supplies by cruelly ravaging the surrounding lands.

It has been thought that the famous picture of the sufferings of the people of England during the anarchy of Stephen's reign, which was written in the neighbouring city of Peterborough, where the last of the English Chronicles was now drawing to its close, gained its vividness from the writer's personal knowledge of the horrors of this time; and this is probable, though he speaks in general terms. His pitiful account runs thus in part: "Every powerful man made his castles and held them against him [the king]; and they filled the land full of castles. They cruelly oppressed the wretched men of the land with castle-works. When the castles were made, they filled them with devils and evil men. Then took they those men that they thought had any property ... and put them in prison for their gold and silver, and tortured them with unutterable torture; for never were martyrs so tortured as they were. They hanged them up by the feet and smoked them with foul smoke; they hanged them by the thumbs or by the head and hung armour on their feet; they put knotted strings about their heads and writhed them so that they went into the brain. They put them in dungeons in which were adders, and snakes, and toads, and killed them so.... Then was corn dear, and flesh, and cheese, and butter; for there was none in the land. Wretched men died of hunger; some went seeking alms who at one while were rich men; some fled out of the land. Never yet had more wretchedness been in the land, nor ever did heathen men do worse than they did; for oftentimes they forbore neither church nor churchyard, but took all the property that was therein and then burned the church and all together.... However a man tilled, the earth bare no corn; for the land was all fordone by such deeds; and they said openly that Christ and his saints slept."

Geoffrey de Mandeville's career of plundering and sacrilege was not destined to continue long. Towards the end of the summer of 1144, he was wounded in the head by an arrow, in an attack on a fortified post which the king had established at Burwell to hold his raids in check; and soon after he died. His body was carried to the house of the Templars in London, but for twenty years it could not be received into consecrated ground, for he had died with his crimes unpardoned and under the ban of the Church, which was only removed after these years by the efforts of his younger son, a new Earl of Essex. To the great power for which Geoffrey was playing, to his independent principality, or to his possibly even higher ambition of controlling the destinies of the crown of England, there was no successor. His eldest son, Ernulf, shared his father's fall and condemnation, and was disinherited, though from him there descended a family holding for some generations a minor position in Oxfordshire. Twelve years after the death of Geoffrey, his second son—also Geoffrey—was made Earl of Essex by Henry II, and his faithful service to the king, and his brother's after him, were rewarded by increasing possessions and influence that almost rivalled their father's; but the wilder designs and unscrupulous methods of the first Earl of Essex perished with him.

The years 1144 and 1145 were on the whole prosperous for Stephen. A number of minor successes and minor accessions from the enemy made up a general drift in his favour. Even the Earl of Gloucester's son Philip, with a selfishness typical of the time, turned against his father; but the most important desertion to the king was that of the Earl of Chester, who joined him in 1146 and made a display of zeal, real or pretended, in his service. Starting with greater power and a more independent position than Geoffrey de Mandeville, and perhaps less openly bartering his allegiance to one side and the other at a constantly rising price, he had still pursued the same policy and with even greater success. His design was hardly less than the carving out of a state for himself from western and northern England, and during much of this disjointed time he seems to have carried himself with no regard to either side. To go over to the king so soon after the fall of the Earl of Essex was, it is likely, to take some risk, and as in the former case there was a party at the court which influenced Stephen against him. His refusal, notwithstanding his zeal, to restore castles and lands belonging to the king, and his attempt to induce Stephen to aid him against the Welsh, which was considered a plot to get possession of the king's person, led to his arrest. Again Stephen followed his habitual policy of forcing the surrender of his prisoner's castles, or certain of them, and then releasing him; and again the usual result followed, the instant insurrection of the earl. His real power had hardly been lessened by giving up the king's castles,—to which he had been forced,—and it was not easy to attack him. On a later visit of the young Henry to England, he obtained from him, and even from the king of Scotland, to whom he had long been hostile, large additions to his coveted principality in the west and north; but Stephen at once bid higher, and for a grant including the same possessions and more he abandoned his new allies. On Henry's final visit, in 1153, when the tide was fairly turning in his favour, another well-timed treason secured the earl his winnings and great promises for the future; but in this same year he died, poisoned, as it was believed, by one whose lands he had obtained. Out of the breaking up of England and the helplessness of her rulers arose no independent feudalism. Higher titles and wider lands many barons did gain, but the power of the king emerged in the end still supreme, and the worst of the permanent evils of the feudal system, a divided state, though deliberately sought and dangerously near, was at last averted.

With the death of Pope Innocent II, in September, 1143, a new period opened in the relation of the English Church and of the English king towards the papacy. Innocent had been on the whole favourable to Stephen's cause. His successor, Celestine II, was as favourable to Anjou, but his papacy was so short that nothing was done except to withhold a renewal of Henry of

Winchester's commission as legate. Lucius II, who succeeded in March, 1144, sent his own legate to England; but he was not a partisan of either side, and seems even—perhaps by way of compensation—to have taken steps towards creating an independent archbishopric in the south-west in Henry's favour. His papacy again lasted less than a year, and his successor, Eugenius III, whose reign lasted almost to the end of Stephen's, was decidedly unfriendly. Henry of Winchester was for a time suspended; and the king's candidate for the archbishopric of York, William Fitz Herbert, afterwards St. William of York,—whose position had long been in doubt, for though he had been consecrated he had not received his pallium,—was deposed, and in his place the Cistercian Abbot of Fountains, Henry Murdac, was consecrated by the Cistercian pope. This was the beginning of open conflict. Henry Murdac could not get possession of his see, and Archbishop Theobald was refused permission to attend a council summoned by the pope at Reims for March, 1148. He went secretly, crossing the channel in a fishing boat, and was enthusiastically received by the pope. The Bishop of Winchester was again suspended, and other bishops with him; several abbots were deposed; and Gilbert Foliot, a decided partisan of Matilda's, was designated Bishop of Hereford. The pope was with difficulty persuaded to postpone the excommunication of Stephen himself, and steps were actually taken to reopen before the Roman court the question of his right to the throne. Stephen, on his side, responded with promptness and vigour. He refused to acknowledge the right of the pope to reopen the main question. The primate was banished and his temporalities confiscated. Most of the English clergy were kept on the king's side, and in some way—there is some evidence that the influence of Queen Matilda was employed—the serious danger which threatened Stephen from the Church in the spring of 1148 was averted. Peace was made in November with Archbishop Theobald, who had ineffectually tried an interdict, and he was restored to his see and revenues. The practical advantage, on the whole, remained with the king; but in the course of these events a young man, Thomas Becket, in the service of the archbishop, acquired a training in ideas and in methods which was to serve him well in a greater struggle with a greater king.

In the spring of the next year, young Henry of Anjou made an attempt on England, and found his enemies still too strong for him. In the interval since his first visit, Robert of Gloucester, the wisest of the leaders of the Angevin cause, had died in his fortress of Bristol in 1174; and in February of 1148, Matilda herself had given up her long and now apparently hopeless struggle in England, and gone back to the home of her husband, though she seems to have encouraged her son in his new enterprise by her presence in England at least for a time.[43] The older generation was disappearing from the field; the younger was preparing to go on with the conflict. In 1149 Henry was sixteen years old, a mature age in that time, and it might well have been thought that it was wise to put him forward as leader in his own cause. The plan for this year seems to have been an attack on Stephen from the north by the king of Scotland in alliance with the Earl of Chester, and Henry passed rapidly through western England to Carlisle, where he was knighted by King David. Their army, which advanced to attack Lancaster, accomplished nothing, because, as has been related, the allegiance of Ralph of Chester, on whom they depended, had been bought back by Stephen; and Stephen himself, waiting with his army at York, found that he had nothing to do. The Scottish force withdrew, and Henry, again disappointed, was obliged to return to Normandy.

Three years later the young Henry made another and finally successful attempt to win his grandfather's throne, but in the interval great changes had occurred. Of these one fell in the year next following, 1150. Soon after Henry's return from England, his father had handed over to him the only portion of his mother's inheritance which had yet been recovered, the duchy of Normandy, and retired himself to his hereditary dominions. Geoffrey had never shown, so far as we know, any interest in his wife's campaigns in England, and had confined his attention to Normandy, in which one who was still primarily a count of Anjou would naturally have the most concern; and of all the efforts of the family this was the only one which was successful. Now while still a young man, with rare disregard of self, he gave up his conquest to his son, who had been brought up to consider himself as belonging rather to England than to Anjou. On the other side of the channel, during this year 1150, Stephen seems to have decided upon a plan which he bent every effort in the following years to carry out, but unsuccessfully,—the plan of securing a formal recognition of his son Eustace as his successor in the throne, or even as king with him. At least this is the natural explanation of the reconciliation which took place near the close of the year, between Eustace and his father on one side and Henry Murdac on the other, by which the archbishop was at last admitted to his see of York, and then set off immediately for Rome to persuade the pope to recognize Eustace, and even to consecrate the young man in person.

In England the practice of crowning the son king in the father's lifetime had never been followed, as it had been in some of the continental states, notably in France; but the conditions were now exactly those which would make such a step seem desirable to the holder of the crown. By this means the Capetian family had maintained undisputed possession of the throne through turbulent times with little real power of their own, and they were now approaching the point when they could feel that the custom was no longer necessary. The decision to attempt this method of securing the succession while still in possession of power, rather than to leave it to the uncertain chances that would follow his death, was for Stephen natural and wise. It is interesting to notice how indispensable the consent of the Church was considered, as the really deciding voice in the matter, and it was this that Stephen was not able to secure. The pope—this was about Easter time of 1151—rejected almost with indignation the suggestion of Murdac, on the ground of the violated oath, and forbade any innovation to be made concerning the crown of England, because this was a subject of litigation; he also directed, very probably at this time, the Archbishop of Canterbury, it was said at the suggestion of Thomas Becket, to refuse to crown Eustace.

With his duchy of Normandy, Henry had inherited at the same time the danger of trouble with the king of France, for his father had greatly displeased Louis by laying siege to the castle of a seditious vassal of Anjou who happened to be a favourite of the king. It would seem that this state of things suggested to Eustace an attack on Normandy in alliance with King Louis, but the attempt was fruitless. Twice during the summer of 1151 French armies invaded Normandy; the first led by the king himself. Both invasions were met by Henry at the head of his troops, but no fighting occurred on either occasion. On the second invasion, Louis was ill of a fever in Paris, and negotiations for peace were begun, the Church interesting itself to this end. Geoffrey and Henry certainly had no wish for war. The king's friend, who had been captured, was handed over to him; the Norman Vexin was surrendered to France; and in return Louis recognized Henry as Duke of Normandy and accepted his homage. Henry at once ordered an assembly of the Norman barons, on September 14, to consider the invasion of England; but his plans were interrupted by the sudden death of his father a week before this date. Geoffrey was then in his thirty-ninth year. The course of his life had been marked out for him by the plans of others, and it is obscured for us by the deeper interest of the struggle in England, and by the greater brilliancy of his son's history; but in the conquest of Normandy he had accomplished a work which was of the highest value to his house, and of the greatest assistance to the rapid success of his son on a wider field.

Events were now steadily moving in favour of Henry. At the close of 1151, the death of his father added the county of Anjou to his duchy of Normandy. Early in 1152 a larger possession than these together, and a most brilliant promise of future power, came to him through no effort of his own. We have seen how at the beginning of the reign of Stephen, when Henry himself was not yet five years old, Eleanor, heiress of Aquitaine, had been married to young Louis of France, who became in a few weeks, by the death of his father, King Louis VII. Half a lifetime, as men lived in those days, they had spent together as man and wife, with no serious lack of harmony. The marriage, however, could never have been a very happy one. Incompatibility of temper and tastes must long have made itself felt before the determination to dissolve the marriage was reached. Masculine in character, strong and full of spirit, Eleanor must have looked with some contempt on her husband, who was losing the energy of his younger days and passing more and more under the influence of the darker and more superstitious elements in the religion of the time, and she probably did not hesitate to let her opinion be known. She said he was a monk and not a king. To this, it is likely, was added the fact—it may very possibly have been the deciding consideration—that during the more than fourteen years of the marriage but two daughters had been born, and the Capetian house still lacked an heir. Whatever may have been the reason, a divorce was resolved upon not long after their return in 1149 from the second crusade. The death in January, 1152, of Louis VI's great minister, Suger, whose still powerful influence, for obvious political reasons, had hindered the final steps, made the way clear. In March an assembly of clergy, with many barons in attendance, declared the marriage void on the convenient and easily adjustable principle of too near relationship, and Eleanor received back her great inheritance.

It was not likely that a woman of the character of Eleanor and of her unusual attractions, alike of person and possessions, would quietly accept as final the position in which this divorce had left her. After escaping the importunate wooings of a couple of suitors who sought to intercept her return to her own dominions, she sent a message to Henry of Anjou, and he responded at once. In the third week of May they were married at Poitiers, two months after the divorce. In a few weeks' time, by two brief ecclesiastical ceremonies, the greatest feudal state of France, a quarter of the kingdom, had been transferred from the king to an uncontrollable vassal who practically held already another quarter. The king of France was reduced as speedily from a position of great apparent power and promise to the scanty territories of the Capetian domain, and brought face to face with the danger of not distant ruin to the plans of his house. To Henry, at the very beginning of his career, was opened the immediate prospect of an empire greater than any which existed at that time in Europe under the direct rule of any other sovereign. If he could gain England, he would bear sway, as king in reality if not in name, from Scotland to the Pyrenees, and from such a beginning what was there that might not be gained? Why these hopes were never realized, how the Capetian kings escaped this danger, must fill a large part of our story to the death of Henry's youngest son, King John. At the date of his marriage Henry had just entered on his twentieth year.

Eleanor was nearly twelve years older. If she had sought happiness in her new marriage, she did not find it, at least not permanently; and many later years were spent in open hostility with Henry, or closely confined in his prisons; but whatever may have been her feelings towards him, she found no occasion to regard her second husband with contempt. Their eldest son, William, who did not survive infancy, was born on August 17, 1153, and in succession four other sons were born to them and three daughters.

The first and most obvious work which now lay before Henry was the conquest of England, and the plans which had been earlier formed for this object and deferred by these events were at once taken up. By the end of June the young bridegroom was at Barfleur preparing to cross the channel with an invading force. But he was not to be permitted to enjoy his new fortunes unchallenged. Louis VII in particular had reasons for interfering, and the law was on his side. The heiress Eleanor had no right to marry without the consent of her feudal suzerain. A summons, it is said, was at once served on Henry to appear before the king's court and answer for his conduct,[44] and this summons, which Henry refused to obey, was supported by a new coalition. Louis and Eustace were again in alliance, and they were joined by Henry's own brother Geoffrey, who could make considerable trouble in the south of Henry's lands, by Robert of Dreux, Count of Perche, and by Eustace's cousin Henry, Count of Champagne. Stephen's brother Theobald had died at the beginning of the year, and his great dominions had been divided, Champagne and Blois being once more separated, never to be reunited until they were absorbed at different dates into the royal domain. This coalition was strong enough to check Henry's plan of an invasion of England, but it did not prove a serious danger, though the allies are said to have formed a plan for the partition of all the Angevin empire among themselves. For some reason their campaign does not seem to have been vigorously pushed. The young duke was able to force his brother to come to terms, and he succeeded in patching up a rather insecure truce with King Louis. On this, however, he dared to rely enough—or perhaps he trusted to the situation as he understood it—to venture at last, in January, 1153, on his long-deferred expedition to recover his mother's kingdom. Stephen had begun the siege of the important fortress of Wallingford, and a new call for aid had come over to Normandy from the hard-pressed garrison.

In the meantime, during the same days when the divorce and remarriage of Eleanor of Aquitaine were making such a change in the power and prospects of his competitor for the crown, Stephen had made a new attempt to secure the possession of that crown firmly to his son Eustace. A meeting of the great council of the kingdom, or of that part which obeyed Stephen, was called at London early in April, 1152. This body was asked to sanction the immediate consecration of Eustace as king. The barons who were present were ready to agree, and they swore allegiance to him and probably did homage, which was as far as the barons by themselves could go. The prelates, however, under the lead of the Archbishop of Canterbury,—Henry of Winchester is not mentioned in this case,—flatly refused to perform the consecration. The papal prohibition of any such act still held good, and the clergy of England had been given, as they would recall the past, no reason to disobey the pope in the interests of King Stephen. The king, in great anger, appealed to force against them, but without avail. Temporary imprisonment of the prelates at the council, in a house together, even temporary confiscation of the baronies of some of them, did not move them, and Stephen was obliged to postpone his plan once more. The archbishop again escaped to the continent to await the course of events, and Stephen appealed to the sword to gain some new advantage to balance this decided rebuff. Then followed the vigorous siege of Wallingford, which called Henry into England at the beginning of January.

The force which Henry brought with him crossed the channel in thirty-six ships, and was estimated at the time at 140 men-at-arms and 3000 foot-soldiers, a very respectable army for that day; but the duke's friends in England very likely formed their ideas of the army he would bring from the breadth of his territories, and they expressed their disappointment. Henry was to win England, however, not by an invasion, but by the skill of his management and by the influence of events which worked for him here as on the continent without an effort of his own. Now it was that Ralph of Chester performed his final change of sides and sold to Henry, at the highest price which treason reached in any transaction of this long and favourable time, the aid which was so necessary to the Angevin success. Henry's first attempt was against the important castle of Malmesbury, midway between Bristol and Wallingford, and Stephen was not able to prevent its fall. Then the garrison of Wallingford was relieved, and the intrenched position of Stephen's forces over against the castle was invested. The king came up with an army to protect his men, and would gladly have joined battle and settled the question on the spot, but once more his barons refused to fight. They desired nothing less than the victory of one of the rivals, which would bring the chance of a strong royal power and of their subjection to it. Apparently Henry's barons held the same view of the case, and assisted in forcing the leaders to agree to a brief truce, the advantage of which would in reality fall wholly to Henry.

From Wallingford Henry marched north through central England, where towns and castles one after another fell into his hands. From Wallingford also, Eustace withdrew from his father, greatly angered by the truce which had been made, and went off to the east on an expedition of his own which looks much like a plundering raid. Rashly he laid waste the lands of St. Edmund, who was well known to be a fierce protector of his own and to have no hesitation at striking even a royal robber. Punishment quickly followed the offence. Within a week Eustace was smitten with madness and died on August 17, a new and terrible warning of the fate of the sacrilegious. This death changed the whole outlook for the future. Stephen had no more interest in continuing the war than to protect himself. His wife had now been dead for more than a year. His next son, William, had never looked forward to the crown, and had never been prominent in the struggle. He had been lately married to the heiress of the Earl of Surrey, and if he could be secured in the quiet and undisputed possession of this inheritance and of the lands which his father had granted him, and of the still broader lands in Normandy and England which had belonged to Stephen before he seized the crown, then the advantage might very well seem to the king, near the close of his stormy life, greater than any to be gained from the desperate struggle for the throne. The Archbishop of Canterbury, who had by some means returned to England, proposed peace, and undertook negotiations between the king and the duke, supported by Henry of Winchester. Henry of Anjou could well afford to wait. The delay before he could in this way obtain the crown would probably not be very long and would be amply compensated by a peaceful and undisputed succession, while in the meantime he could give himself entirely to the mission which, since he had landed in England, he had loudly proclaimed as his of putting an end to plundering and oppression. On November 6 the rivals met at Winchester to make peace, and the terms of their agreement were recited in a great council of the kingdom, probably the first which was in any sense a council of the whole kingdom that had met in nearly or quite fifteen years. First, the king formally recognized before the assembly the hereditary right of Henry to the kingdom of England. Then the duke formally agreed that Stephen should hold the throne so long as he should live; and king, and bishops, and barons bound themselves with an oath that on Stephen's death Henry should succeed peacefully and without any contradiction. It was also agreed under oath, that all possessions which had been seized by force should be restored to their rightful owners, and that all castles which had been erected since the death of Henry I should be destroyed, and the number of these was noted at the time as 1115, though a more credible statement gives the number as 375. The treaty between the two which had no doubt preceded these ceremonies in the council contained other provisions. Stephen promised to regard Henry as a son—possibly he formally adopted him—and to rule England by his advice. Henry promised that William should enjoy undisturbed all the possessions which he had obtained with his wife or from his father, and all his father's private inheritance in England and Normandy. Allegiance and homage were paid by Henry to Stephen as king and by William to Henry, and Henry's barons did homage to Stephen and Stephen's to Henry, with the usual reservation. The king's Flemish mercenaries were to be sent home, and order was to be established throughout the land, the king restoring to all their rights and resuming himself those which had been usurped during the disorders of civil strife.

This programme began at once to be carried out. The war came to an end. The "adulterine" castles were destroyed, not quite so rapidly as Henry desired, but still with some energy. The unprincipled baron, friend of neither side and enemy of all his neighbours, deprived of his opportunity by the union of the two contending parties, was quickly reduced to order, and we hear no more of the feudal anarchy from which the defenceless had suffered so much during these years. Henry and Stephen met again at Oxford in January, 1154; they journeyed together to Dover, but as they were returning, Henry learned of a conspiracy against his life among Stephen's Flemish followers, some of whom must still have remained in England, and thought it best to retire to Normandy, where he began the resumption of the ducal domains with which his father had been obliged to part in the time of his weakness. Stephen went on with the work of restoration in England, but not for long. The new day of peace and strong government was not for him. On October 25, 1154, he died at Dover, "and was buried where his wife and his son were buried, at Faversham, the monastery which they had founded."

Out of this long period of struggle the crown gained nothing. Out of the opportunity of feudal independence and aggrandizement which the conflict offered them, the barons in the end gained nothing. One of the parties to the strife, and one only, emerged from it with great permanent gains of power and independence, the Church. The one power which had held back the English Church from taking its share in that great European movement by which within a century the centralized, monarchical Church had risen up beside the State, indeed above it, for it was now an international and imperial Church, — the restraining force which had held the English Church in check, — had been for a generation fatally weakened. With a bound the Church sprang forward and took the place in England and in the world which it would otherwise have reached more slowly during the reign of Henry. It had been prepared by experience and by the growth of its own convictions, to find its place at once alongside of the continental national churches in the new imperial system. Unweakened by the disorganization into which the State was falling, it was ready to show itself at home the one strong and steady institution in the confusion of the time, and to begin at once to exercise the rights it claimed but had never been able to secure. It began to fill its own great appointments according to its own rules, and to neglect the feudal duties which should go with them. Its jurisdiction, which had been so closely watched, expanded freely and ecclesiastical courts and cases rapidly multiplied. It called its own councils and legislated without permission, and even asserted its exclusive right to determine who should be king. Intercourse with the papal curia grew more untrammelled, and appeals to Rome especially increased to astonishing frequency. With these gains in practical independence, the support on which it all rested grew strong at the same time.—its firm belief in the Hildebrandine system. If a future king of England should ever recover the power over the Church which had been lost in the reign of Stephen, he would do so only by a struggle severer than any of his predecessors had gone through to retain it; and in these events Thomas Becket, who was to lead the defence of the Church against such an attack, had been trained for his future work.

Monasticism also flourished while the official Church was growing strong, and many new religious houses and new orders even were established in the country. More of these "castles of God," we are told by one who himself dwelt in one of them, were founded during the short reign of Stephen than during the one hundred preceding years. In the buildings which these monks did not cease to erect, the severer features of the Norman style were beginning to give way to lighter and more ornamental forms. Scholars in greater numbers went abroad. Books that still hold their place in the intellectual or even in the literary history of the world were written by subjects of the English king. Oxford continued to grow towards the later University, and students there listened eagerly to the lectures on Roman law of the Italian Vacarius until these were stopped by Stephen. In spite of the cruelties of the time, the real life of England went on and was scarcely even checked in its advance to better things.

[41] See Rössler, Kaiserin Mathilde, 287 ff.

[42] William of Malmesbury, sec. 497.

[43] See the Athenaeum, February 6, 1904, p. 177.

[44] But see Lot, Fidèles ou Vassaux (1904), 205-212.

CHAPTER XII.
THE KING'S FIRST WORK

Henry of Anjou, for whom the way was opened to the throne of his grandfather so soon after the treaty with Stephen, was then in his twenty-second year. He was just in the youthful vigour of a life of more than usual physical strength, longer in years than the average man's of the twelfth century, and brilliant in position and promise in the eyes of his time. But his life was in truth filled with annoying and hampering conflict and bitter disappointment. Physically there was nothing fine or elegant about him, rather the contrary. In bodily and mental characteristics there was so much in common between the Angevin house and the Norman that the new blood had made no great changes, and in physique and in spirit Henry II continued his mother's line quite as much as his father's. Certainly, as a modern writer has remarked, he could never have been called by his father's name of "the Handsome." He was of middle height, strongly built, with square shoulders, broad chest, and arms that reminded men of a pugilist. His head was round and well shaped, and he had reddish hair and gray eyes which seemed to flash with fire when he was angry. His complexion also was ruddy and his face is described as fiery or lion-like. His hands were coarse, and he never wore gloves except when necessary in hawking. His legs were hardly straight. They were made for the saddle and his feet for the stirrups. He was heedless of his person and his clothes, and always cared more for action and deeds than for appearances.

In the gifts of statesmanship and the abilities which make a great ruler Henry seemed to his own time above the average of kings, and certainly this is true in comparison with the king who was his rival during so much of his reign, Louis VII of France. Posterity has also agreed to call him one of the greatest, some have been inclined to say the greatest, of English sovereigns. The first heavy task that fell to him, the establishment of peace and strong government in England, he fully achieved; and this work was thankfully celebrated by his contemporaries. All his acts give us the impression of mental and physical power, and no recasting of balances is ever likely to destroy the impression of great abilities occupied with great tasks, but we need perhaps to be reminded that to his age his position made him great, and that even upon us its effect is magnifying. Except in the pacification of England he won no signal success, and the schemes to which he gave his best days ended in failure or barely escaped it. It is indeed impossible to say that in his long reign he had before him any definite or clear policy, except to be a strong king and to assert vigorously every right to which he believed he could lay claim. The opportunity which his continental dominions offered him he seems never to have understood, or at least not as it would have been understood by a modern sovereign or by a Philip Augustus. It is altogether probable that the successful welding together of the various states which he held by one title or another into a consolidated monarchy would have been impossible; but that the history of his reign gives no clear evidence that he saw the vision of such a result, or studied the means to accomplish it, forces us to classify Henry, in one important respect at least, with the great kings of the past and not with those of the coming age. In truth he was a feudal king. Notwithstanding the severe blows which he dealt feudalism in its relation to the government of the state, it was still feudalism as a system of life, as a source of ideals and a guide to conduct, which ruled him to the end. He had been brought up entirely in a feudal atmosphere, and he never freed himself from it. He was determined to be a strong king, to be obeyed, and to allow no infringement of his own rights,—indeed, to push them to the farthest limit possible,—but there seems never to have been any conflict in his mind between his duties as suzerain or vassal and any newer conception of his position and its opportunities.

It was in England that Henry won his chief and his only permanent success. And it was indeed not a small success. To hold under a strong government and to compel into good order, almost unbroken, a generation which had been trained in the anarchy and license of Stephen's reign was a great achievement. But Henry did more than this. In the machinery of centralization, he early began a steady and systematic development which threatened the defences of feudalism, and tended rapidly toward an absolute monarchy. In this was his greatest service to England. The absolutism which his work threatened later kings came but little nearer achieving, and the danger soon passed away, but the centralization which he gave the state grew into a permanent and beneficent organization. In this work Henry claimed no more than the glory of following in his grandfather's footsteps, and the modern student of the age is more and more inclined to believe that he was right in this, and that his true fame as an institution maker should be rather that of a restorer than of a founder. He put again into operation what had been already begun; he combined and systematized and broadened, and he created the conditions which encouraged growth and made it fruitful: but he struck out no new way either for himself or for England.

In mind and body Henry overflowed with energy. He wearied out his court with his incessant and restless activity. In learning he never equalled the fame of his grandfather, Henry Beauclerc, but he loved books, and his knowledge of languages was such as to occasion remark. He had the passionate temper of his ancestors without the self-control of Henry I, and sometimes raved in his anger like a maniac. In matters of morals also he placed no restraints upon himself. His reputation in this regard has been kept alive by the romantic legend of Rosamond Clifford; and, though the pathetic details of her story are in truth romance and not history, there is no lack of evidence to show that Eleanor had occasion enough for the bitter hostility which she felt towards him in the later years of his life. But Henry is not to be reckoned among the kings whose policy or public conduct were affected by his vices. More passionate and less self-controlled than his grandfather, he had something of his patience and tenacity of purpose, and a large share of his diplomatic skill; and the slight scruples of conscience, which on rare occasions interfered with an immediate success, arose from a very narrow range of ethical ideas.

An older man and one of longer training in statecraft and the management of men might easily have doubted his ability to solve the problem which lay before Henry in England. To control a feudal baronage was never an easy task. To re-establish a strong control which for nearly twenty years had been greatly relaxed would be doubly difficult. But in truth the work was more than half done when Henry came to the throne. Since the peace declared at Winchester much had been accomplished, and most of all perhaps in the fact that peace deprived the baron of the even balancing of parties which had been his opportunity. On all sides also men were worn out with the long conflict, and the material, as well as the incentive, to continue it under the changed conditions was lacking. It is likely too that Henry had made an impression in England, during the short time that he had stayed there, very different from that made by Stephen early in his reign; for it is clear that he knew what he wanted and how to get it, and that he would be satisfied with nothing less. Nor did there seem to be anything to justify a fear that arrangements which had been made during the war in favour of individual men were likely to be disturbed. So secure indeed did everything seem that Henry was in no haste to cross to England when the news of Stephen's death reached him.

The Duke of Normandy had been occupied with various things since his return from England in April, with the recovery of the ducal lands, with repressing unimportant feudal disorders, and with negotiations with the king of France. On receiving the news he finished the siege of a castle in which he was engaged, then consulted his mother, whose counsel he often sought to the end of her life, in her quiet retreat near Rouen, and finally assembled the barons of Normandy. In about a fortnight he was ready at Barfleur for the passage, but bad winds kept back the unskilful sailors of the time for a month. In England there was no disturbance. Everybody, we are told, feared or loved the duke and expected him to become king, and even the Flemish troops of Stephen kept the peace. If any one acted for the king, it was Archbishop Theobald, but there is no evidence that there was anything for a regent to do. At last, at the end of the first week in December, Henry landed in England and went up at once to Winchester. There he took the homage of the English barons, and from thence after a short delay he went on to London to be crowned. The coronation on the 19th, the Sunday before Christmas, must have been a brilliant ceremony. The Archbishop of Canterbury officiated in the presence of two other archbishops and seventeen bishops, of earls and barons from England and abroad, and an innumerable multitude of people.

Henry immediately issued a coronation charter, but it is, like Stephen's, merely a charter of general confirmation. No specific promises are made. The one note of the charter, the keynote of the reign for England thus early struck, is "king Henry my grandfather." The ideal of the young king, an ideal it is more than likely wholly satisfactory to his subjects, was to reproduce that reign of order and justice, the time to which men after the long anarchy would look back as to a golden age. Or was this a declaration, a notice to all concerned, flung out in a time of general rejoicing when it would escape challenge, that no usurpation during Stephen's reign was to stand against the rights of the crown? That time is passed over as a blank. No man could plead the charter as guaranteeing him in any grant or privilege won from either side during the civil war. To God and holy Church and to all earls and barons and all his men, the king grants, and restores and confirms all concessions and donations and liberties and free customs which King Henry his grandfather had given and granted to them. Also all evil customs which his grandfather abolished and remitted he grants to be abolished and remitted. That is all except a general reference to the charter of Henry I. Neither Church nor baron could tell from the charter itself what rights had been granted or what evil customs had been abolished. But in all probability no one at the moment greatly cared for more specific statement. The proclamation of a general policy of return to the conditions of the earlier age was what was most desired.

The first work before the young king would be to select those who should aid him in the task of government in the chief offices of the state. He probably already had a number of these men in mind from his knowledge of England and of the leaders of his mother's party. In the peace with

Stephen, Richard de Lucy had been put in charge of the Tower and of Windsor castle. He now seems to have been made justiciar, perhaps the first of Henry's appointments, as he alone signs the coronation charter though without official designation. Within a few days, however, Robert de Beaumont, Earl of Leicester, was apparently given office with the same title, and together they fill this position for many years, Robert completing in it the century and more of faithful service which his family had rendered to every successive king. The family of Roger of Salisbury was also restored to the important branch of the service which it had done so much to create, in the person of Nigel, Bishop of Ely, who was given charge of the exchequer. The most important appointment in its influence on the reign was that to the chancellorship. Archbishop Theobald, who was probably one of Henry's most intimate counsellors, had a candidate in whose favour he could speak in the strongest terms and whose services in the past the king would gratefully recall. This was the young Thomas Becket, who had done so much to prevent the coronation of Eustace.

Immediately after his coronation, at Christmas time, Henry held at Bermondsey the first of the great councils of his reign. Here the whole state of the kingdom was discussed, and it was determined to proceed with the expulsion of Stephen's mercenaries, and with the destruction of the unlawful castles. The first of these undertakings gave no trouble, and William of Ypres disappears from English history. The second, especially with what went with it, — the resumption of Stephen's grants to great as well as small, — was a more difficult and longer process. To begin it in the proper way, the king himself set out early in 1155 for the north. For some reason he did not think it wise at this time to run the risk of a quarrel with Hugh Bigod, and it was probably on this journey at Northampton that he gave him a charter creating him Earl of Norfolk, the title which he had obtained from Stephen. The expedition was especially directed against William of Aumale, Stephen's Earl of Yorkshire, and he was compelled to surrender a part of his spoils including the strong castle of Scarborough. William Peverel of the Peak also, who was accused of poisoning the Earl of Chester, and who knew that there were other reasons of condemnation against him, took refuge in a monastery, making profession as a monk when he heard of Henry's approach, and finally fled to the continent and abandoned everything to the king. Some time after this, but probably during the same year, another of Stephen's earls, William of Arundel or Sussex, obtained a charter of confirmation of the third penny of his county.

One of the interesting features of Henry's first year is the frequency of great councils. Four were held in nine months. It was the work of resumption, and of securing his position, which made them necessary. The expressed support of the baronage, as a whole, was of great value to him as he moved against one magnate and then another, and demanded the restoration of royal domains or castles. The second of these councils, which was held in London in March, and in which the business of the castles was again taken up, did not, however, secure the king against all danger of resistance. Roger, Earl of Hereford, son of Miles of Gloucester, who had been so faithful to Henry's mother, secretly left the assembly determined to try the experiment of rebellion rather than to surrender his two royal castles of Hereford and Gloucester. In this attitude he was encouraged by Hugh Mortimer, a baron of the Welsh Marches and head of a Conquest family of minor rank which was now rising to importance, who was also ready to risk rebellion. Roger did not persist in his plans. He was brought to a better mind by his kinsman, the Bishop of Hereford, Gilbert Foliot, and gave up his castles. Mortimer ventured to stand a siege in his strongholds, one of which was Bridgenorth where Robert of Bellême had tried to resist Henry I in similar circumstances, but he was forced to surrender before the middle of the summer. This was the only armed opposition which the measures of resumption excited, because they were carried out by degrees and with wise caution in the selection of persons as well as of times. It was probably in this spirit that in January of the next year Henry regranted to Aubrey de Vere his title of Earl of Oxford and that of the unfaithful Earl of Essex to the younger Geoffrey de Mandeville. It was twenty years after Henry's accession and in far different circumstances that he first found himself involved in conflict with a dangerous insurrection of the English barons.

Before the submission of Hugh Mortimer the third of the great councils of the year had been held at Wallingford early in April, and there the barons had been required to swear allegiance to Henry's eldest son William, and in case of his death to his brother Henry who had been born a few weeks before. The fourth great council met at Winchester in the last days of September, and there a new question of policy was discussed which led ultimately to events of great importance in the reign, and of constantly increasing importance in the whole history of England to the present day,—the conquest of Ireland. Apparently Henry had already conceived the idea, to which he returns later in the case of his youngest son, of finding in the western island an appanage for some unprovided member of the royal house. Now he thought of giving it to his youngest brother William. Religious and political prejudice and racial pride have been so intensely excited by many of the statements and descriptions in the traditional account of Henry's first steps towards the conquest, which is based on contemporary records or what purports to be such, that evidence which no one would think of questioning if it related to humdrum events on the dead level of history has been vigorously assailed, and almost every event in the series called in question. The writer of history cannot narrate these events as they seem to him to have occurred without warning the reader that some element of doubt attaches to his account, and that whatever his conclusions, some careful students of the period will not agree with him.

A few days before Henry landed in England to be crowned, Nicholas Breakspear, the only Englishman who ever became pope, had been elected Bishop of Rome and had taken the name of Hadrian IV. He was the son of an English clerk, who was later a monk at St. Albans, and had not seemed to his father a very promising boy; but on his father's death he went abroad, studied at Paris, and was made Abbot of St. Rufus in Provence. Then visiting Rome because of trouble, with his monks, he attracted the notice of the pope, was made cardinal and papal legate, and finally was himself elected pope in succession to Anastasius IV. We cannot say, though we may think it likely, that the occupation of the papal throne by a native Englishman made it seem to Henry a favourable time to secure so high official sanction for his new enterprise. Nor is it possible to say what was the form of Henry's request, or the composition of the embassy which seems certainly to have been sent, or the character of the pope's reply, though each of these has been made the subject of differing conjectures for none of which is there any direct evidence in the sources of our knowledge. The most that we can assert is what we are told by John of Salisbury, the greatest scholar of the middle ages.

John was an intimate friend of the pope's and spent some months with him in very familiar intercourse in the winter of 1155-1156. He relates in a passage at the close of his Metalogicus, which he wrote, if we may judge by internal evidence, on learning of Hadrian's death in 1159, and which there is no reason to doubt, that at his request the pope made a written grant of Ireland to Henry to be held by hereditary right. He declares that the ground of this grant was the ownership of all islands conveyed to the popes by the Donation of Constantine, and he adds that Hadrian sent Henry a ring by which he was to be invested with the right of ruling in Ireland. Letter and ring, he says, are preserved in England at the time of his writing. The so called Bull "Laudabiliter" has been traditionally supposed to be the letter referred to by John of Salisbury, but it does not quite agree with his description, and it makes no grant of the island to the king.[45] The probability is very strong that it is not even what it purports to be, a letter of the pope to the king expressing his approval of the enterprise, but merely a student's exercise in letter writing. But the papal approval was certainly expressed at a later time by Pope Alexander III. No doubt can attach, however, to the account of John of Salisbury. As he describes the grant it would correspond fully with papal ideas current at the time, and it would be closely parallel with what we must suppose was the intention of an earlier pope in approving William's conquest of England. If Henry had asked for anything more than the pope's moral assent to the enterprise, he could have expected nothing different from this, nor does it seem that he could in that case have objected to the terms or form of the grant described by John of Salisbury.

The expedition, however, for which Henry had made these preparations was not actually undertaken. His mother objected to it for some reason which we do not know, and he dropped the plan for the present. About the same time Henry of Winchester, who had lived on into a new age, which he probably found not wholly congenial, left England without the king's permission and went to Cluny. This gave Henry a legal opportunity, and he at once seized and destroyed his castles. No other event of importance falls within the first year of the reign. It was a great work which had been done in this time. To have plainly declared and successfully begun the policy of reigning as a strong king, to have got rid of Stephen's dangerous mercenaries without trouble, to have recovered so many castles and domains without exciting a great rebellion, and to have restored the financial system to the hands best fitted to organize and perfect it, might satisfy the most ambitious as the work of a year. "The history of the year furnishes," in the words of the greatest modern student of the age, "abundant illustration of the energy and capacity of a king of two-and-twenty."

Early in January, 1156, Henry crossed to Normandy. His brother Geoffrey was making trouble and was demanding that Anjou and Maine should be assigned to him. We are told an improbable story that their father on his deathbed had made such a partition of his lands, and that Henry had been required blindly to swear that he would carry out an arrangement which was not made known to him. If Henry made any such promise as heir, he immediately repudiated it as reigning sovereign. He could not well do otherwise. To give up the control of these two counties would be to cut his promising continental empire into two widely separated portions. Geoffrey attempted to appeal to arms in the three castles which had been given him earlier, but was quickly forced to submit. All this year and until April of the next, 1157, Henry remained abroad, and before his return to England he was able to offer his brother a compensation for his disappointment which had the advantage of strengthening his own position. The overlordship of the county of Britanny had, as we know, been claimed by the dukes of Normandy, and the claim had sometimes been allowed. To Henry the successful assertion of this right would be of great value as filling out his occupation of western France. Just at this time Britanny had been thrown into disorder and civil strife by a disputed succession, and the town of

Nantes, which commanded the lower course of the Loire, so important a river to Henry, refused to accept either of the candidates. With the aid of his brother, Geoffrey succeeded in planting himself there as Count of Nantes, in a position which promised to open for the house of Anjou the way into Britanny.

The greater part of the time of his stay abroad Henry spent in passing about from one point to another in his various provinces, after the usual custom of the medieval sovereign. In Eleanor's lands he could exert much less direct authority than in England or Normandy; the feudal baron of the south was more independent of his lord; but the opposition which was later to be so disastrous had not yet developed, and the year went by with nothing to record. Soon after his coming to Normandy he had an interview with Louis VII who then accepted his homage both for his father's and his wife's inheritance. If Louis had at one time intended to dispute the right of Eleanor to marry without his consent, he could not afford to continue that policy, so strong was Henry now. It was the part of wisdom to accept what could not be prevented, to arrange some way of living in peace with his rival, and to wait the chances of the future.

It is in connexion with this expedition to Normandy that there first appears in the reign of Henry II the financial levy known as "scutage" — a form of taxation destined to have a great influence on the financial and military history of England, and perhaps even a greater on its constitutional history. The invention of this tax was formerly attributed to the statesmanship of the young king, but we now know that it goes back at least to the time of his grandfather. The term "scutage" may be roughly translated "shield money," and, as the word implies, it was a tax assessed on the knight's fee, and was in theory a money payment accepted or exacted by the king in place of the military service due him under the feudal arrangements. The suggestion of such a commutation no doubt arose in connexion with the Church baronies, whose holders would find many reasons against personal service in the field, especially in the prohibition of the canon law, and who in most cases preferred not to enfeoff on their lands knights enough to meet their military obligations to the king. In such cases, when called on for the service, they would be obliged to hire the required number of knights, and the suggestion that they should pay the necessary sum to the king and let him find the soldiers would be a natural one and probably agreeable to both sides. The scutage of the present year does not seem to have gone beyond this practice. It was confined to Church lands, and the wider application of the principle, which is what we may attribute to Henry II or to some minister of his, was not attempted.

Returning to England in April, 1157, Henry took up again the work which had been interrupted by the demands of his brother Geoffrey. He was ready now to fly at higher game. Stephen's son William, whose great possessions in England and Normandy his father had tried so carefully to secure in the treaty which surrendered his rights to the crown, was compelled to give up his castles, and Hugh Bigod was no longer spared but was forced to do the same. David of Scotland had died before the death of Stephen, and his kingdom had fallen to his grandson Malcolm IV. The new king had too many troubles at home to make it wise for him to try to defend the gains which his grandfather had won from England, and before the close of this year he met Henry at Chester and gave up his claim on the northern counties, received the earldom of Huntingdon, and did homage to his cousin, but for what, whether for his earldom or his kingdom, was not clearly stated. Wales Stephen had practically abandoned, but Henry had no mind to do this, and a campaign during the summer in which there was some sharp fighting forced Owen, the prince of North Wales, to become his man, restored the defensive works of the district, and protected the Marcher lords in their occupation. The Christmas court was held at Lincoln; but warned perhaps by the recent ill luck of Stephen in defying the local superstition, Henry did not attempt to wear his crown in the city. Crown wearing and ceremony in general were distasteful to him, and at the next Easter festival at Worcester, together with the queen, he formally renounced the practice.

Half of the year 1158 Henry spent in England, but the work which lay before him at his accession was now done. Much work of importance and many events of interest concern the island kingdom in the later years of the reign, but these arise from new occasions and belong to a new age. The age of Stephen was at an end, the Norman absolutism was once more established, and the influence of the time of anarchy and weakness was felt no longer. It was probably the death of his brother and the question of the occupation of Nantes that led Henry to cross to Normandy in August. He went first of all, however, to meet the king of France near Gisors. There it was agreed that Henry's son Henry, now by the death of his eldest brother recognized as heir to the throne, should marry Louis's daughter Margaret. The children were still both infants, but the arrangement was made less for their sakes than for peace between their fathers and for substantial advantages which Henry hoped to gain. First he desired Louis's permission to take possession of Nantes, and later, on the actual marriage of the children, was to come the restoration of the Norman Vexin which Henry's father had been obliged to give up to France in the troubles of his time. Protected in this way from the only opposition which he had to fear, Henry had no difficulty in forcing his way into Nantes and in compelling the count of Britanny to recognize his possession. This diplomatic success had been prepared, possibly secured, by a brilliant embassy undertaken shortly before by Henry's chancellor Thomas Becket. One of the biographers of the future saint, one indeed who dwells less upon his spiritual life and miracles than on his external history, rejoices in the details of this magnificent journey, the gorgeous display, the lavish expenditure, the royal generosity, which seem intended to impress the French court with the wealth of England and the greatness of his master, but which lead us to suspect the chancellor of a natural delight in the splendours of the world.

With his feet firmly planted in Britanny, in a position where he could easily take advantage of any future turn of events to extend his power, Henry next turned his attention to the south where an even greater opportunity seemed to offer. The great county of Toulouse stretched from the south-eastern borders of Eleanor's lands towards the Mediterranean and the Rhone over a large part of that quarter of France. A claim of some sort to this county, the exact nature of which we cannot now decide from the scanty and inconsistent accounts of the case which remain to us, had come down to Eleanor from the last two dukes of Aquitaine, her father and grandfather. The claim had at any rate seemed good enough to Louis VII while he was still the husband of the heiress to be pushed, but he had not succeeded in establishing it. The rights of Eleanor were now in the hands of Henry and, after consulting with his barons, he determined to enforce them in a military campaign in the summer of 1159.

By the end of June the attacking forces were gathering in the south. The young king of Scotland was there as the vassal of the king of England and was knighted by his lord. Allies were secured of the lords to the east and south, especially the assistance of Raymond Berenger who was Count of Barcelona and husband of the queen of Aragon, and who had extensive claims and interests in the valley of the Rhone. His daughter was to be married to Henry's son Richard, who had been born a few months before. Negotiations and interviews with the king of France led to no result, and at the last moment Louis threw himself into Toulouse and prepared to stand a siege with the Count, Raymond V, whose rights he now looked at from an entirely different point of view. This act of the king led to a result which he probably did not anticipate. Apparently the feudal spirit of Henry could not reconcile itself to a direct attack on the person of his suzerain. He withdrew from the siege, and the expedition resulted only in the occupation of some of the minor towns of the county. Here Thomas the chancellor appears again in his worldly character. He had led to the war a body of knights said to have been 700 in number, the finest and best-equipped contingent in the field. Henry's chivalry in refusing to fight his suzerain seemed to him the height of folly, and he protested loudly against it. This chivalry indeed did not prevent the vassal from attacking some of his lord's castles in the north, but no important results were gained, and peace was soon made between them.

Far more important in permanent consequences than the campaign itself were the means which the king took to raise the money to pay for it. It was at this time, so far as our present evidence goes and unless a precedent had been made in a small way in a scutage of 1157 for·the campaign in Wales, that the principle of scutage was extended from ecclesiastical to lay tenants in chief. Robert of Torigny, Abbot of Mont-Saint-Michel, tells us that Henry, having regard to the length and difficulty of the way, and not wishing to vex the country knights and the mass of burgesses and rustics, took from each knight's fee in Normandy sixty shillings Angevin (fifteen English), and from all other persons in Normandy and in England and in all his other lands what he thought best, and led into the field with him the chief barons with a few of their men and a great number of paid knights.

Our knowledge of the treasury accounts of this period is not sufficient to enable us to explain every detail of this taxation, but it is sufficient to enable us to say that the statement of the abbot is in general accurate. The tax on the English knight's fee was heavier than that on the Norman; payment does not seem to have been actually required from all persons outside the strict feudal bond, nor within it for that matter; and the exact relationship between payment and service in the field we cannot determine. Two things, however, of interest in the history of taxation in relation both to earlier and later times seem clear. In the first place a new form of land-tax had been discovered of special application to the feudal community, capable of transforming a limited and somewhat uncertain personal service into a far more satisfactory money payment, capable also of considerable extension and, in the hands of an absolute king, of an arbitrary development which apparently some forms of feudal finance had already undergone. This was something new,—that is, it was as new as anything ever is in constitutional history. It was the application of an old process to a new use. In the second place large sums of money were raised, in a purely arbitrary way, it would seem, both as to persons paying and sums paid, from members of the non-feudal community and also from some tenants in chief who at the same time paid scutage. These payments appear to have rested on the feudal principle of the gracious or voluntary aid and to have been called "dona," though the people of that time were in general more accurate in the distinctions they made between things than in the use of the terms applied to them. There was nothing new about this form of taxation. Glimpses which we get here and there of feudalism in operation lead us to suspect that, in small matters and with much irregularity of application to persons, it was in not infrequent use. These particular payments, pressing as they did heavily on the Church and exciting its vigorous objection, carry us back with some interest to the beginning of troubles between Anselm and the Red King over a point of the same kind.

In theory and in strict law these "gifts" were voluntary, both as to whether they should be made at all and as to their amount, but under a sovereign so strong as Henry II or William Rufus, the king must be satisfied. Church writers complained, with much if not entire justice, that this tax was "contrary to ancient custom and due liberty," and they accused Thomas the chancellor of suggesting it. As a matter of fact this tax was less important in the history of taxation than the extension of the principle of scutage which accompanied it. The contribution which it made to the future was not so much in the form of the tax as in the precedent of arbitrary taxation, established in an important instance of taxation at the will of the king. This precedent carried over and applied to scutage in its new form becomes in the reign of Henry's son one of the chief causes of revolutionary changes, and thus constitutes "the scutage of Toulouse" of 1159, if we include under that term the double taxation of the year, one of the great steps forward of the reign of Henry.

At the close of the Toulouse campaign an incident of some interest occurred in the death of Stephen's son William and the ending of the male line of Stephen's succession. His Norman county of Mortain was at once taken in hand by Henry as an escheated fief, and was not filled again until it was given years afterwards to his youngest son. To Boulogne Henry had no right, but he could not afford to allow his influence in the county to decline, though the danger of its passing under the influence of Louis VII was slight. Stephen's only living descendant was his daughter Mary, now Abbess of Romsey. The pope consented to her marriage to a son of the Count of Flanders, and Boulogne remained in the circle of influence in which it had been fixed by Henry I. The wide personal possessions of William in England were apparently added to the royal domain which had already increased so greatly since the death of Stephen.

A year later the other branch of Stephen's family came into a new relationship to the politics of France and England. At the beginning of October, 1160, Louis's second wife died, leaving him still without a male heir. Without waiting till the end of any period of mourning, within a fortnight, he married the daughter of Stephen's brother, Theobald of Blois, sister of the counts Henry of Champagne and Theobald of Blois, who were already betrothed to the two daughters of his marriage with Eleanor. This opened for the house of Blois a new prospect of influence and gain, and for the king of England of trouble which was in part fulfilled. Henry saw the probable results, and at once responded with an effort to improve his frontier defences. The marriage of the young Henry and Margaret of France was immediately celebrated, though the elder of the two was still a mere infant. This marriage gave Henry the right to take possession of the Norman Vexin and its strong castles, and this he did. The war which threatened for a moment did not break out, but there was much fortifying of castles on both sides of the frontier.

It is said that the suggestion of this defensive move came from Thomas Becket. However this may be, Thomas was now near the end of his career of service to the state as chancellor, and was about to enter a field which promised even greater usefulness and wider possibilities of service. Archbishop Theobald of Canterbury died on April 18, 1161. For some months the king gave no sign of his intentions as to his successor. Then he declared his purpose. Thomas, the chancellor, was about to cross to England to carry out another plan of Henry's. The barons were to be asked to swear fealty to the young Henry as the direct heir to the crown. Born in February, 1155, Henry was in his eighth year when this ceremony was performed. Some little time before he had been committed by his father to the chancellor to be trained in his courtly and brilliant household, and there he became deeply attached to his father's future enemy. The swearing of fealty to the heir, to which the barons were now accustomed, was performed without objection, Thomas himself setting the example by first taking the oath.

This was his last service of importance as chancellor. Before his departure from Normandy on this errand, the king announced to him his intention to promote him to the vacant primacy. The appointment would be a very natural one. Archbishop Theobald is said to have hoped and prayed that Thomas might succeed him, and the abilities which the chancellor had abundantly displayed would account for a general expectation of such a step, but Thomas himself hesitated. We are dependent for our knowledge of the details of what happened at this time on the accounts of Thomas's friends and admirers, but there is no reason to doubt their substantial accuracy. It is clear that there were better grounds in fact for the hesitation of Thomas than for the insistence of Henry, but they were apparently concealed from the king. His mother is said to have tried to dissuade him, and the able Bishop of Hereford, Gilbert Foliot, records his own opposition. But the complete devotion to the king's will and the zealous services of Thomas as chancellor might well make Henry believe, if not that he would be entirely subservient to his policy when made archbishop, at least that Church and State might be ruled by them together in full harmony and co-operation, and the days of

William and Lanfranc be brought back. Becket read his own character better and knew that the days of Henry I and Anselm were more likely to return, and that not because he recognized in himself the narrowness of Anselm, but because he knew his tendency to identify himself to the uttermost with whatever cause he adopted.

Thomas had come to the chancellorship at the age of thirty-seven. He had been a student, attached to the household of Archbishop Theobald, and he must long have looked forward to promotion in the Church as the natural field of his ambition, and in this he had just taken the first step in his appointment to the rich archdeaconry of Canterbury by his patron. As chancellor, however, he seems to have faced entirely about. He threw himself into the elegant and luxurious life of the court with an abandon and delight which, we are tempted to believe, reveal his natural bent. The family of a wealthy burgher of London in the last part of the reign of Henry I may easily have been a better school of manners and taste than the court of Anjou. Certainly in refinement, and in the order and elegance of his household as it is described, the chancellor surpassed the king. Provided with an ample income both from benefices which he held in the Church and from the perquisites of his office, he indulged in a profusion of expenditure and display which the king probably did not care for and certainly did not equal, and collected about himself such a company of clerks and laymen as made his household a better place for the training of the children of the nobles than the king's. In the king's service he spent his money with as lavish a hand as for himself, in his embassy to the French court or in the war against Toulouse. He had the skill to avoid the envy of either king or courtier, and no scandal or hint of vice was breathed against him. The way to the highest which one could hope for in the service of the state seemed open before him, and he felt himself peculiarly adapted to enjoy and render useful such a career. One cannot help speculating on the interesting but hopeless problem of what the result would have been if Becket had remained in the line of secular promotion and the primacy had gone to the next most likely candidate, Gilbert Foliot, whose type of mind would have led him to sympathize more naturally with the king's views and purposes in the questions that were so soon to arise between Church and State in England.

The election of Becket to the see of Canterbury seems to have followed closely the forms which had come into use since the compromise between Henry I and Anselm, and which were soon after described in the Constitutions of Clarendon. The justiciar, Richard de Lucy, with three bishops went down to Canterbury and made known the will of the king and summoned the monks to an election. Some opposition showed itself among them, apparently because of the candidate's worldly life and the fact that he was not a monk, but they gave way to the clearly expressed will of the king. The prior and a deputation of the monks went up to London; and there the formal election took place "with the counsel of" the bishops summoned for the purpose, and was at once confirmed by the young prince acting for his father. At the same time Henry, Bishop of Winchester, made a formal demand of those who were representing the king that the archbishop should be released from all liability for the way in which he had handled the royal revenues as chancellor and treasurer, and this was agreed to. On the next Sunday but one, June 3, 1162, Thomas was consecrated Archbishop at Canterbury by the Bishop of Winchester, as the see of London was vacant. As his first official act the new prelate ordained that the feast in honour of the Trinity should be henceforth kept on the anniversary of his consecration.

[45] See the review of the whole controversy in Thatcher, Studies Concerning Adrian IV (1903).

CHAPTER XIII.
KING AND ARCHBISHOP

Thomas Becket, who thus became the head of the English Church, was probably in his forty-fourth year, for he seems to have been born on December 21, 1118. All his past had been a training in one way or another for the work which he was now to do. He had had an experience of many sides of life. During his early boyhood, in his father's house in London, he had shared the life of the prosperous burgher class; he had been a student abroad, and though he was never a scholar, he knew something of the learned world from within; he had been taken into the household of Archbishop Theobald, and there he had been trained, with a little circle of young men of promise of his own age, in the strict ideas of the Church; he had been employed on various diplomatic missions, and had accomplished what had been intrusted to him, we are told, with skill and success; last of all, he had been given a high office in the state, and had learned to know by experience and observation the life of the court, its methods of doing or preventing business, and all its strength and weakness.

As Archbishop of Canterbury, Thomas Becket became almost the independent sovereign of a state within the state. Lanfranc had held no such place, nor had Anselm. No earlier archbishop indeed had found himself at his consecration so free from control and so strong. The organization apart from the state, the ideal liberty of the Church, to which Anselm had looked forward somewhat vaguely, had been in some degree realized since his time. The death of Henry I had removed the restraining hand which had held the Church within its old bounds. For a generation afterwards it was free—free as compared with any earlier period—to put into practice its theories and aspirations, and the new Archbishop of Canterbury inherited the results still unquestioned and undiminished. Henry II had come to the throne young and with much preliminary work to be done. Gradually, it would seem, the reforms necessary to recover the full royal power, and to put into most effective form the organization of the state, were taking shape in his mind. It is possible, it is perhaps more than possible, that he expected to have from his friend Thomas as archbishop sympathy and assistance in these plans, or at least that he would be able to carry them out with no opposition from the Church. This looks to us now like a bad reading of character. At any rate no hope was ever more completely disappointed. In character, will, and ideals, at least as these appear from this time onward, sovereign and primate furnished all the conditions of a most bitter conflict. But to understand this conflict it is also necessary to remember the strength of Becket's position, the fact that he was the ruler of an almost independent state.

What was the true and natural character of Thomas Becket, what were really the ideals on which he would have chosen to form his life if he had been entirely free to shape it as he would, is a puzzle which this is not the place to try to solve. Nor can we discuss here the critical questions, still unsettled, which the sources of our knowledge present. Fortunately no question affects seriously the train of events, and, in regard to the character of the archbishop, we may say with some confidence that, whatever he might have chosen for himself, he threw himself with all the ardour of a great nature into whatever work he was called upon to do. As chancellor, Thomas's household had been a centre of luxurious court life. As archbishop his household was not less lavishly supplied, nor less attractive; but its elegance was of a more sober cast, and for himself Thomas became an ascetic, as he had been a courtier, and practised in secret, according to his biographers, the austerities and good works which became the future saint.

Six months after the consecration of the new archbishop, King Henry crossed from Normandy to England, at the end of January, 1163, but before he did so word had come to him from Becket which was like a declaration of principles. Henry had hoped to have him at the same time primate of the Church and his own chancellor. Not merely would this add a distinction to his court, but we may believe that the king would regard it as a part of the co-operation between Church and State in the reforms he had in mind. To Thomas the retention of his old office would probably mean a pledge not to oppose the royal will in the plans which he no doubt foresaw. It would also interfere seriously with the new manner of life which he proposed for himself, and he firmly declined to continue in the old office. In other ways, unimportant as yet, the policy of the primate as it developed was coming into collision with the king's interests, in his determined pushing of the rights of his Church to every piece of land to which it could lay any claim, in some cases directly against the king, and in his refusal to allow clerks in the service of the State to hold preferments in the Church, of which he had himself been guilty; but all these things were still rather signs of what might be expected than important in themselves. There was for several months no breach between the king and the archbishop.

For some time after his return to England Henry was occupied, as he had been of late on the continent, with minor details of government of no permanent importance. The treaty of alliance with Count Dietrich of Flanders was renewed. Gilbert Foliot was translated to the important bishopric of London. A campaign in South Wales brought the prince of that country to terms, and was followed by homage from him and other Welsh princes rendered at a great council held at Woodstock during the first week of July, 1163. It was at this meeting that the king first met with open and decided opposition from the archbishop, though this was still in regard to a special point and not to a general line of policy. The revenue of the state which had been left by the last reign in a disordered condition was still the subject of much concern and careful planning. Recently, as our evidence leads us to believe, the king had given up the Danegeld as a tax which had declined in value until it was no longer worth collecting. At Woodstock he made a proposition to the council for an increase in the revenue without an increase in the taxation. It was that the so-called "sheriffs aid," a tax said to be of two shillings on the hide paid to the sheriffs by their counties as a compensation for their services, should be for the future paid into the royal treasury for the use of the crown. That this demand was in the direction of advance and reform can hardly be questioned, especially if, as is at least possible, it was based on the declining importance of the sheriffs as purely local officers, and their increasing responsibilities as royal officers on account of the growing importance of the king's courts and particularly of the itinerant justice courts. So decided a change, however, in the traditional way of doing business could only be made with consent asked and obtained. There is no evidence that opposition came from any one except Becket. He flatly refused to consent to any such change, as he had a right to do so far as his own lands were concerned, and declared that this tax should never be paid from them to the public treasury. The motive of his opposition does not appear and is not easy to guess. He stood on the historical purpose of the tax and refused to consider any other use to which it might be put. Henry was angry, but apparently he had to give up his plan. At any rate unmistakable notice had been served on him that his plans for reform were likely to meet with the obstinate opposition of his former chancellor.

This first quarrel was the immediate prelude to another concerning a far more important matter and of far more lasting consequences. Administration and jurisdiction, revenue and justice, were so closely connected in the medieval state that any attempt to increase the revenue, or to improve and centralize the administrative machinery, raised at once the question of changes in the judicial system. But Henry II was not interested in getting a larger income merely, or a closer centralization. His whole reign goes to show that he had a high conception of the duty of the king to make justice prevail and to repress disorder and crime But this was a duty which he could not begin to carry out without at once encountering the recognized rights and still wider claims of the Church. Starting from the words of the apostle against going to law before unbelievers, growing at first as a process of voluntary arbitration within the Church, adding a criminal side with the growth of disciplinary powers over clergy and members, and greatly stimulated and widened by the legislation of the early Christian emperors, a body of law and a judicial organization had been developed by the Church which rivalled that of the State in its own field and surpassed it in scientific form and content. In the hundred years since William the Conqueror landed in England this system had been greatly perfected. The revival of the Roman law in the schools of Italy had furnished both model and material, but more important still the triumph of the Cluniac reformation, of the ideas of centralization and empire, had given an immense stimulus to this growth, and led to clearer conceptions than ever before of what to do and how to do it. When the state tardily awoke to the same consciousness of opportunity and method, it found a large part of what should have been its own work in the hands of a rival power.

In no state in Christendom had the line between these conflicting jurisdictions been clearly drawn. In England no attempt had as yet been made to draw it; the only legislation had been in the other direction. The edict of William I, separating the ecclesiastical courts from the temporal, and giving them exclusive jurisdiction in spiritual causes, must be regarded as a beneficial regulation as things then were. The same thing can hardly be said of the clause in Stephen's charter to the Church by which he granted it jurisdiction over all the clergy; yet under this clause the Church had in fifteen years drawn into its hands, as nearly as we can judge, more business that should naturally belong to the state than in the three preceding reigns. This rapid attainment of what Anselm could only have wished for, this enlarged jurisdiction of the Church, stood directly in the way of the plans of the young king as he took up the work of restoring the government of his grandfather. He had found out this fact before the death of Archbishop Theobald and had taken some steps to bring the question to an issue at that time, but he had been obliged to cross to France and had not since been able to go on with the matter. Now the refusal of Archbishop Thomas to grant his request about the sheriff's aid probably did not make him any less ready to push what he believed to be the clear rights of the state against the usurpations of the clergy.

As the state assumed more and more the condition of settled order under the new king, and the courts were able to enforce the laws everywhere, the failures of justice which resulted from the separate position of the clergy attracted more attention. The king was told that there had been during his reign more than a hundred murders by clerks and great numbers of other crimes, for none of which had it been possible to inflict the ordinary penalties. Special cases began to be brought to his attention. The most important of these was the case of Philip of Broi, a man of some family and a canon of Bedford, who, accused of the murder of a knight, had cleared himself by oath in the bishop's court. Afterwards the king's justice in Bedford summoned him to appear in his court and answer to the same charge, but he refused with insulting language which the justice at once repeated to the king as a contempt of the royal authority. Henry was very angry and swore "by the eyes of God," his favourite oath, that an insult to his minister was an insult to himself and that the canon must answer for it in his court. "Not so," said the archbishop, "for laymen cannot be judges of the clergy. If the king complains of any injury, let him come or send to Canterbury, and there he shall have full justice by ecclesiastical authority." This declaration of the archbishop was the extreme claim of the Church in its simplest form. Even the king could not obtain justice for a personal injury in his own courts, and the strength of Becket's position is shown by the fact that, in spite of all his anger, Henry was obliged to submit. He could not, even then, get the case of the murder reopened, and in the matter of the insult to his judge the penalties which he obtained must have seemed to him very inadequate.

It seems altogether probable that this case had much to do with bringing Henry to a determination to settle the question, what law and what sovereign should rule in England. So long as such things were possible, there could be no effective centralization and no supremacy of the national law. Within three months of the failure of his plan of taxation in the council at Woodstock the king made a formal demand of the Church to recognize the right of the State to punish criminous clerks. The bishops were summoned to a conference at Westminster on October 1. To them the king proposed an arrangement, essentially the same as that afterwards included in the Constitutions of Clarendon, by which the question of guilt or innocence should be determined by the Church court, but once pronounced guilty the clerk should be degraded by the Church and handed over to the lay court for punishment. The bishops were not at first united on the answer which they should make, but Becket had no doubts, and his opinion carried the day. One of his biographers, Herbert of Bosham, who was his secretary and is likely to have understood his views, though he was if possible of an even more extreme spirit than his patron, records the speech in which the archbishop made known to the king the answer of the Church. Whether actually delivered or not, the speech certainly states the principles on which Becket must have stood, and these are those of the reformers of Cluny in their most logical form. The Church is not subject to an earthly king nor to the law of the State alone: Christ also is its king and the divine law its law. This is proved by the words of our Lord concerning the "two swords." But those who are by ordination the clergy of the Church, set apart from the nations of men and peculiarly devoted to the work of God, are under no earthly king. They are above kings and confer their power upon them, and far from being subject to any royal jurisdiction they are themselves the judges of kings. There can be no doubt but that Becket in his struggle with the king had consciously before him the model of Anselm; but these words, whether he spoke them to the king's face or not, forming as they did the principles of his action and accepted by the great body of the clergy, show how far the English Church had progressed along the road into which Anselm had first led it.

Henry's only answer to the argument of the archbishop was to adopt exactly the position of his grandfather in the earlier conflict, and to inquire whether the bishops were willing to observe the ancient customs of the realm. To this they made answer together and singly that they were, "saving their order." This was of course to refuse, and the conference came to an end with no other result than to define more clearly the issue between Church and State. In the interval which followed Becket was gradually made aware that his support in the Church at large was not so strong as he could wish. The terror of the king's anger still had its effect in England, and some of the bishops went over to his side and tried to persuade the archbishop to some compromise. The pope, Alexander III, who had taken refuge in France from the Emperor and his antipope, saw more clearly than Becket the danger of driving another powerful sovereign into the camp of schism and rebellion and counselled moderation. He even sent a special representative to England, with letters to Becket to this effect, and with instructions to urge him to come to terms with the king.

At last Becket was persuaded to concede the form of words desired, though his biographers asserted that he did this on the express understanding that the concession should be no more than a form to save the honour of the king. He had an interview with Henry at Oxford and engaged that he would faithfully observe the customs of the realm. This promise Henry received gladly, though not, it was noticed, with a return of his accustomed kindness to the archbishop; and he declared at once that, as the refusal of Thomas to obey the customs of the realm had been public, so the satisfaction made to his honour must be public and the pledge be given in the presence of the nobles and bishops of the kingdom. To this Becket apparently offered no objection, nor to the proposal which followed, according to his secretary at the suggestion of the archbishop's enemies, but certainly from Henry's point of view the next natural step, that after the promise had been given, the customs of the realm should be put into definite statement by a "recognition," or formal inquiry, that there might be no further danger of either civil or clerical courts infringing on the jurisdiction of the other.

For this double purpose, to witness the archbishop's declaration and to make the recognition, a great council met at Clarendon, near Salisbury, towards the end of January, 1164. Some questions both of what happened at this council and of the order of events are still unsettled, but the essential points seem clear. Becket gave the required promise with no qualifying phrase, and was followed by each of the bishops in the same form. Then came the recognition, whether provided for beforehand or not, by members of the council who were supposed to know the ancient practice, for the purpose of putting into definite form the customs to which the Church had agreed. The document thus drawn up, which has come down to us known as the Constitutions of Clarendon, records in its opening paragraph the fact and form of this agreement and the names of the consenting bishops. It is probable, however, that this refers to the earlier engagement, and that after the customs were reduced to definite statement, no formal promise was made. The archbishop in the discussion urged his own ignorance of the customs, and it is quite possible that, receiving his training in the time of Stephen and believing implicitly in the extreme claims of the Church, he was really ignorant of what could be proved by a historical study of the ancient practice. The king demanded that the bishops should put their seals to this document, but this they evidently avoided. Becket's secretary says that he temporized and demanded delay. Henry had gained, however, great advantage from the council, both in what he had actually accomplished and in position for the next move.

To all who accepted the ideas which now ruled the Church there was much to complain of, much that was impossible in the Constitutions of Clarendon. On the question of the trial of criminous clerks, which had given rise to these difficulties, it was provided, according to the best interpretation, that the accused clerk should be first brought before a secular court and there made to answer to the charge. Whatever he might plead, guilty or not guilty, he was to be transferred to the Church court for trial and, if found guilty, for degradation from the priesthood; he was then to be handed over to the king's officer who had accompanied him to the bishop's court for sentence in the king's court to the state's punishment of his crime.[46] Becket and his party regarded this as a double trial and a double punishment for a single offence. But this was not all. The Constitutions went beyond the original controversy. Suits to determine the right of presentation to a living even between two clerks must be tried in the king's court, as also suits to determine whether a given fee was held in free alms or as a lay fee. None of the higher clergy were to go out of the kingdom without the king's permission, nor without his consent were appeals to be taken from ecclesiastical courts to the pope, his barons to be excommunicated or their lands placed under an interdict. The feudal character of the clergy who held in chief of the king was strongly insisted on. They must hold their lands as baronies, and answer for them to the royal justices, and perform all their feudal obligations like other barons; and if their fiefs fell vacant, they must pass into the king's hand and their revenues be treated as domain revenues during the vacancy. A new election must be made by a delegation summoned by the king, in his chapel, and with his consent, and the new prelate must perform liege homage and swear fealty to the king before his consecration.

In short, the Constitutions are a codification of the ancient customs on all those points where conflict was likely to arise between the old ideas of the Anglo-Norman State and the new ideas of the Hildebrandine Church. For there can be little doubt that Henry's assertion that he was but stating the customs of his grandfather was correct. There is not so much proof in regard to one or two points as we should like, but all the evidence that we have goes to show that the State was claiming nothing new, and about most of the points there can be no question. Nor was this true of England only. The rights asserted in the Constitutions had been exercised in general in the eleventh and early twelfth centuries by every strong state in Europe. The weakness of Henry's position was not in its historical support, but in the fact that history had been making since his grandfather's day. Nor was the most important feature of the history that had been made in the interval the fact that the State in its weakness had allowed many things to slip out of its hands. For Henry's purpose of recovery the rise of the Church to an equality with the State, its organization as an international monarchy, conscious of the value of that organization and powerful to defend it, was far more important. The Anglo-Norman monarchy had been since its beginning the strongest in Europe. Henry II was in no less absolute control of the State than his ancestors. But now there stood over against the king, as there never had before, a power almost as strong in England as his own. Thomas understood this more clearly than Henry did. He not merely believed in the justice and necessity of his cause, but he believed in his ability to make it prevail. Thomas may have looked to Anselm as his model and guide of conduct, but in position he stood on the results of the work which Anselm had begun, and he was even more convinced than his predecessor had been of the righteousness of his cause and of his power to maintain it. This conflict was likely to be a war of giants, and at its beginning no man could predict its outcome.

Even if the council of Clarendon closed, as we have supposed it did, with no definite statement on Thomas's part of his attitude towards the Constitutions, and not, as some accounts imply, with a flat refusal to accept them, he probably left the council fully determined not to do so. He carried away with him an official copy of the Constitutions as evidence of the demands which had been made and shortly afterwards he suspended himself from his functions because of the promise which he had originally given to obey them, and applied to the pope for absolution. For some months matters drifted with no decisive events. Both sides made application to the pope. The archbishop attempted to leave England without the knowledge of the king, but failed to make a crossing. The courts were still unable to carry out the provisions of the Constitutions. Finally a case arose involving the archbishop's own court, and on his disregard of the king's processes he was summoned to answer before the curia regis at Northampton on October 6.

It is to be regretted that we have no account of the interesting and dramatic events of this assembly from a hand friendly to the king and giving us his point of view. In the biographies of the archbishop, written by clerks who were not likely to know much feudal law, it is not easy to trace out the exact legal procedure nor always to discover the technical right which we may be sure the king believed was on his side in every step he took. At the outset it was recorded that as a mark of his displeasure Henry omitted to send to the archbishop the customary personal summons to attend the meeting of the court and summoned him only through the sheriff, but, though the omission of a personal summons to one of so high rank would naturally be resented by his friends, as he was to go, not as a member of the court, but as an accused person to answer before it, the omission was probably quite regular. Immediately after the organization of the court, Becket was put on his trial for neglect to obey the processes of the king's court in the earlier case. Summoned originally on an appeal for default of judgment, he had neither gone to the court himself nor sent a personal excuse, but he had instructed his representatives to plead against the legality of the appeal. This he might have done himself if personally before the court, but, as he had not come, there was technically a refusal to obey the king's commands which gave Henry his opportunity. Before the great curia regis the case was very simple. The archbishop seems to have tried to get before the court the same plea as to the illegality of the appeal, but it was ruled out at once, as "it had no place there." In other words, the case was now a different one. It was tried strictly on the ground of the archbishop's feudal obligations, and there he had no defence. Judgment was given against him, and all his movables were declared in the king's mercy.

William Fitz Stephen, one of Becket's biographers who shows a more accurate knowledge of the law than the others, and who was present at the trial, records an interesting incident of the judgment. A dispute arose between the barons and the bishops as to who should pronounce it, each party trying to put the unpleasant duty on the other. To the barons' argument that a bishop should declare the decision of the court because Becket was a bishop, the bishops answered that they were not sitting there as bishops but as barons of the realm and peers of the lay barons. The king interposed, and the sentence was pronounced by the aged Henry, Bishop of Winchester. Becket seems to have submitted without opposition, and the bishops who were present, except Gilbert Foliot of London, united in giving security for the payment of the fine.

A question that inevitably arises at this point and cannot be answered is, why Henry did not rest satisfied with the apparently great advantage he had gained. He had put into operation more than one of the articles of the Constitutions of Clarendon, and against the archbishop in person. Becket had been obliged to recognize the jurisdiction of the curia regis over himself and to submit to its sentence, and the whole body of bishops had recognized their feudal position in the state and had acted upon it. Perhaps the king wished to get an equally clear precedent in a case which was a civil one rather than a misdemeanour. Perhaps he was so exasperated against the archbishop that he was resolved to pursue him to his ruin, but, though more than one thing points to this, it does not seem a reasonable explanation. Whatever may have been his motive, the king immediately,— the accounts say on the same day with the first trial;—demanded that his former chancellor should account for £300 derived from the revenues of the castles of Eye and Berkhampsted held by him while chancellor. Thomas answered that the money had been spent in the service of the state, but the king refused to admit that this had been done by his authority. Again Becket submitted, though not recognizing the right of the court to try him in a case in which he had not been summoned, and gave security for the payment.

Still this was not sufficient. On the next day the king demanded the return of 500 marks which he had lent Becket for the Toulouse campaign, and of a second 500 which had been borrowed of a Jew on the king's security. This was followed at once by a further demand for an account of the revenues of the archbishopric and of all other ecclesiastical fiefs which had been vacant while Thomas was chancellor. To pay the sum which this demand would call for would be impossible without a surrender of all the archbishop's sources of income for several years, and it almost seems as if Henry intended this result. The barons apparently thought as much, for from this day they ceased to call at Becket's quarters. The next day the clergy consulted together on the course to be taken and there was much difference of opinion. Some advised the immediate resignation of the archbishopric, others a firm stand accepting the consequence of the king's anger; and there were many opinions between these two extremes. During the day an offer of 2000 marks in settlement of the claim was sent to the king on the advice of Henry of Winchester, but it was refused, and the day closed without any agreement among the clergy on a common course of action.

The next day was Sunday, and the archbishop did not leave his lodgings. On Monday he was too ill to attend the meeting of the court, much to Henry's anger. The discussions of Saturday and the reflections of the following days had apparently led Becket to a definite decision as to his own conduct. The king was in a mood, as it would surely seem to him, to accept nothing short of his ruin. No support was to be expected from the barons. The clergy, even the bishops, were divided in opinion and it would be impossible to gain strength enough from them to escape anything which the king might choose to demand. We must, I think, explain Becket's conduct from this time on by supposing that he now saw clearly that all concessions had been and would be in vain, and that he was resolved to exert to the utmost the strength of passive opposition which lay in the Church, to put his case on the highest possible grounds, and to gain for the Church the benefits of persecution and for himself the merits, if needs be, of the martyr.

Early the next morning the bishops, terrified by the anger of the king, came to Becket and tried to persuade him to yield completely, even to giving up the archbishopric. This he refused. He rebuked them for their action against him already in the court, forbade them to sit in judgment on him again, himself appealing to the pope, and ordered them, if any secular person should lay hands on him in punishment, to excommunicate him at once. Against this order Gilbert Foliot immediately appealed. The bishops then departed, and Becket entered the monastery church and celebrated the mass of St. Stephen's day, opening with the words of the Psalm, "Princes did sit and speak against me." This was a most audacious act, pointed directly at the king, and a public declaration that he expected and was prepared for the fate of the first martyr. Naturally the anger of the court was greatly increased. From the celebration of the mass, Becket went to the meeting of the court, his cross borne before him in the usual manner, but on reaching the door of the meeting-place, he took it from his cross-bearer and carrying it in his own hands entered the hall. Such an unusual proceeding as this could have but one meaning. It was a public declaration that he was in fear of personal violence, and that any one who laid hands on him must understand his act to be an attack on the cross and all that it signified. Some of the bishops tried to persuade him to abandon this attitude, but in vain. So far as we can judge the mood of Henry, Becket had much to justify his feeling, and if he were resolved not to accept the only other alternative of complete submission, but determined to resist to the utmost, the act was not unwise.

When the bishops reported to the king the primate's order forbidding them to sit in trial of him again, it was seen at once to be a violation of the Constitutions of Clarendon; and certain barons were sent to him to inquire if he stood to this, to remind him of his oath as the king's liege-man, and of the promise, equivalent to an oath, which he had made at Clarendon to keep the Constitutions "in good faith, without guile, and according to law," and to ask if he would furnish security for the payment of the claims against him as chancellor. In reply Becket stood firmly to his position, and renewed the prohibition and the appeal to the pope. The breach of the Constitutions being thus placed beyond question, the king demanded the judgment of the court, bishops and barons together. The bishops urged the ecclesiastical dangers in which they would be placed if they disregarded the archbishop's prohibition, and suggested that instead they should themselves appeal to Rome against him as a perjurer. To this the king at last agreed, and the appeal was declared by Hilary, Bishop of Chichester, who had throughout inclined to the king's side, and who urged upon the archbishop with much vigour the oath which they had all taken at Clarendon under his leadership and which he was now forcing them to violate. Becket's answer to this speech is the weakest and least honest thing that he did during all these days of trial. "We promised nothing at Clarendon," he said, "without excepting the rights of the Church. The very clauses to which you refer, 'in good faith, without guile, and according to law,' are saving clauses, because it is impossible to observe anything in good faith and according to law if it is contrary to the laws of God and to the fealty due the Church. Nor is there any such thing as the dignity of a Christian king where the liberty of the Church which he has sworn to observe has perished."

The court then, without the bishops, found the archbishop guilty of perjury and probably of treason. The formal pronunciation of the sentence in the presence of Becket was assigned to the justiciar, the Earl of Leicester, but he was not allowed to finish. With violent words Thomas interrupted him and bitterly denounced him for presuming as a layman to sit in judgment on his spiritual father. In the pause that followed, Becket left the hall still carrying his cross. As he passed out, the spirit of the chancellor overcame for a moment that of the bishop, and he turned fiercely on those who were saying "perjured traitor" and cried that, if it were not for his priestly robes and the wickedness of the act, he would know how to answer in arms such an accusation. During the night that followed, Becket secretly left Northampton, and by a roundabout way after two weeks succeeded in escaping to the continent in disguise. The next day the court held its last session. After some discussion it was resolved to allow the case to stand as it was, and not even to take the archbishop's fief into the king's hands until the pope should decide the appeal, a resolution which shows how powerful was the Church and how strong was the influence of the bishops who were acting with the king. At the same time an embassy of great weight and dignity was appointed to represent the king before the pope, consisting of the Archbishop of York, the Bishops of London, Chichester, Exeter, and Worcester, two earls and two barons, and three clerks from the king's household. They were given letters to the King of France and to the Count of Flanders which said that Thomas, "formerly Archbishop of Canterbury," had fled the kingdom as a traitor and should not be received in their lands.

In the somewhat uncertain light in which we are compelled to view these events, this quarrel seems unnecessary, and the guilt of forcing it on Church and State in England, at least at this time and in these circumstances, appears to rest with Henry. The long patience of his grandfather, which was willing to wait the slow process of events and carefully shunned the drawing of sharp issues when possible, he certainly does not show in this case. It is more than likely, however, that the final result would have been the same in any case. No reconciliation was possible between the ideas or the characters of the two chief antagonists, and the necessary constitutional growth of the state made the collision certain. It was a case in which either the Church or the State must give way, but greater moderation of action and demand would have given us a higher opinion of Henry's practical wisdom; and the essential justice of his cause hardly excuses such rapid and violent pushing of his advantage. On the other hand Thomas's conduct, which must have been exceedingly exasperating to the hot blood which Henry had inherited, must be severely condemned in many details. We cannot avoid the feeling that much about it was insincere and theatrical, and even an intentional challenging of the fate he seemed to dread. But yet it does not appear what choice was left him between abjectly giving up all that he had been trained to believe of the place of the Church in the world and entering on open war with the king.

The war now declared dragged slowly on for six years with few events that seemed to bring a decision nearer till towards the end of that period. Henry's embassy returned from the pope at Christmas time and reported that no formal judgment had been rendered on the appeal. The king then put in force the ordinary penalty for failure of service and confiscated the archbishop's revenues. He went even further than this in some acts that were justifiable and some that were spiteful. He ordered the confiscation of the revenues of the archbishop's clerks who had accompanied him, prohibited all appeals to the pope, and ordered Becket's relatives to join him in exile. As to the archbishop, whatever one may think of his earlier attitude we can have but little sympathy with his conduct from this time on. He went himself to the pope after the departure of Henry's messengers, but though Alexander plainly inclined to his side, he did not obtain a formal decision. Ther he retired to the abbey of Pontigny in Burgundy, where he resided for some time.

Political events did not wait the settlement of the conflict with the Church, though nothing of great interest occurred before its close. Henry crossed to Normandy in the spring of 1165, where an embassy came to him from the Emperor which resulted in the marriage of his daughter Matilda with Henry the Lion, of the house of Guelf. Two clerks who returned with this embassy to Germany seem to have involved the king in some embarrassment by promises of some kind to support the emperor against the pope. It does not appear, however, that Henry ever intended to recognize the antipope; and, whatever the promises were, he promptly disavowed them. Later in the year two campaigns in Wales are less interesting from a military point of view than as leading to further experiments in taxation. The year 1166 is noteworthy for the beginning of extensive judicial and administrative reforms which must be considered hereafter with the series to which they belong. In that year also Becket began a direct attack upon his enemies in England.

He began by sending to the king three successive warnings, all based on the assumption that in such a dispute the final decision must remain with the Church and that the State must always give way. His next step was the solemn excommunication of seven supporters of the king, mostly clerks, but including Richard of Lucy, the justiciar. The king was warned to expect the same fate himself, and all obedience to the Constitutions of Clarendon was forbidden. The effect of this act was not what Becket anticipated. It led rather to a reaction of feeling against him from its unnecessary severity, and a synod of the clergy of the archbishopric entered an appeal against it. A new embassy was sent to the pope who was then at Rome to get the appeal decided, and was much more favourably received by Alexander who seems to have been displeased with Becket's action. He promised to send legates to Henry to settle the whole question with him. The occupation of Britanny by which it was brought under Henry's direct control and a short and inconclusive war with the king of France took up the interval until the legates reached Normandy in October, 1167. Their mission proved a failure. Becket, who came in person to the inquiry which they held, refused to accept any compromise or to modify in any way his extreme position. On the other side Henry was very angry because they refused to deprive the archbishop.

The year 1168 was a troubled one for Henry, with revolts in Poitou and Britanny, supported by the king of France, and with useless negotiations with Louis. Early in 1169 the pope sent new envoys to try to reconcile king and primate with instructions to bring pressure to bear on both parties. The king of France also came to the meeting and exerted his influence, but the result was a second failure. Becket had invented a new saving clause which he thought the king might be induced to accept. He would submit "saving the honour of God," but Henry understood the point and could see no difference between this and the old reservation. Becket finally stood firmly against the pressure of the envoys and the influence of Louis, and Henry was not moved by the threats which the pope had directed to be made if necessary. A third embassy later in the year seemed for a moment about to find a possible compromise, but ended in another failure, both parties refusing to make any real concession. The interval between these two attempts at reconciliation Becket had used to excommunicate about thirty of his opponents in England, mostly churchmen, including the Bishops of London and Salisbury.

For more than a year longer the quarrel went on, the whole Church suffering from the results, and new points arising to complicate the issue. The danger that England would be placed under an interdict Henry met by most stringent regulations against the admission of any communications from the pope, or any intercourse with pope or archbishop. On the question which arose in the constant negotiations as to the compensation which should be made to Becket for his loss of revenue since he had left England, he showed himself as unyielding as on every other point, and demanded the uttermost farthing. For some time the king had wished to have his son Henry crowned, and on June 14, 1170, that ceremony was actually performed at Westminster by the Archbishop of York, who had, as Henry believed or asserted, a special permission from the pope for the purpose. Of course Becket resented this as a new invasion of his rights and determined to exact for it the proper penalties. Finally, towards the end of July, an agreement was reached which was no compromise; it simply ignored the points in dispute and omitted all the qualifying phrases. The king agreed to receive the archbishop to his favour and to restore him his possessions, and Becket accepted this. The agreement can hardly have been regarded by either side as anything more than a truce. Neither intended to abandon any right for which he had been contending, but both were exhausted by the conflict and desired an interval for recovery, perhaps with a hope of renewing the strife from a better position.

It was December 1 before Thomas actually landed in England. He then came bringing war, not peace. He had sent over, in advance of his own crossing, letters which he had solicited and obtained from the pope, suspending from their functions all the bishops who had taken part in the coronation of the young king, and reviving the excommunications of the Bishops of London and Salisbury. Then, landing at Sandwich, he went on to Canterbury, where he was received with joy. But there was little real joy for Becket or his friends in the short remainder of his life, unless it may have been the joy of conflict and of anticipated martyrdom. To messengers who asked the removal of the sentence against the bishops, he refused any concession except on their unconditional promise to abide by the pope's decision; and the three prelates most affected—York, London, and Salisbury—went over to Normandy to the king. A plan to visit the court of the young king at London was stopped by orders to return to Canterbury. On Christmas day, at the close of a sermon from the text "Peace on earth to men of good-will," he issued new excommunications against some minor offenders, and bitterly denounced, in words that seemed to have the same effect, those who endangered the peace between himself and the king.

It was on the news of this Christmas proclamation, or perhaps on the report of the bishops who had come from England, that Henry gave way to his violent temper, and in an outburst of passion denounced those whom he had cherished and covered with favours, because they could not avenge him of this one priest. On these words four knights of his household resolved to punish the archbishop, and, leaving the court secretly, they went over to England. They were Reginald Fitz Urse, William of Tracy, Hugh of Morville, and Richard le Breton. An attempt to stop them when their departure was observed did not succeed, and, collecting supporters from the local enemies of the archbishop, they forced their way into his presence on the afternoon of December 29. Their reproaches, demands, and threats Becket met with firmness and dignity, refusing to be influenced by fear. Finding that they could gain nothing by words, they withdrew to get their arms, and Becket was hurried into the cathedral by his friends. As they were going up the steps from the north-west transept to the choir, their enemies met them, calling loudly for "the traitor, Thomas Becket." The archbishop turned about and stepped down to the floor of the transept, repelling their accusations with bitter words and accusations of his own, and was there struck down by their swords and murdered; not before the altar, as is sometimes said, though within the doors of his own church.

[46] See Maitland, Henry II and the Criminous Clerks, in his Canon Law in the Church of England (1898). (Engl. Hist., Rev. vii, 224.)

CHAPTER XIV.
CONQUEST AND REBELLION

The martyrdom of Thomas Becket served his cause better than his continuance in life could have done. Even if his murderers foolishly thought to serve the king by their deed, Henry himself was under no delusion as to its effect. He was thunderstruck at the news, and, in a frenzy of horror which was no doubt genuine, as well as to mark his repudiation of all share in the deed, he fasted and shut himself from communication with the court for days. But the public opinion of Europe would not acquit Henry of the guilt. Letters poured in upon the pope denouncing him and demanding his punishment. The interdict of his Norman dominions which had been threatened was proclaimed by the Archbishop of Sens, but suspended again by an appeal to the pope. Events moved slowly in the twelfth century, and before the pope could take any active steps in the case, an embassy which left Normandy almost immediately had time to reach him and to promise on the part of the king his complete submission to whatever the pope should decree after examination of the facts. Immediate punishment of any severity was thus avoided, and the embassy of two cardinals to Normandy which the pope announced could act only after some delay.

In the meanwhile in England Thomas the archbishop was being rapidly transformed into Thomas the saint. Miracles were reported almost at once, and the legend of his saintship took its rise and began to throw a new light over the events of his earlier life. The preparation of his body for the grave had revealed his secret asceticism,—the hair garments next his skin and long unchanged. The people believed him to be a true martyr, and his popular canonization preceded by some time the official, though this followed with unusual quickness even for the middle ages. It was pronounced by the pope in whose reign he had died on February 21, 1173. For generations he remained the favourite saint of England, and his popularity in foreign lands is surprising, though it must be remembered that he was a great and most conspicuous martyr of the official Church, of the new Hildebrandine Church, of the spirit and ideas which were by that date everywhere in command.

This long and bitter struggle between Church and State, unworthy of both the combatants, was now over except for the consequences which were lasting, and the interest of Henry's reign flows back into the political channel. The king did not wait in seclusion the report of the pope's mission. It may have been, as was suggested even at the time, that he was glad of an excuse to escape from Normandy before the envoys' coming and to avoid a meeting with them until time had done something to soften the feeling against him. Before his departure his hold on Britanny was strengthened by the death, in February, 1171, of Conan the candidate whom he had recognized as count. Since 1166 the administration of the country had been practically in his hands; and in that year his son Geoffrey had been betrothed to Constance, the daughter and heiress of Conan. Geoffrey would now succeed to the countship, but he was still a child; and Britanny was virtually incorporated in Henry's continental empire.

The refuge which the repentant Henry may have sought from the necessity of giving an answer to the pope at once, or a kind of preliminary penance for his sin, he found in Ireland. Since he received so early in his reign the sanction of Pope Hadrian IV of his plan of conquest, he had done nothing himself towards that end, but others had. The adventurous barons of the Welsh marches, who were used to the idea of carving out lordships for themselves from the lands of their Celtic enemies, were easily persuaded to extend their civilizing operations to the neighbouring island, where even richer results seemed to be promised. In 1166 Dermot, the dispossessed king of Leinster, who had found King Henry too busily occupied with affairs in France to aid him, had secured with the royal permission the help he needed in Wales, and thus had connected with the future history of Ireland the names of "Strongbow" and Fitzgerald. The native Irish, though the bravest of warriors, were without armour, and their weapons, of an earlier stage of military history, were no match for the Norman; especially had they no defence against the Norman archers. The conquest of Leinster, from Waterford to Dublin, and including those two cities, occupied some years, but was accomplished by a few men. "Strongbow" himself, Richard de Clare, Earl of Pembroke, did not cross over till the end of August, 1170, when the work was almost completed. He married the daughter of Dermot and was recognized as his heir, but the death of his father-in-law in the next spring was followed by a general insurrection against the new rulers, and this was hardly under control when the earl was summoned to England to meet the king.

Henry could not afford to let the dominion of Ireland, to which he had looked forward for himself, slip from his hands, nor to risk the danger that an independent state might be formed so close to England by his own vassals. Already the Earl of Pembroke was out of favour; it was said that his lands had been forfeited, and he might easily become a rebel difficult to subdue in his new possessions. At the moment he certainly had no thought of rebellion, and he at once obeyed the summons to England. Henry had crossed from Normandy early in September, 1171, had paid a brief visit to Winchester, where Henry of Blois, once so powerful in Church and State, was now dying, and then advanced with his army through southern Wales into Pembrokeshire whence he crossed to Ireland in the middle of October. As he passed from Waterford to Cashel, and then again from Waterford to Dublin, chiefs came in from all sides, many of whom had never submitted to the Norman invaders, and acknowledged his overlordship. Only in the remoter parts of the west and north did they remain away, except Roderick of Connaught, the most powerful of the Irish kings, who was not yet ready to own himself a vassal, but claimed the whole of Ireland for himself. The Christmas feast Henry kept in Dublin, and there entertained his new subjects who were astonished at the splendour of his court.

A few weeks later a council of the Irish Church was held at Cashel, and attended by all the prelates of the island except the Archbishop of Armagh whose age prevented his coming. The bishops swore allegiance to Henry, and each of them is said to have made a formal declaration, written and sealed, recognizing the right of Henry and his heirs to the kingdom of Ireland. The canons adopted by the council, putting into force rules of marriage and morals long established in practice in the greater part of Christendom, reveal the reasons that probably led the Church to favour the English conquest and even to consider it an especially pious act of the king. A report of Henry's acceptance by the Irish kings and of the acts of the council was sent at once to the pope, who replied in three letters under date of September 20, 1172, addressed to Henry, to the Irish bishops, and to the Irish kings, approving fully of all that had been done.

It is not clear that Henry had in mind any definite plan for the political government of the conquest which he had made. The allegiance of those princes who were outside the territories occupied by the Norman adventurers could have been no more than nominal, and no attempt seems to have been made to rule them. Meath was granted as a fief to Hugh of Lacy on the service of fifty knights. He was also made governor of Dublin and justiciar of Ireland, but this title is the only evidence that he was to be regarded as the representative of the king. Waterford and Wexford were made domain towns, as well as Dublin, and the earl of Pembroke, who gave up the royal rights which he might inherit from King Dermot, was enfeoffed with Leinster on the service of a hundred knights. Plainly the part of Ireland which was actually occupied was not treated in practice as a separate kingdom, whatever may have been the theory, but as a transplanted part of England under a very vague relationship. As a matter of fact, it was a purely feudal colony, under but the slightest control by a distant overlord, and doomed both from its situation in the midst of an alien, only partly civilized, and largely unconquered race, and from its own organization or lack of organization, to speedy troubles.

Henry returned to England at Easter time, and went on almost at once to meet the papal legates in Normandy. By the end of May his reconciliation with the Church was completed. First, Henry purged himself by solemn oath in the cathedral at Avranches of any share in the guilt of Thomas's assassination, and then the conditions of reconciliation were sworn to by himself and by the young king. These conditions are a very fair compromise, though Becket could never have agreed to them nor probably would Henry have done so but for the murder. The Church insisted on the one thing which was most essential to its real interests, the freedom of appeals to the pope. The point most important to the State, which had led originally to the quarrel—the question of the punishment of criminous clerks by the lay courts—was passed over in silence, a way out of the difficulty being found by requiring of the king a promise which he could readily make, that he would wholly do away with any customs which had been introduced against the churches of the land in his time. This would not be to his mind renouncing the Constitution of Clarendon. The temporalities of Canterbury and the exiled friends of the archbishop were to be restored as before the quarrel, and Henry promised not to withdraw his obedience from the catholic pope or his successors. The other conditions were of the nature of penance. The king promised to assume the cross at the next Christmas for a crusade of three years, and in the meantime to provide the Templars with a sum of money which in their judgment would be sufficient to maintain 200 knights in the Holy Land for a year.

Henry no doubt felt that he had lost much, but in truth he had every reason to congratulate himself on the lightness of his punishment for the crime to which his passionate words had led. He did not get all which he had set out to recover from the Church, but his gains were large and substantial. The agreement is a starting-point of some importance in the legal history of England. It may be taken as the beginning, with more full consciousness of field and boundaries, of the development of two long lines of law and jurisdiction, running side by side for many generations, each encroaching somewhat on the occupied or natural ground of the other, but with no other conflict of so serious a character as this. The criminal jurisdiction of the state did not recover quite all that the Constitutions of Clarendon had demanded. Clerks accused of the worst offences, of felonies, except high treason, were tried and punished by the Church courts, and from this arose the privilege known as benefit of clergy with all its abuses, but in all minor offences no distinction was made between clerk and layman. In civil cases also, suits which involved the right of property, even the right of presentation to livings, the state courts had their way. Two large fields of law, on the other hand,—marriage, and wills,—the Church, much to its profit, had entirely to itself.

The interval of peace for Henry was not a long one. Hardly was he freed from one desperate struggle when he found himself by degrees involved in another from which he was never to find relief. The policy which he was to follow towards his sons had been already foreshadowed in the coronation of the young Henry in 1170, but we do not find it easy to account for it or to reconcile it with other lines of policy which he was as clearly following. The conflict of ideas, the subtle contradictions of the age in which he lived, must have been reflected in the mind of the king whose dominions themselves were an empire of contrasts. Of all the middle ages there is perhaps no period that saw the ideal which chivalry had created of the wholly "courteous" king and prince more nearly realized in practice than the last half of the twelfth century—the brave warrior and great ruler, of course, but always also the generous giver, who considered "largesse" one of the chiefest of virtues and first of duties, and bestowed with lavish hand on all comers money and food, robes and jewels, horses and arms, and even castles and fiefs, recognizing the natural right of each one to the gift his rank would seem to claim. That such an ideal was actually realized in any large number of cases it would be absurd to maintain. It is not likely that any one ever sought to equal in detail the extravagant squandering of wealth in gifts which figures in the poetry of the age—the rich mantles which Arthur hung about the halls at a coronation festival to be taken by any one, or the thirty bushels of silver coins tumbled in a heap on the floor from which all might help themselves. But these poems record the ideal, and probably no other age saw more men, from kings down to simple knights, who tried to pattern themselves on this model and to look on wealth as an exhaustless store of things to be given away. But in the mind of kings who reigned in a world more real than the romances of chivalry, this duty had always to contend with natural ambition and with their responsibility for the welfare of the lands they ruled. The last half of the twelfth century saw these considerations grow rapidly stronger. The age that formed and applauded the young Henry also gave birth to Philip Augustus.

The marriage with Eleanor added to the strange mixture of blood in the Norman-Angevin house a new and warmer strain. It showed itself, careless, luxurious, self-indulgent, restless at any control, in her sons. But the marriage had also its effect on the husband and father. It gave a strong impetus to the conquest, which had already begun, of the colder and slower north by the ideals of duty and manners which had blossomed out into a veritable theory of life in the more tropical south. Henry could not keep himself from the spell of these influences, though they never controlled him as they did his children. It seems impossible to doubt, however, that he really believed it to be his duty to give his sons the position that belonged to them as princes, where they could form courts of their own, surrounded by their barons and knights, and display the virtues which belonged to their station. They had a rightful claim to this, which the ruling idea of conduct befitting a king would not allow him to deny. The story of Henry's waiting on his son at table after his coronation "as seneschal" and the reply of the young king to those who spoke of the honour done him, that it was a proper thing for one who was only the son of a count to wait on the son of a king, is significant of deeper things than mere manners. But, though he might be under the spell of these ideals, to partition his kingdom in very truth, to divest himself of power, to make his sons actually independent in the provinces which he gave them, was impossible to him. The power of his empire he could not break up. The real control of the whole, and even the greater part of the revenues, must remain in his hands. The conflict of ideas in his mind, when he tried to be true to them all in practice, led inevitably to a like conflict of facts and of physical force.

The coronation of the young Henry as king of England, considered by itself, seems an unaccountable act. Stephen had tried to secure the coronation of his son Eustace in his own lifetime, but there was a clear reason of policy in his case. The Capetian kings of France had long followed the practice, but for them also it had plainly been for many generations of the utmost importance for the security of the house. There had never been any reason in Henry's reign why extraordinary steps should seem necessary to secure the succession, and there certainly was none fifteen years after its beginning. No explanation is given us in any contemporary account of the motives which led to this coronation, and it is not likely that they were motives of policy. It is probable that it was done in imitation of the French custom, under the influence of the ideas of chivalry. But even if the king looked on this as chiefly a family matter, affecting not much more than the arrangements of the court, he could not keep it within those limits. His view of the position to which his sons were entitled was the most decisive influence shaping the latter half of his reign and through its effect on their characters almost as decisive for another generation.

Not long after his brother's coronation Richard received his mother's inheritance, Aquitaine and Poitou; Geoffrey was to be Count of Britanny by his marriage with the heiress; Normandy, Maine, and Anjou were assigned to the young king; while the little John, youngest of the children of Henry and Eleanor, received from his father only the name "Lackland" which expresses well enough Henry's idea that his position was not what it ought to be so long as he had no lordship of his own. Trouble of one kind had begun with the young king's coronation, for Louis of France had been deeply offended because his daughter Margaret had not been crowned queen of England at the same time. This omission was rectified in August, 1172, at Winchester, when Henry was again crowned, and Margaret with him. But more serious troubles than this were now beginning.

Already while Henry was in Ireland, the discontent of the young king had been noticed and reported to him. It had been speedily discovered that the coronation carried with it no power, though the young Henry was of an age to rule according to the ideas of the time, — of the age, indeed, at which his father had begun the actual government of Normandy. But he found himself, as a contemporary called him, "our new king who has nothing to reign over." It is probable, however, that the scantiness of the revenues supplied him to support his new dignity and to maintain his court had more to do with his discontent than the lack of political power. The courtly virtue of "largesse," which his father followed with some restraint where money was concerned, was with him a more controlling ideal of conduct. A brilliant court, joyous and gay, given up to minstrelsy and tournaments, seemed to him a necessity of life, and it could not be had without much money. Contemporary literature shows that the young king had all those genial gifts of manner, person, and spirit, which make their possessors universally popular. He was of more than average manly beauty, warm-hearted, cordial, and generous. He won the personal love of all men, even of his enemies, and his early death seemed to many, besides the father whom he had so sorely tried, to leave the world darker. Clearly he belongs in the list of those descendants of the Norman house, with the Roberts and the Stephens, who had the gifts which attract the admiration and affection of men, but at the same time the weakness of character which makes them fatal to themselves and to their friends. To a man of that type, even without the incentive of the spirit of the time, no amount of money could be enough. It is hardly possible to doubt that the emptiness of his political title troubled the mind of the young Henry far less than the emptiness of his purse.[47]

There was no lack of persons, whose word would have great influence with the young king, to encourage him in his discontent and even in plans of rebellion. His father-in-law, Louis VII, would have every reason to urge him on to extremes, those of policy because of the danger which threatened the Capetian house from the undivided Angevin power, those of personal feeling because of the seemingly intentional slights which his daughter Margaret had suffered. Eleanor, at once wife and mother, born probably in 1122, had now reached an age when she must have felt that she had lost some at least of the sources of earlier influence and consideration. Proud and imperious of spirit, she would bitterly resent any lack of attention on her husband's part, and she had worse things than neglect to excite her anger. From the beginning, we are told, while Henry was still in Ireland, she had encouraged her son to believe himself badly treated by his father. The barons, many of them at least, through all the provinces of Henry's empire, were restless under his strong control and excited by the evidence, constantly increasing as the judicial and administrative reforms of the reign went on, that the king was determined to confine their independence within narrower and narrower limits. Flattering offers of support no doubt came in at any sign that the young king would head resistance to his father.

The final step of appealing directly to armed force the young Henry did not take till the spring of 1173. A few weeks after his second coronation he was recalled to Normandy, but was allowed to go off at once to visit his father-in-law, ostensibly on a family visit. Louis was anxious to see his daughter. Apparently it was soon after his return that he made the first formal request of his father to be given an independent position in some one of the lands which had been assigned to him, urged, it was said, by the advice of the king of France and of the barons of England and Normandy. The request was refused, and he then made up his mind to rebel as soon as a proper opportunity and excuse should offer. These he found in the course of the negotiations for the marriage of his brother John about the beginning of Lent, 1173.

Marriage was the only way by which Henry could provide for his youngest son a position equal to that which he had given to the others, and this he was now planning to do by a marriage which would at the same time greatly increase his own power. The Counts of Maurienne in the kingdom of Burgundy had collected in their hands a variety of fiefs east of the Rhone extending from Geneva on the north over into the borders of Italy to Turin on the south until they commanded all the best passes of the western Alps. The reigning count, Humbert, had as yet no son. His elder daughter, a child a little younger than John, would be the heiress of his desirable lands. The situation seems naturally to have suggested to him the advantage of a close alliance with one whose influence and alliances were already so widely extended in the Rhone valley as Henry's. It needed no argument to persuade Henry of the advantage to himself of such a relationship. He undoubtedly looked forward to ruling the lands his son would acquire by the marriage as he ruled the lands of Geoffrey and of his other sons; and to command the western Alps would mean not merely a clear road into Italy if he should wish one, but also, of more immediate value, a strategic position on the east from which he might hope to cut off the king of France from any further interference in the south like that which earlier in his reign had compelled him to drop his plans against Toulouse. Belley, which would pass into his possession when this treaty was carried out, was not very far from the eastern edge of his duchy of Aquitaine. South-eastern France would be almost surrounded by his possessions, and it was not likely that anything could prevent it from passing into his actual or virtual control. Whether Henry dreamed of still wider dominion, of interference even in Italy and possibly of contending for the empire itself with Frederick Barbarossa, as some suspected at the time and as a few facts tend to show, we may leave unsettled, since the time never came when he could attempt seriously to realize such a dream.

The more probable and reasonable objects of his diplomacy seemed about to be attained at once. At Montferrand in Auvergne in February he met the Count of Maurienne, who brought his daughter with him, and there the treaty between them was drawn up and sworn to. At the same place appeared his former ally the king of Aragon and his former opponent the Count of Toulouse. Between them a few days later at Limoges peace was made; any further war would be against Henry's interests. The Count of Toulouse also frankly recognized the inevitable, and did homage and swore fealty to Henry, to the young Henry, and to his immediate lord, Richard, Duke of Aquitaine. From the moment of apparent triumph, however, dates the beginning of Henry's failure. Humbert of Maurienne, who was making so magnificent a provision for the young couple, naturally inquired what Henry proposed to do for John. He was told that three of the more important Angevin castles with their lands would be granted him. But the nominal lord of these castles was the young king, and his consent was required. This he indignantly refused, and his anger was so great that peaceable conference with him was no longer possible. He was now brought to the pitch of rebellion, and as they reached Chinon on their return to Normandy, he rode off from his father and joined the king of France. On the news Eleanor sent Richard and Geoffrey to join their brother, but was herself arrested soon after and held in custody.

Both sides prepared at once for war. Henry strengthened his frontier castles, and Louis called a great council of his kingdom, to which came his chief vassals, including the Counts of Flanders and Boulogne, whose long alliance with England made their action almost one of rebellion. There it was decided to join the war against the elder king of England. The long list of Henry's vassals who took his son's side, even if we deduct the names of some whose wavering inclination may have been fixed by the promises of lands or office which the younger Henry distributed with reckless freedom, reveals a widespread discontent in the feudal baronage. The turbulent lords of Aquitaine might perhaps be expected to revolt on every occasion, but the list includes the oldest names and leading houses of England and Normandy. Out of the trouble the king of Scotland hoped to recover what had been held of the last English king, and it may very well have seemed for a moment that the days of Stephen were going to return for all. The Church almost to a man stood by the king who had so recently tried to invade its privileges, and Henry hastened to strengthen himself with this ally by filling numerous bishoprics which had for a long time been in his hands. Canterbury was with some difficulty included among them. An earlier attempt to fill the primacy had failed because of a dispute about the method of choice, and now another failed because the archbishop selected refused to take office. At last in June Richard, prior of St. Martin's at Dover, was chosen, but his consecration was delayed for nearly a year by an appeal of the young king to the pope against a choice which disregarded his rights. The elder Henry had on his side also a goodly list of English earls: the illegitimate members of his house, Hamelin of Surrey, Reginald of Cornwall, and William of Gloucester; the earls of Arundel, Pembroke, Salisbury, Hertford, and Northampton; the son of the traitor of his mother's time, William de Mandeville, Earl of Essex; and William of Beaumont, Earl of Warwick, whose cousins of Leicester and Meulan were of the young king's party. The new men of his grandfather's making were also with him and the mass of the middle class.

The war was slow in opening. Henry kept himself closely to the defensive and waited to be attacked, appearing to be little troubled at the prospect and spending his time mostly in hunting. Early in July young Henry invaded Normandy with the Counts of Flanders and Boulogne, and captured Aumale, Eu, and a few other places, but the Count of Boulogne was wounded to the death, and the campaign came to an end. At the same time King Louis entered southern Normandy and laid siege to Verneuil, one ward of which he took and burnt by a trick that was considered dishonourable, and from which he fled in haste on the approach of Henry with his army. In the west, at the end of August, Henry's Brabantine mercenaries, of whom he is said to have had several thousand in his service, shut up a number of the rebel leaders in Dol. In a forced march of two days the king came on from Rouen, and three days later compelled the surrender of the castle. A long list is recorded of the barons and knights who were made prisoners there, of whom the most important was the Earl of Chester. A month later a conference was held at Gisors between the two parties, to see if peace were possible. This conference was held, it is said, at the request of the enemies of the king of England; but he offered terms to his sons which surprise us by their liberality after their failure in the war, and which show that he was more moved by his feelings as a father than by military considerations. He offered to Henry half the income of the royal domains in England, or if he preferred to live in Normandy, half the revenues of that duchy and all those of his father's lands in Anjou; to Richard half the revenues of Aquitaine; and to Geoffrey the possession of Britanny on the celebration of his marriage. Had he settled revenues like these on his sons when he nominally divided his lands among them, there probably would have been no rebellion; but now the king of France had much to say about the terms, and he could be satisfied only by the parcelling out of Henry's political power. To this the king of England would not listen, and the conference was broken off without result.

In England the summer and autumn of 1173 passed with no more decisive events than on the continent, but with the same general drift in favour of the elder Henry. Richard of Lucy, the justiciar and special representative of the king, and his uncle, Reginald of Cornwall, were the chief leaders of his cause. In July they captured the town of Leicester, but not the castle. Later the king of Scotland invaded Northumberland, but fell back before the advance of Richard of Lucy, who in his turn laid waste parts of Lothian and burned Berwick. In October the Earl of Leicester landed in Norfolk with a body of foreign troops, but was defeated by the justiciar and the Earl of Cornwall, who took him and his wife prisoners. The year closed with truces in both England and France running to near Easter time. The first half of the year 1174 passed in the same indecisive way. In England there was greater suffering from the disorders incident to such a war, and sieges and skirmishes were constantly occurring through all the centre and north of the land.

By the middle of the year King Henry came to the conclusion that his presence was more needed in the island than on the continent, and on July 8 he crossed to Southampton, invoking the protection of God on his voyage if He would grant to his kingdom the peace which he himself was seeking. He brought with him all his chief prisoners, including his own queen and his son's. On the next day he set out for Canterbury. The penance of a king imposed upon him by the Church for the murder of Thomas Becket he might already have performed to the satisfaction of the pope, but the penance of a private person, of a soul guilty in the sight of heaven, he had still to take upon himself, in a measure to satisfy the world and very likely his own conscience. For such a penance the time was fitting. Whatever he may have himself felt, the friends of Thomas believed that the troubles which had fallen upon the realm were a punishment for the sins of the king.

A personal reconciliation with the martyr, to be obtained only as a suppliant at his tomb, was plainly what he should seek.

As Henry drew near the city and came in sight of the cathedral church, he dismounted from his horse, and bare-footed and humbly, forbidding any sign that a king was present, walked the remainder of the way to the tomb. Coming to the door of the church, he knelt and prayed; at the spot where Thomas fell, he wept and kissed it. After reciting his confession to the bishops who had come with him or gathered there, he went to the tomb and, prostrate on the floor, remained a long time weeping and praying. Then Gilbert Foliot, Bishop of London, made an address to those present, declaring that not by command or knowledge was the king guilty of the murder, but admitting the guilt of the hasty words which had occasioned it. He proclaimed the restoration of all rights to the church of Canterbury, and of the king's favour to all friends of the late archbishop. Then followed the formal penance and absolution. Laying off his outer clothes, with head and shoulders bowed at the tomb, the king allowed himself to be scourged by the clergy present, said to have numbered eighty, receiving five blows from each prelate and three from each monk. The night that followed he spent in prayer in the church, still fasting. Mass in the morning completed the religious ceremonies, but on Henry's departure for London later in the day he was given, as a mark of the reconciliation, some holy water to drink made sacred by the relics of the martyr, and a little in a bottle to carry with him.

The medieval mind overlooked the miracle of Henry's escape from the sanitary dangers of this experience, but dwelt with satisfaction on another which seemed the martyr's immediate response and declaration of forgiveness. It was on Saturday that the king left Canterbury and went up to London, and there he remained some days preparing his forces for the war. On Wednesday night a messenger who had ridden without stopping from the north arrived at the royal quarters and demanded immediate admittance to the king. Henry had retired to rest, and his servants would not at first allow him to be disturbed, but the messenger insisted: his news was good, and the king must know it at once. At last his importunity prevailed, and at the king's bedside he told him that he had come from Ranulf Glanvill, his sheriff of Lancashire, and that the king of Scotland had been overcome and taken prisoner. The news was confirmed by other messengers who arrived the next day and was received by the king and his barons with great rejoicing. The victory was unmistakably the answer of St. Thomas to the penance of Henry, and a plain declaration of reconciliation and forgiveness, for it soon became known that it was on the very day when the penance at

Canterbury was finished, perhaps at the very hour, that this great success was granted to the arms of the penitent king.

The two spots of danger in the English insurrection were the north, where not merely was the king of Scotland prepared for invasion, but the Bishop of Durham, Hugh of Puiset, a connexion of King Stephen, was ready to assist him and had sent also for his nephew, another Hugh of Puiset, Count of Bar, to come to his help with a foreign force; and the east, where Hugh Bigod, the old earl of Norfolk, was again in rebellion and was expecting the landing of the Count of Flanders with an army. It was in the north that the fate of the insurrection was settled and without the aid of the king. The king of Scotland, known in the annals of his country as William the Lion, had begun his invasion in the spring after the expiration of the truce of the previous year, and had raided almost the whole north, capturing some castles and failing to take others such as Bamborough and Carlisle. In the second week of July he attacked Prudhoe castle in southern Northumberland. Encouraged perhaps by the landing of King Henry in England, the local forces of the north now gathered to check the raiding. No barons of high rank were among the leaders. They were all Henry's own new men or the descendants of his grandfather's. Two sheriffs, Robert of Stuteville of Yorkshire and Ranulf Glanvill of Lancashire, probably had most to do with collecting the forces and leading them. At the news of their arrival, William fell back toward the north, dividing up his army and sending detachments off in various directions to plunder the country. The English followed on, and at Alnwick castle surprised the king with only a few knights, his personal guard. Resistance was hopeless, but it was continued in the true fashion of chivalry until all the Scottish force was captured.

This victory brought the rebellion in England to an end. On hearing the news Henry marched against the castle of Huntingdon, which had been for some time besieged, and it at once surrendered. There his natural son Geoffrey, who had been made Bishop of Lincoln the summer before, joined him with reinforcements, and he turned to the east against Hugh Bigod. A part of the Flemish force which was expected had reached the earl, but he did not venture to resist. He came in before he was attacked, and gave up his castles, and with great difficulty persuaded the king to allow him to send home his foreign troops. Henry then led his army to Northampton where he received the submission of all the rebel leaders who were left. The Bishop of Durham surrendered his castles and gained reluctant permission for his nephew to return to France. The king of Scotland was brought in a prisoner. The Earl of Leicester's castles were given up, and the Earl of Derby and Roger Mowbray yielded theirs. This was on the last day of

July. In three weeks after Henry's landing, in little more than two after his sincere penance for the murder of St. Thomas, the dangerous insurrection in England was completely crushed,—crushed indeed for all the remainder of Henry's reign. The king's right to the castles of his barons was henceforth strictly enforced. Many were destroyed at the close of the war, and others were put in the hands of royal officers who could easily be changed. It was more than a generation after this date and under very different conditions that a great civil war again broke out in England between the king and his barons.

But the war on the continent was not closed by Henry's success in England. His sons were still in arms against him, and during his absence the king of France with the young Henry and the Count of Flanders had laid siege to Rouen. Though the blockade was incomplete, an attack on the chief city of Normandy could not be disregarded. Evidently that was Henry's opinion, for on August 6 he crossed the channel, taking with him his Brabantine soldiers and a force of Welshmen, as well as his prisoners including the king of Scotland. He entered Rouen without difficulty, and by his vigorous measures immediately convinced the besiegers that all hope of taking the city was over. King Louis, who was without military genius or spirit, and not at all a match for Henry, gave up the enterprise at once, burned his siege engines, and decamped ignominiously in the night. Then came messengers to Henry and proposed a conference to settle terms of peace, but at the meeting which was held on September 8 nothing could be agreed upon because of the absence of Richard who was in Aquitaine still carrying on the war. The negotiations were accordingly adjourned till Michaelmas on the understanding that Henry should subdue his son and compel him to attend and that the other side should give the young rebel no aid. Richard at first intended some resistance to his father, but after losing some of the places that held for him and a little experience of fleeing from one castle to another, he lost heart and threw himself on his father's mercy, to be received with the easy forgiveness which characterized Henry's attitude toward his children.

There was no obstacle now to peace. On September 30 the kings of England and France and the three young princes met in the adjourned conference and arranged the terms. Henry granted to his sons substantial revenues, but not what he had offered them at the beginning of the war, nor did he show any disposition to push his advantage to extremes against any of those who had joined the alliance against him. The treaty in which the agreement between father and sons was recorded may still be read. It provides that Henry "the king, son of the king," and his brothers and all the barons who have withdrawn from the allegiance of the father shall return to it free and quit from all oaths and agreements which they may have made in the meantime, and the king shall have all the rights over them and their lands and castles that he had two weeks before the beginning of the war. But they also shall receive back all their lands as they had them at the same date, and the king will cherish no ill feeling against them. To Henry his father promised to assign two castles in Normandy suitable for his residence and an income of 15,000 Angevin pounds a year; to Richard two suitable castles and half the revenue of Poitou, but the interesting stipulation is added that Richard's castles are to be of such a sort that his father shall take no injury from them; to Geoffrey half the marriage portion of Constance of Britanny and the income of the whole when the marriage is finally made with the sanction of Rome. Prisoners who had made fine with the king before the peace were expressly excluded from it, and this included the king of Scotland and the Earls of Chester and Leicester. All castles were to be put back into the condition in which they were before the war. The young king formally agreed to the provision for his brother John, and this seems materially larger than that originally proposed. The concluding provisions of the treaty show the strong legal sense of King Henry. He was ready to pardon the rebellion with great magnanimity, but crimes committed and laws violated either against himself or others must be answered for in the courts by all guilty persons. Richard and Geoffrey did homage to their father for what was granted them, but this was excused the young Henry because he was a king. In another treaty drawn up at about the same time as Falaise the king of Scotland recognized in the clearest terms for himself and his heirs the king of England as his liege lord for Scotland and for all his lands, and agreed that his barons and men, lay and ecclesiastic, should also render liege homage to Henry, according to the Norman principle. On these conditions he was released. Of the king of France practically nothing was demanded.

The treaty between the two kings of England established a peace which lasted for some years, but it was not long before complaints of the scantiness of his revenues and of his exclusion from all political influence began again from the younger king and from his court. There was undoubtedly much to justify these complaints from the point of view of Henry the son. Whatever may have been the impelling motive, by establishing his sons in nominal independence, Henry the father had clearly put himself in an illogical position from which there was no escape without a division of his power which he could not make when brought to the test. The young king found his refuge in a way thoroughly characteristic of himself and of the age, in the great athletic sport of that period—the tournament, which differed from modern athletics in the important particular that the gentleman, keeping of course the rules of the game, could engage in it as a means of livelihood. The capturing of horses and armour and the ransoming of prisoners made the tournament a profitable business to the man who was a better fighter than other men, and the young king enjoyed that fame. At the beginning of his independent career his father had assigned to his service a man who was to serve the house of Anjou through long years and in far higher capacity— William Marshal, at that time a knight without lands or revenues but skilled in arms, and under his tuition and example his pupil became a warrior of renown. It was not exactly a business which seems to us becoming to a king, but it was at least better than fighting his father, and the opinion of the time found no fault with it.

[47] Robert of Torigni, Chronicles of Stephen, iv, 305; L'Histoire de Guillaume le Maréchal, 11. 1935-5095.

CHAPTER XV.
HENRY AND HIS SONS

For England peace was now established. The insurrection was suppressed, the castles were in the king's hands, even the leaders of the revolted barons were soon reconciled with him. The age of Henry I returned, an age not so long in years as his, but yet long for any medieval state, of internal peace, of slow but sure upbuilding in public and private wealth, and, even more important, of the steady growth of law and institutions and of the clearness with which they were understood, an indispensable preparation for the great thirteenth century so soon to begin—the crisis of English constitutional history. For Henry personally there was no age of peace. England gave him no further trouble; but in his unruly southern dominions, and from his restless and discontented sons, the respite from rebellion was short, and it was filled with labours.

In 1175 the two kings crossed together to England, though the young king, who was still listening to the suggestions of France and who professed to be suspicious of his father's intentions, was with some difficulty persuaded to go. He also seems to have been troubled by his father's refusal to receive his homage at the same time with his brothers'; at any rate when he finally joined the king on April 1, he begged with tears for permission to do homage as a mark of his father's love, and Henry consented. At the end of the first week in May they crossed the channel for a longer stay in England than usual, of more than two years, and one that was crowded with work both political and administrative. The king's first act marks the new era of peace with the Church, his attendance at a council of the English Church held at London by Archbishop Richard of Canterbury; and his second was a pilgrimage with his son to the tomb of St. Thomas. Soon after the work of filling long-vacant sees and abbacies was begun. At the same time matters growing out of the insurrection received attention. William, Earl of Gloucester, was compelled to give up Bristol castle which he had kept until now. Those who had been opposed to the king were forbidden to come to court unless ordered to do so by him. The bearing of arms in

England was prohibited by a temporary regulation, and the affairs of Wales were considered in a great council at Gloucester.

One of the few acts of severity which Henry permitted himself after the rebellion seems to have struck friend and foe alike, and suggests a situation of much interest to us which would be likely to give us a good deal of insight into the methods and ideas of the time if we understood it in detail. Unfortunately we are left with only a bare statement of the facts, with no explanation of the circumstances or of the motives of the king. Apparently at the Whitsuntide court held at Reading on the first day of June, Henry ordered the beginning of a series of prosecutions against high and low, churchmen and laymen alike, for violations of the forest laws committed during the war. At Nottingham, at the beginning of August, these prosecutions were carried further, and there the incident occurred which gives peculiar interest to the proceedings. Richard of Lucy, the king's faithful minister and justiciar, produced before the king his own writ ordering him to proclaim the suspension of the laws in regard to hunting and fishing during the war. This Richard testified that he had done as he was commanded, and that the defendants trusting to this writ had fearlessly taken the king's venison. We are simply told in addition that this writ and Richard's testimony had no effect against the king's will. It is impossible to doubt that this incident occurred or that such a writ had been sent to the justiciar, but it seems certain that some essential detail of the situation is omitted. To guess what it was is hardly worth while, and we can safely use the facts only as an illustration of the arbitrary power of the Norman and Angevin kings, which on the whole they certainly exercised for the general justice.

From Nottingham the two kings went on to York, where they were met by William of Scotland with the nobles and bishops of his kingdom, prepared to carry out the agreement which was made at Falaise when he was released from imprisonment. Whatever may have been true of earlier instances, the king of Scotland now clearly and beyond the possibility of controversy became the liege-man of the king of England for Scotland and all that pertained to it, and for Galloway as if it were a separate state. The homage was repeated to the young king, saving the allegiance due to the father. According to the English chroniclers all the free tenants of the kingdom of Scotland were also present and did homage in the same way to the two kings for their lands. Some were certainly there, though hardly all; but the statement shows that it was plainly intended to apply to Scotland the Norman law which had been in force in England from the time of the Conquest, by which every vassal became also the king's vassal with an allegiance paramount to all other feudal obligations. The bishops of

Scotland as vassals also did homage, and as bishops they swore to be subject to the Church of England to the same extent as their predecessors had been and as they ought to be. The treaty of Falaise was again publicly read and confirmed anew by the seals of William and his brother David. There is nothing to show that King William did not enter into this relationship with every intention of being faithful to it, nor did he endeavour to free himself from it so long as Henry lived. The Norman influence in Scotland was strong and might easily increase. It is quite possible that a succession of kings of England who made that realm and its interests the primary objects of their policy might have created from this beginning a permanent connexion growing constantly closer, and have saved these two nations, related in so many ways, the almost civil wars of later years.

From these ceremonies at York Henry returned to London, and there, before Michaelmas, envoys came to him to announce and to put into legal form another significant addition to his empire, significant certainly of its imposing power though the reasons which led to this particular step are not known to us. These envoys were from Roderick, king of Connaught, who, when Henry was in Ireland, had refused all acknowledgment of him, and they now came to make known his submission. In a great council held at Windsor the new arrangement was put into formal shape. In the document there drawn up Roderick was made to acknowledge himself the liege-man of Henry and to agree to pay a tribute of hides from all Ireland except that part which was directly subject to the English invaders. On his side Henry agreed to recognize Roderick as king under himself as long as he should remain faithful, and also the holdings of all other men who remained in his fealty. Roderick should rule all Ireland outside the English settlement, at least for the purposes of the tribute, and should have the right to claim help from the English in enforcing his authority if it should seem necessary. Such an arrangement would have in all probability only so much force as Roderick might be willing to allow it at any given time, and yet the mere making of it is a sign of considerable progress in Ireland and the promise of more. At the same council Henry appointed a bishop of Waterford, who was sent over with the envoys on their return to be consecrated.

At York the king had gone on with his forest prosecutions, and there as before against clergy as well as laity. Apparently the martyrdom of Archbishop Thomas had secured for the Church nothing in the matter of these offences. The bishops did not interfere to protect the clergy, says one chronicler; and very likely in these cases the Church acknowledged the power rather than the right of the king. At the end of October a papal legate, Cardinal Hugo, arrived in England, but his mission accomplished nothing of importance that we know of, unless it be his agreement that Henry should have the right to try the clergy in his own courts for violations of the forest law. This agreement at any rate excited the especial anger of the monastic chroniclers who wrote him down a limb of Satan, a robber instead of a shepherd, who seeing the wolf coming abandoned his sheep. In a letter to the pope which the legate took with him on his return to Rome, Henry agreed not to bring the clergy in person before his courts except for forest offences and in cases concerning the lay services due from their fiefs. On January 25, 1176, a great council met at Northampton, and there Henry took up again the judicial and administrative reforms which had been interrupted by the conflict with Becket and by the war with his sons.

The task of preserving order in the medieval state was in the main the task of repressing and punishing crimes of violence. Murder and assault, robbery and burglary, fill the earliest court records, and on the civil side a large proportion of the cases, like those under the assizes of Mort d'Ancestor and Novel Disseisin, concerned attacks on property not very different in character. The problem of the ruler in this department of government was so to perfect the judicial machinery and procedure as to protect peaceable citizens from bodily harm and property from violent entry and from fraud closely akin to violence. An additional and immediate incentive to the improvement of the judicial system arose from the income which was derived from fines and confiscations, both heavier and more common punishments for crime than in the modern state. It would be unfair to a king like Henry II, however, to convey the impression that an increase of income was the only, or indeed the main, thing sought in the reform of the courts. Order and security for land and people were always in his mind to be sought for themselves, as a chief part of the duty of a king, and certainly this was the case with his ministers who must have had more to do than he with the determining and perfecting of details.

This is not the place to describe the judicial reforms of the reign in technical minuteness or from the point of view of the student of constitutional history. The activity of a great king, the effect on people and government are the subjects of interest here. The series of formal documents in which Henry's reforming efforts are embodied opens with the Constitutions of Clarendon in 1164. Of the king's purpose in this—not new legislation, but an effort to bring the clergy under responsibility to the state for their criminal acts according to the ancient practice,—and of its results, we have already had the story. The second in the series, the Assize of Clarendon, the first that concerns the civil judicial system, though we have good reason to suspect that it was not actually Henry's first attempt at reform, dates from early in the year 1166. It dealt with the detection and punishment of crime, and greatly improved the means at the command of the state for these purposes. In 1170, to check the independence of the sheriffs and their abuse of power for private ends, of which there were loud complaints, he ordered strict inquiry to be made, by barons appointed for the purpose, into the conduct of the sheriffs and the abuses complained of, and removed a large number of them, appointing others less subject to the temptations which the local magnate was not likely to resist. This was a blow at the hold of the feudal baronage on the office, and a step in its transformation into a subordinate executive office, which was rapidly going on during the reign. In 1176, in the Assize of Northampton, the provisions of the Assize of Clarendon for the enforcement of criminal justice were made more severe, and new enactments were added. In 1181 the Assize of Arms made it compulsory on knights and freemen alike to keep in their possession weapons proportionate to their income for the defence of king and realm. In 1184 the Assize of the Forest enforced the vexatious forest law and decreed severe penalties for its violation. In the year before the king's death, in 1188, the Ordinance of the Saladin Tithe regulated the collection of this new tax intended to pay the expenses of Henry's proposed crusade.

This list of the formal documents in which Henry's reforms were proclaimed is evidence of no slight activity, but it gives, nevertheless, a very imperfect idea of his work as a whole. That was nothing less than to start the judicial organization of the state along the lines it has ever since followed. He did this by going forward with beginnings already made and by opening to general and regular use institutions which, so far as we know, had up to this time been only occasionally employed in special cases. The changes which the reign made in the judicial system may be grouped under two heads: the further differentiation and more definite organization of the curia regis and the introduction of the jury in its undeveloped form into the regular procedure of the courts both in civil and criminal cases.

Under the reign of the first Henry we noticed the twofold form of the king's court, the great curia regis, formed by the barons of the whole kingdom and the smaller in practically permanent session, and the latter also acting as a special court for financial cases—the exchequer. Now we have the second Henry establishing, in 1178, what we may call another small curia regis—apparently of a more professional character—to be in permanent session for the trial of cases. The process of differentiation, beginning in finding a way for the better doing of financial business, now goes a step further, though to the men of that time—if they had thought about it at all—it would have seemed a classification of business, not a dividing up of the king's court. The great curia regis, the exchequer, and the permanent trial court, usually meeting at Westminster, were all the same king's court; but a step had really been taken toward a specialized judicial system and an official body of judges.

In the reign of Henry I we also noticed evidence which proved the occasional, and led us to suspect the somewhat regular employment of itinerant justices. This institution was put into definite and permanent form by his grandson. The kingdom was at first divided into six circuits, to each of which three justices were sent. Afterwards the number of justices was reduced. These justices, though not all members of the small court at Westminster, were all, it is likely, familiar with its work, and to each circuit at least one justice of the Westminster court was probably always assigned. What they carried into each county of the kingdom as they went the round of their districts was not a new court and not a local court; it was the curia regis itself, and that too in its administrative as well as in its judicial functions indeed it is easy to suspect that it was quite as much the administrative side of its work,—the desire to check the abuses of the sheriffs by investigation on the spot, and to improve the collection of money due to the crown, as its judicial,—as the wish to render the operation of the law more convenient by trying cases in the communities where they arose, that led to the development of this side of the judicial system. Whatever led to it, this is what had begun, a new branch of the judicial organization.

It was in these courts, these king's courts,—the trial court at Westminster and the court of the itinerant justices in the different counties,—that the institution began to be put into regular use that has become so characteristic a distinction of the Anglo-Saxon judicial system—the jury. The history of the jury cannot here be told. It is sufficient to say that it existed in the Frankish empire of the early ninth century in a form apparently as highly developed as in the Norman kingdom of the early twelfth. From Charles the Great to Henry II it remained in what was practically a stationary condition. It was only on English soil, and after the impulse given to it by the broader uses in which it was now employed that it began the marvellous development from which our liberty has gained so much. At the beginning it was a process belonging to the sovereign and used solely for his business, or employed for the business of others only by his permission in the special case. What Henry seems to have done was to generalize this use, to establish certain classes of cases in which it might always be employed by his subjects, but in his courts only. In essence it was a process for getting local knowledge to bear on a doubtful question of fact of interest to the government. Ought A to pay a certain tax? The question is usually to be settled by answering another: Have his ancestors before him paid it, or the land which he now holds? The memory of the neighbours can probably determine this, and a certain number of the men likely to know are summoned before the officer representing the king, put on oath, and required to say what they know about it.

In its beginning that is all the jury was. But it was a process of easy application to other questions than those which interested the king. The question of fact that arose in a suit at law—was the land in dispute between A and B actually held by the ancestor of B?—could be settled in the same way by the memory of the neighbours, and in a way much more satisfactory to the party whose cause was just than by an appeal to the judgment of heaven in the wager of battle. If the king would allow the private man the use of this process, he was willing to pay for the privilege. Such privilege had been granted since the Conquest in particular cases. A tendency at least in Normandy had existed before Henry II to render it more regular. This tendency Henry followed in granting the use of the primitive jury generally to his subjects in certain classes of cases, to defendants in the Great Assize to protect their freehold, to plaintiffs in the three assizes of Mort d'Ancestor, Novel Disseisin, and Darrein Presentment to protect their threatened seisin. As a process of his own, as a means of preserving order, he again broadened its use in another way in the Assize of Clarendon, finding in it a method of bringing local knowledge to the assistance of the government in the detection of crime, the function of the modern grand jury and its origin as an institution.

The result of Henry's activities in this direction—changes we may call them, but hardly innovations, following as they do earlier precedents and lying directly in line with the less conscious tendencies of his predecessors,—this work of Henry's was nothing less than to create our judicial system and to determine the character and direction of its growth to the present day. In the beginning of these three things, of a specialized and official court system, of a national judiciary bringing its influence to bear on every part of the land, and of a most effective process for introducing local knowledge into the trial of cases, Henry had accomplished great results, and the only ones that he directly sought. But two others plainly seen after the lapse of time are of quite equal importance. One of these was the growth at an early date of a national common law.

Almost the only source of medieval law before the fourteenth century was custom, and the strong tendency of customary law was to break into local fragments, each differing in more or less important points from the rest. Beaumanoir in the thirteenth century laments the fact that every castellany in France had a differing law of its own, and Glanville still earlier makes a similar complaint of England. But the day was rapidly approaching in both lands when the rise of national consciousness under settled governments, and especially the growth of a broader and more active commerce, was to create a strong demand for a uniform national law. What influences affected the forming constitutions of the states of Europe because this demand had to be met by recourse to the imperial law of Rome, the law of a highly centralized absolutism, cannot here be recounted. From these influences, whether large or small, from the necessity of seeking uniformity in any ready-made foreign law, England was saved by the consequences of Henry's action. The king's court rapidly created a body of clear, consistent, and formulated law. The itinerant justice as he went from county to county carried with him this law and made it the law of the entire nation. From these beginnings arose the common law, the product of as high an order of political genius as the constitution itself, and now the law of wider areas and of more millions of men than ever obeyed the law of Rome.

One technical work, at once product and monument of the legal activity of this generation, deserves to be remembered in this connexion, the Treatise on the Laws of England. Ascribed with some probability to Ranulf Glanvill, Henry's chief justiciar during his last years, it was certainly written by some one thoroughly familiar with the law of the time and closely in touch with its enforcement in the king's court. To us it declares what that law was at the opening of its far-reaching history, and in its definiteness and certainty as well as in its arrangement it reveals the great progress that had been made since the law books of the reign of Henry I. That progress continued so rapid that within a hundred years Glanvill's book had become obsolete, but by that time it had been succeeded by others in the long series of great books on our common law. Nor ought we perhaps entirely to overlook another book, as interesting in its way, the Dialogue of the Exchequer. Written probably by Richard Fitz Neal, of the third generation of that great administration family founded by Roger of Salisbury and restored to office by Henry II, the book gives us a view from within of the financial organization of the reign as enlightening as is Glanvill's treatise on the common law.

But besides the growth of the common law, these reforms involved and carried with them as a second consequence a great change in the machinery of government and in the point of view from which it was regarded. We have already seen how in the feudal state government functions were undifferentiated and were exercised without consciousness of inconsistency by a single organ, the curia regia, in which, as in all public activities, the leading operative element was the feudal baronage. The changes in the judicial system which were accomplished in the reign of Henry, especially the giving of a more fixed and permanent character to the courts, the development of legal procedure into more complicated and technical forms, and the growth of the law itself in definiteness and body, — these changes meant the necessity of a trained official class and the decline of the importance of the purely feudal baronage in the carrying on of government. This was the effect also of the gradual transformation of the sheriff into a more strictly ministerial officer and the diminished value of feudal levies in war as indicated by the extension of scutage. In truth, at a date relatively as early for this transformation as for the growth of a national law, the English state was becoming independent of feudalism. The strong Anglo-Norman monarchy was attacking the feudal baron not merely with the iron hand by which disorder and local independence were repressed, but by finding out better ways of doing the business of government and so destroying practically the whole foundation on which political feudalism rested. Of the threatening results of these reforms the baronage was vaguely conscious, and this feeling enters as no inconsiderable element into the troubles that filled the reign of Henry's youngest son and led to the first step towards constitutional government.

For a moment serious business was now interrupted by a bit of comedy, at least it seems comedy to us, though no doubt it was a matter serious enough to the actors. For many years there had been a succession of bitter disputes between the Archbishops of Canterbury and York over questions of precedence and various ceremonial rights, or to state it more accurately the Archbishops of York had been for a long time trying to enforce an exact equality in such matters with the Archbishops of Canterbury. At mid-Lent, 1776 Cardinal Hugo, the legate, held a council of the English Church in London, and at its opening the dispute led to actual violence. The cardinal took the seat of the presiding officer, and Richard of Canterbury seated himself on his right hand. The Archbishop of York on entering found the seat of honour occupied by his rival, and unwilling to yield, tried to force himself in between Richard and the cardinal. One account says that he sat down in Richard's lap. Instantly there was a tumult. The partisans of Canterbury seized the offending archbishop, bishops we are told even leading the attack, dragged him away, threw him to the floor, and misused him seriously. The legate showed a proper indignation at the disorder caused by the defenders of the rights of Canterbury, but found himself unable to go on with the council.

For a year past the young king had been constantly with his father, kept almost a prisoner, as his immediate household felt and as we may well believe. Now he began to beg permission to go on a pilgrimage to the famous shrine of St. James of Compostella, and Henry at last gave his consent, though he knew the pilgrimage was a mere pretext to escape to the continent. But the younger Henry was detained at Portchester some time, waiting for a fair wind; and Easter coming on, he returned to Winchester, at his father's request, to keep the festival with him. In the meantime, Richard and Geoffrey had landed at Southampton, coming to their father with troubles of their own, and reached Winchester the day before Easter Sunday. Henry and his sons were thus together for the feast, much to his joy we are told; but it is not said that Queen Eleanor, who was then imprisoned in England, very likely in Winchester itself, was allowed any part in the celebration. Richard's visit to England was due to a dangerous insurrection in his duchy, and he had come to ask his father's help. Henry persuaded the young king to postpone his pilgrimage until he should have assisted his brother to re-establish peace in Aquitaine, and with this understanding they both crossed to the continent about a fortnight after Easter, but young Henry on landing at once set off with his wife to visit the king of France. Richard was now nearly nineteen years old, and in the campaign that followed he displayed great energy and vigour and the skill as a fighter for which he was afterwards so famous, putting down the insurrection almost without assistance from his brother, who showed very little interest in any troubles but his own. The young king, indeed, seemed to be making ready for a new breach with his father. He was collecting around him King Henry's enemies and those who had helped him in the last war, and was openly displaying his discontent. An incident which occurred at this time illustrates his spirit. His vice-chancellor, Adam, who thought he owed much to the elder king, attempted to send him a report of his son's doings; but when he was detected, the young Henry, finding that he could not put him to death as he would have liked to do because the Bishop of Poitiers claimed him as a clerk, ordered him to be sent to imprisonment in Argentan and to be scourged as a traitor in all the towns through which he passed on the way.

About the same time an embassy appeared in England from the Norman court of Sicily to arrange for a marriage between William II of that kingdom and Henry's youngest daughter, Joanna. The marriages of each of Henry's daughters had some influence on the history of England before the death of his youngest son. His eldest daughter Matilda had been married in 1168 to Henry the Lion, head of the house of Guelf in Germany, and his second daughter, Eleanor, to Alphonso III of Castile, in 1169 or 1170. The ambassadors of King William found themselves pleased with the little princess whom they had come to see, and sent back a favourable report, signifying also the consent of King Henry. In the following February she was married and crowned queen at Palermo, being then a little more than twelve years old. Before the close of this year, 1176, Henry arranged for another marriage to provide for his youngest son John, now ten years old. The infant heiress of Maurienne, to whom he had been years before betrothed, had died soon after, and no other suitable heiress had since been found whose wealth might be given him. The inheritance which his father had now in mind was that of the great Earl Robert of Gloucester, brother and supporter of the Empress Matilda, his father's mother. Robert's son William had only daughters. Of these two were already married, Mabel to Amaury, Count of Evreux, and Amice to Richard of Clare, Earl of Hertford. Henry undertook to provide for these by pensions on the understanding that all the lands of the earldom should go to John on his marriage with the youngest daughter Isabel. To this plan Earl William agreed. The marriage itself did not take place until after the death of King Henry.

An income suitable for his position had now certainly been secured for the king's youngest son, for in addition to the Gloucester inheritance that of another of the sons of Henry I, Reginald, Earl of Cornwall who had died in 1175, leaving only daughters, was held by Henry for his use, and still earlier the earldom of Nottingham had been assigned him. At this time, however, or very soon after, a new plan suggested itself to his father for conferring upon him a rank and authority proportionate to his brothers'. Ireland was giving more and more promise of shaping itself before long into a fairly well-organized feudal state. If it seems to us a turbulent realm, where a central authority was likely to secure little obedience, we must remember that this was still the twelfth century, the height of the feudal age, and that to the ruler of Aquitaine Ireland might seem to be progressing more rapidly to a condition of what passed as settled order than to us. Since his visit to the island, Henry had kept a close watch on the doings of his Norman vassals there and had held them under a firm hand. During the rebellion of 1173 he had had no trouble from them. Indeed, they had served him faithfully in that struggle and had been rewarded for their fidelity. In the interval since the close of the war some advance in the Norman occupation had been made. There seemed to be a prospect that both the south-west and the north-east— the southern coast of Munster and the eastern coast of Ulster—might be acquired. Limerick had been temporarily occupied, and it was hoped to gain it permanently. Even Connaught had been successfully invaded. Possibly it was the hope of securing himself against attacks of this sort which he may have foreseen that led Roderick of Connaught to acknowledge himself Henry's vassal by formal treaty. If he had any expectation of this sort, he was disappointed; for the invaders of Ireland paid no attention to the new relationship, nor did Henry himself any longer than suited his purpose.

We are now told that Henry had formed the plan of erecting Ireland into a kingdom, and that he had obtained from Alexander III permission to crown whichever of his sons he pleased and to make him king of the island. Very possibly the relationship with Scotland, which he had lately put into exact feudal form, suggested the possibility of another subordinate kingdom and of raising John in this way to an equality with Richard and Geoffrey. At a great council held at Oxford in May, 1177, the preliminary steps were taken towards putting this plan into operation. Some regulation of Irish affairs was necessary. Richard "Strongbow," Earl of Pembroke and Lord of Leinster, who had been made justiciar after the rebellion, had died early in 1176, and his successor in office, William Fitz Adelin, had not proved the right man in the place. There were also new conquests to be considered and new homages to be rendered, if the plan of a kingdom was to be carried out. His purpose Henry announced to the council, and the Norman barons, some for the lordships originally assigned them, some for new ones like Cork and Limerick, did homage in turn to John and to his father, as had been the rule in all similar cases. Hugh of Lacy, Henry's first justiciar, was reappointed to that office, but there was as yet no thought of sending John, who was then eleven years old, to occupy his future kingdom.

It was a crowded two years which Henry spent in England. Only the most important of the things that occupied his attention have we been able to notice, but the minor activities which filled his days make up a great sum of work accomplished. Great councils were frequently held; the judicial reforms and the working of the administrative machinery demanded constant attention; the question of the treatment to be accorded to one after another of the chief barons who had taken part in the rebellion had to be decided; fines and confiscations were meted out, and finally the terms on which the offenders were to be restored to the royal favour were settled. The castles occasioned the king much anxiety, and of those that were allowed to stand the custodians were more than once changed. The affairs of Wales were frequently considered, and at last the king seemed to have arranged permanent relations of friendship with the princes of both north and south Wales. In March, 1177, a great council decided a question of a kind not often coming before an English court. The kings of Castile and Navarre submitted an important dispute between them to the arbitration of King Henry, and the case was heard and decided in a great council in London—no slight indication of the position of the English king in the eyes of the world.

Ever since early February, 1177, Henry had been planning to cross over to Normandy with all the feudal levies of England. There were reasons enough for his presence there, and with a strong hand. Richard's troubles were not yet over, though he had already proved his ability to deal with them alone. Brittany was much disturbed, and Geoffrey had not gone home with Richard, but was still with his father. The king of France was pressing for the promised marriage of Adela and Richard, and it was understood that the legate, Cardinal Peter of Pavia, had authority to lay all Henry's dominions under an interdict if he did not consent to an immediate marriage. The attitude of the young Henry was also one to cause anxiety, and his answers to his father's messages were unsatisfactory. One occasion of delay after another, however, postponed Henry's crossing, and it was the middle of August before he landed in Normandy. We hear much less of the army that actually went with him than of the summons of the feudal levies for the purpose, but it is evident that a strong force accompanied him. The difficulty with the king of France first demanded attention. The legate consented to postpone action until Henry, who had determined to try the effect of a personal interview, should have a conference with Louis. This took place on September 21, near Nonancourt, and resulted in a treaty to the advantage of Henry. He agreed in the conference that the marriage should take place on the original conditions, but nothing was said about it in the treaty. This concerned chiefly a crusade, which the two kings were to undertake in close alliance, and a dispute with regard to the allegiance of the county of Auvergne, which was to be settled by arbitrators named in the treaty, After this success Henry found no need of a strong military force. Various minor matters detained him in France for nearly a year, the most important of which was an expedition into Berri to force the surrender to him of the heiress of Déols under the feudal right of wardship. July 15, 1178, Henry landed again in England for another long stay of nearly two years. As in his previous sojourn this time was occupied chiefly in a further development of the judicial reforms already described.

While Henry was occupied with these affairs, events in France were rapidly bringing on a change which was destined to be of the utmost importance to England and the Angevin house. Louis VII had now reigned in France for more than forty years. His only son Philip, to be known in history as Philip Augustus, born in the summer of 1165, was now nearly fifteen years old, but his father had not yet followed the example of his ancestors and had him crowned, despite the wishes of his family and the advice of the pope. Even so unassertive a king as Louis VII was conscious of the security and strength which had come to the Capetian house with the progress of the last hundred years. Now he was growing ill and felt himself an old man, though he was not yet quite sixty, and he determined to make the succession secure before it should be too late. This decision was announced to a great council of the realm at the end of April, 1179, and was received with universal applause. August 15 was appointed as the day for the coronation, but before that day came the young prince was seriously ill, and his father was once more deeply anxious for the future. Carried away by the ardour of the chase in the woods of Compiegne, Philip had been separated from his attendants and had wandered all one night alone in the forest, unable to find his way. A charcoal-burner had brought him back to his father on the second day, but the strain of the unaccustomed dread had been too much for the boy, and he had been thrown into what threatened to be a dangerous illness. To Louis's troubled mind occurred naturally the efficacy of the new and mighty saint, Thomas of Canterbury, who might be expected to recall with gratitude the favours which the king of France had shown him while he was an exile. The plan of a pilgrimage to his shrine, putting the king practically at the mercy of a powerful rival, was looked upon by many of Louis's advisers with great misgiving, but there need have been no fear. Henry could always be counted upon to respond in the spirit of chivalry to demands of this sort having in them something of an element of romance. He met the royal pilgrim on his landing, and attended him during his short stay at Canterbury and back to Dover. This first visit of a crowned king of France to England, coming in his distress to seek the aid of her most popular saint, was long remembered there, as was also his generosity to the monks of the cathedral church. The intercession of St. Thomas availed. The future king of France recovered, selected to become—it was believed that a vision of the saint himself so declared—the avenger of the martyr against the house from which he had suffered death.

Philip recovered, but Louis fell ill with his last illness. As he drew near to Paris on his return a sudden shock of paralysis smote him. His whole right side was affected, and he was unable to be present at the coronation of his son which had been postponed to November 1. At this ceremony the house of Anjou was represented by the young King Henry, who as Duke of Normandy bore the royal crown, and who made a marked impression on the assembly by his brilliant retinue, by the liberal scale of his expenditure and the fact that he paid freely for everything that he took, and by the generosity of the gifts which he brought from his father to the new king of France. The coronation of Philip II opens a new era in the history both of France and England, but the real change did not declare itself at once. What seemed at the moment the most noteworthy difference was made by the sudden decline in influence of the house of Blois and Champagne, which was attached to Louis VII by so many ties, and which had held so high a position at his court, and by the rise of Count Philip of Flanders to the place of most influential counsellor, almost to that of guardian of the young king. With the crowning of his son, Louis's actual exercise of authority came to an end; the condition of his health would have made this necessary in any case, and Philip II was in fact sole king. His first important step was his marriage in April, 1180, to the niece of the Count of Flanders, Isabel of Hainault, the childless count promising an important cession of the territory of south-western Flanders to France to take place on his own death, and hoping no doubt to secure a permanent influence through the queen, while

Philip probably intended by this act to proclaim his independence of his mother's family.

These rapid changes could not take place without exciting the anxious attention of the king of England. His family interests, possibly also his prestige on the continent, had suffered to some extent in the complete overthrow and exile of his son-in-law Henry the Lion by the Emperor Frederick I, which had occurred in January, 1180, a few weeks before the marriage of Philip II, though as yet the Emperor had not been able to enforce the decision of the diet against the powerful duke. Henry of England would have been glad to aid his son-in-law with a strong force against the designs of Frederick, which threatened the revival of the imperial power and might be dangerous to all the sovereigns of the west if they succeeded, but he found himself between somewhat conflicting interests and unable to declare himself with decision for either without the risk of sacrificing the other. Already, before Philip's marriage, the young Henry had gone over to England to give his father an account of the situation in France, and together they had crossed to Normandy early in April. But the marriage had taken place a little later, and May 29 Philip and his bride were crowned at St. Denis by the Archbishop of Sens, an intentional slight to William of Blois, the Archbishop of Reims. Troops were called into the field on both sides and preparations made for war, while the house of Blois formed a close alliance with Henry. But the grandson of the great negotiator, Henry I, had no intention of appealing to the sword until he had tried the effect of diplomacy. On June 28 Henry and Philip met at Gisors under the old elm tree which had witnessed so many personal interviews between the kings of England and France. Here Henry won another success. Philip was reconciled with his mother's family; an end was brought to the exclusive influence of the Count of Flanders; and a treaty of peace and friendship was drawn up between the two kings modelled closely on that lately made between Henry and Louis VII, but containing only a general reference to a crusade. Henceforth, for a time, the character of Henry exercised a strong influence over the young king of France, and his practical statesmanship became a model for Philip's imitation.

At the beginning of March, 1182, Henry II returned to Normandy. Events which were taking place in two quarters required his presence. In France, actual war had broken out in which the Count of Flanders was now in alliance with the house of Blois against the tendency towards a strong monarchy which was already plainly showing itself in the policy of young Philip, Henry's sons had rendered loyal and indispensable assistance to their French suzerain in this war, and now their father came to his aid with his diplomatic skill. Before the close of April he had made peace to the advantage of Philip. His other task was not so easily performed.

Troubles had broken out again in Richard's duchy. The young duke was as determined to be master in his dominions as his father in his, but his methods were harsh and violent; he was a fighter, not a diplomatist; the immorality of his life gave rise to bitter complaints; and policy, methods, and personal character combined with the character of the land he ruled to make peace impossible for any length of time. Now the troubadour baron, Bertran de Born, who delighted in war and found the chosen field for his talents in stirring up strife between others, in a ringing poem called on his brother barons to revolt. Henry, coming to aid his son in May, 1182, found negotiation unsuccessful, and together in the field they forced an apparent submission. But only for a few months.

In the next act of the constantly varied drama of the Angevin family in this generation the leading part is taken by the young king. For some time past the situation in France had almost forced him into harmony with his father, but this was from no change of spirit. Again he began to demand some part of the inheritance that was nominally his, and fled to his customary refuge at Paris on a new refusal. With difficulty and by making a new arrangement for his income, his father was able to persuade him to return, and Henry had what satisfaction there could be to him in spending the Christmas of 1182 at Caen with his three sons, Henry, Richard, and Geoffrey, and with his daughter Matilda and her exiled husband, the Duke of Saxony. This family concord was at once broken by Richard's flat refusal to swear fealty to his elder brother for Aquitaine. Already the Aquitanian rebels had begun to look to the young Henry for help against his brother, and Bertran de Born had been busy sowing strife between them. In the rebellion of the barons that followed, young Henry and his brother Geoffrey acted an equivocal and most dishonourable part. Really doing all they could to aid the rebels against Richard, they repeatedly abused the patience and affection of their father with pretended negotiations to gain time. Reduced to straits for money, they took to plundering the monasteries and shrines of Aquitaine, not sparing even the most holy and famous shrine of Rocamadour, Immediately after one of the robberies, particularly heinous according to the ideas of the time, the young king fell ill and grew rapidly worse. His message, asking his father to come to him, was treated with the suspicion that it deserved after his recent acts, and he died with only his personal followers about him, striving to atone for his life of sin at the last moment by repeated confession and partaking of the sacrament, by laying on William Marshal the duty of carrying his crusader's cloak to the Holy Land, and by ordering the clergy present to drag him with a rope around his neck on to a bed of ashes where he expired.

CHAPTER XVI.
HENRY OUTGENERALLED

The prince who died thus pitifully on June 11, 1183, was near the middle of his twenty-ninth year. He had never had an opportunity to show what he could do as a ruler in an independent station, but if we may trust the indications of his character in other directions, he would have belonged to the weakest and worst type of the combined houses from which he was descended. But he made himself beloved by those who knew him, and his early death was deeply mourned even by the father who had suffered so much from him. Few writers of the time saw clearly enough to discern the frivolous character beneath the surface of attractive manners, and to the poets of chivalry lament was natural for one in whom they recognized instinctively the expression of their own ideal. His devoted servant, William Marshal, carried out the mission with which he had been charged, and after an absence of two years on a crusade for Henry the son, he returned and entered the service of Henry the father.

The death of a king who had never been more than a king in name made no difference in the political situation. It was a relief to Richard who once more and quickly got the better of his enemies. It must also in many ways have been a relief to Henry, though he showed no disposition to take full advantage of it. The king had learned many things in the experience of the years since his eldest son was crowned, but the conclusions which seem to us most important, he appears not to have drawn. He had had indeed enough of crowned kings among his sons, and from this time on, though Richard occupied clearly the position of heir to the crown, there was no suggestion that he should be made actually king in the lifetime of his father. There is evidence also that after the late war the important fortresses both of Aquitaine and Britanny passed into the possession of Henry and were held by his garrisons, but just how much this meant it is not easy to say. Certainly he had no intention of abandoning the plan of parcelling out the great provinces of his dominion among his sons as subordinate rulers. It almost seems as if his first thought after the death of his eldest son was that now there was an opportunity of providing for his youngest. He sent to Ranulf Glanvill, justiciar of England, to bring John over to Normandy, and on their arrival he sent for Richard and proposed to him to give up Aquitaine to his brother and to take his homage for it. Richard asked for a delay of two or three days to consult his friends, took horse at once and escaped from the court, and from his duchy returned answer that he would never allow Aquitaine to be possessed by any one but himself.

The death of young Henry led at once to annoying questions raised by Philip of France. His sister Margaret was now a widow without children, and he had some right to demand that the lands which had been ceded by France to Normandy as her marriage portion should be restored. These were the Norman Vexin and the important frontier fortress of Gisors. In the troublous times of 1151 Count Geoffrey might have felt justified in surrendering so important a part of Norman territory and defences to the king of France in order to secure the possession of the rest to his son, but times were now changed for that son, and he could not consent to open up the road into the heart of Normandy to his possible enemies. He replied to Philip that the cession of the Vexin had been final and that there could be no question of its return. Philip was not easily satisfied, and there was much negotiation before a treaty on the subject was finally made at the beginning of December, 1183. At a conference near Gisors Henry did homage to Philip for all his French possessions, a liberal pension was accepted for Margaret in lieu of her dower lands, and the king of France recognized the permanence of the cession to Normandy on the condition that Gisors should go to one of the sons of Henry on his marriage with Adela which was once more promised. This marriage in the end never took place, but the Vexin remained a Norman possession.

The year 1184 was a repetition in a series of minor details, family quarrels, foreign negotiations, problems of government, and acts of legislation, of many earlier years of the life of Henry. After Christmas, 1183, angered apparently by a new refusal of Richard to give up Aquitaine to John, or to allow any provision to be made for him in the duchy, Henry gave John an army and permission to make war on his brother to force from him what he could. Geoffrey joined in to aid John, or for his own satisfaction, and together they laid waste parts of Richard's lands. He replied in kind with an invasion of Britanny, and finally Henry had to interfere and order all his sons over to England that he might reconcile them. In the spring of the year he found it necessary to try to make peace again between the king of France and the Count of Flanders. The agreement which he had arranged in 1182 had not really settled the difficulties that had arisen. The question now chiefly concerned the lands of Vermandois, Amiens, and Valois, the inheritance which the Countess of Flanders had brought to her husband. She had died just before the conclusion of the peace in 1182, without heirs, and it had been then agreed that the Count should retain possession of the lands during his life, recognizing certain rights of the king of France. Now he had contracted a second marriage in the evident hope of passing on his claims to children of his own. Philip's declaration that this marriage should make no difference in the disposition of these lands which were to prove the first important accession of territory made by the house of Capet since it came to the throne, was followed by a renewal of the war, and the best efforts of Henry II only succeeded in bringing about a truce for a year.

Still earlier in the year died Richard, Archbishop of Canterbury, and long disputes followed between the monks of the cathedral church and the suffragan bishops of the province as to the election of his successor. The monks claimed the exclusive right of election, the bishops claimed the right to concur and represented on this occasion the interests of the king. After a delay of almost a year, Baldwin, Bishop of Worcester, was declared elected, but no final settlement was made of the disputed rights to elect. In legislation the year is marked by the Forest Assize, which regulated the forest courts and re-enacted the forest law of the early Norman kings in all its severity. One of its most important provisions was that hereafter punishments for forest offences should be inflicted strictly upon the body of the culprit and no longer take the form of fines. Not merely was the taking of game by private persons forbidden, but the free use of their own timber on such of their lands as lay within the bounds of the royal forests was taken away. The Christmas feast of the year saw another family gathering more complete than usual, for not merely were Richard and John present, but the Duke and Duchess of Saxony, still in exile, with their children, including the infant William, who had been born at Winchester the previous summer, and whose direct descendants were long afterwards to come to the throne of his grandfather with the accession of the house of Hanover. Even Queen Eleanor was present at this festival, for she had been released for a time at the request of her daughter Matilda.

One more year of the half decade which still remained of life to Henry was to pass with only a slight foreshadowing, near its close, of the anxieties which were to fill the remainder of his days. The first question of importance which arose in 1185 concerned the kingdom of Jerusalem. England had down to this time taken slight and only indirect part in the great movement of the crusades. The Christian states in the Holy Land had existed for nearly ninety years, but with slowly declining strength and defensive power. Recently the rapid progress of Saladin, creating a new Mohammedan empire, and not merely displaying great military and political skill, but bringing under one bond of interest the Saracens of Egypt and Syria, whose conflicts heretofore had been among the best safeguards of the Christian state, threatened the most serious results. The reigning king of Jerusalem at this moment was Baldwin IV, grandson of that Fulk V, Count of Anjou, whom we saw, more than fifty years before this date, handing over his French possessions to his son Geoffrey, newly wedded to Matilda the Empress, and departing for the Holy Land to marry its heiress and become its king. Baldwin was therefore the first cousin of Henry II, and it was not unnatural that his kingdom should turn in the midst of the difficulties that surrounded it to the head of the house of Anjou now so powerful in the west. The embassy which came to seek his cousin's help was the most dignified and imposing that could be sent from the Holy Land, with Heraclius the patriarch of Jerusalem at its head, supported by the grand-masters of the knights of the Temple and of the Hospital. The grand-master of the Templars died at Verona on the journey, but the survivors landed in England at the end of January, 1185, and Henry who was on his way to York turned back and met them at Reading. There Heraclius described the evils that afflicted the Christian kingdom so eloquently that the king and all the multitude who heard were moved to sighs and tears. He offered to Henry the keys of the tower of David and of the holy sepulchre, and the banner of the kingdom, with the right to the throne itself.

To such an offer in these circumstances there was but one reply to make, and a king like Henry could never have been for a moment in doubt as to what it should be. His case was very different from his grandfather's when a similar offer was made to him. Not merely did the responsibility of a far larger dominion rest on him, with greater dangers within and without to be watched and overcome, but a still more important consideration was the fact that there was no one of his sons in whose hands his authority could be securely left. His departure would be the signal for a new and disastrous civil war, and we may believe that the character of his sons was a deciding reason with the king. But such an offer, made in such a way, and backed by the religious motives so strong in that age, could not be lightly declined. A great council of the kingdom was summoned to meet in London about the middle of March to consider the offer and the answer to be made. The king of Scotland and his brother David, and the prelates and barons of England, debated the question, and advised Henry not to abandon the duties which rested upon him at home. It is interesting to notice that the obligations which the coronation oath had imposed on the king were called to mind as determining what he ought to do, though probably no more was meant by this than that the appeal which the Church was making in favour of the crusade was balanced by the duty which he had assumed before the Church and under its sanction to govern well his hereditary kingdom. Apparently the patriarch was told that a consultation with the king of France was necessary, and shortly after they all crossed into Normandy. Before the meeting of the council in London Baldwin IV had closed his unhappy reign and was succeeded by his nephew Baldwin V, a child who never reached his majority. In France the embassy succeeded no better. At a conference between the kings the promise was made of ample aid in men and money, but the great hope with which the envoys had started, that they might bring back with them the king of England, or at least one of his sons, to lead the Christian cause in Palestine, was disappointed; and Heraclius set out on his return not merely deeply grieved, but angry with Henry for his refusal to undertake what he believed to be his obvious religious duty.

Between the meeting of the council in London and the crossing into Normandy, Henry had taken steps to carry out an earlier plan of his in regard to his son John. He seems now to have made up his mind that Richard could never be induced to give up Aquitaine or any part of it, and he returned to his earlier idea of a kingdom of Ireland. Immediately after the council he knighted John at Windsor and sent him to take possession of the island, not yet as king but as lord (dominus). On April 25 he landed at Waterford, coming, it is said, with sixty ships and a large force of men-at-arms and foot-soldiers. John was at the time nearly nineteen years old, of an age when men were then expected to have reached maturity, and the prospect of success lay fair before him; but he managed in less than six months to prove conclusively that he was, as yet at least, totally unfit to rule a state. The native chieftains who had accepted his father's government came in to signify their obedience, but he twitched their long beards and made sport before his attendants of their uncouth manners and dress, and allowed them to go home with anger in their hearts to stir up opposition to his rule. The Archbishop of Dublin and the barons who were most faithful to his father offered him their homage and support, but he neglected their counsels and even disregarded their rights. The military force he had brought over, ample to guard the conquests already made, or even to increase them, he dissipated in useless undertakings, and kept without their pay that he might spend the money on his own amusements, until they abandoned him in numbers, and even went over to his Irish enemies. In a few months he found himself confronted with too many difficulties, and gave up his post, returning to his father with reasons for his failure that put the blame on others and covered up his own defects. Not long afterwards died Pope Lucius III, who had steadily refused to renew, or to put into legal form, the permission which Alexander III had granted to crown one of Henry's sons king of Ireland; and to his successor, Urban III, new application was at once made in the special interest of John, and this time with success. The pope is said even to have sent a crown made of peacock's feathers intertwined with gold as a sign of his confirmation of the title.

John was, however, never actually crowned king of Ireland, and indeed it is probable that he never revisited the island. In the summer of the next year, 1186, news came, in the words of a contemporary, "that a certain Irishman had cut off the head of Hugh of Lacy." Henry is said to have rejoiced at the news, for, though he had never found it possible to get along for any length of time without the help of Hugh of Lacy in Ireland, he had always looked upon his measures and success with suspicion. Now he ordered John to go over at once and seize into his hand Hugh's land and castles, but John did not leave England. At the end of the year legates to Ireland arrived in England from the pope, one object of whose mission was to crown the king of Ireland, but Henry was by this time so deeply interested in questions that had arisen between himself and the king of France because of the death of his son Geoffrey, the Count of Britanny, that he could not give his attention to Ireland, and with the legates he crossed to Normandy instead, having sent John over in advance.

Affairs in France had followed their familiar course since the conference between Henry and Philip on the subject of the crusade in the spring of 1185. Immediately after that meeting Henry had proceeded with great vigour against Richard. He had Eleanor brought over to Normandy, and then commanded Richard to surrender to his mother all her inheritance under threat of invasion with a great army. Richard, whether moved by the threat or out of respect to his mother, immediately complied, and, we are told,[43] remained at his father's court "like a well-behaved son," while Henry in person took possession of Aquitaine. In the meantime the war between Philip II and the Count of Flanders had gone steadily on, the king of England declining to interfere again. At the end of July, 1185, the count had been obliged to yield, and had ceded to Philip Amiens and most of Vermandois, a very important enlargement of territory for the French monarchy. This first great success of the young king of France was followed the next spring by the humiliation and forced submission of the Duke of Burgundy.

In all these events the king of England had taken no active share. He was a mere looker-on, or if he had interfered at all, it was rather to the advantage of Philip, while the rival monarchy in France had not merely increased the territory under its direct control, but taught the great vassals the lesson of obedience, and proclaimed to all the world that the rights of the crown would be everywhere affirmed and enforced. It was clearly the opening of a new era, yet Henry gave not the slightest evidence that he saw it or understood its meaning for himself. While it is certain that Philip had early detected the weakness of the Angevin empire, and had formed his plan for its destruction long before he was able to carry it out, we can only note with surprise that Henry made no change in his policy to meet the new danger of which he had abundant warning. He seems never to have understood that in Philip Augustus he had to deal with a different man from Louis VII. That he continued steadily under the changed circumstances his old policy of non-intervention outside his own frontiers, of preserving peace to the latest possible moment, and of devoting himself to the maintenance and perfection of a strong government wherever he had direct rule, is more creditable to the character of Henry II than to the insight of a statesman responsible for the continuance of a great empire, and offered the realization of a great possibility. To Philip Augustus it was the possibility only which was offered; the empire was still to be created: but while hardly more than a boy, he read the situation with clear insight and saw before him the goal to be reached and the way to reach it, and this he followed with untiring patience to the end of his long reign.

When Henry returned to England at the end of April, 1186, he abandoned all prospect of profiting by the opportunity which still existed, though in diminished degree, of checking in its beginning the ominous growth of Philip's power, an opportunity which we may believe his grandfather would not have overlooked or neglected. By the end of the summer all chance of this was over, and no policy of safety remained to Henry but a trial of strength to the finish with his crafty suzerain, for Philip had not merely returned successful from his Burgundian expedition, but he had almost without effort at concealment made his first moves against the Angevin power. His opening was the obvious one offered him by the dissensions in Henry's family, and his first move was as skilful as the latest he ever made. Richard was now on good terms with his father; it would even appear that he had been restored to the rule of Aquitaine; at any rate Henry's last act before his return to England in April had been to hand over to Richard a great sum of money with directions to subdue his foes. Richard took the money and made successful and cruel war on the Count of Toulouse, on what grounds we know not. Geoffrey, however, offered himself to Philip's purposes. Henry's third son seems to have been in character and conduct somewhat like his eldest brother, the young king. He had the same popular gifts and attractive manners; he enjoyed an almost equal renown for knightly accomplishments and for the knightly virtue of "largesse"; and he was, in the same way, bitterly dissatisfied with his own position. He believed that the death of his brother ought to improve his prospects, and his mind was set on having the county of Anjou added to his possessions. When Richard and his father refused him this, he turned to France and betook himself to Paris. Philip received him with open arms, and they speedily became devoted friends. Just what their immediate plans were we cannot say. They evidently had not been made public, and various rumours were in circulation. Some said that Geoffrey would hold Britanny of Philip; or he had been made sereschal of France, an office that ought to go with the county of Anjou; or he was about to invade and devastate Normandy. It is probable that some overt action would have been undertaken very shortly when suddenly, on August 19, Geoffrey died, having been mortally hurt in a tournament, or from an attack of fever, or perhaps from both causes. He was buried in Paris, Philip showing great grief and being, it is said, with difficulty restrained from throwing himself into the grave.

The death of Geoffrey may have made a change in the form of Philip's plans, and perhaps in the date of his first attempt to carry them out, but not in their ultimate object. It furnished him, indeed, with a new subject of demand on Henry. There had been no lack of subjects in the past, and he had pushed them persistently: the question of Margaret's dower lands, — the return of the Norman Vexin, — and of the payment of her money allowance, complicated now by her second marriage to Bela, king of Hungary; the standing question of the marriage of Philip's sister Adela; the dispute about the suzerainty of Auvergne still unsettled; and finally Richard's war on the Count of Toulouse. Now was added the question of the wardship of Britanny. At the time of his death one child had been born to Geoffrey of his marriage with Constance, — a daughter, Eleanor, who was recognized as the heiress of the county. Without delay Philip sent an embassy to Henry in England and demanded the wardship of the heiress, with threats of war if the demand was not complied with. The justice of Philip's claim in this case was not entirely clear since he was not the immediate lord of Britanny, but kings had not always respected the rights of their vassals in the matter of rich heiresses, and possibly Geoffrey had actually performed the homage to Philip which he was reported to be planning to do. In any case it was impossible for Henry to accept Philip's view of his rights, but war at the moment would have been inconvenient, and so he sent a return embassy with Ranulf Glanvill at its head, and succeeded in getting a truce until the middle of the winter. Various fruitless negotiations followed, complicated by an attack made by the garrison of Gisors on French workmen found building an opposing castle just over the border. Henry himself crossed to Normandy about the middle of February, 1187, but personal interviews with Philip led to no result, and the situation drifted steadily toward war. The birth of a posthumous son to Geoffrey in March—whom the Bretons insisted on calling Arthur, though Henry wished to give him his own name, a sure sign of their wish for a more independent position—brought about no change. Philip had protected himself from all danger of outside interference by an alliance with the Emperor Frederick Barbarossa and was determined on war. By the middle of May both sides were ready. Henry divided his army into four divisions and adopted a purely defensive policy.

Philip's attack fell on the lands of disputed allegiance on the eastern edge of the duchy of Aquitaine near his own possessions, and after a few minor successes he laid siege to the important castle of Châteauroux. This was defended by Richard in person, with his brother John, but Philip pressed the siege until Henry drew near with an army, when he retired a short distance and awaited the next move. Negotiations followed, in the course of which the deep impression that the character of Philip had already made on his great vassals is clearly to be seen.[49] Henry's desire was to avoid a battle, and this was probably the best policy for him; it certainly was unless he were willing, as he seems not to have been, to bring on at once the inevitable mortal struggle between the houses of Capet and Anjou. Unimportant circumstances on both sides came in to favour Henry's wish and to prevent a battle, and finally Henry himself, by a most extraordinary act of folly, threw into the hands of Philip the opportunity of gaining a greater advantage for his ultimate purposes than he could hope to gain at that time from any victory. Henry's great danger was Richard. In the situation it was incumbent on him from every consideration of policy to keep Richard satisfied, and to prevent not merely the division of the Angevin strength, but the reinforcement of the enemy with the half of it. He certainly had had experience enough of Richard's character to know what to expect. He ought by that time to have been able to read Philip Augustus's. And yet he calmly proceeded to a step from which, it is hardly too much to say, all his later troubles came through the suspicion he aroused in Richard's mind,—a step so unaccountable that we are tempted to reject our single, rather doubtful account of it. He wrote a letter to Philip proposing that Adela should be married to John, who should then be invested with all the French fiefs held by the house of Anjou except Normandy, which with the kingdom of England should remain to Richard. [50] If Henry was blind enough to suppose that the Duke of Aquitaine could be reconciled to such an arrangement, Philip saw at once what the effect of the proposal would be, and he sent the letter to Richard.

The immediate result was a treaty of peace to continue in force for two years, brought about apparently by direct negotiations between Richard and Philip, but less unfavourable to Henry than might have been expected. It contained, according to our French authorities, the very probable agreement that the points in dispute between the two kings should be submitted to the decision of the curia regis of France, and Philip was allowed to retain the lordships of Issoudun and Fréteval, which he had previously occupied, as pledges for the carrying out of the treaty. The ultimate result of Philip's cunning was that Richard deserted his father and went home with the king of France, and together they lived for a time in the greatest intimacy. Philip, it seemed, now loved Richard "as his own soul," and showed him great honour. Every day they ate at table from the same plate, and at night they slept in the same bed. One is reminded of Philip's ardent love for Geoffrey, and certain suspicions inevitably arise in the mind. But at any rate the alarm of Henry was excited by the new intimacy, and he did not venture to go over to England as he wished to do until he should know what the outcome was to be. He sent frequent messengers to Richard, urging him to return and promising to grant him everything that he could justly claim, but without effect. At one time Richard pretended to be favourably inclined, and set out as if to meet his father, but instead he fell upon the king's treasure at Chinon and carried it off to Aquitaine to use in putting his own castles into a state of defence. His father, however, forgave even this and continued to send for him, and at last he yielded. Together they went to Angers, and there in a great assembly Richard performed liege homage to his father once more and swore fealty to him "against all men," a fact which would seem to show that Richard had in some formal way renounced his fealty while at Philip's court, though we have no account of his doing so. During this period, in September, 1187, an heir was born to King Philip, the future Louis VIII.

As this year drew to its close frequent letters and messengers from the Holy Land made known to the west one terrible disaster after another. Saladin with a great army had fallen on the weak and divided kingdom and had won incredible successes. The infant king, Baldwin V, had died before these events began, and his mother Sibyl was recognized as queen. She immediately, against the expressed wish of the great barons, gave the crown to her husband, Guy of Lusignan. He was a brave man and an earnest defender of the Holy Land, but he could not accomplish the impossible task of maintaining a kingdom, itself so weak, in the face of open and secret treachery. In October the news reached Europe of the utter defeat of the Christians, of the capture of the king, and worse still of the true Cross by the infidels. The pope, Urban III, died of grief at the tidings. His successor, Gregory VIII, at once urged Europe to a new crusade in a long and vigorous appeal. Very soon afterwards followed the news of the capture of Jerusalem by Saladin. The Emperor Frederick was anxious to put himself at the head of the armies of Christendom, as he was entitled to do as sovereign of the Holy Roman Empire, and lead them to recover the holy places. But while most princes delayed and waited to know what others would do, the impulsive and emotional Richard took the cross the next morning, men said, after he had learned the news. This he did without the knowledge of his father who was shocked to learn of it, and shut himself up for days, understanding more clearly than did his son what the absence of the heir to the throne on such a long and uncertain expedition would mean at such a time.

The advisability, the possibility even, of such a crusade would all depend upon Philip, and the movements of Philip just then were very disquieting. About the beginning of the new year, 1188, he returned from a conference with the Emperor Frederick, which in itself could bode no good to the father-in-law and supporter of Henry the Lion, and immediately began collecting a large army, "impudently boasting," says the English chronicler of Henry's life, "that he would lay waste Normandy and the other lands of the king of England that side the sea, if he did not return to him Gisors and all that belonged to it or make his son Richard take to wife Adela the daughter of his father Louis." Philip evidently did not intend to drop everything to go to the rescue of Jerusalem nor was he inclined at any expense to his own interests to make it easy for those who would. Henry who was already at the coast on the point of crossing to England, at once turned back when he heard of Philip's threats, and arranged for a conference with him on January 21. Here was the opportunity for those who were urging on the crusade. The kings of France and England with their chief barons were to be together while the public excitement was still high and the Christian duty of checking the Saracen conquest still keenly felt. The Archbishop of Tyre, who had come to France on this mission, gave up all his other undertakings as soon as he heard of the meeting and resolved to make these great princes converts to his cause. It was not an easy task. Neither Henry nor Philip was made of crusading material, and both were far more interested in the tasks of constructive statesmanship which they had on hand than in the fate of the distant kingdom of Jerusalem. A greater obstacle than this even was their fear of each other, of what evil one might do in the absence of the other, the unwillingness of either to pledge himself to anything definite until he knew what the other was going to do, and the difficulty of finding any arrangement which would bind them both at once. It is practically certain that they yielded at last only to the pressure of public opinion which must have been exceedingly strong in the excitement of the time and under the impassioned eloquence of a messenger direct from the scene of the recent disasters. It was a great day for the Church when so many men of the highest rank, kings and great barons, took the cross, and it was agreed that the spot should be marked by a new church, and that it should bear the name of the Holy Field.

Whatever may be true of Philip, there can, I think, be no doubt that, when Henry took the cross, he intended to keep his vow. It was agreed between them that all things should remain as they were until their return; and

Henry formally claimed of his suzerain the protection of his lands during his absence, and Philip accepted the duty.[51] A few days after taking the cross Henry held an assembly at Le Mans and ordered a tax in aid of his crusade. This was the famous Saladin tithe, which marks an important step in the history of modern taxation. It was modelled on an earlier tax for the same purpose which had been agreed upon between France and England in 1166, but it shows a considerable development upon that, both in conception and in the arrangements for carrying out the details of the tax. The ordinance provided for the payment by all, except those who were themselves going on the crusade, of a tenth, a "tithe," of both personal property and income, precious stones being exempt and the necessary tools of their trade of both knights and clerks. Somewhat elaborate machinery was provided for the collection of the tax, and the whole was placed under the sanction of the Church. A similar ordinance was shortly adopted by Philip for France, and on February 11, Henry, then in England, held a council at Geddington, in Northamptonshire, and ordained the same tax for England.

In the meantime the crusade had received a check, and partly, at least, through the fault of its most eager leader, Richard of Poitou. A rebellion had broken out against him, and he was pushing the war with his usual rapidity and his usual severities, adopting now, however, the interesting variation of remitting all other penalties if his prisoners would take the cross. If Richard was quickly master of the rebellion, it served on the one hand to embitter him still more against his father, from the report, which in his suspicious attitude he was quick to believe, that Henry's money and encouragement had supported the rebels against him; and on the other, to lead to hostilities with the Count of Toulouse. The count had not neglected the opportunity of Richard's troubles to get a little satisfaction for his own grievances, and had seized some merchants from the English lands. Richard responded with a raid into Toulouse, in which he captured the chief minister of the count and refused ransom for him. Then the count in his turn arrested a couple of English knights of some standing at court, who were returning from a pilgrimage to St. James of Compostella. Still Richard refused either ransom or exchange, and an appeal to the king of France led to no result. Richard told his father afterwards that Philip had encouraged his attack on the count. Soon, however, his rapid successes in Toulouse, where he was taking castle after castle, compelled Philip to more decided interference; probably he was not sorry to find a reason both to postpone the crusade and to renew the attack on the Angevin lands. First he sent an embassy to Henry in England to protest against Richard's doings, and received the reply that the war was against Henry's will, and that he could not justify it. With a great army Philip then invaded Auvergne, captured Châteauroux and took possession of almost all Berri. An embassy sent to bring Philip to a better mind was refused all satisfaction, and Henry, seeing that his presence was necessary in France, crossed the channel for the last of many times and landed in Normandy on July 1, 1188.

All things were now, indeed, drawing to a close with Henry, who was not merely worn out and ill, but was plunged into a tide of events flowing swiftly against all the currents of his own life. Swept away by the strong forces of a new age which he could no longer control, driven and thwarted by men, even his own sons, whose ideals of conduct and ambition were foreign to his own and never understood, compelled to do things he had striven to avoid, and to see helplessly the policy of his long reign brought to naught, the coming months were for him full of bitter disasters which could end only, as they did, in heartbreak and death. Not yet, however, was he brought to this point, and he got together a great army and made ready to fight if necessary. But first, true to his policy of negotiation, he sent another embassy to Philip and demanded restitution under the threat of renouncing his fealty. Philip's answer was a refusal to stop his hostilities until he should have occupied all Berri and the Norman Vexin. War was now inevitable, but it lingered for some time without events of importance, and on August 16 began a new three days' conference at the historic meeting-place of the kings near Gisors. This also ended fruitlessly; some of the French even attacked the English position, and then cut down in anger the old elm tree under which so many conferences had taken place. Philip was, however, in no condition to push the war upon which he had determined. The crusading ardour of France which he himself did not feel, and which had failed to bring about a peace at Gisors, expressed itself in another way; and the Count of Flanders and Theobald of Blois and other great barons of Philip notified him that they would take no part in a war against Christians until after their return from Jerusalem.

Philip's embarrassment availed Henry but little, although his own force remained undiminished. A sudden dash at Mantes on August 30, led only to the burning of a dozen or more French villages, for Philip by a very hurried march from Chaumont was able to throw himself into the city, and Henry withdrew without venturing a pitched battle. On the next day Richard, who till then had been with his father, went off to Berri to push with some vigour the attack on Philip's conquests there, promising his father faithful service. A double attack on the French, north and south, was not a bad plan as Philip was then situated, but for some reason not clear to us Henry seems to have let matters drift and made no use of the great army which he had got together. The king of France, however, saw clearly what his next move should be, and he sent to propose peace to Henry on the basis of a restoration of conquests on both sides. Henry was ever ready for peace, and a new conference took place at Chatillon on the Indre, where it was found that Philip's proposition was the exchange of his conquests in Berri for those of Richard in Toulouse, and the handing over to him of the castle of Pacy, near Mantes, as a pledge that the treaty would be kept. It is difficult to avoid the conclusion that Philip knew that this demand would be refused, as it was, and that he had only made the proposal of peace in order to gain time to collect a new force. In this he must now have succeeded, for he immediately took the offensive in Berri and added somewhat to his conquests, probably by hiring the German mercenaries whom we learn he shortly afterwards defrauded of their pay.

In the meantime Richard and Philip were drawing together again, in what way exactly we do not know. We suspect some underhanded work of Philip's which would be easy enough. Evidently Richard was still very anxious about the succession, and it seems to have occurred to him to utilize his father's desire for peace on the basis of Philip's latest proposition, to gain a definite recognition of his rights. At any rate we are told that he brought about the next meeting between the kings, and that he offered to submit the question of the rights or wrongs of his war with Toulouse to the decision of the French king's court. This dramatic and fateful conference which marks the success of Philip's intrigues began on November 18 at Bonmoulins, and lasted three days. Henry was ready to accept the proposal now made that all things should be restored on both sides to the condition which existed at the taking of the cross, but here Richard interposed a decided objection. He could not see the justice of being made to restore his conquests in Toulouse which he was holding in domain, and which were worth a thousand marks a year, to get back himself some castles in Berri which were not of his domain but only held of him. Then Philip for him, evidently by previous agreement, brought forward the question of the succession. The new proposition was that Richard and Adela should be married and that homage should be paid to Richard as heir from all the Angevin dominions. It seems likely, though it is not so stated, that on this condition Richard would have agreed to the even exchange of conquests. As time went on the discussion, which had been at first peaceable and calm, became more and more excited so that on the third day the attendants came armed. On that day harsh words and threats were exchanged. To Richard's direct demand that he should make him secure in the succession, Henry replied that he could not do it in the existing circumstances, for, if he did, he would seem to be yielding to threats and not acting of his own will. Then Richard, crying out that he could now believe things that had seemed incredible to him, turned at once to Philip, threw off his sword, and in the presence of his father and all the bystanders offered him his homage for all the French fiefs, including Toulouse, saying his father's rights during his lifetime and his own allegiance to his father. Philip accepted this offer without scruple, and promised to Richard the restoration of what he had taken in Berri, with Issoudun and all that he had conquered of the English possessions since the beginning of his reign.

To one at least of the historians of the time Richard's feeling about the succession did not seem strange, nor can it to us.[52] For this act of Richard, after which peace was never restored between himself and his father, Henry must share full blame with him. Whether he was actuated by a blind affection for his youngest son, or by dislike and distrust of Richard, or by a remembrance of his troubles with his eldest son, his refusal to recognize Richard as his heir and to allow him to receive the homage of the English and French barons, a custom sanctioned by the practice of a hundred years in England and of a much longer period in France, was a political and dynastic blunder of a most astonishing kind. Nothing could show more clearly how little he understood Philip Augustus or the danger which now threatened the Angevin house. As for Richard, he may have been quick-tempered, passionate, and rash, not having the well-poised mind of the diplomatist or the statesman, at least not one of the high order demanded by the circumstances, and deceived by his own anger and by the machinations of Philip; yet we can hardly blame him for offering his homage to the king of France. Nor can we call the act illegal, though it was extreme and unusual, and might seem almost revolutionary. An appeal to his overlord was in fact the only legal means left him of securing his inheritance, and it bound Philip not to recognize any one else as the heir of Henry. Philip was clearly within his legal rights in accepting the offer of Richard, and the care with which Richard's declaration was made to keep within the law, reserving all the rights which should be reserved, shows that however impulsive his act may have seemed to the bystanders, it really had been carefully considered and planned in advance. The conference broke up after this with no other result than a truce to January 13, and Richard rode off with Philip without taking leave of his father.

For all that had taken place Henry did not give up his efforts to bring back Richard to himself, but they were without avail. He himself, burdened with anxiety and torn by conflicting emotions, was growing more and more ill. The scanty attendance at his Christmas court showed him the opinion of the barons of the hopelessness of his cause and the prudence of making themselves secure with Richard. He was not well enough to meet his enemies in the conference proposed for January 13, and it was postponed first to February 2 and then to Easter, April 9. It was now, however, too late for anything to be accomplished by diplomacy. Henry could not yield to the demands made of him until he was beaten in the field, nor were they likely to be modified. Indeed we find at this time the new demand appearing that John should be made to go on the crusade when Richard did. Even the intervention of the pope, who was represented at the conferences finally held soon after Easter and early in June, by a cardinal legate, in earnest effort for the crusade, served only to show how completely Philip was the man of a new age. To the threat of the legate, who saw that the failure to make peace was chiefly due to him, that he would lay France under an interdict if he did not come to terms with the king of England, Philip replied in defiant words that he did not fear the sentence and would not regard it, for it would be unjust, since the Roman Church had no right to interfere within France between the king and his rebellious vassal and he overbore the legate and compelled him to keep silence.

After this conference events drew swiftly to an end. The allies pushed the war, and in a few days captured Le Mans, forcing Henry to a sudden flight in which he was almost taken prisoner. A few days later still Philip stormed the walls of Tours and took that city. Henry was almost a fugitive with few followers and few friends in the hereditary county from which his house was named. He had turned aside from the better fortified and more easily defended Normandy against the advice of all, and now there was nothing for him but to yield. Terms of peace were settled in a final conference near Colombières on July 4, 1189. At the meeting Henry was so ill that he could hardly sit his horse, though Richard and Philip had sneered at his illness and called it pretence, but he resolutely endured the pain as he did the humiliation of the hour. Philip's demands seem surprisingly small considering the man and the completeness of his victory, but there were no grounds on which he could demand from Henry any great concession. One thing he did insist upon, and that was for him probably the most important advantage which he gained. Henry must acknowledge himself entirely at his mercy, as a contumacious vassal, and accept any sentence imposed on him. In the great task which Philip Augustus had before him, already so successfully begun, of building up in France a strong monarchy and of forcing many powerful and independent vassals into obedience to the crown, nothing could be more useful than this precedent, so dramatic and impressive, of the unconditional submission of the most powerful of all the vassals, himself a crowned king. All rights over the disputed county of Auvergne were abandoned. Richard was acknowledged heir and was to receive the homage of all barons. Those who had given in their allegiance to Richard should remain with him till the crusade, which was to be begun the next spring, and 20,000 marks were to be paid the king of France for his expenses on the captured castles, which were to be returned to Henry.

These were the principal conditions, and to all these Henry agreed as he must. That he intended to give up all effort and rest satisfied with this result is not likely, and words he is said to have used indicate the contrary, but his disease and his broken spirits had brought him nearer the end than he knew. One more blow, for him the severest of all, remained for him to suffer. He found at the head of the list of those who had abandoned his allegiance the name of John. Then his will forsook him and his heart broke. He turned his face to the wall and cried: "Let everything go as it will; I care no more for myself or for the world." On July 6 he died at Chinon, murmuring almost to the last, "Shame on a conquered king," and abandoned by all his family except his eldest son Geoffrey, the son, it was said, of a woman, low in character as in birth.

[48] Gesia Henrici, i. 338.

[49] Gervase of Canterbury, i. 371; Giraldus Cambrensis, De Principis Instructione, iii. 2. (Opera, viii. 231.)

[50] Giraldus Cambrensis, De Principis Instructione. (Opera, viii. 232.)

[51] Ralph de Diceto, ii. 55.

[52] Gervase of Canterbury, i. 435.

CHAPTER XVII.
RICHARD I AND THE CRUSADE

The death of Henry II may be taken to mark the close of an epoch in English history, the epoch which had begun with the Norman Conquest. We may call it, for want of a better name, the feudal age,—the age during which the prevailing organization, ideals, and practices had been Norman-feudal. It was an age in which Normandy and the continental interests of king and barons, and the continental spirit and methods, had imposed themselves upon the island realm. It was a time in which the great force in the state and the chief factor in its history had been the king. The interests of the barons had been on the whole identical with his. The rights which feudal law and custom gave him had been practically unquestioned, save by an always reluctant Church, and baronial opposition had taken the form of a resistance to his general power rather than of a denial of special rights. Now a change had silently begun which was soon to show itself openly and to lead to great results. This change involved only slowly and indirectly the general power of the king, but it takes its beginning from two sources: the rising importance of England in the total dominions of the king, and the disposition to question certain of his rights. Normandy was losing its power over the English baron, or if this is too strong a statement for anything that was yet true, he was beginning to identify himself more closely with England and to feel less interest in sacrifices and burdens which inured only to the benefit of the king and a policy foreign to the country. To the disposition to question the king's actions and demands Henry had himself contributed not a little by the frequency and greatness of those demands, and by the small regard to the privileges of his vassals shown in the development of his judicial reforms and in his financial measures these last indeed under Henry II violated the baronial rights less directly but, as they were carried on by his sons, they attacked them in a still more decisive way. When once this disposition had begun, the very strength of the Norman monarchy was an element of weakness, for it gave to individual complaints a unity and a degree of importance and interest for the country which they might not otherwise have had. In this development the reign of Richard, though differing but little in outward appearance from his father's, was a time of rapid preparation, leading directly to the struggles of his brother's reign and to the first great forward step, the act which marks the full beginning of the new era.

Richard could have felt no grief at the death of his father, and he made no show of any. Geoffrey had gone for the burial to the nunnery of Fontevrault, a favourite convent of Henry's, and there Richard appeared as soon as he heard the news, and knelt beside the body of his father, which was said to have bled on his approach, as long as it would take to say the Lord's prayer. Then we are told he turned at once to business. The first act which he performed, according to one of our authorities, on stepping outside the church was characteristic of the beginning of his reign. One of the most faithful of his father's later servants was William Marshal, who had been earlier in the service of his son Henry. He had remained with the king to the last, and in the hurried retreat from Le Mans he had guarded the rear. On Richard's coming up in pursuit he had turned upon him with his lance and might have killed him as he was without his coat of mail, but instead, on Richard's crying out to be spared, he had only slain his horse, and so checked the pursuit, though he had spared him with words of contempt which Richard must have remembered: "No, I will not slay you," he had said; "the devil may slay you." Now both he and his friends were anxious as to the reception he would meet with from the prince, but Richard was resolved to start from the beginning as king and not as Count of Poitou. He called William Marshal to him, referred to the incident, granted him his full pardon, confirmed the gift to him which Henry had recently made him of the hand of the heiress of the Earl of Pembroke and her rich inheritance, and commissioned him to go at once to England to take charge of the king's interests there until his own arrival. This incident was typical of Richard's action in general. Henry's faithful servants suffered nothing for their fidelity in opposing his son; the barons who had abandoned him before his death, to seek their own selfish advantage because they believed the tide was turning against him, were taught that Richard was able to estimate their conduct at its real worth.

Henry on his death-bed had made no attempt to dispose of the succession. On the retreat from Le Mans he had sent strict orders to Normandy, to give up the castles there in the event of his death to no one but John. But the knowledge of John's treason would have changed that, even if it had been possible to set aside the treaty of Colombières. There was no disposition anywhere to question Richard's right. On July 20 at Rouen he was formally girt with the sword of the duchy of Normandy, by the archbishop and received the homage of the clergy and other barons. He at once confirmed to his brother John, who had joined him, the grants made or promised him by their father: £4000 worth of land in England, the county of Mortain in Normandy, and the hand and inheritance of the heiress of the Earl of Gloucester. To his other brother, Geoffrey, he gave the archbishopric of York, carrying out a wish which Henry had expressed in his last moments; and Matilda, the daughter of Henry the Lion, was given as his bride to another Geoffrey, the heir of the county of Perche, a border land whose alliance would be of importance in case of trouble with France. Two days later he had an interview with King Philip at the old meeting-place near Gisors. There Philip quickly made evident the fact that in his eyes the king of England was a different person from the rebellious Count of Poitou, and he met Richard with his familiar demand that the Norman Vexin should be given up. Without doubt the point of view had changed as much to Richard, and he adopted his father's tactics and promised to marry Adela. He also promised Philip 4000 marks in addition to the 20,000 which Henry had agreed to pay. With these promises Philip professed himself content. He received Richard's homage for all the French fiefs, and the treaty lately made with Henry was confirmed, including the agreement to start on the crusade the next spring.

In the meantime by the command of Richard his mother, Eleanor, was set free from custody in England; and assuming a royal state she made a progress through the kingdom and gave orders for the release of prisoners. About the middle of August Richard himself landed in England with John. No one had any grounds on which to expect a particularly good reign from him, but he was everywhere joyfully received, especially by his mother and the barons at Winchester. A few days later the marriage of John to Isabel of Gloucester was celebrated, in spite of a formal protest entered by Baldwin, Archbishop of Canterbury, because the parties were related within the prohibited degrees. The coronation took place on Sunday, September 3, and was celebrated apparently with much care to follow the old ritual correctly and with much formal pomp and ceremony, so that it became a new precedent for later occasions down to the present day.

Richard was then just coming to the end of his thirty-second year. In physical appearance he was not like either the Norman or the Angevin type, but was taller and of a more delicate and refined cast, and his portrait shows a rather handsome face. In character and ambitions also he was not a descendant of his father's line. The humdrum business of ruling the state, of developing its law and institutions, of keeping order and doing justice, or even of following a consistent and long-continued policy of increasing his power or enlarging his territories, was little to his taste. He was determined, as his father had been, to be a strong king and to put down utterly every rebellion, but his determination to be obeyed was rather a resolution of the moment than a means to any foreseen and planned conclusion. He has been called by one who knew the time most thoroughly "the creation and impersonation of his age," and nothing better can be said. The first age of a self-conscious chivalry, delighting intensely in the physical life, in the sense of strength and power, that belonged to baron and knight, and in the stirring scenes of castle and tournament and distant adventure, the age of the troubadour, of an idealized warfare and an idealized love, the age which had expressed one side of itself in his brother Henry, expressed a more manly side in Richard. He was first of all a warrior; not a general but a fighter. The wild enthusiasm of the hand-to-hand conflict, the matching of skill against skill and of strength against strength, was an intense pleasure to him, and his superiority in the tactics of the battle-field, in the planning and management of a fight, or even of a series of attacks or defences, a march or a retreat, placed him easily in the front rank of commanders in an age when the larger strategy of the highest order of generalship had little place. Of England he had no knowledge. He was born there, and he had paid it two brief visits before his coronation, but he knew nothing of the language or the people. He had spent all his life in his southern dominions, and the south had made him what he was. His interest in England was chiefly as a source of supplies, and to him the crusade was, by the necessities of his nature, of greater importance than the real business of a king. For England itself the period was one during which there was no king, though it was by the authority of an absent king that a series of great ministers carried forward the development of the machinery and law which had begun to be put into organized form in Henry's reign, and carried forward also the training of the classes who had a share in public affairs for the approaching crisis of their history. From this point of view the exceedingly burdensome demands of Richard upon his English subjects are the most important feature of his time.

At the beginning of his reign Richard had, like his father, a great work to do, great at least from his point of view; but the difference between the two tasks shows how thoroughly Henry had performed his. Richard's problem was to get as much money as possible for the expenses of the crusade, and to arrange things, if possible, in such a shape that the existing peace and quiet would be undisturbed during his absence. About the business of raising money he set immediately and thoroughly. The medieval king had many things to sell which are denied the modern sovereign: offices, favour, and pardons, the rights of the crown, and even in some cases the rights of the purchaser himself. This was Richard's chief resource. "The king exposed for sale," as a chronicler of the time said,[53] "everything that he had"; or as another said,[54] "whoever wished, bought of the king his own and others' rights": not merely was the willing purchaser welcome, but the unwilling was compelled to buy wherever possible. Ranulf Glanvill, the great judge, Henry's justiciar and "the eye of the king," was compelled to resign and to purchase his liberty with the great sum, it is asserted, of £15,000. In most of the counties the former sheriffs were removed and fined, and the offices thus vacated were sold to the highest bidder. The Bishop of Durham, Hugh de Puiset, bought the earldom of Northumberland and the justiciarship of England; the Bishop of Winchester and the Abbot of St. Edmund's bought manors which belonged of right to their churches; the Bishop of Coventry bought a priory and the sheriffdoms of three counties; even the king's own devoted follower, William of Longchamp, paid £3000 to be chancellor of the kingdom. Sales like these were not unusual in the practice of kings, nor would they have occasioned much remark at the time, if the matter had not been carried to such extremes, and the rights and interests of the kingdom so openly disregarded. The most flagrant case of this sort was that relating to the liege homage of the king of Scotland, which Henry had exacted by formal treaty from William the Lion and his barons. In December, 1189, King William was escorted to Richard at Canterbury by Geoffrey, Archbishop of York and the barons of Yorkshire, and there did homage for his English lands, but was, on a payment of 10,000 marks, released from whatever obligations he had assumed in addition to those of former Scottish kings. Nothing could show more clearly than this how different were the interests of Richard from his father's, or how little he troubled himself about the future of his kingdom.

Already before this incident, which preceded Richard's departure by only a few days, many of his arrangements for the care of the kingdom in his absence had been made. At a great council held at Pipewell abbey near Geddington on September 15, vacant bishoprics were filled with men whose names were to be conspicuous in the period now beginning. Richard's chancellor, William Longchamp, was made Bishop of Ely; Richard Fitz Nigel, of the family of Roger of Salisbury, son of Nigel, Bishop of Ely, and like his ancestors long employed in the exchequer and to be continued in that service, was made Bishop of London; Hubert Walter, a connexion of Ranulf Glanvill, and trained by him for more important office than was now intrusted to him, became Bishop of Salisbury; and Geoffrey's appointment to York was confirmed. The responsibility of the justiciarship was at the same time divided between Bishop Hugh of Durham and the Earl of Essex, who, however, shortly died, and in his place was appointed William Longchamp. With them were associated as assistant justices five others, of whom two were William Marshal, now possessing the earldom of Pembroke, and Geoffrey Fitz Peter himself afterwards justiciar. At Canterbury, in December, further dispositions were made. Richard had great confidence in his mother, and with good reason. Although she was now nearly seventy years of age, she was still vigorous in mind and body, and she was always faithful to the interests of her sons, and wise and skilful in the assistance which she gave them. Richard seems to have left her with some ultimate authority in the state, and he richly provided for her wants. He assigned her the provision which his father had already made for her, and added also that which Henry I had made for his queen and Stephen for his, so that, as was remarked at the time, she had the endowment of three queens. John was not recognized as heir nor assigned any authority. Perhaps Richard hoped to escape in this way the troubles of his father, but, perhaps remembering also how much a scanty income had had to do with his brother Henry's discontent, he gave him almost the endowment of a king. Besides the grants already made to him in Normandy, and rich additions since his coming to England, he now conferred on him all the royal revenues of the four south-western counties of Cornwall, Devon, Dorset, and Somerset. He already held the counties of Derby and Nottingham. Richard plainly intended that political rights should not go with these grants, but he shows very little knowledge of John's character or appreciation of the temptation which he put in his way in the possession of a great principality lacking only the finishing touches.

John's position was not the only source from which speedy trouble was threatened when Richard crossed to Normandy on December 11. He had prepared another, equally certain, in the arrangement which had been made for the justiciarship. It was absurd to expect Hugh of Puiset and William Longchamp to work in the same yoke. In spirit and birth Hugh was an aristocrat of the highest type. Of not remote royal descent, a relative of the kings both of England and France, he was a proud, worldly-minded, intensely ambitious prelate of the feudal sort and of great power, almost a reigning prince in the north. Longchamp was of the class of men who rise in the service of kings. Not of peasant birth, though but little above it, he owed everything to his zealous devotion to the interests of Richard, and, as is usually the case with such men, he had an immense confidence in himself; he was determined to be master, and he was as proud of his position and abilities as was the Bishop of Durham of his blood. Besides this he was naturally of an overbearing disposition and very contemptuous of those whom he regarded as inferior to himself in any particular. Hugh in turn felt, no doubt, a great contempt for him, but Longchamp had no hesitation in measuring himself with the bishop. Soon after the departure of the king he turned Hugh out of the exchequer and took his county of Northumberland away from him. Other high-handed proceedings followed, and many appeals against his chancellor were carried to Richard in France.

To rearrange matters a great council was summoned to meet in Normandy about the end of winter. The result was that Richard sustained his minister as Longchamp had doubtless felt sure would be the case. The Humber was made a dividing line between the two justiciars, while the pope was asked to make Longchamp legate in England during the absence of the Archbishop of Canterbury, who was going on the crusade. Perhaps Richard now began to suspect that he had been preparing trouble for England instead of peace, for at the same time he exacted an oath from his brothers, Geoffrey, whose troubles with his church of York had already begun, and John, not to return to England for three years; but John was soon after released from his oath at the request of his mother.

Richard was impatient to be gone on the crusade, and he might now believe that England could be safely left to itself; but many other things delayed the expedition, and the setting out was finally postponed, by agreement with Philip, to June 24. The third crusade is the most generally interesting of all the series, because of the place which it has taken in literature; because of the greatness of its leaders and their exploits; of the knightly character of Saladin himself; of the pathetic fate of the old Emperor Frederick Barbarossa, who lost his life and sacrificed most of his army in an attempt to force his way overland through Asia Minor; and of its real failure after so great an expenditure of life and effort and so many minor successes — the most brilliant of all the crusades, the one great crusade of the age of chivalry: but it concerns the history of England even less than does the continental policy of her kings. It belongs rather to the personal history of Richard, and as such it serves to explain his character and to show why England was left to herself during his reign.

Richard and Philip met at Vézelai at the end of June, 1190, to begin the crusade. There they made a new treaty of alliance and agreed to the equal division of all the advantages to be gained in the expedition, and from thence Richard marched down the Rhone to Marseilles, where he took ship on August 7, and, by leisurely stages along the coast of Italy, went on to Messina which he reached on September 23. Much there was to occupy Richard's attention in Sicily. Philip had already reached Messina before him, and many questions arose between them, the most important of which was that of Richard's marriage. Towards the end of the winter Queen Eleanor came to Sicily, bringing with her Berengaria, the daughter of the king of Navarre, whom Richard had earlier known and admired, and whom he had now decided to marry. Naturally Philip objected, since Richard had definitely promised to marry his sister Adela; but now he flatly refused to marry one of whose relations with his father evil stories were told. By the intervention of the Count of Flanders a new treaty was made, and Richard was released from his engagement, paying 10,000 marks to the king of France. Quarrels with the inhabitants of Messina, due partly to the lawlessness of the crusaders and partly to Richard's overbearing disposition, led to almost open hostilities, and indirectly to jealousy on the part of the French. Domestic politics in the kingdom of Sicily were a further source of trouble. Richard's brother-in-law, King William, had died a year before the arrival of the crusaders, and the throne was in dispute between Henry VI, the new king of Germany, who had married Constance, William's aunt and heiress, and Tancred, an illegitimate descendant of the Norman house. Tancred was in possession, and to Richard, no doubt, the support of Sicily at the time seemed more important than the abstract question of right or the distant effect of his policy on the crusade. Accordingly a treaty was made, Tancred was recognized as king, and a large sum of money was paid to Richard; but to Henry VI the treaty was a new cause of hostility against the king of England, added to his relationship with the house of Guelf. The winter in Sicily, which to the modern mind seems an unnecessary waste of time, had added thus to the difficulties of the crusade new causes of ill-feeling between the French and English, and given a new reason for suspicion to the Germans.

It was only on April 10, 1191, that Richard at last set sail on the real crusade. He sent on a little before him his intended bride, Berengaria, with his sister Joanna, the widowed queen of Sicily. The voyage proved a long and stormy one, and it was not until May 6 that the fleet came together, with some losses, in the harbour of Limasol in Cyprus. The ruler of Cyprus, Isaac, of the house of Comnenus, who called himself emperor, showed so inhospitable a mein that Richard felt called upon to attack and finally to overthrow and imprison him and to take possession of the island. This conquest, in a moment of anger and quite in accordance with the character of Richard, though hardly to be justified even by the international law of that time, was in the end the most important and most permanent success of the third crusade. Shortly before his return home Richard gave the island to Guy of Lusignan, to make up to him his loss of the kingdom of Jerusalem; and his descendants and their successors retained it for four centuries, an outpost of Christendom against the advancing power of the Turks. In Cyprus Richard was married to Berengaria, and on June 5 he set sail for Acre, where he arrived on the 8th.

The siege of the important port and fortress of Acre, which had been taken by Saladin shortly before the fall of Jerusalem, had been begun by Guy of Lusignan at the end of August, 1189, as the first step toward the recovery of his kingdom. Saladin, recognizing the importance of the post, had come up with an army a few days later, and had in turn besieged the besiegers. This situation had not materially changed at the time of Richard's arrival. Both the town and the besiegers' camp had remained open to the sea, but though many reinforcements of new crusaders had come to the Christians almost from the beginning of the siege, little real progress had been made; even the arrival of King Philip in April had made no important change. Richard, on landing, found a condition cf things that required the exercise of the utmost tact and skill. Not merely was the military problem one of the greatest difficulty, but the bitter factional dissensions of the native lords of Palestine made a successful issue almost hopeless. Guy of Lusignan had never been a popular king, and during the siege his wife Sibyl and their two daughters had died, while his rival, Conrad marquis of Montferrat, had persuaded his sister Isabel to divorce her husband and to marry him. The result was a conflict for the crown, which divided the interests and embittered the spirits of those whom the crusaders had come to aid. Philip had declared for Conrad. Guy was a man somewhat of Richard's own type, and he would have been attracted to him apart from the natural effect of Philip's action. One who is disposed to deny Richard the qualities of the highest generalship must admit that he handled the difficult and complicated affairs he had to control with great patience and unusual self-command, and that he probably accomplished as much in the circumstances as any one could have done.

The siege was now pressed with more vigour, and before the middle of July, Acre surrendered. Then Philip, whose heart was always in his plans at home, pleaded ill health and returned to France. After this began the slow advance on Jerusalem, Saladin's troops hanging on the line of march and constantly attacking in small bodies, while the crusaders suffered greatly from the climate and from lack of supplies. So great were the difficulties which Richard had not foreseen that at one time he was disposed to give up the attempt and to secure what he could by treaty, but the negotiations failed. The battle of Arsuf gave him an opportunity to exercise his peculiar talents, and the Saracens were badly defeated; but the advance was not made any the easier. By the last day of the year the army had struggled through to within ten miles of the holy city. There a halt was made; a council of war was held on January 13, 1192, and it was decided, much against the will of Richard, to return and occupy Ascalon before attempting to take and hold Jerusalem—probably a wise decision unless the city were to be held merely as material for negotiation. Various attempts to bring the war to an end by treaty had been going on during the whole march; Richard had even offered his sister, Joanna, in marriage to Saladin's brother, whether seriously or not it is hardly possible to say; but the demands of the two parties remained too far apart for an agreement to be reached. The winter and spring were occupied with the refortification of Ascalon and with the dissensions of the factions, the French finally withdrawing from Richard's army and going to Acre. In April the Marquis Conrad was assassinated by emissaries of "the Old Man of the Mountain"; Guy had little support for the throne except from Richard; and both parties found it easy to agree on Henry of Champagne, grandson of Queen Eleanor and Louis VII, and so nephew at once of Philip and Richard, and he was immediately proclaimed king on marrying Conrad's widow, Isabel. Richard provided for Guy by transferring to him the island of Cyprus as a new kingdom. On June 7 began the second march to Jerusalem, the army this time suffering from the heats of summer as before they had suffered from the winter climate of Palestine. They reached the same point as in the first advance, and there halted again; and though all were greatly encouraged by Richard's brilliant capture of a rich Saracen caravan, he himself was now convinced that success was impossible. On his arrival Richard had pushed forward with a scouting party until he could see the walls of the city in the distance, and obliged to be satisfied with this, he retreated in July to Acre. One more brilliant exploit of Richard's own kind remained for him to perform, the most brilliant of all perhaps, the relief of Joppa which Saladin was just on the point of taking when Richard with a small force saved the town and forced the Saracens to retire. On September 2 a truce for three years was made, and the third crusade was at an end. The progress of Saladin had been checked, a series of towns along the coast had been recovered, and the kingdom of Cyprus had been created; these were the results which had been gained by the expenditure of an enormous treasure and thousands of lives. Who shall say whether they were worth the cost.

During all the summer Richard had been impatient to return to England, and his impatience had been due not alone to his discouragement with the hopeless conditions in Palestine, but partly to the news which had reached him from home. Ever since he left France, in fact, messages had been coming to him from one and another, and the story they told was not of a happy situation. Exactly those things had happened which ought to have been expected. Soon after the council in Normandy, William Longchamp had freed himself from his rival Hugh of Durham by placing him under arrest and forcing him to surrender everything he had bought of the king. Then for many months the chancellor ruled England as he would, going about the country with a great train, almost in royal state, so that a chronicler writing probably from personal observation laments the fact that a house that entertained him for a night hardly recovered from the infliction in three years. Even more oppressive on the community as a whole were the constant exactions of money which he had to make for the king's expenses. The return of John to England in 1190, or early in 1191, made at first no change, but discontent with the chancellor's conduct would naturally look to him for leadership, and it is likely John was made ready to head an active opposition by the discovery of negotiations between Longchamp and the king of Scotland for the recognition of Arthur of Britanny as the heir to the kingdom, negotiations begun—so the chancellor said—under orders from Richard. About the middle of summer, 1191, actual hostilities seemed about to begin. Longchamp's attempt to discipline Gerard of Camville, holder of Lincoln castle and sheriff of Lincolnshire, was resisted by John, who seized the royal castles of Nottingham and Tickhill. Civil war was only averted by the intervention of Walter of Coutances, Archbishop of Rouen, who had arrived in England in the spring with authority from the king to interfere with the administration of Longchamp if it seemed to him and the council wise to do so. By his influence peace was made, at an assembly of the barons at Winchester, on the whole not to the disadvantage of John, and embodied in a document which is almost a formal treaty. One clause of this agreement is of special interest as a sign of the trend of thought and as foreshadowing a famous clause in a more important document soon to be drawn up. The parties agreed that henceforth no baron or free tenant should be disseized of land or goods by the king's justices or servants without a trial according to the customs and assizes of the land, or by the direct orders of the king. The clause points not merely forward but backward, and shows what had no doubt frequently occurred since the departure of the king.

About the middle of September a new element of discord was brought into the situation by the landing of Geoffrey, who had now been consecrated Archbishop of York, and who asserted that he, as well as John, had Richard's permission to return. Longchamp's effort to prevent his coming failed; but on his landing he had him arrested at the altar of the Priory of St. Martin's, Dover, where he had taken sanctuary, and he was carried off a prisoner with many indignities. This was a tactical mistake on Longchamp's part. It put him greatly in the wrong and furnished a new cause against him in which everybody could unite. In alarm he declared he had never given orders for what was done and had Geoffrey released, but it was too late. The actors in this outrage were excommunicated, and the chancellor was summoned to a council called by John under the forms of a great council. At the first meeting, held between Reading and Windsor on October 5, he did not appear, but formal complaint was made against him, and his deposition was moved by the Archbishop of Rouen. The meeting was then adjourned to London, and Longchamp, hearing this, left Windsor at the same time and took refuge in the Tower. For both parties, as in former times of civil strife, the support of the citizens of London was of great importance. They were now somewhat divided, but a recognition of the opportunity inclined them to the stronger side; and they signified to John and the barons that they would support them if a commune were granted to the city.[55] This French institution, granting to a city in its corporate capacity the legal position and independence of the feudal vassal, had as yet made no appearance in England. It was bitterly detested by the great barons, and a chronicler of the time who shared this feeling was no doubt right in saying that neither Richard nor his father would have sanctioned it for a million marks, but as he says London found out that there was no king.[56] John was in pursuit of power, and the price which London demanded would not seem to him a large one, especially as the day of reckoning with the difficulty he created was a distant one and might never come. The commune was granted, and Longchamp was formally deposed. John was recognized as Richard's heir, fealty was sworn to him, and he was made regent of the kingdom; Walter of Rouen was accepted as justiciar; and the castles were disposed of as John desired. Longchamp yielded under protest, threatening the displeasure of the king, and was allowed to escape to the continent.

The action of John and the barons in deposing Longchamp made little actual change. John gained less power than he had expected, and found the new justiciar no more willing to give him control of the kingdom than the old one. The action was revolutionary, and if it had any permanent influence on the history of England, it is to be found in the training it gave the barons in concerted action against a tyrannous minister, revolutionary but as nearly as possible under the forms of law. While these events were taking place, Philip was on his way from Tyre to France. He reached home near the close of the year, ready for the business for which he had come, to make all that he could out of Richard's absence. Repulsed in an attempt to get the advantage of the seneschal of Normandy he applied to John, perhaps with more hope of success, offering him the hand of the unfortunate Adela with the investiture of all the French fiefs. John was, of course, already married, but that was a small matter either to Philip, or to him. He was ready to listen to the temptation, and was preparing to cross to discuss the proposition with Philip, when his plans were interrupted by his mother. She had heard of what was going on and hastily went over to England to interfere, where with difficulty John was forced to give up the idea. The year 1192 passed without disturbance. When Longchamp tried to secure his restoration by bribing John, he was defeated by a higher bid from the council. An attempt of Philip to invade Normandy was prevented by the refusal of his barons to serve, for without accusing the king, they declared that they could not attack Normandy without themselves committing perjury. At the beginning of 1193 the news reached England that Richard had been arrested in Germany and that he was held in prison there.

[53] Benedict of Peterborough, ii. 90.

[54] Roger of Howden, iii. 18.

[55] Round, Commune of London, ch. xi.

[56] Richard of Devizes, Chronicles of Stephen, iii. 416.

CHAPTER XVIII.
WAR AND FINANCE

Richard was indeed in prison in Germany. To avoid passing through Toulouse on account of the hostility of the count he had sailed up the Adriatic, hoping possibly to strike across into the northern parts of Aquitaine, and there had been shipwrecked. In trying to make his way in disguise through the dominions of the Duke of Austria he had been recognized and arrested, for Leopold of Austria had more than one ground of hatred of Richard, notably because his claim to something like an equal sovereignty had been so rudely and contemptuously disallowed in the famous incident of the tearing down of his banner from the walls of Acre. But a greater sovereign than Leopold had reason to complain of the conduct of Richard and something to gain from his imprisonment, and the duke was obliged to surrender his prisoner to the emperor, Henry VI.

When the news of this reached England, it seemed to John that his opportunity might at last be come, and he crossed over at once to the continent. Finding the barons of Normandy unwilling to receive him in the place of Richard, he passed on to Philip, did him homage for the French fiefs, and even for England it was reported, took oath to marry Adela, and ceded to him the Norman Vexin. In return Philip promised him a part of Flanders and his best help to get possession of England and his brother's other lands. Roger of Howden, who records this bargain, distinguishes between rumour and what he thought was true, and it may be taken as a fair example of what it was believed John would agree to in order to dispossess his imprisoned brother. He then returned to England with a force of mercenaries, seized the castles of Wallingford and Windsor, prepared to receive a fleet which Philip was to send to his aid, and giving out that the king was dead, he demanded the kingdom of the justices and the fealty of the barons. But nobody believed him; the justices immediately took measures to resist him and to defend the kingdom against the threatened invasion, and civil war began anew. Just then Hubert Walter, Bishop of Salisbury, arrived from Germany, bringing a letter from Richard himself. It was certain that the king was not dead, but the news did not promise an immediate release. The emperor demanded a great ransom and a crowd of hostages of the barons. The justices must at once set about raising the sum, and a truce was made with John until autumn.

The terms of his release which Richard had stated in his letter did not prove to be the final ones. Henry VI was evidently determined to make all that he could out of his opportunity, and it was not till after the middle of the year 1193 that a definite agreement was at last made. The ransom was fixed at 150,000 marks, of which 100,000 were to be on hand in London before the king should go free. It was on the news of this arrangement that Philip sent his famous message to John, "Take care of yourself: the devil is loosed." In John's opinion the best way to take care of himself was to go to Philip's court, and this he did on receiving the warning, either because he was afraid of the view Richard might take of his conduct on his return, or because he suspected that Philip would throw him over when he came to make a settlement with Richard. There were, however, still two obstacles in the way of Richard's return: the money for the ransom must be raised, and the emperor must be persuaded to keep his bargain. Philip, representing John as well, was bidding against the terms to which Richard had agreed. They offered the emperor 80,000 marks, to keep him until the Michaelmas of 1194; or £1000 a month for each month that he was detained; or 150,000 marks, if he would hold him in prison for a year, or give him up to them. Earlier still Philip had tried to persuade Henry to surrender Richard to him, but such a disposition of the case did not suit the emperor's plans, and now he made Philip's offers known to Richard. If he had been inclined to listen, as perhaps he was, the German princes, their natural feeling and interest quickened somewhat by promises of money from Richard, would have insisted on the keeping of the treaty. On February 4, 1194, Richard was finally set free, having done homage to the emperor for the kingdom of England and having apparently issued letters patent to record the relationship,[57] a step towards the realization of the wide-reaching plans of Henry VI for the reconstruction of the Roman Empire, and so very likely as important to him as the ransom in money.

The raising of this money in England and the other lands of the king was not an easy task, not merely because the sum itself was enormous for the time, but also because so great an amount exceeded the experience, or even the practical arithmetic of the day, and could hardly be accurately planned for in advance. It was, however, vigorously taken in hand by Eleanor and the justices, assisted by Hubert Walter, who had now become Archbishop of Canterbury by Richard's direction and who was soon made justiciar, and the burden seems to have been very patiently borne. The method of the Saladin tithe was that first employed for the general taxation by which it was proposed to raise a large part of the sum. All classes, clerical and feudal, burgess and peasant, were compelled to contribute according to their revenues, the rule being one-fourth of the income for the year, and the same proportion of the movable property; all privileges and immunities of clergy and churches as well as of laymen were suspended; the Cistercians even who had a standing immunity from all exactions gave up their whole year's shearing of wool, and so did the order of Sempringham; the plate and, jewels of the churches and monasteries, held to be properly used for the redemption of captives, were surrendered or redeemed in money under a pledge of their restoration by the king. The amount at first brought in proved insufficient, and the officers who collected it were suspected of peculation, possibly with justice, but possibly also because the original calculation had been inaccurate, so that a second and a third levy were found necessary. It was near the end of the year 1193 before the sum raised was accepted by the representatives of the emperor as sufficient for the preliminary payment which would secure the king's release.

Richard, set free on February 4, did not feel it necessary to be in haste, and he only reached London on March 6. There he found things in as unsettled a state as they had been since the beginning of his imprisonment. He had made through Longchamp a most liberal treaty with Philip to keep him quiet during his imprisonment; he had also induced John by a promise of increasing his original grants to return to his allegiance to himself: but neither of these agreements had proved binding on the other parties. John had made a later treaty with Philip, purchasing his support with promises of still more extensive cessions of the land he coveted, and under this treaty the king of France had taken possession of parts of Normandy, while the justiciar of England, learning of John's action, had obtained a degree of forfeiture against him from a council of the barons and had begun the siege of his castles. This war on John was approved by Richard, who himself pushed it to a speedy and successful end. Then on March 30 the king met a great council of the realm at Nottingham. His mother was present, and the justiciar, and Longchamp, who was still chancellor, though he had not been allowed to return to England to remain until now. By this council John was summoned to appear for trial within forty days on pain of the loss of all his possessions and of all that he might expect, including the crown. Richard's chief need would still be money both for the war in France and for further payments on his ransom; and he now imposed a new tax of two shillings on the carucate of land and called out one-third of the feudal force for service abroad. Many resumptions of his former grants were also made, and some of them were sold again to the highest bidders. Two weeks later the king was re-crowned at Winchester, apparently with something less of formal ceremony than in his original coronation, but with much more than in the annual crown-wearings of the Norman kings, a practice which had now been dropped for almost forty years. Whether quite a coronation in strict form or not, the ceremony was evidently regarded as of equivalent effect both by the chroniclers of the time and officially, and it probably was intended to make good any diminution of sovereignty that might be thought to be involved in his doing homage to the emperor for the kingdom

Immediately after this the king made ready to cross to France, where his interests were then in the greatest danger, but he was detained by contrary winds till near the middle of May. In the almost exactly five years remaining of his life Richard never returned to England. He belonged by nature to France, and England must have seemed a very foreign land to him; but in passing judgment on him we must not overlook the fact that England was secure and needed the presence of the king but little, while many dangers threatened, or would seem to Richard to threaten, his continental possessions. Even a Henry I would probably have spent those five years abroad. Richard found the king of France pushing a new attack on Normandy to occupy the lands which John had ceded him, but the French forces withdrew without waiting to try the issue of a battle. Richard had hardly landed before another enemy was overcome, by his own prudence also, and another example given of the goodness of Richard's heart toward his enemies and of his willingness to trust their professions. He had said that his brother would never oppose force with force, and now John was ready to abandon the conflict before it had begun. He came to Richard, encouraged by generous words of his which were repeated to him, and threw himself at his feet; he was at once pardoned and treated as if he had never sinned, except that the military advantages he had had in England through holding the king's castles were not given back to him. Along all the border the mere presence of Richard seemed to check Philip's advance and to bring to a better mind his own barons who had been disposed to aid the enemy. About the middle of June almost all the details of a truce were agreed upon by both sides, but the plan at last failed, because Richard would not agree that the barons who had been on the opposing sides in Poitou should be made to cease all hostilities against each other, for this would be contrary, he said, to the ancient custom of the land. The war went on a few weeks longer with no decisive results. Philip destroyed Evreux, but fell back from Freteval so hastily, to avoid an encounter with Richard, that he lost his baggage, including his official records, and barely escaped capture himself. On November 1 a truce for one year was finally made, much to the advantage Philip, but securing to the king of England the time he needed for preparation.

When Richard crossed to Normandy not to return, he left England in the hands of his new justiciar, Hubert Walter, Archbishop of Canterbury, and soon to be appointed legate of the pope, at once the head of Church and State. No better man could have been found to stand in the place of the king. Nephew of the wife of Glanvill, the great judge of Henry II's time, spending much of his youth in the household of his uncle and some little time also in the service of the king, he was by training and by personal experience fitted to carry on the administration of England along the lines laid down in the previous reign and even to carry forward law and institutions in harmony with their beginnings and with the spirit of that great period. Indeed the first itinerant justices' commission in definite form that has come down to us dates but a few weeks after the king's departure, and is of especial interest as showing a decided progress since the more vague provisions of the Assize of Clarendon. A possible source of danger to a successful ministry lay in the quarrelsome and self-assertive Archbishop of York, the king's brother Geoffrey; but soon after Richard's departure Hubert deprived him of power by a sharp stroke and a skilful use of the administrative weapons with which he was familiar. On complaint of Geoffrey's canons against him he sent a commission of judges to York to examine the case, who ordered Geoffrey's servants to be imprisoned on a charge of robbery, and on the archbishop's refusal to appear before them to answer for himself they decreed the confiscation of his estates. Geoffrey never recovered his position in Richard's time.

The year 1195 in England and abroad passed by with few events of permanent interest. Archbishop Hubert was occupied chiefly with ecclesiastical matters and with the troubles of Geoffrey of York, and conditions in the north were further changed by the closing of the long and stormy career of the bishop, of Durham, Hugh of Puiset. In France the truce was broken by Philip in June, and the war lingered until December with some futile efforts at peace, but with no striking military operations on either side. Early in December the two kings agreed on the conditions of a treaty, which was signed on January 15, 1196. The terms were still unfavourable to Richard; for Philip at last had Gisors and the Norman Vexin ceded to him by competent authority and a part of his other conquests and the overlordship of Angoulême, while Richard on his side was allowed to retain only what he had taken in Berri.

As this treaty transferred to France the old frontier defences of Normandy and opened the way down the Seine to a hostile attack upon Rouen, the question of the building of new fortifications became an important one to both the kings. The treaty contained a provision that Andely should not be fortified. This was a most important strategic position on the river, fitted by nature for a great fortress and completely covering the capital of Normandy. At a point where the Seine bends sharply and a small stream cuts through the line of limestone cliffs on its right bank to join it, a promontory of rock three hundred feet above the water holds the angle, cut off from the land behind it except for a narrow isthmus, and so furnished the feudal castle-builder with all the conditions which he required. The land itself belonged to the Archbishop of Rouen, but Richard, to whom the building of a fortress at the place was a vital necessity, did not concern himself seriously with that point, and began the works which he had planned soon after the signing of the treaty in which he had promised not to do so. The archbishop who was still Walter of Coutances, Richard's faithful minister of earlier days, protested without avail and finally retired to Rome, laying the duchy under an interdict. Richard was no more to be stopped in this case by an interdict than by his own promises, and went steadily on with his work, though in the end he bought off the archbishop's opposition by a transfer to him in exchange of other lands worth intrinsically much more than the barren crag that he had seized. The building occupied something more than a year, and when it was completed, the castle was one of the strongest in the west. Richard had made use in its fortification of the lessons which he learned in the Holy Land, where the art of defence had been most carefully studied under compulsion; and the three wards of the castle, its thick walls and strong towers, and the defences crossing the river and in the town of New Andely at its foot, seemed to make it impregnable. Richard took great pride in his creation. He called it his fair child, and named it Chateau-Gaillard or "saucy castle."

Philip had not allowed all this to go on without considering the treaty violated, but the war of 1196 is of the same wearisome kind as that of the previous year. The year brought with it some trouble in Britanny arising from a demand of Richard's for the wardship of his nephew Arthur, and resulting in the barons of Britanny sending the young prince to the court of Philip. In England the rising of a demagogue in London to protest against the oppression of the poor is of some interest. The king's financial demands had never ceased; they could not cease, in fact, and though England was prosperous from the long intervals of peace she had enjoyed and bore the burden on the whole with great patience, it was none the less heavily felt. In London there was a feeling not merely that the taxes were heavy, but that they were unfairly assessed and collected, so that they rested in undue proportion on the poorer classes. Of this feeling William Fitz Osbert, called "William with the Beard," made himself the spokesman. He opposed the measures of the ruling class, stirred up opposition with fiery speeches, crossed over to the king, and, basing on the king's interest in the subject a boast of his support, threatened more serious trouble. Then the justiciar interfered by force, dragged him out of sanctuary, and had him executed. The incident had a permanent influence in the fact that Hubert Walter, who was already growing unpopular, found his support from the clergy weakened because of his violation of the right of sanctuary. He was also aggrieved because Richard sent over from the continent the Abbot of Caen, experienced in Norman finance, to investigate his declining revenues and to hold a special inquisition of the sheriffs. The inquisition was not held because of the death of the abbot, but later in the year Hubert offered to resign, but finally decided to go on in office for a time longer.

The year 1197 promised great things for Richard in his war with the king of France, but yielded little. He succeeded in forming a coalition among the chief barons of the north, which recalls the diplomatic successes of his ancestor, Henry I. The young Count Baldwin of Flanders and Hainault had grievances of his own against Philip which he was anxious to avenge. Count Philip, who had exercised so strong an influence over King Philip at the time of his accession, had died early in the crusade, and the Count of Hainault on succeeding him had been compelled to give up to France a large strip of territory adjoining Philip's earlier annexation, and on his death Count Baldwin had had to pay a heavy relief. The coalition was joined by the Counts of Boulogne and Blois, and Britanny was practically under the control of Richard. Philip, however, escaped the danger that threatened him by some exercise of his varied talents of which we do not know the exact details. Led on in pursuit of the Count of Flanders until he was almost cut off from return, he purchased his retreat by a general promise to restore the count all his rights and to meet Richard in a conference on the terms of peace. On Richard's side the single advantage gained during the campaign was the capture of the cousin of the French king, Philip of Dreux, the warlike Bishop of Beauvais, whose raids along the border and whose efforts at the court of Henry VI of Germany against his release from imprisonment had so enraged Richard that he refused upon any terms or under any pressure to set him free as long as he lived. The interview between the kings took place on September 17, when a truce for something more than a year was agreed upon to allow time for arranging the terms of a permanent peace.

The year closed in England with an incident of great interest, but one which has sometimes been made to bear an exaggerated importance. At a council of the kingdom held at Oxford on December 7, the justiciar presented a demand of the king that the baronage should unite to send him at their expense three hundred knights for a year's service with him abroad. Evidently it was hoped that the clergy would set a good example. The archbishop himself expressed his willingness to comply, and was followed by the Bishop of London to the same effect. Then Bishop Hugh of Lincoln, being called upon for his answer, to the great indignation of the justiciar, flatly refused on the ground that his church was not liable for service abroad. The Bishop of Salisbury, next called upon, made the same refusal; and the justiciar seeing that the plan was likely to fail dissolved the council in anger. One is tempted to believe that some essential point is omitted from the accounts we have of this incident, or that some serious mistake has been made in them, either in the speech of Bishop Hugh given us in his biography or in the terms of Richard's demand recorded in two slightly different forms. Hubert must have believed that the baronage in general were going to follow the example given them by the two bishops and refuse the required service, or he would not have dissolved the council and reported to the king that his plan had failed. But to refuse this service on the ground that it could not be required except in England was to go against the unbroken practice of more than a hundred years. Nor was there anything contrary to precedent in the demand for three hundred knights to serve a year. The union of the military tenants to equip a smaller force than the whole service due to the lord, but for a longer time than the period of required feudal service, was not uncommon. The demand implied a feudal force due to the king from England of less than three thousand knights, and this was well within his actual rights, though if we accept the very doubtful statement of one of our authorities that their expenses were to be reckoned at the rate of three shillings per day, the total cost would exceed that of any ordinary scutage.

Richard clearly believed, as did his justiciar, that he was making no illegal demand, for he ordered the confiscation of the baronies of the two bishops, and Herbert of Salisbury was obliged to pay a fine. It was only a personal journey to Normandy and the great reputation for sanctity of the future St. Hugh of Lincoln that relieved him from the same punishment. The importance of the right of consent to taxation in the growth of the constitution has led many writers to attach a significance to this incident which hardly belongs to it. Whatever were the grounds of his action, the Bishop of Lincoln could have been acting on no general constitutional principle. He must have been insisting on personal rights secured to him by the feudal law. If his action contributed largely, as it doubtless did, to that change of earlier conditions which led to the beginning of the constitution, it was less because he tried to revive a principle of general application, which as a matter of fact had never existed, than because he established a precedent of careful scrutiny of the king's rights and of successful resistance to a demand possibly of doubtful propriety. It is as a sign of the times, as the mark of an approaching revolution, that the incident has its real interest.

About the time that Richard sent over to England his demand for three hundred knights news must have reached him of an event which would seem to open the way to a great change in continental affairs. The far-reaching plans of the emperor, Henry VI, had been brought to an end by his death in Sicily on September 28, 1197, in the prime of his life. His son, the future brilliant Emperor Frederick II, was still an infant, and there was a prospect that the hold of the Hohenstaufen on the empire might be shaken off. About Christmas time an embassy reached Richard from the princes of Germany, summoning him on the fealty he owed the empire to attend a meeting at Cologne on February 22 to elect an emperor. This he could not do, but a formal embassy added the weight of his influence to the strong Guelfic party; and his favourite nephew, who had been brought up at his court, was elected emperor as Otto IV. The Hohenstaufen party naturally did not accept the election, and Philip of Suabia, the brother of Henry VI, was put up as an opposition emperor, but for the moment the Guelfs were the stronger, and they enjoyed the support of the young and vigorous pope, Innocent III, who had just ascended the papal throne, so that even Philip II's support of his namesake of Suabia was of little avail.

From the change Richard gained in reality nothing. It was still an age when the parties to international alliances sought only ends to be gained within their own territories, or what they believed should be rightfully their territories, and the objects of modern diplomacy were not yet regarded. The truce of the preceding September, which was to last through the whole of the year 1198, was as little respected as the others had been. As soon as it was convenient, the war was reopened, the baronial alliance against the king of France still standing, and Baldwin of Flanders joining in the attack. At the end of September Richard totally defeated the French, and drove their army in wild flight through the town of Gisors, precipitating Philip himself into the river Epte by the breaking down of the bridge under the weight of the fugitives, and capturing a long list of prisoners of distinction, three of them, a Montmorency among them, overthrown by Richard's own lance, as he boasted in a letter to the Bishop of Durham. Other minor successes followed, and Philip found himself reduced to straits in which he felt obliged to ask the intervention of the pope in favour of peace. Innocent III, anxious for a new crusade and determined to make his influence felt in every question of the day, was ready to interfere on his own account; and his legate, Cardinal Peter, brought about an interview between the two kings on January 13, 1199, when a truce for five years was verbally agreed upon, though the terms of a permanent treaty were not yet settled.

In the meantime financial difficulties were pressing heavily upon the king of England. Scutages for the war in Normandy had been taken in

1196 and 1197. In the next year a still more important measure of taxation was adopted, which was evidently intended to bring in larger sums to the treasury than an ordinary scutage. This is the tax known as the Great Carucage of 1198. The actual revenue that the king derived from it is a matter of some doubt, but the machinery of its assessment is described in detail by a contemporary and is of special interest.[58] The unit of the new assessment was to be the carucate, or ploughland, instead of the hide, and consequently a new survey of the land was necessary to take the place of the old Domesday record. To obtain this, practically the same machinery was employed as in the earlier case, but to the commissioners sent into each county by the central government two local knights, chosen from the county, were added to form the body before whom the jurors testified as to the ownership and value of the lands in their neighbourhoods. Thanks to the rapid judicial advance and administrative reforms of the past generation, the jury was now a familiar institution everywhere and was used for many purposes. Its employment in this case to fix the value of real property for taxation, and of personal property as in the Saladin tithe of 1188, though but a revival of its earlier use by William I, marks the beginning of a continuous employment of jurors in taxation in the next period which led to constitutional results—the birth of the representative system, and we may almost say to the origin of Parliament in the proper meaning of the term—results of even greater value in the growth of our civil liberty than any which came from it in the sphere of judicial institutions important as these were.

Now in the spring of 1199 a story reached Richard of the finding of a wonderful treasure on the land of the lord of Chalus, one of his under vassals in the Limousin. We are told that it was the images of an emperor, his wife, sons, and daughters, made of gold and seated round a table also of gold. If the story were true, here was relief from his difficulties, and Richard laid claim to the treasure as lord paramount of the land. This claim was of course disputed, and with his mercenaries the king laid siege to the castle of Chalus. It was a little castle and poorly defended, but it resisted the attack for three days, and on the third Richard, who carelessly approached the wall, was shot by a crossbow bolt in the left shoulder near the neck. The wound was deep and was made worse by the surgeon in cutting out the head of the arrow. Shortly gangrene appeared, and the king knew that he must die. In the time that was left him he calmly disposed of all his affairs. He sent for his mother who was not far away, and she was with him when he died. He divided his personal property among his friends and in charity, declared John to be his heir, and made the barons who were present swear fealty to him. He ordered the man who had shot him to be pardoned and given a sum of money; then he confessed and received the last offices of the Church, and died on April 6, 1199, in the forty-second year of his age.

The twelfth century was drawing to its end when Richard died, but the close of the century was then as always in history a purely artificial dividing line. The real historical epoch closed, a new age began with the granting of the Great Charter. The date may serve, however, as a point from which to review briefly one of the growing interests of England that belongs properly within the field of its political history—its organized municipal life. The twelfth century shows a slow, but on the whole a constant, increase in the number, size, and influence of organized towns in England, and of the commerce, domestic and foreign, on which their prosperity rested. Even in the long disorder of Stephen's reign the interruption of this growth seems to have been felt rather in particular places than in the kingdom as a whole, and there was no serious set-back of national prosperity that resulted from it. Not with the rapidity of modern times, but fairly steadily through the century, new articles appear in commerce; manufactures rise to importance, like that of cloth; wealth and population accumulate in the towns, and they exert an unceasing pressure on the king, or on the lords in whose domain they are, for grants of privileges.

Such grants from the king become noticeably frequent in the reign of Richard and are even more so under John. The financial necessities of both kings and their recklessness, at least that of Richard, in the choice of means to raise money, made it easy for the boroughs to purchase the rights or exemptions they desired. The charters all follow a certain general type, but there was no fixed measure of privilege granted by them. Each town bargained for what it could get from a list of possible privileges of some length. The freedom of the borough; the right of the citizens to have a gild merchant; exemption from tolls, specified or general, within a certain district or throughout all England or also throughout the continental Angevin dominions; exemption from the courts of shire and hundred, or from the jurisdiction of all courts outside the borough, except in pleas of the crown, or even without this exception; the right to farm the revenues of the borough, paying a fixed "firma," or rent, to the king, and with this often the right of the citizens to elect their own reeve or even sheriff to exempt them from the interference of the king's sheriff of the county. This list is not a complete one of the various rights and privileges granted by the charters, but only of the more important ones.

To confer these all upon a town was to give it the fullest right obtained by English towns and to put it practically in the position which London had reached in the charter of Henry I's later years. London, if we may trust our scanty evidence, advanced at one time during this period to a position reached by no other English city, to the position of the French commune. [59] Undoubtedly the word "commune," like other technical words, was sometimes used at the time loosely and vaguely, but in its strict and legal sense it meant a town raised to the position of a feudal vassal and given all the rights as well as duties of a feudal lord, a seigneurie collective populaire, as a French scholar has called it.[60] Thus regarded, the town had a fulness of local independence to be obtained in no other way. To such a position no English city but London attained, and it may be thought that the evidence in London's case is not full enough to warrant us in believing that it reached the exact legal status of a commune.

We find it related as an incident of the struggle between John and Longchamp in 1191, when Longchamp was deposed, that John and the barons conceded the commune of London and took oath to it, and about the same time we have proof that the city had its mayor. Documentary evidence has also been discovered of the existence at the same date of the governing body known on the continent as the échevins. But while the mayor and the échevins are closely associated with the commune, their presence is not conclusive evidence of the existence of a real commune, nor is the use of the word itself, though the occurrence of the two together makes it more probable. Early in 1215, when John was seeking allies everywhere against the confederated barons, he granted a new charter to London, which recognized the right of the citizens to elect their own mayor and required him to swear fealty to the king. If we could be sure that this oath was sworn for the city, it would be conclusive evidence, since the oath of the mayor to the lord of whom the commune as a corporate person "held" was a distinguishing mark of this relationship. The probability that such was the case is confirmed by the fact that a few weeks later, in the famous twelfth clause of the Great Charter, we find London put distinctly in the position of a king's vassal. This evidence is strengthened by a comparison with the corresponding clause of the Articles of the Barons, a kind of preliminary draft of the Great Charter, and much less carefully drawn, where there is added to London a general class of towns whose legal right to the privilege granted it would not have been possible to defend.[61] That London maintained its position among the king's vassals in the legally accurate Great Charter is almost certain proof that it had some right to be classed with them. But even if London was for a time a commune, strictly speaking, it did not maintain the right in the next reign, and that form of municipal organization plays no part in English history.[62] It is under the form of chartered towns, not communes, that the importance of the boroughs in English commercial and public life continued to increase in the thirteenth as it had in the twelfth century.

[57] Ralph de Diceto, ii, 113.

[58] Roger of Howden, iv. 46.

[59] Round, The Commune of London.

[60] Luchaire, Communes Françaises, 97.

[61] Articles of the Barons, c. 32; Stubbs, Select Charters, 393.

[62] See London and the Commune in Engl. Hist. Rev., Oct. 1904.

CHAPTER XIX.
THE LOSS OF NORMANDY

The death of Richard raised a question of succession new in the history of England since the Norman Conquest. The right of primogeniture, the strict succession of the eldest born, carrying with it the right of the son of a deceased elder brother to stand in the place of his father, the principle which was in the end to prevail, had only begun to establish itself. The drift of feeling was undoubtedly towards it, but this appeared strongly in the present crisis only in the northwestern corner of the Angevin dominions in France, where it was supported by still stronger influences. The feudal law had recognized and still recognized, many different principles of succession, and the prevailing feeling in England and Normandy is no doubt correctly represented in an incident recorded by the biographer of William Marshal. On receiving the news of Richard's death at Rouen, William went at once to consult with the archbishop and to agree on whom they would support as heir. The archbishop inclined at first to Arthur, the son and representative of John's elder brother, Geoffrey, but William declared that the brother stood nearer to his father and to his brother than the grandson, or nephew, and the archbishop yielded the point without discussion. Neither in England nor in Normandy did there appear the slightest disposition to support the claims of Arthur, or to question the right of John, though possibly there would have been more inclination to do so if the age of the two candidates had been reversed, for Arthur was only twelve, while John was past thirty.

Neither of the interested parties, however, was in the least disposed to waive any claims which he possessed. John had had trouble with Richard during the previous winter on a suspicion of treasonable correspondence with Philip and because he thought his income was too scanty, and he was in Britanny, even at the court of Arthur, when the news of Richard's death reached him. He at once took horse with a few attendants and rode to Chinon, where the king's treasure was kept, and this was given up without demur on his demand by Robert of Turnharn, the keeper. Certain barons who were there and the officers of Richard's household also recognized his right, on his taking the oath which they demanded, that he would execute his brother's will, and that he would preserve inviolate the rightful customs of former times and the just laws of lands and people. From Chinon John set out for Normandy, but barely escaped capture on the way, for Arthur's party had not been idle in the meantime. His mother with a force from Britanny had brought him with all speed to Angers, where he was joyfully received. William des Roches, the greatest baron of the country and Richard's seneschal of Anjou, had declared for him at the head of a powerful body of barons, who probably saw in a weak minority a better chance of establishing that local freedom from control for which they had always striven than under another Angevin king. At Le Mans Arthur was also accepted with enthusiasm as count a few hours after a cold reception of John and his hasty departure.

There Constance and her son were met by the king of France, who, as soon as God had favoured him by the removal of Richard, — so the French regarded the matter, — seized the county of Evreux and pushed his conquests almost to Le Mans. Arthur did homage to Philip for the counties of Anjou, Maine, and Touraine; Tours received the young count as Angers and Le Mans had done; Philip's right of feudal wardship was admitted, and Arthur was taken to Paris under his secure protection, secure for his own designs and against those of John. Philip could hardly do otherwise than recognize the rights of Arthur. It was perhaps the most favourable opportunity that had ever occurred to accomplish the traditional policy of the Capetians of splitting apart the dominions of the rival Norman or Angevin house. That policy, so long and so consistently followed by Philip almost from his accession to the death of Arthur, in the support in turn of young Henry, Richard, John, and Arthur against the reigning king, was destined indeed never to be realized in the form in which it had been cherished in the past; but the devotion of a part of the Angevin empire to the cause of Arthur was a factor of no small value in the vastly greater success which Philip won, greater than any earlier king had ever dreamed of, greater than Philip himself had dared to hope for till the moment of its accomplishment.

From Le Mans John went direct to Rouen. The barons of Normandy had decided to support him, and on April 25 he was invested with the insignia of the duchy by the archbishop, Walter of Coutances, taking the usual oath to respect the rights of Church and people. His careless and irreverent conduct during the ceremony displeased the clergy, as his refusal to receive the communion on Easter day, a week before, had offended Bishop Hugh of Lincoln, who came a part of the way with him from Chinon. As the lance, the special symbol of investiture, was placed in his hand, he turned to make some jocular remark to his boon companions who were laughing and chattering behind him, and carelessly let it fall, an incident doubtless considered at the time of evil omen, and easily interpreted after the event as a presage of the loss of the duchy. From Normandy John sent over to England to assist the justiciar, Geoffrey Fitz Peter, in taking measures to secure his succession, two of the most influential men of the land, William Marshal and Hubert Walter, Archbishop of Canterbury, who had been in Normandy since the death of Richard, while he himself remained a month longer on the continent, to check, if possible, the current in favour of Arthur. He took Le Mans and destroyed its walls in punishment, and sent a force to aid his mother in Aquitaine; but the threatening attitude of Philip made it impossible for him to accomplish very much. No slight influence on the side of John was the strong support and vigorous action in his favour of that remarkable woman, Eleanor of Aquitaine, then about eighty years of age. She seems never to have cared for her grandson Arthur, and for this his mother was probably responsible. Constance appears to have been a somewhat difficult person, and what was doubtless still more important, she had never identified herself with the interests of her husband's house, but had always remained in full sympathy with the separatist tendencies and independent desires of her own Britanny.[63] She had no right to count on any help from Eleanor in carrying out her ambitions, and Aquitaine was held as securely for John by his mother as Normandy was by the decision of its leading barons.

In England, although no movement in favour of Arthur is perceptible, there was some fear of civil strife, perhaps only of that disorder which was apt to break out on the death of the king, as it did indeed in this case, and many castles were put in order for defence. What disorder there was soon put down by the representatives of the king, whom John had appointed, and who took the fealty of the barons and towns to him. On the part of a considerable number of the barons—the names that are recorded are those of old historic families, Beaumont, Ferrers, Mowbray, De Lacy, the Earls of Clare and Chester—there was found to be opposition to taking the oath of fealty on the ground of injustice committed by the administration. Whether these complaints were personal to each baron, as the language has been taken to mean, or complaints of injustice in individual cases wrought by the general policy of the government, as the number of cases implies, it is hardly possible to say. The probability is that both explanations are true. Certainly the old baronage could easily find grounds enough of complaint in the constitutional policy steadily followed by the government of the first two Angevin kings. The crisis was wisely handled by the three able men whom John had appointed to represent him. They called an assembly of the doubtful barons at Northampton and gave to each one a promise that he should have his right (jus suum). In return for these promises the oaths were taken, but the incident was as ominous of another kind of trouble as the dropping of the lance at Rouen. We can hardly understand the reign of John unless we remember that at its very beginning men were learning to watch the legality of the king's actions and to demand that he respect the limitations which the law placed on his arbitrary will.

On May 25, John landed in England, and on the 27th, Ascension day, he was crowned in Westminster by the Archbishop of Canterbury before a large assembly of barons and bishops. The coronation followed the regular order, and no dissenting voice made itself heard, though a rather unusual display of force seems to have been thought necessary. Two authorities, both years later and both untrustworthy, refer to a speech delivered during the ceremony by the archbishop, in which he emphasized the fact that the English crown was elective and not hereditary. Did not these authorities seem to be clearly independent of one another we should forthwith reject their testimony, but as it is we must admit some slight chance that such a speech was made. One of these accounts, in giving what purports to be the actual speech of Hubert Walter, though it must have been composed by the writer himself, states a reason for it which could not possibly have been entertained at the time.[64] The other gives as its reason the disputed succession, but makes the archbishop refer not to the right of Arthur, but to that of the queen of Castile, a reference which must also be untrue. [65] If such a speech was made, it had reference unquestionably to the case of Arthur, and it must be taken as a sign of the influence which this case certainly had on the development, in the minds of some at least, of something more like the modern understanding of the meaning of election, and as a prelude to the great movement which characterizes the thirteenth century, the rapid growth of ideas which may now without too great violence be called constitutional. If such a speech was made we may be sure also that it was not made without the consent of John, and that it contained nothing displeasing to him. One of his first acts as king was to make Hubert Walter his chancellor, and apparently the first document issued by the new king and chancellor puts prominently forward John's hereditary right, and states the share of clergy and people in his accession in peculiar and vague language.[66]

John had no mind to remain long in England, nor was there any reason why he should. The king of Scotland was making some trouble, demanding the cession of Cumberland and Northumberland, but it was possible to postpone for the present the decision of his claims. William Marshal was at last formally invested with the earldom of Pembroke and Geoffrey Fitz Peter with that of Essex. More important was a scutage, probably ordered at this time, of the unusual rate of two marks on the knight's fee, twenty shillings having been the previous limit as men remembered it. By June 20

John's business in England was done, and by July 1 he was again at Rouen to watch the course of events in the conflict still undecided. On that day a truce was made with Philip to last until the middle of August, and John began negotiations with the Counts of Flanders and Boulogne and with his nephew, Otto IV of Germany, in a search for allies, from whom he gained only promises. On the expiration of the truce Philip demanded the cession of the entire Vexin and the transfer to Arthur of Poitou, Anjou, Maine, and Touraine,—a demand which indicates his determination to go on with the war. For Poitou Philip had already received Eleanor's homage, and she in turn invested John with it as her vassal. In the beginning of the war which was now renewed Philip committed a serious error of policy, to which he was perhaps tempted by the steady drift of events in his favour since the death of Richard. Capturing the castle of Ballon in Maine he razed it to the ground. William des Roches, the leader of Arthur's cause, at once objected since the castle should belong to his lord, and protested to the king that this was contrary to their agreement, but Philip haughtily replied that he should do as he pleased with his conquests in spite of Arthur. This was too early a declaration of intentions, and William immediately made terms with John, carrying over to him Arthur and his mother and the city of Le Mans. A slight study of John's character ought to have shown to William that no dependence whatever could be placed on his promise in regard to a point which would seem to them both of the greatest importance. William took the risk, however, binding John by solemn oath that Arthur should be dealt with according to his counsel, a promise which was drawn up in formal charter. On the very day of his arrival, it is said, Arthur was told of John's intention to imprison him, and he fled away with his mother to Angers; but William des Roches remained for a time in John's service.

The year 1199 closed with a truce preliminary to a treaty of peace which was finally concluded on May 18. Philip II was at the moment in no condition to push the war. He was engaged in a desperate struggle with Innocent III and needed to postpone for the time being every other conflict. Earlier in his reign on a political question he had defied a pope, and with success; but Innocent III was a different pope, and on the present question Philip was wrong. In 1193 he had repudiated his second wife, Ingeborg of Denmark, the day after the marriage, and later married Agnes of Meran whom he had hitherto refused to give up at the demand of the Church. At the close of 1199 France was placed under an interdict until the king should yield, and it was in this situation that the treaty with John was agreed to. Philip for the moment abandoned his attempt against the Angevin empire. John was recognized as rightful heir of the French fiefs, and his homage was accepted for them all, including Britanny, for which Arthur then did homage to John.

These concessions were not secured, however, without some sacrifices on the English side. John yielded to Philip all the conquests which had been made from Richard, and agreed to pay a relief of 20,000 marks for admission to his fiefs. The peace was to be sealed by the marriage of John's niece, the future great queen and regent of France, Blanche of Castile, to Philip's son Louis, and the county of Evreux was to be ceded as her dower. The aged but tireless Eleanor went to Spain to bring her granddaughter, and the marriage was celebrated four days after the signing of the treaty, Louis at the time being thirteen years old and Blanche twelve.

While his mother went to Spain for the young bride, John crossed to England to raise money for his relief. This was done by ordering a carucage at the rate of three shillings on the ploughland. The Cistercian order objected to paying the tax because of the general immunity which they enjoyed, and John in great anger commanded all the sheriffs to refuse them the protection of the courts and to let go free of punishment any who injured them, in effect to put them outside the law. This decree he afterwards modified at the request of Hubert Walter, but he refused an offer of a thousand marks for a confirmation of their charters and liberties, and returned to Normandy in the words quoted by the chronicler, "breathing out threatenings and slaughter against the servants of Christ."

John was now in a position where he should have used every effort to strengthen himself against the next move of Philip, which he should have known was inevitable, and where, if ever, he might hope to do so. Instead of that, by a blunder in morals, in which John's greatest weakness lay, by an act of passion and perfidy, he gave his antagonist a better excuse than he could have hoped for when he was at last ready to renew the war. John had now been for more than ten years married to Isabel of Gloucester, and no children had been born of the marriage. In the situation of the Angevin house he may well have wished for a direct heir and have been ready to adopt the expedient common to sovereigns in such cases. At any rate about this time he procured from the Bishops of Normandy and Aquitaine a divorce, a formal annulling of the marriage on the ground of consanguinity, the question raised at the time of their marriage never, it would seem, having been settled by dispensation. Then he sent off an embassy to ask for a daughter of the king of Portugal. In the meantime he went on a progress through the French lands which had been secured to him by treaty with Philip, and met the beautiful Isabel, daughter of the Count of Angoulême, then twelve years of age, and determined to marry her out of hand. The fact that she was already betrothed to Hugh "the Brown," son and heir of his own vassal the Count of La Marche, and that she was then living in the household of her intended father-in-law, made no more difference to him than his own embassy to Portugal. It seems possible indeed that it was in the very castle of the Count of La Marche that the plan was formed. Isabel's father also did not hesitate in the choice of sons-in-law, and his daughter having been brought home, she was at once married to John. An act of this kind was a most flagrant violation of the feudal contract, nor was the moral blunder saved from being a political one by the fact that the injured house was that of the Lusignans, great barons and long turbulent and unruly vassals of Aquitaine. John had given them now a legal right of appeal to his suzerain and a moral justification of rebellion.

After his marriage John went back to England for the coronation of his queen, which took place on October 8. At Lincoln he received the homage of William of Scotland and made peace with the Cistercians, and then went on a progress through the north as far as Carlisle. In the meantime, as was to be expected, hostilities had begun with the family of the Count of La Marche, and the king sent out a summons to the barons of England to meet him at Portsmouth at Whitsuntide prepared for service abroad. On receipt of this notice the earls held a meeting at Leicester and by agreement replied to the king that they would not go over sea with him unless he restored to them their rights. There is no evidence in the single account we have of this incident that the earls intended to deny their liability to service abroad. It is probable they intended to take their position on the more secure principle that services due to the suzerain who violated the rights of his vassal were for the time being, at least, suspended. If this is so, the declaration of the earls is the first clear evidence we have that the barons of England were beginning to realize their legal right of resistance and to get sight of the great principle which was so soon to give birth to the constitution. The result of the opposition to John's summons we do not know, unless the statement which follows in the chronicle that the king was demanding the castles of the barons, and taking hostages if they retained them, was his answer to their demand. At any rate they appeared as required at Portsmouth ready for the campaign abroad, but John, instead of sending them over to France, took away the money which they had brought to spend in his service, and let them go home.

From the time of John's landing in Normandy, about June 1, 1201, until the same time the next year, he was occupied with negotiating rather than with fighting. Philip was not yet ready to take part himself in the war, but he kept a careful watch of events and made John constantly aware that he was not overlooking his conduct toward his vassals. Several interviews were held between the kings of a not unfriendly character; the treaty of the previous year was confirmed, and John was invited to Paris by Philip and entertained in the royal palace. It was at first proposed that the case between

John and the Lusignans should be tried in his own court as Count of Poitou, but he insisted upon such conditions that the trial was refused. Meanwhile Philip's affairs were rapidly becoming settled and he was able to take up again his plans of conquest. The death of Agnes of Meran made possible a reconciliation with the Church, and the death of the Count of Champagne added the revenues of that great barony to his own through his wardship of the heir. In the spring of 1202 he was ready for action. The barons of Poitou had already lodged an appeal with him as overlord against the illegal acts of John. This gave him a legal opportunity without violating any existing treaty. After an interview with John on March 25, which left things as they were, a formal summons was issued citing John to appear before Philip's court and answer to any charges against him. He neither came nor properly excused himself, though he tried to avoid the difficulty. He alleged that as Duke of Normandy he could not be summoned to Paris for trial, and was answered that he had not been summoned as Duke of Normandy but as Count of Poitou. He demanded a safe conduct and was told that he could have one for his coming, but that his return would depend on the sentence of the court. He said that the king of England could not submit to such a trial, and was answered that the king of France could not lose his rights over a vassal because he happened to have acquired another dignity. Finally, John's legal rights of delay and excuse being exhausted, the court decreed that he should be deprived of all the fiefs which he held of France on the ground of failure of service. All the steps of this action from its beginning to its ending seem to have been perfectly regular, John being tried, of course, not on the appeal of the barons of Poitou which had led to the king's action, but for his refusal to obey the summons, and the severe sentence with which it closed was that which the law provided, though it was not often enforced in its extreme form, and probably would not have been in this case if John had been willing to submit.[67]

The sentence of his court Philip gladly accepted, and invaded Normandy about June 1, capturing place after place with almost no opposition from John. Arthur, now sixteen years old, he knighted, gave him the investiture of all the Angevin fiefs except Normandy, and betrothed him to his own daughter Mary. On August 1 occurred an event which promised at first a great success for John, but proved in its consequences a main cause of his failure, and led to the act of infamy by which he has ever since been most familiarly known. Arthur, hearing that his grandmother Eleanor was at the castle of Mirebeau in Poitou with a small force, laid siege to the castle to capture her as John's chief helper, and quickly carried the outer works. Eleanor had managed, however, to send off a messenger to her son at Le Mans, and John, calling on the fierce energy he at times displayed, covered the hundred miles between them in a day and a night, surprised the besiegers by his sudden attack, and captured their whole force. To England he wrote saying that the favour of God had worked with him wonderfully, and a man more likely to receive the favour of God might well think so. Besides Arthur, he captured Hugh of Lusignan the younger and his uncle Geoffrey, king Richard's faithful supporter in the Holy Land, with many of the revolted barons and, as he reported with probable exaggeration, two hundred knights and more. Philip, who was besieging Arques, on hearing the news, retired hastily to his own land and in revenge made a raid on Tours, which in his assault and John's recapture was almost totally destroyed by fire. The prisoners and booty were safely conveyed to Normandy, and Arthur was imprisoned at Falaise.

Instantly anxiety began to be felt by the friends of Arthur as to his fate. William des Roches, who was still in the service of John, went to the king with barons from Britanny and asked that his prisoner be given up to them. Notwithstanding the written promise and oath which John had given to follow the counsel of William in his treatment of Arthur, he refused this request. William left the king's presence to go into rebellion, and was joined by many of the barons of Britanny; at the end of October they got possession of Angers. It was a much more serious matter that during the autumn and winter extensive disaffection and even open treason began to show themselves among the barons of Normandy. What disposition should be made of Arthur was, no doubt, a subject of much debate in the king's mind, and very likely with his counsellors, during the months that followed the capture. John's lack of insight was on the moral side, not at all on the intellectual, and he no doubt saw clearly that so long as Arthur lived he never could be safe from the designs of Philip. On the other hand he probably did not believe that Philip would seriously attempt the unusual step of enforcing in full the sentence of the court against him, and underestimated both the danger of treason and the moral effect of the death of Arthur. What the fate of the young Count of Britanny really was no one has ever known. The most accurate statement of what we do know is that of an English chronicler[68] who says that he was removed from Falaise to Rouen by John's order and that not long after he suddenly disappeared, and we may add that this disappearance must have been about the Easter of 1203. Many different stories were in circulation at the time or soon after, accounting for his death as natural, or accidental, or a murder, some of them in abundant detail, but in none of these can we have any confidence. The only detail of the history which seems historically probable is one we find in an especially trustworthy chronicler, which represents John as first intending to render Arthur incapable of ruling by mutilation and sending men to Falaise to carry out this plan.[69] It was not done, though Arthur's custodian, Hubert de Burgh, thought it best to give out the report that it had been, and that the young man had died in consequence. The report roused such a storm of anger among the Bretons that Hubert speedily judged it necessary to try to quiet it by evidence that Arthur was still alive, and John is said not to have been angry that his orders had been disobeyed. It is certain, however, that he learned no wisdom from the result of this experiment, and that Arthur finally died either by his order or by his hand.

It is of some interest that in all the contemporary discussion of this case no one ever suggested that John was personally incapable of such a violation of his oath or of such a murder with his own hand. He is of all kings the one for whose character no man, of his own age or later, has ever had a good word. Historians have been found to speak highly of his intellectual or military abilities, but words have been exhausted to describe the meanness of his moral nature and his utter depravity. Fully as wicked as William Rufus, the worst of his predecessors, he makes on the reader of contemporary narratives the impression of a man far less apt to be swept off his feet by passion, of a cooler and more deliberate, of a meaner and smaller, a less respectable or pardonable lover of vice and worker of crimes. The case of Arthur exhibits one of his deepest traits, his utter falsity, the impossibility of binding him, his readiness to betray any interest or any man or woman, whenever tempted to it. The judgment of history on John has been one of terrible severity, but the unanimous opinion of contemporaries and posterity is not likely to be wrong, and the failure of personal knowledge and of later study to find redeeming features assures us of their absence. As to the murder of Arthur, it was a useless crime even if judged from the point of view of a Borgian policy merely, one from which John had in any case little to gain and of which his chief enemy was sure to reap the greatest advantage.

Soon after Easter Philip again took the field, still ignorant of the fate of Arthur, as official acts show him to have been some months later. Place after place fell into his hands with no serious check and no active opposition on the part of John, some opening their gates on his approach, and none offering an obstinate resistance. The listless conduct of John during the loss of Normandy is not easy to explain. The only suggestion of explanation in the contemporary historians is that of the general prevalence of treason in the duchy, which made it impossible for the king to know whom to trust and difficult to organize a sufficient defence to the advance of Philip, and undoubtedly this factor in the case should receive more emphasis than it has usually been given. Other kings had had to contend with extensive treason on the part of the Norman barons, but never in quite the same circumstances and probably never of quite the same spirit. Treason now was a different thing from that of mere feudal barons in their alliance with Louis VII in the reign of Henry I. It might be still feudal in form, but its immediate and permanent results were likely to be very different. It was no temporary defection to be overcome by some stroke of policy or by the next turn of the wheel. It was joining the cause of Philip Augustus and the France which he had done so much already to create; it was being absorbed in the expansion of a great nation to which the duchy naturally belonged, and coming under the influence of rapidly forming ideals of nationality, possibly even induced by them more or less consciously felt. This may have been treason in form, but in real truth it was a natural and inevitable current, and from it there was no return. John may have felt something of this. Its spirit may have been in the atmosphere, and its effect would be paralyzing. Still we find it impossible to believe that Henry I in the same circumstances would have done no more than John did to stem the tide. He seemed careless and inert. He showed none of the energy of action or clearness of mind which he sometimes exhibits. Men came to him with the news of Philip's repeated successes, and he said, "Let him go on, I shall recover one day everything he is taking now"; though what he was depending on for this result never appears. Perhaps he recognized the truth of what, according to one account, William Marshal told him to his face, that he had made too many enemies by his personal conduct,[70] and so he did not dare to trust any one; but we are tempted after all explanation to believe there was in the case something of that moral breakdown in dangerous crises which at times comes to men of John's character.

By the end of August Philip was ready for the siege of the Château-Gaillard, Richard's great fortress, the key to Rouen and so to the duchy. John seems to have made one attempt soon after to raise the siege, but with no very large forces, and the effort failed; it may even have led to the capture of the fort on the island in the river and the town of Les Andelys by the French. Philip then drew his lines round the main fortress and settled down to a long blockade. The castle was commanded by Roger de Lacy, a baron faithful to John, and one who could be trusted not to give up his charge so long as any further defence was possible. He was well furnished with supplies, but as the siege went on he found himself obliged, following a practice not infrequent in the middle ages, to turn out of the castle, to starve between the lines, some hundreds of useless mouths of the inhabitants of Les Andelys, who had sought refuge there on the capture of the town by the French. Philip finally allowed them to pass his lines. Chateau-Gaillard was at last taken not by the blockade, but by a series of assaults extending through about two weeks and closing with the capture of the third or inner ward and keep on March 6, 1204, an instance of the fact of which the history of medieval times contains abundant proof, that the siege appliances of the age were sufficient for the taking of the strongest fortress unless it were in a situation inaccessible to them. In the meantime John, seeing the hopelessness of defending Normandy with the resources left him there, and even, it is said, fearing treasonable designs against his person, had quitted the duchy in what proved to be a final abandonment and crossed to England on December 5. He landed with no good feeling towards the English barons whom he accused of leaving him at the mercy of his enemies, and he ordered at once a tax of one-seventh of the personal property of clergy and laymen alike. This was followed by a scutage at the rate of two marks on the knight's fee, determined on at a great council held at Oxford early in January. But, notwithstanding these taxes and other ways of raising money, John seems to have been embarrassed in his measures of defence by a lack of funds, while Philip was furnished with plenty to reinforce the victories of his arms with purchased support where necessary, and to attract John's mercenaries into his service.

After the fall of Chateau-Gaillard events drew rapidly to a close. John tried the experiment of an embassy headed by Hubert Walter and William Marshal to see if a peace could be arranged, but Philip naturally set his terms so high that nothing was to be lost by going on with the war, however disastrous it might prove. He demanded the release of Arthur, or, if he were not living, of his sister Eleanor, with the cession to either of them of the whole continental possessions of the Angevins. In the interview Philip made known the policy that he proposed to follow in regard to the English barons who had possessions in Normandy, for he offered to guarantee to William Marshal and his colleague, the Earl of Leicester, their Norman lands if they would do him homage. Philip's wisdom in dealing with his conquests, leaving untouched the possessions and rights of those who submitted, rewarding with gifts and office those who proved faithful, made easy the incorporation of these new territories in the royal domain. By the end of May nearly all the duchy was in the hands of the French, the chief towns making hardly a show of resistance, but opening their gates readily on the offer of favourable terms. For Rouen, which was reserved to the last, the question was a more serious one, bound as it was to England by commercial interests and likely to suffer injury if the connexion were broken. Philip granted the city a truce of thirty days on the understanding that it should be surrendered if the English did not raise the siege within that time. The messengers sent to the king in England returned with no promise of help, and on June 24 Philip entered the capital of Normandy.

With the loss of Normandy nothing remained to John but his mother's inheritance, and against this Philip next turned. Queen Eleanor, eighty-two years of age, had closed her marvellous career on April 1, and no question of her rights stood in the way of the absorption of all Aquitaine in France. The conquest of Touraine and Poitou was almost as easy as that of Normandy, except the castles of Chinon and Loches which held out for a year, and the cities of Niort, Thouars, and La Rochelle. But beyond the bounds of the county of Poitou Philip made no progress. In Gascony proper where feudal independence of the old type still survived the barons had no difficulty in perceiving that Philip Augustus was much less the sort of king they wished than the distant sovereign of England. No local movement in his favour or national sympathy prepared the way for an easy conquest, nor was any serious attempt at invasion made. Most of the inheritance of Eleanor remained to her son, though not through any effort of his, and the French advance stopped at the capture of the castles of Loches and Chinon in the summer of 1205. John had not remained in inactivity in England all this time, however, without some impatience? but efforts to raise sufficient money for any considerable undertaking or to carry abroad the feudal levies of the country had all failed. At the end of May, 1205, he did collect at Portchester what is described as a very great fleet and a splendid army to cross to the continent, but Hubert Walter and William Marshal, supported by others of the barons, opposed the expedition so vigorously and with so many arguments that the king finally yielded to their opposition though with great reluctance.

The great duchy founded three hundred years before on the colonization of the Northmen, always one of the mightiest of the feudal states of France, all the dominions which the counts of Anjou had struggled to bring together through so many generations, the disputed claims on Maine and Britanny recognized now for a long time as going with Normandy, a part even of the splendid possessions of the dukes of Aquitaine;—all these in little more than two years Philip had transferred from the possession of the king of England to his own, and all except Britanny to the royal domain. If we consider the resources with which he began to reign, we must pronounce it an achievement equalled by few kings. For the king of England it was a corresponding loss in prestige and brilliancy of position. John has been made to bear the responsibility of this disaster, and morally with justice; but it must not be forgotten that, as the modern nations were beginning to take shape and to become conscious of themselves, the connexion with England would be felt to be unnatural, and that it was certain to be broken. For England the loss of these possessions was no disaster; it was indeed as great a blessing as to France. The chief gain was that it cut off many diverting interests from the barons of England, just at a time when they were learning to be jealous of their rights at home and were about to enter upon a struggle with the king to compel him to regard the law in his government of the country, a struggle which determined the whole future history of the nation.

[63] See Walter of Coventry, ii. 196.

[64] Matth. Paris, ii. 455.

[65] Rymer, Foedera, i. 140.

[66] Rymer, Foedera, i. 75.

[67] But see Guilhiermoz, Bibliothèque de l'Ecole des Chartes, lx. (1899), 45-85, whose argument is, however, not convincing.

[68] Roger of Wendover, iii. 170.

[69] Ralph of Coggeshall, 139-141.

[70] L'Histoire de Guillaume la Maréchal, ll. 12737-12741.

CHAPTER XX.
CONFLICT WITH THE PAPACY

The loss of the ancient possessions of the Norman dukes and the Angevin counts marks the close of an epoch in the reign of John; but for the history of England and for the personal history of the king the period is more appropriately closed by the death of Archbishop Hubert Walter on July 13, 1205, for the consequences which followed that event lead us directly to the second period of the reign. Already at the accession of John one of the two or three men of controlling influence on the course of events, trained not merely in the school of Henry II, but by the leading part he had played in the reign of Richard, there is no doubt that he had kept a strong hand on the government of the opening years of the new reign, and that his personality had been felt as a decided check by the new king. We may believe also that as one who had been brought up by Glanvill, the great jurist of Henry's time, and who had a large share in carrying the constitutional beginnings of that time a further stage forward, but who was himself a practical statesman rather than a lawyer, he was one of the foremost teachers of that great lesson which England was then learning, the lesson of law, of rights and responsibilities, which was for the world at large a far more important result of the legal reforms of the great Angevin monarch than anything in the field of technical law. It is easy to believe that a later writer records at least a genuine tradition of the feeling of John when he makes him exclaim on hearing of the archbishop's death, "Now—for the first time am I king of England." In truth practically shut up now for the first time to his island kingdom, John was about to be plunged into that series of quarrels and conflicts which fills the remainder of his life.

For the beginning of the conflict which gives its chief characteristic to the second period of his reign, the conflict with the pope and the Church, John is hardly to be blamed, at least not from the point of view of a king of England. With the first scene of the drama he had nothing to do; in the second he was doing no more than all his predecessors had done with scarcely an instance of dispute since the Norman Conquest. There had long been two questions concerning elections to the see of Canterbury that troubled the minds of the clergy. The monks of the cathedral church objected to the share which the bishops of the province had acquired in the choice of their primate, and canonically they were probably right. They also objected, and the bishops, though usually acting on the side of the king, no doubt sympathized with them, to the virtual appointment of the archbishop by the king. This objection, though felt by the clergy since the day when Anselm had opened the way into England to the principles of the Hildebrandine reformation, had never yet been given decided expression in overt act or led to any serious struggle with the sovereign; and it is clear that it would not have done so in this instance if the papal throne had not been filled by Innocent III. That great ecclesiastical statesman found in the political situation of more than one country of Europe opportunities for the exercise of his decided genius which enabled him to attain more nearly to the papacy of Gregory VII's ideal than had been possible to any earlier pope, and none of his triumphs was greater than that which he won from the opportunity offered him in England.

On Archbishop Hubert's death a party of the monks of Canterbury determined to be beforehand with the bishops and even with the king. They secretly elected their subprior to the vacant see, and sent him off to Rome to be confirmed before their action should be known, but the personal vanity of their candidate betrayed the secret, and his boasting that he was the elect of Canterbury was reported back from the continent to England to the anger of the monks, who then sent a deputation to the king and asked permission in the regular way to proceed to an election. John gave consent, and suggested John de Grey, Bishop of Norwich, as his candidate, since he was "alone of all the prelates of England in possession of his counsels." The bishop was elected by the chapter; both bishops and monks were induced to withdraw the appeals they had made to Rome on their respective rights, and, on December 11, the new archbishop was enthroned and invested with the fiefs of Canterbury by the king. Of course the pallium from the pope was still necessary, and steps were at once taken to secure it. Innocent took plenty of time to consider the situation and did not render his decision until the end of March, 1206, declaring then against the king's candidate and ordering a deputation of the monks to be sent him, duly commissioned to act for the whole chapter. King and bishops were also told to be represented at the final decision. The pope's action postponed the settlement of the question for six months, and the interval was spent by John in an effort to recover something of his lost dominions, undertaken this time with some promise of success because of active resistance to Philip in Poitou. On this occasion no objection to the campaign was made by the barons, and with a large English force John landed at La Rochelle on June 7. Encouraged by his presence the insurrection spread through the greater part of Poitou and brought it back into his possession. He even invaded Anjou and held its capital for a time, and reached the borders of Maine, but these conquests he could not retain after Philip took the field against him in person; but on his side Philip did not think it wise to attempt the recovery of Poitou. On October 26 a truce for two years was proclaimed, each side to retain what it then possessed, but John formally abandoning all rights north of the Loire during the period of the truce.

John did not return to England until near the middle of December, but even at that date Innocent III had not decided the question of the Canterbury election. On December 20 he declared against the claim of the bishops and against the first secret election by the monks, and under his influence the deputation from Canterbury elected an Englishman and cardinal highly respected at Rome both for his character and for his learning, Stephen of Langton. The representatives of the king at Rome refused to agree to this election, and the pope himself wrote to John urging him to accept the new archbishop, but taking care to make it clear that the consent of the king was not essential, and indeed he did not wait for it. After correspondence with John in which the king's anger and his refusal to accept Langton were plainly expressed, on June 17, 1207, he consecrated Stephen archbishop. John's answer was the confiscation of the lands of the whole archbishopric, apparently those of the convent as well as those of the archbishop, and the expulsion of the monks from the country as traitors, while the trial in England of all appeals to the pope was forbidden.

Before this violent proceeding against the Canterbury monks, the financial necessities of John had led to an experiment in taxation which embroiled him to almost the same extent with the northern province. Not the only one, but the chief source of the troubles of John's reign after the loss of Normandy, and the main cause of the revolution in which the reign closed, is to be found in the financial situation of the king. The normal expenses of government had been increasing rapidly in the last half century. The growing amount and complexity of public and private business, to be expected in a land long spared the ravages of war, which showed itself in the remarkable development of judicial and administrative machinery during the period, meant increased expenses in many directions not to be met by the increased income from the new machinery. The cost of the campaigns in France was undoubtedly great, and the expense of those which the king desired to undertake was clearly beyond the resources of the country, at least beyond the resources available to him by existing methods of taxation. Nor was John a saving and careful housekeeper who could make a small income go a long ways. The complete breakdown of the ordinary feudal processes of raising revenue, the necessity forced upon the king of discovering new sources of income, the attempt within a single generation to impose on the country something like the modern methods and regularity of taxation, these must be taken into account as elements of decided importance in any final judgment we may form of the struggles of John's reign and their constitutional results. Down to this date a scutage had been imposed every year since the king's accession, at the rate of two marks on the fee except on the last occasion when the tax had been twenty shillings. Besides these there had been demanded the carucage of 1200 and the seventh of personal property of 1204, to say nothing of some extraordinary exactions. But these taxes were slow in coming in; the machinery of collection was still primitive, and the amount received in any year was far below what the tax should have yielded.

At a great council held in London on January 8 the king asked the bishops and abbots present to grant him a tax on the incomes of all beneficed clergy. The demand has a decidedly modern sound. Precedents for taxation of this sort had been made in various crusading levies, in the expedients adopted for raising Richard's ransom, and in the seventh demanded by John in 1204, which was exacted from at least a part of the clergy, but these were all more or less exceptional cases, and there was no precedent for such a tax as a means of meeting the ordinary expenses of the state. The prelates refused their consent, and the matter was deferred to a second great council to be held at Oxford a month later. This council was attended by an unusually large number of ecclesiastics, and the king's proposition, submitted to them again, was again refused. The council, however, granted the thirteenth asked, to be collected of the incomes and personal property of the laity. But John had no mind to give up his plan because it had not been sanctioned by the prelates in general assembly, and he proceeded, apparently by way of individual consent, doubtless practically compulsory as usual, to collect the same tax from the whole clergy, the Cistercians alone excepted. A tax of this kind whether of laity or clergy was entirely non-feudal, foreign both in nature and methods to the principles of feudalism, and a long step toward modern taxation, but it was some time before the suggestion made by it was taken up by the government as one of its ordinary resources. Archbishop Geoffrey of York, the king's brother, who since the death of his father seemed never to be happy unless in a quarrel with some one, took it upon himself to oppose violently the taxation of his clergy, though he had enforced the payment of a similar tax for Richard's ransom. Finding that he could not prevent it he retired from the country, excommunicating the despoilers of the church, and his lands were taken in hand by the king.

The expulsion of the monks of Canterbury was a declaration of war against the Church and the pope, and the Church was far more powerful, more closely organized, and more nearly actuated by a single ideal, than in the case of any earlier conflict between Church and State in England, and the pope was Innocent III, head of the world in his own conception of his position and very nearly so in reality. There was no chance that a declaration of war would pass unanswered, but the pope did not act without deliberation. On the news of what the king had done he wrote to the Bishops of London, Ely, and Worcester, directing them to try to persuade John to give way, and if he obstinately continued his course, to proclaim an interdict. This letter was written on August 27, but the interdict was not actually put into force until March 24,1208, negotiations going on all the winter, and John displaying, as he did throughout the whole conflict, considerable ability in securing delay and in keeping opponents occupied with proposals which he probably never intended to carry out. At last a date was set on which the interdict would be proclaimed if the king had not yielded by that time, and he was given an opportunity of striking the first blow which he did not neglect. He ordered the immediate confiscation of the property of all the clergy who should obey the interdict.

The struggle which follows exhibits, as nothing else could do so well, the tremendous power of the Norman feudal monarchy, the absolute hold which it had on state and nation even on the verge of its fall. John had not ruled during these eight years in such a way as to strengthen his personal position. He had been a tyrant; he had disregarded the rights of batons as well as of clergy; he had given to many private reasons of hatred; he had lost rather than won respect by the way in which he had defended his inheritance in France his present cause, if looked at from the point of view of Church and nation and not from that of the royal prerogative alone, was a bad one. The interdict was a much dreaded penalty, suspending some of the most desired offices of religion, and, while not certainly dooming all the dying to be lost in the world to come, at least rendering their state to the pious mind somewhat doubtful; and, though the effect of the spiritual terrors of the Church had been a little weakened by their frequent use on slight occasions, the age was still far distant when they could be disregarded. We should expect John to prove as weak in the war with Innocent as he had in that with Philip, and at such a test to find his power crumbling without recovery. What we really find is a successful resistance kept up for years, almost without expressed opposition, a great body of the clergy reconciling themselves to the situation as best they could; a period during which the affairs of the state seem to go on as if nothing were out of order, the period of John's greatest tyranny, of almost unbridled power. And when he was forced to yield at last, it was to a foreign attack, to a foreign attack combined, it is true, with an opposition at home which had been long accumulating, but no one can say how long this opposition might have gone on accumulating before it would have grown strong enough to check the king of itself.

The interdict seems to have been generally observed by the clergy. The Cistercians at first declared that they were not bound to respect it, but they were after a time forced by the pope to conform. Baptism and extreme unction were allowed; marriages might be celebrated at the church door; but no masses were publicly said, and all the ordinary course of the sacraments was intermitted; the dead were buried in unconsecrated ground, and the churches were closed except to those who wished to make offerings. Nearly all the bishops went into exile. Two only remained in the end, both devoted more to the king than to the Church; John de Grey, Bishop of Norwich, employed during most of the time in secular business in Ireland, and Peter des Roches, appointed Bishop of Winchester in 1205, destined to play a leading part against the growing liberties of the nation in the next reign, and now, as a chronicler says, occupied less with defending the Church than in administering the king's affairs. The general confiscation of Church property must have relieved greatly the financial distress of the king, and during the years when these lands were administered as part of the royal domains, we hear less of attempts at national taxation. John did not stop with confiscation of the goods of the clergy. Their exemption from the jurisdiction of the ordinary courts of the state was suspended, and they were even in some cases denied the protection of the laws. It is said that once there came to the king on the borders of Wales officers of one of the sheriffs, leading a robber with his hands bound behind his back, who had robbed and killed a priest, and they asked the king what should be done with him. "He has killed one of my enemies. Loose him and let him go," ordered John. After the interdict had been followed by the excommunication of the king, Geoffrey, Archdeacon of Norwich, urged upon his associates at the exchequer that it was not safe for those who were in orders to remain in the service of an excommunicate king, and left the court without permission and went home. John hearing this sent William Talbot after him with a band of soldiers, who arrested the archdeacon, and loaded him with chains, and threw him into prison. There shortly after by the command of the king he was pressed to death. It was by acts like these, of which other instances are on record, that John terrorized the country and held it quiet under his tyranny.

Even the greatest barons were subjected to arbitrary acts of power of the same kind. On the slightest occasion of suspicion the king demanded their sons or other relatives, or their vassals, as hostages, a measure which had been in occasional use before, but which John carried to an extreme. The great earl marshal himself, who, if we may trust his biographer, was never afraid to do what he thought honour demanded, and was always able to defend himself in the king's presence with such vigorous argument that nothing could be done with him, was obliged to give over to the king's keeping first his eldest and then his second son. The case of William de Braóse is that most commonly cited. He had been a devoted supporter of John and had performed many valuable services in his interest, especially at the time of the coronation. For these he had received many marks of royal favour, and was rapidly becoming both in property and in family alliances one of the greatest barons of the land. About the time of the proclamation of the interdict a change took place in his fortunes. For some reason he lost the favour of the king and fell instead under his active enmity. According to a formal statement of the case, which John thought well to put forth afterwards, he had failed to pay large sums which he had promised in return for the grants that had been made him; and the records support the accusation.[71] According to Roger of Wendover the king had a personal cause of anger. On a demand of hostages from her husband, the wife of William had rashly declared to the officers that her sons should never be delivered to the king because he had basely murdered his nephew Arthur, whom he was under obligation to guard honourably, and it is impossible to believe that it was merely delay in paying money that excited the fierce persecution that followed William with his family took refuge in Ireland, where he was received by William Marshal and the Lacies, but John pursued him thither, and he was again obliged to fly. His wife and son, attempting to escape to Scotland, were seized in Galloway by a local baron and delivered to John, who caused them to be starved to death in prison.

It may seem strange at the present day that the absolutism of the king did not bring about a widespread rebellion earlier than it did. One of the chief causes of his strength is to be found in the bands of mercenary soldiers which he maintained, ready to do any bidding at a moment's notice, under the command of men who were entirely his creatures, like Gerald of Athies, a peasant of Touraine, who with some of his fellows was thought worthy of mention by name in the Great Charter. The cost of keeping these bands devoted to his service was no doubt one of the large expenses of the reign. Another fact of greater permanent interest that helped to keep up the king's power is the lack of unity among the barons, of any feeling of a common cause, but rather the existence of jealousies, and open conflicts even, which made it impossible to bring them together in united action in their own defence. The fact is of especial importance because it was the crushing tyranny of John that first gave rise to the feeling of corporate unity in the baronage, and the growth of this feeling is one of the great facts of the thirteenth century.

At the beginning of 1209 Innocent III had threatened the immediate excommunication of John, but the king had known how to keep him, and the bishops who represented him in the negotiations, occupied with one proposition of compromise after another until almost the close of the year. The summer was employed in settling affairs with Scotland, which down to this time had not been put into form satisfactory to either king. A meeting at the end of April led to no result, but in August, after armies of the two countries had faced each other on the borders, a treaty was agreed upon. William the Lion was not then in a condition to insist strongly on his own terms, and the treaty was much in favour of John. The king of Scotland promised to pay 15,000 marks, and gave over two of his daughters to John to be given in marriage by him. In a later treaty John was granted the same right with respect to Alexander, the heir of Scotland, arrangements that look very much like a recognition of the king of England as the overlord of Scotland. In Wales also quarrels among the native chieftains enabled John to increase his influence in the still unconquered districts. In November the long-deferred excommunication fell upon the unrepentant king, but it could not be published in England. There were no bishops left in the country who were acting in the interests of the pope, and John took care that there should be no means of making any proclamation of the sentence in his kingdom. The excommunication was formally published in France, and news of it passed over to England, but no attention was paid to it there. For the individual, excommunication was a more dreaded penalty than the interdict. The interdict might compel a king to yield by the public fear and indignation which it would create, but an excommunication cut him off as a man completely from the Church and all its mercies, cast him out of the community of Christians, and involved in the same awful fate all who continued to support him, or, indeed, to associate with him in any way. Even more than the interdict, the excommunication reveals the terrible strength of the king. When the time came for holding the Christmas court of 1209, the fact that it had been pronounced was generally known, but it made no difference in the attendance. All the barons are said to have been present and to have associated with the king as usual, though there must have been many of them who trembled at the audacity of the act, and who would have withdrawn entirely from him if they had dared. On his return from the north John had demanded and obtained a renewal of homage from all the free tenants of the country. The men of Wales had even been compelled to go to Woodstock to render it. It is quite possible that this demand had been made in view of the excommunication that was coming; the homage must certainly have been rendered by many who knew that the sentence was hanging over the king's head.

The year 1210 is marked by an expedition of John with an army to Ireland. Not only were William de Braóse and his wife to be punished, but the Lacies had been for some time altogether too independent, and the conduct of William Marshal was not satisfactory. The undertaking occasioned the first instance of direct taxation since the lands of the Church had been taken in hand, a scutage, which in this case at least would have a warrant in strict feudal law. The clergy also were compelled to pay a special and heavy tax, and the Jews throughout the kingdom—perhaps an act of piety on the part of the king to atone somewhat for his treatment of the Church—were arrested and thrown into prison and forced to part with large sums of money. It was on this occasion that the often-quoted incident occurred of the Jew of Bristol who endured all ordinary tortures to save his money, or that in his charge, until the king ordered a tooth to be drawn each day so long as he remained obstinate. As the eighth was about to be pulled, "tardily perceiving," as the chronicler remarks, "what was useful," he gave up and promised the 10,000 marks demanded.

John landed in Ireland about June 20, and traversed with his army all that part of the country which was occupied by Anglo-Norman settlers without finding any serious opposition. William Marshal entertained his host for two days with all loyalty. The Lacies and William de Braóse's family fled before him from one place to another and finally escaped out of the island to Scotland. Carrickfergus, in which Hugh de Lacy had thought to stand a siege, resisted for a few days, and then surrendered. At Dublin the native kings of various districts, said by Roger of Wendover to have been more than twenty in number, including the successor of Roderick, king of Connaught, who had inherited a greatly reduced power, came in and did homage and swore fealty to John. At the same time, we are told, the king introduced into the island the laws and administrative system of England, and appointed sheriffs.[72] John's march through the island and the measures of government which he adopted have been thought to mark an advance in the subjection of Ireland to English rule, and to form one of the few permanent contributions to English history devised by the king. On his departure Bishop John de Grey was left as justiciar, and toward the end of August John landed in England to go on with the work of exacting money from the clergy and the Jews that he had begun before he left the country.

The two years which followed John's return from Ireland, from August, 1210 to August 1212, form the period of his highest power. No attempt at resistance to his will anywhere disturbed the peace of England. Llewelyn, Prince of north Wales, husband of John's natural daughter Joanna, involved in border warfare with the Earl of Chester, was not willing to yield to the authority of the king, but two expeditions against him in 1211 forced him to make complete submission. A contemporary annalist remarks with truth that none of John's predecessors exercised so great an authority over Scotland, Wales, or Ireland as he, and we may add that none exercised a greater over England. The kingdom was almost in a state of blockade, and not only was unauthorized entrance into the country forbidden, but departure from it as well, except as the king desired. During these two years John's relations with the Church troubled him but little. Negotiations were kept up as before, but they led to nothing. On his return from the Welsh campaign the king met representatives of the pope at Northampton, one of whom was the Roman subdeacon Pandulf, whom John met later in a different mood. We have no entirely trustworthy account of the interview, but it was found impossible to agree upon the terms of any treaty which would bring the conflict to an end. The pope demanded a promise of complete obedience from John on all the questions that had caused the trouble, and restoration to the clergy of all their confiscated revenues, and to one or both of these demands the king refused to yield. Now it is that we begin to hear of threats of further sentences to be issued by the pope against John, or actually issued, releasing his subjects from their allegiance and declaring the king incapable of ruling, but if any step of that kind was taken, it had for the present no effect. The Christmas feast was kept as usual at Windsor, and in Lent of the next year John knighted young Alexander of Scotland, whose father had sent him to London to be married as his liege lord might please, though "without disparagement."

In the spring of 1212 John seems to have felt himself strong enough to take up seriously a plan for the recovery of the lands which he had lost in France. The idea he had had in mind for some years was the formation of a great coalition against Philip Augustus by combining various enemies of his or of the pope's. In May the Count of Boulogne, who was in trouble with the king of France, came to London and did homage to John. Otto IV, the Guelfic emperor and John's nephew, was now in as desperate conflict with the papacy as if he were a Ghibelline, and Innocent was supporting against him the young Hohenstaufen Frederick, son of Henry VI and Constance of Sicily. Otto therefore was ready to promise help to any one from whom he could hope for aid in return, or to take part in any enterprise from which a change of the general situation might be expected. Ferdinand of Portugal, just become Count of Flanders by marriage with Jeanne, the heiress of the crusading Count Baldwin, the emperor Baldwin of the new Latin empire, had at the moment of his accession been made the victim of Philip Augustus's ceaseless policy of absorbing the great fiefs in the crown, and had lost the two cities of Aire and St. Omer. He was ready to listen to John's solicitations, and after some hesitation and delay joined the alliance, as did also most of the princes on the north-east between France and Germany. John laboured long and hard with much skill and final success, at a combination which would isolate the king of France and make it possible to attack him with overwhelming force at once from the north and the south. With a view, in all probability, to calling out the largest military force possible in the event of a war with France, John at this time ordered a new survey to be taken of the service due from the various fiefs in England. The inquest was made by juries of the hundreds, after a method very similar to that lately employed in the carucage of 1198, and earlier in the Domesday survey by William the Conqueror, though it was under the direction of the sheriffs, not of special commissioners. The interesting returns to this inquiry have been preserved to us only in part.[73] If John hoped to be able to attack his enemy abroad in the course of the year 1212, he was disappointed in the end. His combination of allies he was not able to complete. A new revolt of the Welsh occupied his attention towards the end of the summer and led him to hang twenty-eight boys, hostages whom they had given him the year before. Worst of all, evidence now began to flow in to the king from various quarters of a serious disaffection among the barons of the kingdom and of a growing spirit of rebellion, even, it was said, of an intention to deprive him of the crown. We are told that on the eve of his expedition against the Welsh a warning came to him from the king of Scotland that he was surrounded by treason, and another from his daughter in Wales to the same effect. Whatever the source of his information, John was evidently convinced—very likely he needed but little to convince him—of a danger which he must have been always suspecting. At any rate he did not venture to trust himself to his army in the field, but sent home the levies and carefully guarded himself for a time. Then he called for new declarations of loyalty and for hostages from the barons; and two of them, Eustace de Vescy and Robert Fitz Walter, fled from the country, the king outlawing them and seizing their property. About the same time a good deal of public interest was excited by a hermit of Yorkshire, Peter of Pontefract, who was thought able to foretell the future, and who declared that John would not be king on next Ascension day, the anniversary of his coronation. It was probably John's knowledge of the disposition of the barons, and possibly the hope of extorting some information from him, that led him, rather unwisely, to order the arrest of the hermit, and to question him as to the way in which he should lose the crown. Peter could only tell him that the event was sure, and that if it did not occur, the king might do with him what he pleased. John took him at his word, held him in prison, and hanged him when the day had safely passed.

By that 23d of May, however, a great change had taken place in the formal standing of John among the sovereigns of the world, a change which many believed fulfilled the prediction of Peter, and one which affected the history of England for many generations. As the year 1212 drew to its close, John was not merely learning his own weakness in England, but he was forced by the course of events abroad to recognize the terrible strength of the papacy and the small chance that even a strong king could have of winning a victory over it.[74] His nephew Otto IV had been obliged to retire, almost defeated, before the enthusiasm which the young Frederick of Hohenstaufen had aroused in his adventurous expedition to recover the crown of Germany. Raymond of Toulouse, John's brother-in-law, had been overwhelmed and almost despoiled of his possessions in an attempt to protect his subjects in their right to believe what seemed to them the truth. For the moment the vigorous action which John had taken after the warnings received on the eve of the Welsh campaign had put an end to the disposition to revolt, and had left him again all powerful. He had even been able to extort from the clergy formal letters stating that the sums he had forced them to pay were voluntarily granted him. But he had been made to understand on how weak a foundation his power rested. He must have known that Philip Augustus had for some time been considering the possibility of an invasion of England, whether invited by the barons to undertake it or not, and he could hardly fail to dread the results to himself of such a step after the lesson he had learned in Normandy of the consequences of treason. The situation at home and abroad forced upon him the conclusion that he must soon come to terms with the papacy, and in November he sent representatives to Rome to signify that he would agree to the proposals he had rejected when made by Pandulf early in the previous year.[75] Even in this case John may be suspected, as so often before, of making a proposition which he did not intend to carry out, or at least of trying to gain time, for it was found that the embassy could not make a formally binding agreement; and it is clear that Innocent III, while ready to go on with the negotiations and hoping to carry them to success, was now convinced that he must bring to bear on John the only kind of pressure to which he would yield.

There is reason to believe that after his reconciliation with the king of England Innocent III had all the letters in which he had threatened John with the severest penalties collected so far as possible and destroyed.[76] It is uncertain, however, whether before the end of 1212 he had gone so far as to depose the king and to absolve his subjects from their allegiance, though this is asserted by English chroniclers. But there is no good ground to doubt that in January, 1213, he took this step, and authorized the king of France to invade England and deprive John of his kingdom. Philip needed no urging. He collected a numerous fleet, we are told, of 1500 vessels, and a large army. In the first week of April he held a great council at Soissons, and the enterprise was determined on by the barons and bishops of France. At the same council arrangements were made to define the legal relations to France of the kingdom to be conquered, The king of England was to be Philip's son, Louis, who could advance some show of right through his wife, John's niece, Blanche of Castile but during his father's lifetime he was to make no pretension to any part of France, a provision which would leave the duchy of Aquitaine in Philip's hands, as Normandy was. Louis was to require an oath of his new subjects that they would undertake nothing against France, and he was to leave to his father the disposal of the person of John and of his private possessions. Of the relationship between the two countries when Louis should succeed to the crown of France, nothing was said. Preparations were so far advanced that it was expected that the army would embark before the end of May.

In the meantime John was taking measures for a vigorous defence. Orders were sent out for all ships capable of carrying at least six horses to assemble at Portsmouth by the middle of Lent. The feudal levies and all men able to bear arms were called out for April 21. The summons was obeyed by such numbers that they could not be fed, and all but the best armed were sent home, while the main force was collected on Barham Down, between Canterbury and Dover, with outposts at the threatened ports. John has been thought by some to have had a special interest in the development of the fleet; at any rate he knew how to employ here the defensive manoeuvre which has been more than once of avail to England, and he sent out a naval force to capture and destroy the enemy's ships in the mouth of the Seine and at Fécamp, and to take and burn the town of Dieppe. It was his plan also to defend the country with the fleet rather than with the army, and to attack and destroy the hostile armament on its way across the channel. To contemporaries the preparations seemed entirely sufficient to defend the country, not merely against France, but against any enemy whatever, provided only the hearts of all had been devoted to the king.

While preparations were being made in France for an invasion of England under the commission of the pope, Innocent was going on with the effort to bring John to his terms by negotiation. The messengers whom the king had sent to Rome returned bringing no modification of the papal demands. At the same time Pandulf, the pope's representative, empowered to make a formal agreement, came on as far as Calais and sent over two Templars to England to obtain permission for an interview with John, while he held back the French fleet to learn the result. The answer of John to Pandulf's messengers would be his answer to the pope and also his defiance of Philip. There can be no doubt what his answer would have been if he had had entire confidence in his army, nor what it would have been if Philip's fleet had not been ready. He yielded only because there was no other way out of the situation into which he had brought himself, and he made his submission complete enough to insure his escape. He sent for Pandulf, and on May 13 met him at Dover and accepted his terms. Four of his chief barons, as the pope required, the Earl of Salisbury, the Count of Boulogne, and the Earls Warenne and Ferrers, swore on the king's soul that he would keep the agreement, and John issued letters patent formally declaring what he had promised. Stephen Langton was to be accepted as Archbishop of Canterbury, and all the exiled bishops, monks, and laymen were to be reinstated, and full compensation made them for their financial losses. Two days later John went very much further than this: at the house of the Templars near Dover in the presence of the barons he surrendered the kingdom to the pope, confirming the act by a charter witnessed by two bishops and eleven barons, and received it back to be held as a fief, doing homage to Pandulf as the representative of the pope, and promising for himself and his heirs the annual payment of 700 marks for England and 300 for Ireland in lieu of feudal service.

Whether this extraordinary act was demanded by Innocent or suggested by John, the evidence does not permit us to say. The balance of probabilities, however, inclines strongly to the opinion that it was a voluntary act of the king's. There is nothing in the papal documents to indicate any such demand, and it is hardly possible that the pope could have believed that he could carry the matter so far. On the other hand, John was able to see clearly that nothing else would save him. He had every reason to be sure that no ordinary reconciliation with the papacy would check the invasion of Philip or prevent the treason of the barons. If England were made a possession of the pope, the whole situation would take on a different aspect. Not only would all Europe think Innocent justified in adopting the most extreme measures for the defence of his vassal, but also the most peculiar circumstances only would justify Philip in going on with his attack, and without him disaffection at home was powerless. We should be particularly careful not to judge this act of John's by the sentiment of a later time. There was nothing that seemed degrading to that age about becoming a vassal. Every member of the aristocracy of Europe and almost every king was a vassal. A man passed from the classes that were looked down upon, the peasantry and the bourgeoisie, into the nobility by becoming a vassal. The English kings had been vassals since feudalism had existed in England, though not for the kingdom, and only a few years before Richard had made even that a fief of the empire. There is no evidence that John's right to take this step was questioned by any one, or that there was any general condemnation of it at that time. One writer a few years later says that the act seemed to many "ignominious," but he records in the same sentence his own judgment that John was "very prudently providing for himself and his by the deed."[77] Even in the rebellion against John that closed his reign no objection was made to the relationship with the papacy, nor was the king's right to act as he did denied, though his action was alleged by his enemies to be illegal because it did not have the consent of the barons. John's charter of concession, however, expressly affirms this consent, and the barons on one occasion seem to have confirmed the assertion.[78]

[71] See J.H. Round's article on William in Dict. Nat. Biogr., vi. 229.

[72] See C.L. Falkiner in Proc. Royal Irish Acad., xxiv. c. pt. 4 (1903).

[73] See Round, Commune of London, 261-277.

[74] Ralph of Coggeshall, 164-165.

[75] Walter of Coventry, ii, lviii. n. 4.

[76] Innocent III, Epp. xvi. 133. (Rymer, Foedera, i. 116.)

[77] Walter of Coventry, ii. 210.

[78] Rymer, Foedera, i. 120.

CHAPTER XXI.
THE GREAT CHARTER

The king of France may have been acting, as he would have the world believe, as the instrument of heaven to punish the enemy of the Church, but he did not learn with any great rejoicing of the conversion of John from the error of his ways. Orders were sent him at once to abstain from all attack on one who was now the vassal of the pope, and he found it necessary in the end to obey, declaring, it is said, that the victory was after all his, since it was due to him that the pope had subdued England. The army and fleet prepared for the invasion, he turned against his own vassal who had withheld his assistance from the undertaking, the Count of Flanders, and quickly occupied a considerable part of the country. Count Ferdinand in his extremity turned to King John and he sent over a force under command of his brother, William Longsword, Earl of Salisbury, which surprised the French fleet badly guarded in the harbour of Damme and captured or destroyed 400 ships. If Philip had any lingering hope that he might yet be able to carry out his plan of invasion, he was forced now to abandon it, and in despair of preserving the rest of his fleet, or in a fit of anger, he ordered it to be burned.

The Archbishop of Canterbury landed in England in July, accompanied by five of the exiled bishops, and a few days later met the king. On the 20th at Winchester John was absolved from his excommunication, swearing publicly that he would be true to his agreement with the Church, and taking an additional oath in form somewhat like the coronation oath, which the archbishop required or which perhaps the fact of his excommunication made necessary, "that holy Church and her ministers he would love, defend, and maintain against all her enemies to the best of his power, that he would renew the good laws of his predecessors, and especially the laws of King Edward, and annul all bad ones, and that he would judge all men according to just judgments of his courts and restore to every man his rights." It is doubtful if we should regard this as anything more than a renewal of the coronation oath necessary to a full restoration of the king from the effects of the Church censure, but at any rate the form of words seems to have been noticed by those who heard it, and to have been referred to afterwards when the political opposition to the king was taking share, a sure sign of increasing watchfulness regarding the mutual rights of king and subjects. [79]

The king was no longer excommunicate, but the kingdom was still under the interdict, and the pope had no intention of annulling it until the question of compensation for their losses was settled to the satisfaction of the bishops and others whose lands had been in the hands of the king. That was not an easy question to settle. It was not a matter of arrears of revenue merely, for John had not been content with the annual income of the lands, but he had cut down forests and raised money in other extraordinary ways to the permanent injury of the property. In the end only a comparatively small sum was paid, and in all probability a full payment would have been entirely beyond the resources of the king, but at the beginning John seems to have intended to carry out his agreement in good faith. There is no reason to doubt the statement of a chronicler of the time that on the next day after his absolution the king sent out writs to all the sheriffs, ordering them to send to St. Albans at the beginning of August the reeve and four legal men from each township of the royal domains, that by their testimony and that of his own officers the amount of these losses might be determined. This would be to all England a familiar expedient, a simple use of the jury principle, with nothing new about it except the bringing of the local juries together in one place, nor must it be regarded as in any sense a beginning of representation. It has no historic connexion with the growth of that system, and cannot possibly indicate more than that the idea of uniting local juries in one place had occurred to some one. We have no evidence that this assembly was actually held, and it is highly probable that it was not. Nor can anything more be said with certainly of writs which were issued in November of this year directing the sheriffs to send four discreet men from each county to attend a meeting of the council at Oxford. John himself was busily occupied with a plan to transport the forces he had collected into Poitou to attack the king of France there, and he appointed the justiciar, Geoffrey Fitz Peter, and the Bishop of Winchester, Peter des Roches, as his representatives during his absence. These two held a great council at St. Albans in August at which formal proclamation was made of the restoration of good laws and the abolition of bad ones as the king had promised, the good laws now referred to being those of Henry I; and all sheriffs and other officers were strictly enjoined to abstain from violence and injustice for the future, but no decision was reached as to the sum to be paid the clergy.

In the meantime John was in difficulties about his proposed expedition to Poitou. When he was about to set out, he found the barons unwilling. They declared that the money they had provided for their expenses had all been used up in the long delay, and that if they went, the king must meet the cost, while the barons of the north refused, according to one account, because they were not bound by the conditions of their tenure to serve abroad. In this they were no doubt wrong, if services were to be determined, as would naturally be the case, by custom; but their refusal to obey the king on whatever ground so soon after he had apparently recovered power by his reconciliation with the Church is very noteworthy. In great anger the king embarked with his household only and landed in Jersey, as if he would conquer France alone, but he was obliged to return. His wrath, however, was not abated, and he collected a large force and marched to the north, intending to bring the unwilling barons to their accustomed obedience; but his plan was interrupted by a new and more serious opposition. Archbishop Stephen Langton seems to have returned to England determined to contend as vigorously for the rights of the laity as for those of the Church. We are told by one chronicler that he had heard it said that on August 25, while the king was on the march to the north, Stephen was presiding over a council of prelates and barons at St. Paul's, and that to certain of them he read a copy of Henry I's coronation charter as a record of the ancient laws which they had a right to demand of the king. There may be difficulties in supposing that such an incident occurred at this exact date, but something of the kind must have happened not long before or after. If we may trust the record we have of the oath taken by John at the time of his absolution, it suggests that the charter of Henry I was in the mind of the man who drew it up. Now, at any rate, was an opportunity to interfere in protection of clearly defined rights, and to insist that the king should keep the oath which he had just sworn. Without hesitation the archbishop went after the king, overtook him at Northampton, where John was on the 28th, and reminded him that he would break his oath if he made war on any of his barons without a judgment of his court. John broke out into a storm of rage, as he was apt to do; "with great noise" he told the archbishop to mind his own business and let matters of lay jurisdiction alone, and moved on to Nottingham. Undismayed, Langton followed, declaring that he would excommunicate every one except the king who should take part in the attack, and John was obliged again to yield and to appoint a time for the court to try the case.

The attempt to settle the indemnity to be paid the clergy dragged on through the remainder of the year, and was not then completed. Councils were held at London, Wallingford, and Reading, early in October, November, and December respectively, in each of which the subject was discussed, and left unsettled, except that after the Reading council the king paid the archbishop and the bishops who had been exiled 15,000 marks. At the end of September a legate from the pope, Cardinal Nicholas, landed in England, and to him John repeated the surrender of the crown and his homage as the pope's vassal. Along with the question of indemnity, that of filling up the vacant sees was discussed, and with nearly as little result. The local officers of the Church were disposed to make as much as possible out of John's humiliation and the chapters to assert the right of independent election. The king was not willing to allow this, and pope and legate inclined to support him. On October 14 the justiciar, Geoffrey Fitz Peter, died. John's exclamation when he heard the news, as preserved in the tradition of the next generation,—"When he gets to hell, let him greet Hubert Walter," and, as earlier in the case of Hubert himself, "Now by the feet of God am I first king and lord of England,"—and, more trustworthy perhaps, the rapid decline of events after Geoffrey's death towards civil war and revolution, lead us to believe that like many a great judge he exercised a stronger influence over the actual history of his age than appears in any contemporary record.

It was near the middle of February, 1214, before John was able to carry out in earnest his plan for the recovery of Poitou. At that time he landed at La Rochelle with a large army and a full military chest, but with very few English barons of rank accompanying him. Since the close of actual war between them Philip had made gains in one way or another within the lands that had remained to John, and it was time for the Duke of Aquitaine to appear to protect his own, to say nothing of any attempt to recover his lost territories. At first his presence seemed all that was necessary; barons renewed their allegiance, those who had done homage to Philip returned and were pardoned, castles were surrendered, and John passed through portions of Poitou and Angoulème, meeting with almost no resistance. A dash of Philip's, in April, drove him back to the south, but the king of France was too much occupied with the more serious danger that threatened him from the coalition in the north to give much time to John, and he returned after a few days, leaving his son Louis to guard the line of approach to Paris. Then John returned to the field, attacked the Lusignans, took their castles, and forced them to submit. The Count of La Marche was the Hugh the Brown from whom years before he had stolen his bride, Isabel of Angoulème, and now he proposed to strengthen the new-made alliance by giving to Hugh's eldest son Isabel's daughter Joanna. On June 11 John crossed the Loire, and a few days later entered Angers, whose fortifications had been destroyed by the French. The occupation of the capital of Anjou marks the highest point of his success in the expedition. To protect and complete his new conquest, John began at once the siege of La Roche-au-Moine, a new castle built by William des Roches on the Loire, which commanded communications with the south. Against him there Louis of France advanced to raise the siege.

John wished to go out and meet him, but the barons of Poitou refused, declaring that they were not prepared to fight battles in the field, and the siege had to be abandoned and a hasty retreat made across the river. Angers at once fell into the hands of Louis, and its new ramparts were destroyed.

It was about July first that Louis set out to raise the siege of La Roche-au-Moine, and on the 27th the decisive battle of Bouvines was fought in the north before John had resolved on his next move. The coalition, on which John had laboured so long and from which he hoped so much, was at last in the field. The emperor Otto IV, the Counts of Flanders, Boulogne, Holland, Brabant, and Limburg, the Duke of Lorraine, and others, each from motives of his own, had joined their forces with the English under the Earl of Salisbury, to overthrow the king of France. To oppose this combination Philip had only his vassals of northern France, without foreign allies and with a part of his force detached to watch the movements of the English king on the Loire. The odds seemed to be decidedly against him, but the allies, attacking at a disadvantage the French army which they believed in retreat, were totally defeated near Bouvines. The Earl of Salisbury and the Counts of Flanders and Boulogne with many others were taken prisoners, and the triumph of Philip was as complete as his danger had been great. The popular enthusiasm with which the news of this victory was received in northern France shows how thorough had been the work of the monarchy during the past century and how great progress had been made in the creation of a nation in feeling and spirit as well as in name under the Capetian king. The general rejoicing was but another expression of the force before which in reality the English dominion in France had fallen.

The effects of the battle of Bouvines were not confined to France nor to the war then going on. The results in German history—the fall of Otto IV, the triumph of Frederick II—we have no occasion to trace. In English history its least important result was that John was obliged to make peace with Philip. The treaty was dated on September 18. A truce was agreed upon to last for five years from the following Easter, everything to remain in the meantime practically as it was left at the close of the war. This might be a virtual recognition by John of the conquests which Philip had made, but for him it was a much more serious matter that the ruin of his schemes left him alone, unsupported by the glamour of a brilliant combination of allies, without prestige, overwhelmed with defeat, to face the baronial opposition which in the past few years had been growing so rapidly in strength, in intelligent perception of the wrongs that had been suffered, and in the knowledge of its own power.

About the middle of October John returned to England to find that the disaffection among the barons, which had expressed itself in the refusal to serve in Poitou, had not grown less during his absence. The interdict had been removed on July 2, John having given security for the payment of a sum as indemnity to the Church which was satisfactory to the pope, but the rejoicing over this relief was somewhat lessened by the fact that the monastic houses and the minor clergy were unprovided for and received no compensation for their losses. The justiciar whom the king had appointed on the eve of his departure, the Bishop of Winchester, Peter des Roches, naturally unpopular because he was a foreigner and out of sympathy with the spirit of the barons, had ruled with a strong hand and sternly repressed all expression of discontent, but his success in this respect had only increased the determination to have a reckoning with the king. In these circumstances John's first important act after his return brought matters to a crisis. Evidently he had no intention of abandoning any of his rights or of letting slip any of his power in England because he had been defeated in France, and he called at once for a scutage from those barons who had not gone with him to Poitou. This raised again the question of right, and we are told that it was the northern barons who once more declared that their English holdings did not oblige them to follow the king abroad or to pay a scutage when he went, John on his side asserting that the service was due to him because it had been rendered to his father and brother. In this the king was undoubtedly right. He could, if he had known it, have carried back his historical argument a century further, but in general feudal law there was justification enough for the position of the barons to warrant them in taking a stand on the point if they wished to join issue with the king. This they were now determined to do. We know from several annalists that after John's return the barons came to an agreement among themselves that they would demand of the king a confirmation of the charter of Henry I and a re-grant of the liberties contained in it. In one account we have the story of a meeting at Bury St. Edmunds, on pretence of a pilgrimage, in which this agreement was made and an oath taken by all to wage war on the king if he should refuse their request which they decided to make of him in form after Christmas. Concerted action there must have been, and it seems altogether likely that this account is correct.

The references to the charter of Henry I in the historians of the time prove clearly enough the great part which that document played at the origin of the revolution now beginning. It undoubtedly gave to the discontented barons the consciousness of legal right, crystallized their ideas, and suggested the method of action, but it is hardly possible to believe that a simple confirmation of this charter could now have been regarded as adequate. The charter of Henry I is as remarkable a document for the beginning of the twelfth as the Great Charter is for the beginning of the thirteenth century, but no small progress had taken place in two directions in the intervening hundred years. In one direction the demands of the crown—we ought really to say the demands of the government—were more frequent, new in kind, and heavier in amount than at the earlier date. The reorganization of the judicial and administrative systems had enlarged greatly the king's sphere of action at the expense of the baron's. All this, and it forms together a great body of change, was advance, was true progress, but it seemed to the baron encroachment on his liberties and denial of his rights, and there was a sense in which his view was perfectly correct. It was partly due to these changes, partly to the general on-going of things, that in the other direction the judgment of the baron was more clear, his view of his own rights and wrongs more specific than a hundred years before, and, by far most important of all, that he had come to a definite understanding of the principle that the king, as lord of his vassals, was just as much under obligation to keep the law as the baron was. Independent of these two main lines of development was the personal tyranny of John, his contemptuous disregard of custom and right in dealing with men, his violent overriding of the processes of his own courts in arbitrary arrest and cruel punishment. The charter of Henry I would be a suggestive model; a new charter must follow its lines and be founded on its principles, but the needs of the barons would now go far beyond its meagre provisions and demand the translation of its general statements into specific form.

According to the agreement they had made the barons came together at London soon after January 1, 1215, with some show of arms, and demanded of the king the confirmation of the charter of Henry I. John replied that the matter was new and important, and that he must have some time for consideration, and asked for delay until the octave of Easter, April 26. With reluctance the barons made this concession, Stephen Langton, William Marshal, and the Bishop of Ely becoming sureties for the king that he would then give satisfaction to all. The interval which was allowed him John used in a variety of attempts to strengthen himself and to prepare for the trial of arms which he must have known to be inevitable. On the 21st of the previous November he had issued a charter granting to the cathedral churches and monasteries throughout England full freedom of election, and this charter he now reissued a few days after the meeting with the barons. If this was an attempt to separate the clergy from the cause of the barons, or to bring the archbishop over wholly to his own side, it was a failure. About the same time he adopted a familiar expedient and ordered the oath of allegiance to himself against all men to be taken throughout the country, but he added a new clause requiring men to swear to stand by him against the charter. [80] Since the discussion of the charter had begun a general interest in its provisions had been excited, and the determination to secure the liberties it embodied had grown rapidly, so that now the king quickly found, by the opposition it aroused, that in this peculiar demand he had overshot the mark, and he was obliged to recall his orders. Naturally John turned at once to the pope, who was now under obligation to protect him from his enemies, but his envoy was followed by Eustace de Vescy, who argued strongly for the barons' side. The pope's letters to England in reply did not afford decisive support to either party, though more in favour of the king's, who was exhorted, however, to grant "just petitions" of the barons. On Ash Wednesday John went so far as to assume the cross of the crusader, most likely to secure additional favour from the pope, who was very anxious to renew the attempt that had failed in the early part of his reign, no doubt having in mind also the personal immunities it would secure him. For troops to resist the barons in the field the king's reliance was chiefly, as it had been during all his reign, on soldiers hired abroad, and he made efforts to get these into his service from Flanders and from Poitou, promising great rewards to knights who would join him from thence, as well as from Wales.

John's preparations alarmed the barons, and they determined not to wait for April 26, the appointed day for the king's answer. They came together in arms at Stamford, advanced from thence to Northampton, and then on to Brackley to be in the neighbourhood of the king, who was then at Oxford. Their array was a formidable one. The list recorded gives us the names of five earls, forty barons, and one bishop, Giles de Braóse, who had family wrongs to avenge; and while the party was called the Northerners, because the movement had such strong support in that part of England, other portions of the country were well represented. Annalists of the time noticed that younger men inclined to the side of the insurgents, while the older remained with the king. This fact in some cases divided families, as in the case of the Marshals, William the elder staying with John, while William the younger was with the barons. That one abode in the king's company does not indicate, however, that his sympathies in this struggle were on that side. Stephen Langton was in form with the king and acted as his representative in the negotiations, though it was universally known that he supported the reforms asked for. It is probable that this was true also of the Earl of Pembroke. These two were sent by John to the barons to get an exact statement of their demands, and returned with a "schedule," which was recited to the king point by point. These were no doubt the same as the "articles" presented to the king afterwards, on which the Great Charter was based. When John was made to understand what they meant, his hot, ancestral temper swept him away in an insane passion of anger. "Why do they not go on and demand the kingdom itself?" he cried, and added with a furious oath that he would never make himself a slave by granting such concessions.

When the barons received their answer, they decided on immediate war. As they viewed the case, this was a step justified by the feudal law. It was their contention that the reforms they demanded had been granted and recognized as legal by former kings. In other words, their suzerain was denying them their hereditary rights, acknowledged and conceded by his predecessors. To the feudal mind the situation which this fact created was simple and obvious. They were no longer bound by any fealty to him. It was their right to make war upon him until he should consent to grant them what was their due. Their first step was to send to the king the formal diffidatio prescribed for such cases, withdrawing their fealty and notifying him of their intention to begin war. Then choosing Robert Fitz Walter their commander, under the title of Marshal of the Army of God and Holy Church, they began the siege of Northampton, but were unable to take it from lack of siege machinery. On May 17 the barons, having in the meantime rejected several unsatisfactory proposals of the king, entered London at the request of the chief citizens, though the tower was still held by John's troops. The great strength of the barons at this time as against the king was not, however, their possession of London, or the forces which had taken the field in their cause, but the fact that John had practically no part of England with him beyond the ground commanded by the castles still held by his foreign soldiers. Pleas ceased in the exchequer, we are told, and the operations of the sheriffs, because no one could be found who would pay the king anything or show him any obedience, and many of the barons, who up to this time had stood with him, now joined the insurgents. No help could be had for some time from the pope. Langton refused to act at the king's request and excommunicate his enemies. There was nothing for John to do but to yield and trust that time would bring about some change to relieve him of the obligations he must assume.

On June 8 John granted a safe conduct to representatives of the barons to negotiate with him to hold good until the 11th, and later extended the period until the 15th. He was then at Windsor, and the barons from London came to Staines and camped in the field of Runnymede. The "Articles" were presented to the king in form, and now accepted by him, and on the basis of them the Great Charter was drawn up and sealed on June 15, 1215.

In the history of constitutional liberty, of which the Great Charter is the beginning, its specific provisions are of far less importance than its underlying principle. What we to-day consider the great safeguards of Anglo-Saxon liberty are all conspicuously absent from the first of its creative statutes, nor could any of them have been explained in the meaning we give them to the understanding of the men who framed the charter. Consent to taxation in the modern sense is not there; neither taxation nor consent. Trial by jury is not there in that form of it which became a check on arbitrary power, nor is it referred to at all in the clause which has been said to embody it. Parliament, habeas corpus, bail, the independence of the judiciary, are all of later growth, or existed only in rudimentary form. Nor can the charter be properly called a contract between king and nation. The idea of the nation, as we now hold it, was still in the future, to be called into existence by the circumstances of the next reign. The idea of contract certainly pervades the document, but only as the expression of the always existent contract between the suzerain and his vassals which was the foundation of all feudal law. On the other hand, some of the provisions of our civil liberty, mainly in the interest of individual rights, are plainly present. That private property shall not be taken for public use without just compensation, that cruel and unusual punishments shall not be inflicted nor excessive fines be imposed, that justice shall be free and fair to all, these may be found almost in modern form.

But it is in none of these directions that the great importance of the document is to be sought. All its specific provisions together as specific provisions are not worth, either in themselves or in their historical influence, the one principle which underlies them all and gives validity to them all— the principle that the king must keep the law. This it was that justified the barons in their rebellion. It was to secure this from a king who could not be bound by the ordinary law that the Great Charter was drawn up and its clauses put into the form in which they stand. In other words, the barons contended that the king was already bound by the law as it stood, and that former kings had recognized the fact. In this they were entirely correct. The Great Charter is old law. It is codification, or rather it is a selection of those points of the existing law which the king had constantly violated, for the purpose of stating them in such form that his specific pledge to regard them could be secured, and his consent to machinery for enforcing them in case he broke his pledge. The source of the Great Charter, then, of its various provisions and of its underlying principle, must be sought in the existing law that regulated the relations between the king and the barons—the feudal law.

From beginning to end the Great Charter is a feudal document. The most important of its provisions which cannot be found in this law, those which may perhaps be called new legislation, relate to the judicial system as recently developed, which had proved too useful and was probably too firmly fixed to be set aside, though it was considered by the barons to infringe upon their feudal rights and had been used in the past as an engine of oppression and extortion. In this one direction the development of institutions in England had already left the feudal system behind. In financial matters a similar development was under rapid way, but John's effort to push forward too fast along that line was one cause of the insurrection and the charter, and of the reaction in this particular which it embodies. As a statement of feudal law the Great Charter is moderate, conservative, and carefully regardful of the real rights of the king. As a document born in civil strife it is remarkable in this respect, or would be were this not true of all its progeny in Anglo-Saxon history. Whoever framed it must have been fair-minded and have held the balance level between king and insurgents. Its provisions in regard to wardship and marriage have been called weak. They are not weak; they are just, and as compared with the corresponding provisions of the charter of Henry I they are less revolutionary, and leave to the king what belonged to him historically—the rights which all English kings had exercised and which in that generation Philip of France also had repeatedly exercised, even against John himself.

But the chief feature of the Great Charter apart from all its specific enactments, that on which it all rests, is this, that the king has no right to violate the law, and if he attempts to do so, may be constrained by force to obey it. That also is feudal law. It was the fundamental conception of the whole feudal relationship that the suzerain was bound to respect the recognized rights of his vassal, and that if he would not, he might be compelled to do so; nor was it in England alone that this idea was held to include the highest suzerain, the lord paramount of the realm.[81] Clause 61 which to the modern mind seems the most astonishing of the whole charter, legalizing insurrection and revolution, contains nothing that was new, except the arrangement for a body of twenty-five barons who were to put into orderly operation the right of coercion. It is certainly not necessary to show by argument the supreme importance of this principle. It is the true corner-stone of the English constitution. It was the preservation of this right, its development into new forms to meet the changing needs of the state, that created and protected constitutional liberty, and it was the supreme service of the Great Charter, far beyond any accomplished by any one clause or by all specific clauses together, to carry over from feudalism this right and to make it the fostering principle of a new growth in which feudalism had no share.[82]

It may be that the barons believed they were demanding nothing in the Great Charter that had not been granted by former kings or that the king was not bound by the law to observe. It may be possible to prove that this belief was historically correct in principle if not in specific form; but the king could not be expected to take the same view of the case. He had been compelled to renounce many things that he had been doing through his whole reign, and some things, as he very well knew, that had been done by his father and brother before him. He may honestly have believed that he had been forced to surrender genuine royal rights. He certainly knew that if he faithfully kept its provisions, the task of raising the necessary money to carry on the government, already not easy, would become extremely difficult if not impossible. It is not likely that John promised to be bound by the charter with any intention of keeping his promise. He had no choice at the moment but to yield, and if he yielded, the forces of the barons would probably scatter, and the chances favour such a recovery of his strength that with the help of the pope he could set the charter aside. At first nothing could be done but to conform to its requirements, and orders were sent throughout the country for the taking of the oath in which all men were to swear to obey the twenty-five barons appointed guardians of the charter. Juries were to be chosen to inquire into grievances, and some of the foreign troops were sent home. Suspicions began to be felt, however, in regard to the intentions of the king during the negotiations concerning details which followed the signing of the charter. A council called to meet at Oxford about the middle of July, he refused to attend. Nor were provocations and violations of the spirit of the charter wanting on the part of the barons. Certain of the party, indeed, "Trans-Humbrians" they are called, probably the extreme enemies of the king, had withdrawn from the conference at Runnymede, and now refused to cease hostilities because they had had no part in making peace. The royal officers were maltreated and driven off, and the king's manors plundered.

By August John was rapidly preparing for a renewal of the war. He sent out orders to get the royal castles ready for defence. His emissaries were collecting troops in Flanders and Aquitaine. Philip Augustus's Count of Britanny, Peter of Dreux, was offered the honour of Richmond, which former counts had held, if he would come to John's aid with a body of knights. Money does not seem to have been lacking through the struggle that followed, and John's efforts to collect mercenary troops were abundantly successful. Dover was appointed as the gathering-place of his army, both as a convenient landing-place for those coming from abroad and for strategic reasons. As it became evident that the charter had not brought the conflict to an end, the barons were obliged to consider what their next step should be. In clause 61 of the charter in regard to coercing the king, they had bound themselves not to depose him, but the arrangements made in that clause were never put into operation, nor could they be. There was only one way of dealing with a king who obstinately insisted on his rights, as he regarded them, against the law, and that was by deposition. The leaders of the barons now decided that this step was necessary, and an effort was made to unite all barons in taking it, but those who had been with the king before refused, and some members of the baronial party itself were not willing to go so far, nor were the clergy. The pope was making his position perfectly plain. Before the meeting at Runnymede he had ordered the excommunication of the disturbers of the king and kingdom; and when this sentence was published later, the barons might pretend that the king was the worst disturber of the kingdom, but they really knew what the pope intended. In September the Bishop of Winchester and Pandulf, representing the pope, suspended Archbishop Langton because of his refusal to enforce the papal sentences. By the end of the month the news reached England of Innocent's bull against the charter itself, declaring it null and void, and forbidding the king to observe it or the barons to require it to be kept under penalty of excommunication. Doubtless John expected this from the pope, and if his own view of the charter were correct, Innocent's action would be entirely within his rights. No vassal had a right to enter into any agreement which would diminish the value of his fief, and John had done this if the rights that he was exercising in 1213 were really his. It was apparently about this time that the insurgent barons determined to transfer their allegiance to Louis of France. We are told that they selected him because, if he were king of England, most of John's mercenaries would leave his service since they were vassals of France; but Louis was really the only one available who could be thought to represent in any way the old dynasty, and it would certainly be remembered that he had been proposed for the place in 1213. Negotiations were begun to induce him to accept, but in the meantime John had secured a sufficient force to take the offensive, and was beginning to push the war with unusual spirit and vigour. A part of his force he sent to relieve Northampton and Oxford, besieged by the barons, and he himself with the rest set out to take Rochester castle which was held against him. Repulsed at first, he succeeded in a second attempt to destroy the bridge across the Medway to cut off communication with London, and began a regular siege which he pressed fiercely. The garrison was not large, but they defended themselves with great courage, having reason to fear the consequences of yielding, and prolonged the siege for seven weeks. Even after the keep had been in part taken by undermining the wall they maintained themselves in what was left until they were starved into surrender. It was only the threat that his mercenaries would leave him for fear of reprisals that kept John from hanging his prisoners. During this siege the barons in London had remained in a strange inactivity, making only one half-hearted attempt to save their friends, seemingly afraid to meet the king in the field, and accused of preferring the selfish security and luxury of the capital. This was their conduct during the whole of the winter while their strongholds were captured and their lands devastated in all parts of England by the forces of their enemy, for John continued his campaign. Soon after the capture of Rochester he marched through Windsor to the north of London and, leaving a part of his army under the Earl of Salisbury to watch the barons and to lay waste their lands in that part of the country, he passed himself through the midlands to the north, destroying everything belonging to his enemies that he could find and not always distinguishing carefully between friends and foes. England had not for generations suffered such a harrying as it received that winter. So great was the terror created by the cruelties practised that garrisons of the barons' castles, it is said, fled on the news of the king's approach, leaving the castles undefended to fall into his hands. The march extended as far as Scotland. Berwick was taken and burnt, and the parts of the country about were laid waste in revenge for the favour which King Alexander had shown the barons. In March, 1216, John returned to the neighbourhood of London, leaving a new track of devastation further to the east, and bringing with him a great store of plunder.

During the winter the barons had kept up their negotiations with Louis, and an agreement had finally been made. They had pledged themselves to do homage to Louis and accept him as king, and had sent to France twenty-four hostages "of the noblest of the land" in pledge of their fidelity. Louis in return sent over small bodies of men to their aid and promised himself to follow in person in the spring. To this step the barons were indeed driven, unless they were prepared to submit, because of the strength the king had gained since the signing of the charter and their own comparative weakness. Why this change had taken place so soon after the barons had been all-powerful cannot now be fully explained, but so far as we can see the opinion of a contemporary that they would have been overcome but for the aid of the French is correct. Against the invasion of Louis, John had two lines of defence, the pope and the fleet. Innocent, who had once favoured a transfer of the English crown to Louis, must now oppose it. When he learned how far preparations for the expedition had gone, he sent a legate, Cardinal Gualo, to France to forbid any further step. Gualo was received by Philip and his son at Melun on April 25. There before the king and the court the case was argued between the cardinal and a knight representing Louis, as if it were a suit at law to be decided in the ordinary way. Louis's case was skilfully constructed to deprive the legate of his ground of interference, but his assertions were falsehoods or misrepresentations. John had been condemned to death for the murder of Arthur—the first occasion on which we hear of this—and afterwards rejected by the barons of England for his many crimes, and they were making war on him to expel him from the kingdom. John had surrendered the kingdom to the pope without the consent of the barons, and if he could not legally do this, he could by the attempt create a vacancy, which the barons had filled by the choice of Louis. The legate, apparently unable to meet these unexpected arguments, asserted that John was a crusader and therefore under the protection of the apostolic see. For Louis it was answered that John had been making war on him long before he took the cross and had continued to do so since, so that Louis had a right to go on with the war. The legate had no answer to this, though it was false, but he prohibited Louis from going and his father from allowing him to go. Louis, denying the right of his father to interfere with his claims in a land not subject to the king of France, and sending an embassy to argue his case before the pope, went on with his preparations. Philip Augustus carefully avoided anything that would bring him into open conflict with Innocent and threw the whole responsibility on his son.

Louis landed in England in the Isle of Thanet on May 21. John had collected a large and strong fleet to prevent his crossing, but a storm just at the moment had dispersed it and left the enemy a clear passage. John, then at Canterbury, first thought to attack the French with his land forces, but fearing that his hired troops would be less loyal to a mere paymaster than to the heir and representative of their suzerain in France, he fell back and left the way open for Louis's advance to London. Soon after landing, Louis sent forward a letter to the Abbot of St. Augustine's in Canterbury, who, he feared, was about to excommunicate him. In this letter which was possibly intended also for general circulation, he repeated the arguments used against the legate with some additional points of the same sort, and explained the hereditary claim of his wife and his own right by the choice of the barons. The document is a peculiar mixture of fact and falsehood, but it was well calculated to impose on persons to whom the minor details of history would certainly be unknown. Rochester castle fell into the hands of the French with no real resistance; and on June 2, Louis was welcomed in London with great rejoicing, and at once received the homage of the barons and of the mayor. Louis's arrival seemed to turn the tide for the moment against the king. He retreated into the west, while the barons took the field once more, and with the French gained many successes in the east and north, particularly against towns and castles. On June 25, Louis occupied Winchester. Barons who had been until now faithful to the king began to come in and join the French as their rapid advance threatened their estates; among them was even John's brother, the Earl of Salisbury. Early in July Worcester was captured and Exeter threatened, and John was forced back to the borders of Wales. This marks, however, the limit of Louis's success. Instead of pushing his advance rapidly forward against the one important enemy, the king himself, he turned aside to undertake some difficult sieges, and made the further mistake of angering the English barons by showing too great favour to his French companions. Dover castle seemed to the military judgment of the French particularly important as "key of England," and for more than three months Louis gave himself up to the effort to take it.

For the first of these months, till the end of August, John remained inactive on the borders of Wales. The death of Innocent III made no change in the situation. His successor Honorius III continued his English policy. With the beginning of September the king advanced as if to raise the siege of Windsor, but gave up the attempt and passed on east into Cambridgeshire, ravaging horribly the lands of his enemies. The barons pursued him, and he fell back on Lincoln from which as a centre he raided the surrounding country for more than a fortnight. On October 9, he marched eastwards again to Lynn which, like most of the towns, was favourable to him, and there he brought on a dysentery by overeating. From that time his physical decline was rapid. His violent passions, utterly unbridled, tore him to pieces more and more fiercely as he recognized his own loss of strength and learned of one misfortune after another. He would not rest, and he would not listen to counsel. On the 11th he went on to Wisbech, and on the next day he insisted on crossing the Wash, without knowing the crossing or regarding the tide. He himself passed in safety, but he lost a part of his troops and all his baggage with his booty, money, and jewels. At night at Swineshead abbey, hot with anger and grief, and feverish from his illness, he gave way to his appetite again, as always, and ate to excess of peaches and new cider. After a rest of a day he pushed on with difficulty to Sleaford. There messengers reached him from his garrison in Dover asking his permission to surrender if he could not relieve them at once, and the news brought on a new passion of anger. He insisted on going one stage further to Newark, although he had already recognized that his end was near. There three days later, on the 19th of October, he died. The teachings of the Church which he had slighted and despised during his life he listened to as his end drew near, and he confessed and received the communion. He designated his son Henry, now nine years old, as his heir, and especially recommended him to the care of the Earl of Pembroke, and appointed thirteen persons by name to settle his affairs and to distribute his property according to general directions which he left. At his desire he was buried in Worcester cathedral and in the habit of a monk.

It has already been suggested that the reigns of Richard and John form a period of transition to a new age. That period closes and the new age opens with the granting of the Great Charter and the attempted revolution which followed. The reign of John was the culmination of a long tendency in English history, most rapid since the accession of his father, towards the establishment of an absolutism in which the rights of all classes would disappear and the arbitrary will of the king be supreme. The story of his reign should reveal how very near that result was of accomplishment. A monarchy had been forming in the last three reigns, and very rapidly in the reign of John, capable of crushing any ordinary opposition, disregarding public opinion and traditional rights, possessing in the new judicial system, if regarded as an organ of the king's will alone, an engine of centralization, punishment, and extortion, of irresistible force, and developing rapidly in financial matters complete independence of all controlling principles. Though the barons were acting rather from personal and selfish motives, freedom for all classes depended on the speedy checking of this steady drift of two generations. The reigns of Richard and John may be called transitional because it is in them that the barons came to see clearly the principles on which successful resistance could be founded and the absolutist tendency checked. The embodiment of these principles in permanent form in the Great Charter to be accepted by the sovereign and enforced in practice, introduces an age, the age of constitutional growth, new in the history of England, and in the form and importance of its results new in the history of the world.

APPENDIX ON AUTHORITIES 1066-1216

While the material on which the history of any period of the Middle Ages is based is scanty as compared with the abundant supply at the service of the writer of modern history, the number of the original sources for the Norman and early Angevin period is so great as to render impossible any attempt to characterize them all in this place. The more important or more typical chroniclers have been selected to give an idea of the nature of the material on which the narrative rests.

The medieval chronicler did not content himself with writing the history of his own time. He was usually ambitious to write a general history from the beginning of the world or from the Christian era at least, and in comparatively few cases began with the origin of his own land. For a knowledge of times before his own he had to depend on his predecessors in the same line, and often for long periods together the new book would be only an exact copy or a condensation of an older one. If several earlier writers were at hand, the new text might be a composite one, resting on them all, but really adding nothing to our knowledge. As the writer drew nearer to his own time, local tradition or the documents preserved in his monastery might give him information on new points or fuller information on others. On such matters his narrative becomes an independent authority of more or less value, and much that is important has been preserved to us in such additions to the earlier sources. Sometimes for a longer or shorter period before his own day the writer may be using materials all of which have been lost to us, and in such a case he is for our purposes an original and independent authority, although in reality he is not strictly original. Then follows a period, sometimes a long one, sometimes only a very few years, in which his narrative is contemporary and written from his own knowledge or from strictly first-hand materials. This is usually the most valuable portion for the modern writer of history.

A large mass of material of great value cannot be described here. It is made up of records primarily of value for constitutional history, charters, writs, laws, and documentary material of all kinds, from which often new facts are obtained for narrative history or light of great value thrown on doubtful points, especially of chronology or of the history of individuals. Of such a kind are the various monastic cartularies, law-books like Glanvill's, records like the Patent, Close, and Charter Rolls, collections of letters, and modern collections of documents like T. Rymer's Foedera or J.H. Round's Calendar of Documents Preserved in France.

The Saxon Chronicle (with translation by B. Thorpe in the Rolls Series (1861), or C. Plummer's Two Saxon Chronicles, 1892-99) continues during the first part of this period with its earlier characteristics unchanged, though more full than for all but the last of the preceding age. The Conquest had no effect on its language, and it continued to be written in English until the end. The Worcester chronicle closes with the year 1079, while the Peterborough book goes on to the coronation of Henry II in 1154. Practically a contemporary record for the whole period, though not preserved to us in a strictly contemporary form throughout, it is of especial value for the indications it gives of the feelings of the English at a time when they were not often recorded.

William, called of Poitiers, though a Norman, chaplain of William I and Archdeacon of Lisieux, wrote a biography of the king, Gesta Willelmi Duels Normannorum et Regis Anglice (in Migne's Patrologia Latina,149), of much value for the period immediately following the Conquest. It has been thought that he was not present at the battle of Hastings, but the account of William's movements between the battle and his coronation contains several indications of first—hand knowledge, matters of detail likely to be noted by an eye—witness; and though he was a strong partisan and panegyrist of the king, his statements of what happened may generally be accepted. His comments and opinions, however, must be used with the greatest caution. His work originally ended in 1071, but the last part is now wanting, and it ends abruptly in the spring of 1067. The entire book was used, however, by Orderic Vitalis as one of the chief sources of his narrative, and in that form we probably have all the main facts it contained.

William of Malmesbury, born probably between 1090 and 1096, devoted himself from early life to the study of history, seemingly attracted to it, as he tells us himself, by the pleasure which the record of the past gave him and by its ethical value as a collection of practical examples of virtues and vices. This confession gives the key to the character of his work. He prided himself on his Latin style, and with some justice. He regarded himself not as a mere chronicler, but as a historian of a higher rank, the disciple and first continuator of Bede. The accurate telling of facts in their chronological order was to him less important than a well-written and philosophical account of events selected for their importance or interest and narrated in such a way as to bring out the character of the actors or the meaning of the history. That he succeeded in these objects cannot be questioned. His work is of a higher literary and philosophical character than any written since his master Bede, or for some time after himself. On this account, however, it gives less direct information as to the events of the time in which he lived than we could wish, though it is a contemporary authority of considerable value on the reign of Henry I, and of even more value on the first years of Stephen.

His political history is contained in two works, the Gesta Regum, which closes with the year 1128, and the Historia Novella, which continues the narrative to December, 1142 (W. Stubbs, Rolls Series, 1887-89). A third work, the Gesta Pontificum (N.E.S.A. Hamilton, Rolls Series, 1870), also contains some notices of value for the political history. William boasted a friendship with Robert, Earl of Gloucester, who was his patron, and his sympathies were with the Empress's party in the civil war, but he had also personal relations with Roger of Salisbury and Henry of Winchester, and was no blind partisan.

EADMER, a monk of Canterbury, stands with William of Malmesbury in the forefront of the historians of the twelfth century. His work, less pretentious than William's, is simpler and more straightforward. Eadmer was of Saxon birth and was brought up from childhood in Christ Church, Canterbury. Affectionately attached to Anselm from an early time, he became his chaplain on his appointment as archbishop and was with him almost constantly in his visits to court, in his troubled dealings with his sovereigns, and in his exile abroad. With Anselm's successor, Archbishop Ralph, he stood in equally close relations, and he was honoured and respected in the ecclesiastical world of his time. He writes throughout the greater part of his history, calmly and soberly, of the things that he had seen and in which he had taken part. His chief work, the Historia Novorum (M. Rule, Rolls Series, 1884), begins with the Conquest, but his main interest before the days of Anselm is in the personality and doings of Lanfranc. In the more detailed portion of his work his point of view is always the ecclesiastical. This is the interest which he desires to set forth most fully, but the policy of the Church involved itself so closely in his day with that of the State that the history of the one is almost of necessity that of the other, and in the Historia Novarum we have a contemporary history of English affairs, as they came into touch with the Church, of the greatest value from the accession of Henry I to 1121, and one which preserves a larger proportion of the important formal documents of the time than was usual with twelfth century historians. He wrote also in the latter part of this period a Vita Anselmi in which the religious was even more the leading interest than in his history, but it adds something to our knowledge of the time.

One of the best authorities for the period from the Conquest to 1141 is the Historia Ecclesiastica of ORDERIC VITALIS (A. le Prevost, Societe de l'Histoire de France, 1838-55). Born in England in 1075, of a Norman father, a clerk, and an English mother, he was sent by his father at the age of ten to the monastery of St. Evroul, and there he spent his life. The atmosphere in this monastery was favourable to study. It had an extensive library, and Orderic had at his command good sources of information, though he himself took no part in the events he describes. He paid some visits to England in which he obtained information, and as he always looked upon himself as an Englishman, his history naturally includes England as well as Normandy. He began to write about 1123, and from that date on he may be regarded as a contemporary authority, but from the Conquest the book has in many places the value of an original account. It is an exasperating book to use because of the extreme confusion in which the facts are arranged, or left without arrangement, the account of a single incident being often in two widely separated places. But the book rises much above the level of mere annals, and while perhaps not reaching that of the philosophical historian, gives the reader more of the feeling that a living man is writing about living men than is usual in medieval books. It reveals in the writer a lively imagination, which, while it does not affect the historical value of the narrative, gives it a pictorial setting. Orderic's interest in the minuter details of life and in the personality of the men of his time imparts a strong human element to the book; nor is the least useful feature of the work the writer's critical judgment on men and events, generally on moral grounds, but often assisting our knowledge of character and the causes of events.

HENRY, ARCHDEACON OF HUNTINGDON's Historia Anglorum (T. Arnold, Rolls Series, 1879) becomes original, to our present knowledge at least, with the closing of the manuscript of the Saxon chronicle which he had been following, probably in 1121, and his narrative is contemporary from the last years of that decade to the coronation of Henry II. He adds, however, surprisingly little to our knowledge of the twenty-five years during which he was writing the history of his own time. He had an active imagination and loved to embellish the facts which he had learned with little details that he thought likely to be true. The main value of the original portion of his history lies in its confirmation of what we learn from other sources.

The chronicle of FLORENCE OF WORCESTER (B. Thorpe, Engl. Hist. Soc., 1848-49) is continued by John of Worcester as a source of primary importance to 1141 and by others afterwards. Florence himself died in 1118, but at what point before this his own work breaks off it does not seem possible to determine. There is at no point any real change in the character of the chronicle. The continental chronicle which Florence had been using as the groundwork of his account, that of Marianus Scotus, ends with 1082, but his manuscript of the Saxon chronicle probably went on for some distance further, and about the time of Florence's death much use is made of Eadmer. The account is annalistic throughout, even in the full treatment of Stephen's reign; but in its original portions, or what seem to us original, it has the value of a contemporary record, giving us further insight into the feelings of the English in William's reign and the feelings and sufferings of the people of the south-west in Stephen's time.

An interesting chronicle of Stephen's reign is that by an unknown author known as the Gesta Stephani (R. Hewlett, Rolls Series, Chronicles of Stephen, Henry II, and Richard I, iii, 1866), which existed at the beginning of the seventeenth century in a single manuscript since lost. It has been conjectured with some probability that it was written by a chaplain of the king's brother, Henry, Bishop of Winchester. Certainly the author had very good sources of information, writes often from personal knowledge, and though a strong partisan of Stephen's, is not blind to his weaknesses and faults. While the first part of the narrative was not written precisely at the date, the work has all the value of a contemporary account from 1135, and from 1142 to 1147 it is almost our only authority. The manuscript from which it was first printed in 1619 had been injured, and the book as it now exists breaks off in the middle of a sentence in 1147.

ROBERT OF TORIGNI (R. Hewlett, Rolls Series. Chronicles of Stephen, etc., iv, 1889) spent his life as a monk in Normandy, in the abbey of Bec till 1154 and afterwards as abbot of the monastery of Mont Saint Michel. He made apparently but two visits to England, of which we know no particulars, but as a monk of Normandy, living in two of its most famous monasteries, he was interested in the doings of the English kings, particularly in their continental policy, and more especially in the deeds of the two great Henries. He began to write as a young man, and by 1139, about the time he reached the age of thirty, he seems to have completed his account of the reign of Henry I, which he wrote as an additional, an eighth? book to the History of the Normans of William of Jumieges. His more extended chronicle he had begun before leaving Bec, and he carried the work with him to Mont-Saint-Michel. Down to 1100 this is the chronicle of Sigebert of Gemblours with additions, and it becomes a wholly original chronicle only with 1147. Though of great value for the knowledge of facts, especially between 1154 and 1170, the chronicle never rises above the character of annals and was carelessly constructed, especially as to chronology; it was perhaps worked up by monks of his house from a somewhat rough first draft of memoranda by the abbot. The book closes at the end of 1185, shortly before the death of Robert.

The writer of the twelfth century who comes the nearest to looking upon the task of the historian as a modern writer would is WILLIAM OF NEWBURGH (R. Hewlett, Rolls Series, Chronicles of Stephen, etc., i, and ii, 1884-85). His purpose is not merely to record what happened, with a rather clear conception of the duty of the historian to be accurate and to use the best sources, but to make a selection of the facts, using the more important and those that will show the drift and meaning of the age, and combining them into something like an explanatory account of the period; and this he does with constant critical judgment of men and measures and great breadth of historical view. His Historia Rerum Anglicarum, which may be said to begin with the reign of Stephen, after a brief introduction on the three preceding reigns, appears to have been composed as a whole within two or three years at the close of the twelfth century. The probability is that no part of it is original, in the sense that it was written solely from first-hand knowledge; but the sources from which he derived his material for the period from 1154 to 1173, and at later dates, have not come down to us, and he must have drawn from some personal knowledge in the last portion of his work. It is throughout, however, a critical commentary of great value on the history, and an interpretation of it by a man of clear, impartial, and broad judgment, and one not too far removed from the time of which he wrote to be out of sympathy with it.

For the last half of the reign of Henry II we have the advantage of a valuable and in some respects very interesting and attractive chronicle. This is the Gesta Regis Henrici Secundi, associated with the name of BENEDICT OF PETERBOROUGH (Rolls Series, 2 vols.). Benedict, however, was not the author, and no certain evidence as to who he was can be derived from any source, nor does the chronicle itself supply many of those incidental indications from which it is often possible to learn much regarding the author of an anonymous book. The tentative suggestion of Bishop Stubbs that it may have been written by Richard Fitz Neal, the author of the Dialogus de Scaccario, is now generally regarded as inadmissible. The work begins in 1170, and from a date a year or two later is evidently contemporaneous to its close in 1192, with perhaps a slight interruption at 1177. It is written in a simple and straightforward way, and with a sure touch, unusual accuracy of statement, and a clear understanding of constitutional details; it suggests an interesting personality in its author, with whom we constantly desire a closer acquaintance. Whoever he was, he possessed good sources of information, though apparently too great consideration for king or court keeps him sometimes from saying all he knows or believes, and he has inserted in his work many letters and important documents.

The work known by the name of Benedict was taken up into his own and carried forward to 1201 by an almost equally important chronicler, ROGER OF HOWDEN (W. Stubbs, Rolls Series, 1868-71). The writer was a northerner who began his history with 732, using for all the first part of it northern historians, with some slight additions between 1149 and 1169. From 1170 he copies nearly all the Gesta Regis Henrici, adding to it occasionally original information and some documents, but the knowledge of value which we derive from his additions is disappointingly small considering that he held official positions under the king and was employed by him on various missions. From 1192 to its close the work is an original and contemporary history, carefully written and of great value, and containing an even larger proportion of documents than Benedict. The chronicle excites less interest in the personality of its author than does its predecessor; is of a somewhat more solemn type, and shows more plainly the traits of the ordinary ecclesiastical writer in its sympathy with current superstitions and its frequent moralizing.

RALPH DE DICETO, Dean of St. Paul's during the last ten years of Henry II's reign and the whole of Richard's, began soon after he became dean a chronicle which he called Imagines Historiarum, or Outlines of History (W. Stubbs, Rolls Series, 1876). It begins with 1148, to which date he had brought down an abstract of earlier chronicles from the creation. To about 1183 the work is based on the writings of others, but from 1162 it becomes more full and contains much that is original in form at least. From 1183 to its close in 1202 it is a contemporary account of the highest value, especially for the reign of Richard. Ralph stood in close relations with Richard Fitz Neal, from 1189 Bishop of London, for forty years treasurer of the kingdom, and himself the author of historical books, and with William Longchamp King Richard's representative. From his official position also he possessed unusually good opportunities of information and means of forming those judgments on affairs which are a feature of his chronicle. He has embodied many important documents in his narrative though sometimes not with the true historian's feeling of the importance of the exact language in such cases. His statements of fact and of opinion both greatly aid our understanding of his times, and his writing has, like Benedict of Peterborough, a straightforward air which itself carries weight.

While the more important chroniclers were writing the secular history of the reigns of Henry II and Richard I, a monk of Christ Church, Canterbury, of the name of GERVASE (W. Stubbs, Rolls Series, 1879-80), was also writing a chronicle in which he was chiefly interested to preserve the history of the troubles and ecclesiastical controversies of his house and of the archbishopric. Incidentally, however, he gives us some information concerning political events and considerable confirmatory evidence. He began writing about 1188, and his principal chronicle becomes contemporary soon after that date. It exactly covers a century, opening with the accession of Henry I and closing with the death of Richard I. A minor chronicle, entitled Gesta Regum, begun after the close of the other, starts with the mythical Brutus, the Trojan who gave his name to Britain, and comes rapidly down to the accession of John, abridging earlier works. For the reign of John it is a contemporary chronicle, not very full, but of real value. Gervase writes always as a monk, and even more narrowly, as a monk of Canterbury, influenced by the feelings of his order and monastery. His attitude towards the kings under whom he writes is unsympathetic, and his interest in political matters is always very slight, but his references to them are not on that account without a value of their own.

RALPH, abbot of the Cistercian monastery of Coggeshall from 1207 to 1218, when he resigned because of illness, wrote a Chronicon Anglicanum (J. Stevenson, Rolls Series, 1875), which extends from 1066 to 1223. To 1186 the entries are brief annals: with 1187 the history becomes more full, but the writer's interest is chiefly in the crusade, of which important and interesting accounts are given from excellent sources; and comparatively little is recorded concerning the history of England proper before the accession of John. For the reign of John the book is one of our most important and trustworthy contemporary sources. Ralph was greatly interested in mythical tales, especially in wonderful occurrences in nature, and he records these at length as he heard of them, but this habit does not affect the character of his historical record proper. As a historian he is very well informed, though he gives but few documents; he saw clearly the essential point of things and had a sense of accuracy.

A compilation from earlier historical works made, in the form in which we have it, at the end of the thirteenth or the beginning of the fourteenth century and known by the name of WALTER OF COVENTRY (W. Stubbs, Rolls Series, 1872-73), has preserved a continuation of Roger of Howden which is of great value. This is a chronicle of John's reign and the early years of Henry III, from 1202 to 1226, probably written in the monastery of Barnwell about the time the narrative closes, and original and practically contemporary at least from 1212. From 1202 to 1208 the entries are brief and annalistic, with occasionally a suggestive comment. With 1209 the notices begin to be longer, and with 1212 they form a detailed narrative. The writer has a better opinion of John, at least of his ability, than other chroniclers of the time, does not attribute his misfortunes to the king's faults, and has little sympathy with the cause of the barons. He is accurate in his statements, clear in his narrative, and shows a tendency to reflect on the causes and relations of the leading facts.

Besides these, most important of the primary authorities, there are a number of others of hardly less value. SIMEON OF DURHAM's Historia Regum (T. Arnold, Rolls Series, 1882-85) becomes an independent chronicle from 1119 to 1129 and is continued by JOHN OF HEXHAM (ed. with Simeon of Durham) to 1154 in a narrative not contemporary, but in many places original, while RICHARD OF HEXHAM (Chronicles of Stephen, etc., iii), perhaps John's predecessor as prior, wrote a contemporary history covering the time from the death of Henry I to early in 1139. All these are of especial value for the affairs of northern England. About the same time Master GEOFFREY GAIMAR, the Trouvère, wrote a chronicle in French verse which is mainly a translation from the Saxon chronicle and other earlier writers (T.D. Hardy and C.T. Martin, Rolls Series, 1888-89). It closes with the death of William Rufus, and is chiefly of interest as giving a glimpse of the opinion held by laymen of the noble class about that king. Valuable evidence regarding the Becket controversy is collected in the seven volumes in the Rolls Series, entitled Materials for the History of Thomas Becket (J.C. Robertson, 1875-85). They contain nine contemporary lives of the archbishop and one later one. and three volumes of letters of Becket and others. On the conquest of Ireland there is an important French poem called the Song of Dermot and the Earl (G.H. Orpen, 1892) that was written in the next century, but based on a contemporary narrative; and GIRALDUS CAMBRENSIS (J.S. Brewer, J.F. Dimock, and G.P. Warner, Rolls Series, 186191) gives a lively contemporary account of the Conquest, and descriptions of Ireland as well as of Wales. He also wrote later a book called De Principis Instructione, an avowed attack on Henry II and his sons, against whom he had the grievance of disappointed ambition. The book relates in passing many incidents that fill out our knowledge of the period, and it possesses some value from the very fact of its unfriendly criticism. This, but not much more than this, is also true of RALPH NIGER's contemporary chronicles of Henry II's reign, written in a spirit very unfriendly to the king (R. Anstruther, Caxton Society, 1851). An account of Richard's crusade is preserved in the Itinerarium Regis Ricardi (W. Stubbs, Rolls Series, Chronicles of Richard I, 1864), which is no more than a translation from a contemporary French poem. A biography of St. Hugh, Bishop of Lincoln, who died in 1200, was written after his death by his chaplain and contains many incidental references to public affairs—a few of great value (J.F. Dimock, Rolls Series, 1864). Another biography, written in French verse not quite contemporary, but based on information from a companion of the subject, is the Histoire de Guillaume le Maréchal (P. Meyer, Soc. Hist. de France, 1891-1901). It follows the life of William Marshal through the reigns of Henry II, Richard, and John, and to his death in 1219. It relates many facts, gives much information as to life and manners and suggestions of interpretation from a layman's point of view. Foreign chronicles, of value on the foreign policy of the English kings, are that of GEOFFREY, Prior of VIGEOIS (in Bouquet's Recueil des Historiens de France), on nearly the whole of Henry II's reign, the contemporary histories of Philip Augustus by RIGORD, and GUILLAUME LE BRETON, and the Histoire des Ducs de Normandie (all in the collections of the Soc. Hist. de France). The last is original and contemporary on the reign of John. Collections of letters like those of Lanfranc, and monastic annals like those of Burton, Waverley, and Dunstable, aid materially in filling out our knowledge. A great school of historical writing was rising into prominence as this period closed, in the monastery of St. Albans. Its first great historiographer, ROGER OF WENDOVER (H.O. COXE, Engl. Hist. Soc., 1841-44), probably did not begin to write his chronicle until after the death of John, but his account of that king's reign, written not long after its close, is original and has the practical value of a contemporary narrative.

Of secondary authorities of importance who have written on this period at any length the list is unfortunately short.

First and foremost for every student of Norman and early Angevin history is the work of Bishop STUBBS. With a more direct, personal interest in the growth of institutions, still in his Constitutional History and in his prefaces to the volumes he edited for the Master of the Rolls he discussed the narrative history of the whole age and very fully the reigns of Henry II and his two sons. The characteristic of Bishop Stubbs's work, which makes it of especial value to the student of the present generation, is the remarkable clearness with which he saw the essential meaning of his material and its bearing on the problem under discussion. While he generally neglected a wide range of material of great value to the historian of institutions—the charters and legal documents—and did not always formulate clearly in his mind the exact problem to be solved, yet the keenness with which he detected in imperfect material the real solution is often marvellous. Again and again the later student finds but little more to do than to prove more fully and from a wider range of material the intuitive conclusions of his master.

For the reigns of the Conqueror and of William II we have the benefit of the minute studies of EDWARD A. FREEMAN in his History of the Norman Conquest and his Reign of William Rufus. The faults of Mr. Freeman's work are very serious, and they mar too greatly the results of long and patient industry and much enthusiasm for his subject. The neglect of unprinted material and of almost all that is strictly constitutional in character, and the personal bias arising from his strongly held theory of Teutonic influence in early English history, make every conclusion one to be accepted with caution, but his long books on these reigns furnish a vast store of fact and suggestion of the greatest importance to the student. The Norman Conquest closes with a summary history to the death of Stephen, which is of considerable value.

The second volume of Sir JAMES RAMSAY's Foundations of England and his Angevin Empire together form a continuous history of the whole age from 1066 to 1216. These books are to be noticed for their careful inclusion of details and their bringing all the sources together that bear on successive facts, so as to furnish an almost complete index to the original authorities.

Miss KATE NORGATE has written two books which form a continuous history from the accession of Stephen to the death of John—England under the Angevin Kings and John Lackland. In the first book the influence of John Richard Green is clearly traceable both in the style and in the selection of facts for treatment. It contains many discussions of difficult questions that must be taken into account in forming a final opinion. The second book is a sober and careful study of John's career that brings out some new points of detail, especially in his last years, but gives little attention to constitutional changes.

Three scholars whose work does not bear immediately upon the political history, or bears only upon portions of it, but who have yet contributed greatly by their studies to our understanding of it, are Professor F.W. MAITLAND, Professor FELIX LIEBERMANN, and Mr. HORACE ROUND. Professor Maitland's field is that of legal history, in which he has done as great a work as that of Stubbs in constitutional history, and incidentally has thrown much light on problems which Stubbs discusses. His intimate knowledge and his scientific caution of statement give to any conclusion that he puts in positive form an almost final authority. Of Dr. Liebermann it is to be said that probably no living man has so complete a knowledge of the material which the historian of this period must use, whether that be the original material of the age itself or the scattered work of secondary authorities of different ages and many languages. His own work has been mainly devoted to the preparation of scientifically edited texts, mostly of legal material, but also of extracts from a considerable range of chronicles— work unrivalled in its thoroughness and in its approach to finality. Scattered in the introductions to these texts is a mass of information on points of all kinds, which no student of the times can neglect; while an occasional formal article, like that on Anselm and Archbishop Hugh of Lyons, awakens regret that they are so few. The work of Mr. Round has nearly all appeared in short studies on isolated topics. In Geoffrey de Mandeville he has written one book on the reign of Stephen that approaches the character of narrative history. In his Feudal England and Commune of London many articles on problems of this age have been collected in a form convenient for reference. Mr. Round's knowledge of the history of persons and families is unsurpassed; he subjects the material he uses to a minuteness of analysis that is unusual; and he has settled, so far as the evidence admits of it, some important questions and a large number of minor problems, both of the history of events and of institutions.

We owe to foreign scholars many studies of value on particular questions of Norman and Angevin history, like M. CHARLES BÉMONT's on the trial of King John for the murder of Arthur, and a few long works of first importance. Dr. H. BÖHMER's Kirche und Staat in England und der Normandie im XI und XII Jahrhundert is of great interest on the conflict of Anselm with Henry I and the consequences that flowed from it. O. RÖESSLER's Kaiserin Mathilde is of particular value for the foreign policy of Henry I and for the reign of Stephen, though inclined to attach too much weight to what are really conjectures. M.A. LUCHAIRE's contribution to E. Lavisse's Histoire de France is a very interesting piece of work, dealing fully with the French side of English foreign relations, and of especial value for the first three Angevin kings. The same subject is receiving also minute and careful treatment in Dr. ALEXANDER CARTELLIERI's Philip II Augustus, Koenig van Frankreich, the first volume of which goes to the death of Henry II, while M. PETIT-DUTAILLIS's Étude sur la Vie et la Règne de Louis VIII is useful for the last years of John.

It is impossible in a bibliography of this kind to speak of all the long list of monographs and special studies, English and foreign, which alone make possible the writing of a history of this age, and to which the writer must acknowledge his obligations in general terms.